WHERE A HUNDRED SOLDIERS WERE KILLED

WHERE A HUNDRED SOLDIERS WERE KILLED

The Struggle for the

Powder River Country in 1866

and the Making of the Fetterman Myth

JOHN H. MONNETT

University of New Mexico Press

Albuquerque

First paperbound printing, 2010
Paperbound ISBN: 978-0-8263-4504-2

Library of Congress Cataloging-in-Publication Data
Monnett, John H.
Where a hundred soldiers were killed : the struggle for the
Powder River country in 1866 and the making of the
Fetterman myth / John H. Monnett.
          p. cm.
Includes bibliographical references and index.
ISBN 978-0-8263-4503-5 (cloth) : alk. paper)
1. Fetterman Fight, Wyo., 1866.   2. Powder River Expedition, 1865.
3. United States Army. Infantry Regiment, 18th. I. Title.
          E83.866.M674 2008
          973.8'1—dc22
                2008023197

Designed and typeset by Mina Yamashita
Composed in Adobe Garamond Pro, bringing together elements of
Claude Garamond's Garamond and Robert Granjon's Granjon
in a contemporary typeface by Robert Slimbach.
Printed by Thomson-Shore, Inc. on 55# Natures Natural.

For the students of

Chief Dull Knife College

CONTENTS

LIST OF ILLUSTRATIONS

Maps

I object to all the propositions to write what is called a history of the battle . . . But if a true history is written, what will become of the reputation of half of those who have acquired reputation, and deserve it for their gallantry, but who, if their mistakes and casual misconduct were made public, would NOT be so well thought of?

—Wellington

ACKNOWLEDGMENTS

THIS BOOK HAS BEEN IN THE MAKING for the better part of twenty years. A great many organizations and individuals have, during that time, contributed to the effort. State historical societies were indispensable. I would like to thank the staffs of the South Dakota State Historical Society, Nebraska State Historical Society, Montana Historical Society, Minnesota Historical Society, Oklahoma Historical Society, Ohio Historical Society, and Wyoming State Archives. The Western History Department of Denver Public Library was magnificent as usual. I am likewise grateful to the staffs of the libraries at Yale, University of Oklahoma, University of Wyoming, University of Montana, University of Indiana, and University of Arizona, as well as the Fulmer Public Library (Sheridan, Wyoming), the Douglas Public Library (Douglas, Wyoming), the Newberry Library (Chicago), the archives of the U.S. Army at Carlisle Barracks in Carlisle, Pennsylvania, and the Southwest Museum in Los Angeles. The National Archives and Records Administration was vital for obtaining official records of Fort Phil Kearny and its many historical characters central to the Powder River story. Thanks also to the staff of the National Anthropological Archives at the Smithsonian, especially Candice Greene for putting me onto the important winter counts pertaining to the Powder River country in the 1850s and 1860s.

Many individuals brought this project to life. It would not have been completed without their valued assistance. The folks at the Fort Phil Kearny/ Bozeman Trail Association, of which I am a "silent" member, and the personnel at Fort Phil Kearny Historic Site were wonderful. Interpretative programs, tours, and displays are of first quality and important to an understanding of the struggle for the Powder River country. Thanks also to Bob Reece and Friends of the Little Bighorn Battlefield Association for their virtual tour interpretations of the Fetterman battlefield as it looks today. I wish to extend thanks to my colleagues at Metropolitan State College of Denver for reading portions of the manuscript, especially James Drake,

Jennifer Wynot Garza, Monys Hagan, Todd Laugen, Stephen Leonard, and Laura McCall. They offered valuable suggestions and put me onto some obscure sources. Shannon D. Smith, whose research on Henry Carrington's two wives is exemplary and unique, shared her thoughts regarding Lt. George Washington Grummond at a recent meeting of the Western History Association. We discovered that both of us, over the years, had reached parallel conclusions regarding his character. Appreciation also goes to my colleague Rebecca Hunt, a master "Googler" as well as an accomplished historian at the University of Colorado–Denver. One day she sat down at the computer in my office and five minutes later told me the name of the school where Margaret Carrington was educated. Thanks to my department chairman, Stephen Leonard, who put up with my frustrations over the project during the past several years. He kept me on the right track as did our administrative assistant, Gloria Kennison, who kept the printer operating. I extend my gratitude also to Robert Larson for his input on the manuscript and to Margot Liberty for her astute insights about the modern Cheyennes and their conflicts regarding how they wish to remember their history. Jerry Keenan generously offered his insights on the Wagon Box fight while John D. McDermott graciously provided me with some interesting material on Capt. Frederick Brown, and Jeff Broome provided me with interesting information on buffalo hunting. These people are longtime friends as well as learned historians. My appreciation also goes to Luther Wilson, executive director of the University of New Mexico Press, friend and fly-fishing partner, for his staff's wonderfully adept production of the book.

Students in my Native Americans in American History classes inspired me immeasurably on this project as did many of the staff and students of Chief Dull Knife College in Lame Deer, Montana. I was an invited guest speaker at their annual cultural celebration in 2003 and met many interesting people I consider to be my friends. Professor Alonzo Spang and Conrad Fisher, dean of cultural affairs, deserve special thanks along with college president Richard Little Bear; his contributions to the present-day tribal college system are a source of awe for me. The late Ted Rising Son deserves my thanks and admiration for a variety of reasons. He remembered his ancestors like no other. Former director of the Little Wolf Writing and History Center, Catherine Feher-Elston, and her students, especially Glenda

Littlebird, may have inspired this project the most. To them this book is dedicated. Of course I owe a debt of gratitude to my wife, Linda, for her patience and efforts to make the manuscript at least halfway legible and to my son, Darren, who puts up with me and joins me with camera in hand in my excursions to such exotic places as the Powder River country.

—John H. Monnett
Boulder, Colorado

PROLOGUE

Rethinking Frontier Military History

THIS BOOK IS A NEW INTERPRETATION of the events surrounding the Powder River country and Fort Phil Kearny in 1866, particularly the annihilation of seventy-nine soldiers of the 18th U.S. Infantry and 2nd U.S. Cavalry and two civilians under the command of Capt. William Judd Fetterman on December 21, 1866. Two parallel stories are told here: that of the military, which was chronicled by author Dee Brown in 1962 and whose conclusions are now out of date in light of newer research, and that of the Lakotas, Cheyennes, and Arapahos, whose composite voices are often silent in the secondary source literature. Following that seminal year of "Red Cloud's War," 1866, the shock of the American public over the eighty-one whites killed at the hands of Lakotas, Arapahos, and Cheyennes demanded that someone take the blame for what the press called a disaster. What was a disaster for the U.S. Army, of course, constituted one of the greatest victories in their history for the Indians of the northern plains against American troops. Within a month of the fight, in order to fend off widespread criticism of his leadership, the commander at Fort Phil Kearny, Col. Henry B. Carrington, began casting blame and responsibility for the army's defeat on the dead commander of the tactical forces in the battle, Capt. William J. Fetterman. Carrington spent the remainder of his life pointing blame away from himself and onto Fetterman. For well over a century the Carrington version of the story of that year has stood largely unchallenged in the popular imagination.

Carrington's story was told in a published memoir written by his first wife, Margaret, in 1868: *Ab-sa-ra-ka: Home of the Crows*. It was told again in 1910 in a book by his second wife, Frances, in *My Army Life*. The first attempt at a fuller story of the military experience at Fort Phil Kearny was Dee Brown's *Fort Phil Kearny: An American Saga* (1962), later retitled *The Fetterman Massacre* over Brown's objection. Brown's book has stood as the definitive secondary study of the U.S. Army in the Powder River country of Wyoming (part of Dakota Territory in 1866) until the present day. This study challenges the Carringtons' and Dee Brown's assertions and conclusions. In 1966 in a chapter of his book *Indian Fights*, researcher J. W. Vaughn suggested that Fetterman was not to blame and that Carrington may have actually ordered Fetterman to pursue Indians over a precipice known as Lodge Trail Ridge, an order that resulted in his demise and that of eighty men of his command. More recently, historian Shannon D. Smith in a journal article suggested the same possibility and placed blame elsewhere. This study goes a step further in synthesizing the post–Dee Brown era research and in reanalyzing the original source material in a book-length study. I find some agreement and some disagreement with the more recent research. But I do find a significant amount of original source documentation that, when juxtaposed and reexamined alongside Indian original sources, points blame if not responsibility away from William J. Fetterman. In addition this study employs ethnohistorical methodologies and environmental histories to more fully explain the role of Fort Phil Kearny in the greater context of the Powder River country and the importance of that region during the 1860s. A thorough synthesis of all Indian sources on the war in the Powder River country in 1866 also finds corroboration with white documentation in revising some of the myths and inaccuracies of the traditional Carrington and Dee Brown stories, and again points blame elsewhere than Fetterman. Synthesis of the Indian original sources also brings to light new conclusions regarding the roles of several Indian leaders in that conflict, especially Crazy Horse, which have previously not been considered in depth.

Events like the Fetterman fight can illuminate the significance of frontier military history and Native American history and their relevance to how culturally diverse peoples interpret the complex American story. As such, a base of philosophical assumptions is pertinent to an understanding of the multicultural and gendered nature of the military frontier of the West. The Fetterman story continues to fascinate because, like Custer and the Battle of Little Bighorn, no one will ever know the complete details of what happened simply because one contingent in the fight was annihilated with no one left alive to tell the tale from the perspectives of those participants. In such cases historians—inevitably—speculate. Much of military history is necessarily speculative in nature, and the military history of the West after the Civil War, like the great sectional conflict itself as well as modern wars, is a classic example of intense speculation. "Several million words, or so it sometimes seems," writes Pulitzer Prize–winning military historian James M. McPherson, "have been written about which Confederate general was responsible for losing the Battle of Gettysburg."[1] Where does the true responsibility lie for the aborted Bay of Pigs invasion? How can we meaningfully evaluate the events of Operation Iraqi Freedom? Military history engages at least two, and often more, antagonist groups with different points of view as to right and wrong and each with different visions for the future of the land being fought over. Often there is no single definitive answer so scholars postulate, speculate, "choose sides," and offer possible alternative explanations based on the same body of original source evidence. In interpreting great battles, military historians usually suggest motivations for commanders' decisions and enemy commanders' responses to those decisions. Explanations for defeat are even more intensively analytical. As such the validity of the military historian's methodology often comes into question among other more agenda-driven scholars of the social sciences who regard speculation as a literary device appropriate only for the novelist and of little worth for illuminating problems of the present day.

Frequently military historians are pushed to the periphery of what might be considered "relevant" historical research. Why is it significant to analyze a battle simply to reflect on why and how it was won or lost? After all, military historians write about war, and the very concept of war has rightly come into question in the twenty-first century. Are there not more important social issues upon which to focus meaningful historical research? But experience as a military historian has shown me over the years that a majority of serious scholars of this subfield, and I definitely include myself in the mix, are among the most vocal antiwar activists in Western civilization. Like an MD studying the physiology of disease, our purposes are not to glorify war or disease but to show them up for what they are and to perhaps trick ourselves into believing that in some small manner we are paving the way for the eventual eradication of both. So we speculate.

Our task is made more difficult if our research specialty involves wars of conquest and colonialism of indigenous peoples. Similar difficulties are encountered by British, French, Spanish, Japanese, and German military historians who write about their nations' imperial past. Colonialism is a rightfully discredited sociopolitical system in the twenty-first century. A conflict of cultures is too simplistic an explanation for such wars. These were wars of politics involving questions of sovereignty and land usage. Consequently the history of a region like the American West in this regard presents ethical problems for the military historian. How many millions of words, how many hundreds, even thousands of books and articles over the past century and a quarter have advanced differing speculative arguments regarding who was to blame for Lt. Col. George Custer's demise at Little Bighorn—perhaps more even than Gettysburg? Or was it, to paraphrase western military historian Robert M. Utley, a matter of Custer's losing simply because the Indians won? If so, much of the interest and intrigue of one of the most hotly debated topics in western history has lost its luster because we have taken away the allure of speculation. But there are many who say, "Who cares. Why are such things important?" Custer is an antiquarian anachronism in the twenty-first century. So is Capt. William J. Fetterman. After all, both Custer and Fetterman lost. Speculation over why they lost is a meaningless intellectual exercise when we consider five hundred years of colonialism that culminated in the deaths of millions of indigenous people. Aside from the antiquarian *intrigue* of trying to solve a most interesting yet comparatively unimportant mystery that never will be completely solved, these critics might be right. What is the *significance* of George Custer and William Fetterman, if any, in the collective psyche of Americans today, both Indian and non-Indian? Have they become symbols of something larger than what they were and what they did? Is not the story of colonial conquest, loss of land, and sovereignty more important? Are Custer and Fetterman not merely symbols of that colonialism and conquest? And are not some Indian people emphasizing a desire to decolonize their history in the twenty-first century?

There is no question that Indians of the Western Hemisphere and indigenous peoples everywhere were horribly exploited by Euro-American conquerors who had different visions for the future use of indigenous people's lands. Five hundred years of history reveal the greatest depopulation and sometimes outright genocide in the history of the world. Ethnohistorians today find the demography and epidemiology of Indian depopulation and recovery a rich field for research. My fifteen-week classes on Native Americans in American history do not begin to allow me the time to tell the full story of those incomprehensible population statistics. For many years the history of the American expansion movement was written strictly from the viewpoint of the victors, with Indian peoples (among others) reduced to the status of "savages," elements of a dangerous untamed environment with a "frontier line" separating savagery and civilization that demanded conquest and civilizing or extermination, all justified by the precepts and perceived inevitability of manifest destiny. Their voices went unheard. In 1971 all that changed. Dee Brown published *Bury My Heart at Wounded Knee: An Indian History of the American West*. Although the historical methodology is marginal and the narrative contains factual errors and serious omissions, the book was nevertheless nothing short of revolutionary. More than any other volume of its day, *Bury My Heart at Wounded Knee*, a national bestseller and social phenomenon, revised many people's ways of thinking regarding Indians' roles in American history. It inspired serious scholars to think about new ways to look at and reinterpret the history of the American West and all of its ethnically diverse peoples converging in a defined geographical region. Brown reversed the old genre western psychology. He took the "black hats" off the Indians and put them on the whites, and took the "white hats" off the whites and put them on the Indians. This simple reversal became a shocking new interpretation based on an old body of knowledge. It was history written *about* the losers. But it still employed the same old literary device of good guys in white hats and bad guys in black hats.

In the twenty-first century most serious scholars of the military frontier agree that it is no longer appropriate to tell the story of this important era in American history strictly from the viewpoint of the conquering races. Inclusion and convergence of diverse peoples in the West is far more meaningful. Problems do arise, however, given the comparative scarcity of Indian original sources. Their voices are often too silent in the early records. Where they do exist they are usually filtered through the cultural lenses of white interviewers who befriended some of the surviving Indian veterans of the Indian Wars during the early twentieth century. Scholars like George B. Grinnell and George F. Hyde were ethnographically oriented. Both included elements of Indian culture, thinking, and worldviews in their final products derived from their many interviews and correspondences. Hyde's work is amazing in that he was almost blind by his twenties. Perhaps that is why he was known to colleagues for being impatient and cranky. Still he sought the truth and had little patience for myth. Others, like John Neihardt and

Thomas Marquis, while not ethnographers by training should have been eth-nographers. Today the writing of frontier military history has appropriately grown more ethically complex. As all of Western American history relies more now than ever on interdisciplinary approaches, so too should western military history encourage ethnohistorical methodology to be employed in examining indigenous viewpoints.

Regrettably, much literature still prevails from strictly the perspective of the U.S. Army, although this trend is rapidly changing. Such literature does not fare well with ethnohistorians. Conversely, ethnohistories have tradition-ally been written mostly from the Indian viewpoint and, in large part today, still are written from that viewpoint. My experience behind podiums around the West over thirty years convinces me that many military "buffs" do not read the ethnohistories even though such works would give them a broader perspective on the subject. Among writers, polarization of thought also con-tinues in regards to documented history versus ethnohistorical methodolo-gies. Methodology still unfortunately separates historians and ethnologists far too often. The results still define peoples of the West as good guys in white hats and bad guys in black hats rather than acknowledging that peoples in the West simply wore different hats.

How much can military historians rely on latter-day oral histories more than a century removed from the events in question? Many historians think we cannot rely on such sources. Historian Ned Blackhawk points out that family histories highlight "the power of narrative both to define a people's essence and to instill a deep sense of cultural pride."[2] But how far can we go in assigning individual actions played out in known events through assumptions based not on specific evidence but on known cultural customs, practices, family traditions, and beliefs? More than a small amount of ethnohistori-cal writing over the years has reflected the notion that we can rely on such reconstructions as valid evidence. My research corroborating written docu-ments with evidence of art, such as depicted in the winter counts of the Plains Indians, does indeed convince me that such artistic records *do* qualify as origi-nal source historical documents. Latter-day oral family stories two or three generations removed from the events in question, however, can be another matter. Sometimes fabricated stories told by whites creep into Indian oral tra-dition as well as secondary documentary history. Yellowstone historian Lee H. Whittlesey found that in over a century of storytelling by national park guides of one ilk or another, "there are a great number of so-called 'Indian stories' that can be dismissed as tales made up by whites, probably to explain what Indians 'should have thought' about Yellowstone." Whittlesey argues that "Indian stories" actually originated by whites are "written too slickly and [have] too much perfectly balanced drama . . . to ring true as real Indian legend."[3] Of course military documents can also be misleading and sometimes self-serving. Usually written as "official reports" of one form or another, now housed in the National Archives, documents by officers often attempted to put themselves and their immediate commands in the best light possible during an age, technically speaking, of a "peacetime army" when opportunities for combat were infrequent and promotions slow. Sometimes officers' reports conflicted with those of other officers' reports and with Indian accounts and reminiscences of enlisted men written years later. Less frequently officers' reports were condemnatory of fellow officers in order to cast blame for a failed action away from themselves and onto another person. With all the controversy surrounding the Fetterman fight, this action is rife with such reports and reminiscences. Military historians have always argued among themselves, not unlike the officers of the military units they study. Today, with the inclusion of ethnohistory, that is, anthropology, sociology, and archaeology assimilated with military history, the academic debate becomes far more comprehensive and interdisciplinary than in the past. Sometimes each tries to reject the validity of the other.

So who is right? Perhaps military historians and ethnohistorians will never agree on all things. But in different ways both are right and eventually both must shake hands, come together, and accept the precepts of each other's work. Anthropology today *is* an essential ingredient in interpreting the historical record. Modern oral testimony is likewise useful to demonstrate how modern peoples retain pride and reverence for their history and their heroes. Among many Indian people today oral tradition holds greater weight than among non-Indians. According to Lydia Whirlwind Soldier, a Lakota, "The oral tradition is sometimes considered as legend or myth [by non-Indians], without the credibility that these stories deserve. Most tribal members who have heard our relatives tell the stories, however, read the non-Indians' historical accounts with doubt and sometimes disbelief."[4] Anthropologists have often used as a guidepost to test the validity of oral tradition a contrasting of that tradition against eyewitness accounts, written or otherwise.[5] Gordon M. Day argues that "the validity of the oral tradition is enhanced by its goodness of fit with the historical data." He refers to such methodology as "oral history as complement."[6] More recently modern oral tradition has become more acceptable in ethnohistory whereas academic historians still emphasize corroboration of modern testimony with older or eyewitness testimony. Ethnohistorians emphasize that Indians know their history better than non-Indians.[7]

Ethnohistorical methodology is therefore appropriate to some degree in writing frontier military history. The *way* that it is applied is a critical factor. Due to the popularity of their subject matter, frontier military historians find themselves needing to appeal to different and often wider audiences of general readers than ethnohistorians and are thus usually cautious in employing latter-day oral testimony. It has always been my firm belief that meaningful interpretation of frontier military history must balance *all* antagonists' viewpoints to some extent within the same work. As such, Gordon M. Day's strategy rings true: ethnohistorical methodologies and latter-day family histories should be corroborated with multiple sources of evidence when possible. This approach in no way moderates my basic belief that Indian histories, oral or written, can stand alone if proper comprehensive historical methodology is utilized.

During the 1980s and 1990s the field of American Indian history exploded. Almost immediately scholars recognized that the subject required multidisciplinary research approaches. There was an effort to move beyond the old, timeworn topic of America's Indian Wars. During the late 1980s ethnohistorians Melissa L. Meyer and Russell Thornton wrote, "Historians continue to devote more attention to Indian white conflict, Indian resistance leaders, and federal policy than they do such questions as Indian family life, economic activity, cultural persistence, and political change . . . Sophisticated studies of tribal social structure, reservation culture, and labor patterns will lead us away from a preoccupation with past conflict and policy to a fuller picture of the Indian's historical experience."[8] Currently, some Native American scholars are emphasizing a need to "decolonize" Indian history and focus on the roots of contemporary problems in the tribal communities. An Internet discussion on H-AmIndian reflected this trend. Native American scholar Devon Mihesuah argues that scholars have a responsibility to the Indian communities they study and that "authors need to be accountable to tribes." Scholars should focus research on topics dictated by tribal agendas. "More practical and useful studies," she argues, are needed, "instead of more-of-the-same about topics we've seen repeatedly."[9] In 1991 Vine Deloria Jr. commented that "we need to eliminate useless or repetitive research and focus on actual community needs; it is both unethical and wasteful to plow familiar ground continually."[10]

Certainly times have changed. By the first decade of the twenty-first century the new Indian history has rightly made tremendous strides. Unfortunately military historians of the West have been among the last of the scholars of Native America to embrace these multidisciplinary evolutions, thus pushing their work even further to the periphery of the field. Presumably for some, we are at the forefront of plowing the wasteful and familiar ground to which Mihesuah and Deloria have alluded. Still, interest and curiosity in the frontier military period remains high. Beginning in 1985 the D'Arcy McNickle Center for the History of the American Indian, founded in 1972 at the Newberry Library, began compiling bibliographies of virtually all aspects of research topics, papers, and books produced in recent years that deal with Indian history. The bibliographies demonstrate that the resistance period of Indians in American history is alive and well and still of immense interest to both scholars and the general public today. The catalog offerings of university presses have continued to reflect the same interest.

During the early twenty-first century an unusual number of immaculately scholarly books have appeared on the so-called French and Indian Wars and on conflicts with eastern tribes during the colonial and early national periods. The continued interest is not just restricted to the far West. Recent biographies of Crazy Horse, Victorio, Gall, and a forthcoming offering from Yale by Robert Utley on the life and times of Geronimo are all products of the twenty-first century. Perhaps most important, what many of the new Indian historians fail to mention in their focus on decolonization is that Indian people throughout the Western Hemisphere share a five-hundred-year history with non-Indian people. Much of that story involves colonization as does much of the history of non-Indian peoples in the hemisphere. In all cultures throughout the Americas, diverse groups of peoples remember and share with pride the stories of their resistance and revolutionary heroes, and research and revision continue to "repeatedly" focus on those heroes and their times. A nation remembers its tragedies as well as its mistakes. As such the accomplishments of a people are never placed grossly out of proportion to their entire history. In essence Indians and non-Indian military buffs look at this topic quite differently. Non-Indians focus more on campaigns, strategies, and tactics. Indians focus more on long-range results such as loss of land and sovereignty.

My own conversations with Indian students in my classes and on the Northern Cheyenne Indian Reservation reflect strong pride in their historical heroes in the American West. Readers of all ethnicities simply find the topic interesting and of everlasting importance for numerous reasons. Recently a student attending Chief Dull Knife College in Lame Deer, Montana, wrote me following a visit celebrating, in part, the great odyssey made by the Northern Cheyennes from Indian Territory (Oklahoma) back to their homelands in Montana, a topic on which I had recently written a book. As I drove along the highway between Busby and Lame Deer I worried the Cheyennes would not find that topic timely and relevant. I soon discovered the young lady in question was going through some tough times. "It's times like these," she wrote to me, "when I'm having a hard time, that I think about my ancestors. They fought so hard to get me where I am today . . . I think about what my ancestors went through, like having to run through the winter with their little ones and losing many on the way that makes me feel stronger and more willing to carry on. Your book touched my heart and is in my mind when I feel downhearted and unmotivated. You're doing great things for our people and one day I feel that I will too."[11] Although I am embarrassed to write of this experience, I can assure my readers the above statement is not presented here as an attempt to "toot my own horn," so to speak. Rather it is a simple illustration that challenges the axiom that research on "more of the same" type of topics is "wasteful," or worse, "unethical." Given the elements of cultural pride in and honor of one's history, military historians of the frontier, through revision and inclusion of multiple viewpoints, can indeed be "accountable to the people they study," as Professor Mihesuah asserts, and, I might add, to *all* the people they study.[12]

But what constitutes the non-Indian side of this story, and is it a story still worthy of telling? When an element of mystery is interjected into history, the speculation over "what really happened"—even though possibly, at any given point, unanswerable—remains nonetheless irresistible and will stimulate further research, further speculation, and further interpretation regardless of its importance in shedding light on contemporary issues. When formulating speculative scenarios, the historian's thesis is only definitive until replaced by another. The classic example in western history is again, of course, the Battle of Little Bighorn. Newly proclaimed "definitive" interpretations have proliferated for over a century. Although often neglected, another example is the Fetterman fight. The view of Col. Henry Carrington, commander at Fort Phil Kearny in 1866, has been generally accepted for well over a century without question until now. But the debate over why the so-called Fetterman disaster happened in the first place has confused the larger story of the struggle for the Powder River country among several groups of peoples who converged in that land, including Lakotas, Cheyennes, Arapahos, Shoshonis, and Crows as well as Euro-Americans.

This book presents an alternative vision of the struggle for the Powder River country in 1866 between Indian factions that lived and hunted there and the ambitions of the federal government, including the U.S. Army, as to the proper use of the region. Of course the struggle for the Powder River country involved many different peoples over a much longer period of time, beginning in earnest in the 1840s and extending through the 1870s. A comprehensive history of the entire struggle would take multiple volumes, an endeavor that may, in the future, be in the offing. But I have limited this book primarily to 1866 because the history of that year is so crowded. Eighteen sixty-six was the seminal year for control of this important geophysical region. The year was climaxed by the invasion of the Powder River country and the construction of three new forts in the prized land by the U.S. Army that culminated with the famous Fetterman fight, a battle the Lakotas and Cheyennes call "Where a Hundred Soldiers Were Killed" or "Hundred in the Hand." Events of the late 1850s and the years following 1866 and through the next decade constitute the cause-and-effect relationships to that watershed year. But the story is vast and requires some preliminary overview of events as well as an analysis of cultural and environmental developments and changes before 1866 that helped provoke conflict. To understand the Fetterman fight alone is not sufficient to understand the bitter war that was fought in that year, the previous two years, 1864–65, and again in 1867 and into 1868. Consequently a general overview of events preceding and following the Fetterman fight is likewise considered in this study.

Again, the traditional view of the conflict in 1866 is Dee Brown's *Fort Phil Kearny: An American Saga* (1962), later retitled *The Fetterman Massacre*. It has stood for almost half a century. Brown accepts Carrington's explanation of the event and, like the colonel, blames Fetterman's alleged disobedience of orders as the cause of what the government considered to be a calamity for the U.S. Army in the West.

But problems exist with the work. Puzzlingly, unlike Brown's more famous book, *Bury My Heart at Wounded Knee*, *Fort Phil Kearny* gives short shrift to the Indian side of the Powder River story. Brown's book is basically about the tenure of the post commander in 1866, Col. Henry B. Carrington, about his experiences and those of his family during the months they were stationed at Fort Phil Kearny. Brown emphasizes how Carrington successfully endeavored for most of his life to clear his name of any wrongdoing for the annihilation of Fetterman and eighty men on December 21, 1866. This study takes issue with some of Brown's interpretations and conclusions in several ways while not necessarily blaming Colonel Carrington. It also goes beyond Brown's work in relating the Indian side of the story more fully.

I also focus on important previous errors of omission. Almost always the importance of the Powder River country is explained quickly and simply with a brief sentence or two stating that the region was a prized hunting area with plenty of game. This notion needs a more thorough examination. Building upon ethnohistorical methodology, environmental history, and scientific sources, I include here information on the geophysical changes on the Great Plains in the two decades before 1866. This time was a period of significant climatic and ecological change that redistributed native peoples and the animals they hunted in many ways. This environmental dimension to the ethnohistory of the tribes of the region, not previously broadly examined, paints a more complete picture of the immense social, political, and military importance of the Powder River country to different peoples.

More eyewitness Indian testimonies to the Fetterman fight exist than for any engagement in Plains Indian Wars history other than Little Bighorn and Wounded Knee. Yet all of them taken together (Lakota and Cheyenne) have never before been presented in total in timeline fashion alongside the movements of the American soldiers who died on what came to be called Massacre Ridge. By blending these original-source Indian accounts to a fuller potential and comparatively examining their agreements and discrepancies with military documents, different conclusions may be drawn from those of Dee Brown. Although Brown and others have largely focused on the personalities of Henry Carrington and to a far lesser extent on the other officers at Fort

Phil Kearny in 1866, this study stresses also the roles played by Indian leaders, particularly Red Cloud and Crazy Horse of the Oglalas, Miniconjou leaders like High Backbone, and the sometimes neglected Cheyennes. Recently the roles of women at Fort Phil Kearny have come to light.[13] My findings often conflict with other traditional and recent accounts regarding the roles of several of these important Indian figures.

But for many the story of Fort Phil Kearny and the Fetterman fight *is* the clash of personalities among the junior officers at the fort with their commanding officer, Col. Henry Carrington. The story simply cannot be told without examining this dimension. The traditional view as detailed by Dee Brown and based on Carrington's reports and testimonies portrays Capt. William J. Fetterman as an arrogant, disobedient officer, whose lack of respect for his commanding officer led to his foolish demise and the destruction of his command at the hands of perhaps two thousand Lakota, Cheyenne, and Arapaho warriors. Often the words used to describe his character are "arrogant" and "fire-eater." This study departs noticeably from that stereotype. Another major purpose is to synthesize research conducted after Dee Brown's book was published. My findings dispute the notion that Fetterman was arrogant and personally or primarily to blame for the first annihilation of a sizeable battalion of the U.S. Army in the West. I suggest the blame lies squarely on the shoulders of Lt. George Washington Grummond, who died with Fetterman along with Capt. Frederick Brown.

By revising the view of William J. Fetterman's character I also find that a body of myth has been perpetuated. This study concludes with an interpretive essay that considers that body of myth. This examination adds a dimension to the Fetterman legacy by presenting underused multidisciplinary information that hopefully illuminates the *significance* of the Fetterman story through an examination of the power not only of myth but of historical irony as well, as vehicles for keeping alive false images and stereotypes of past events and personalities.

As with Custer, the Fetterman story relating to its key figures likewise presents enough discrepancies to warrant new considerations and differing interpretations. On balance, for both Indian and white participants who shaped the story of the struggle for the Powder River country of 1866, these alternative views, I hope, will stimulate further interest and debate over this significant period of American history on the northern plains. Certainly there will be disagreement with my views. I hope readers *will* ponder the questions that may be raised, and perhaps arrive at different viewpoints from mine. As James McPherson has stated regarding his own work, "I welcome disagreement and dialog, for that is how scholarship and understanding advance."[14] Ultimately though, like the story of the Little Bighorn, we shall probably never completely solve all the mysteries of the struggle for the Powder River country despite our views and biases, however passionate. But then, speculating on those mysteries is what makes the story all the more interesting and perhaps all the more responsible to the descendents of the people involved.

INTRODUCTION

And so they perished on that barren hill
Beside the Peno. And the Winter strode
Numb-footed down that bloody stretch of road
At twilight, when a squadron came to read
The corpse-writ rune of battle, deed by deed,
Between the Ridge's summit and the ford.
The blizzard broke at dusk. All night it roared
Round Fort Phil Kearny mourning for the
Slain.

—John G. Neihardt[1]

MASSACRE RIDGE AS IT WAS CALLED throughout the last century still looks austere in the new one. On a bitter cold December day the biting wind cuts to the bone like an icy blade as it did in 1866, one of the worst Decembers on record in the Powder River country. Down below the hill in the ravine beneath an open plateau sheltered by ridges the scrawny hardwoods are devoid of summer foliage and patches of hard rotten snow cling tight to shaded places. The interpreters in the visitor center at Fort Phil Kearny State Historic Site will tell you the dogwoods were thicker along Peno Creek in 1866, but viewing this harsh Wyoming landscape in winter, it is hard to believe. Here on December 21, 1866, a well-organized force of perhaps two thousand Oglala and Miniconjou Lakotas, perhaps a few Brulés, Northern Cheyennes, and Arapahos destroyed a detachment of forty-nine federal troops of companies A, C, E, and H of the 18th U.S. Infantry; twenty-seven troopers of Company C, 2nd U.S. Cavalry; and two civilians, James S. Wheatley and Isaac Fisher, under the command of Capt. William J. Fetterman. In addition, captains Fetterman and Frederick H. Brown and 2nd Lt. George Washington Grummond, all officers of the 18th Infantry, lost their lives. The troops had been decoyed over Lodge Trail Ridge above their isolated post, Fort Phil Kearny, near modern Story, Wyoming, at the time a part of the large Dakota Territory. The annihilation of the eighty-one men of Fetterman's command was the worst defeat for the U.S. Army in the far West to that time. The fight was only exceeded by the fabled Battle of Little Bighorn a decade later. The casualties accounted for more deaths along the Bozeman Trail between Fort Laramie and Montana than all other deaths along the trail combined during a three-year period. The Fetterman casualties totaled about 8 percent of the army's killed-in-action during a half-century of Indian warfare in the trans-Mississippi West.[2]

Details of the "Fetterman massacre," as it was called, did not reach the East rapidly because the military posts in the Powder River country were about as isolated on the North American continent as could be found anywhere three years before the completion of the transcontinental railway. Newspaper war correspondents would not make their way to remote army posts until 1867.[3] Riders had to travel through heavy snow in subzero weather to Fort Laramie on the Platte River Road some 236 miles below Fort Phil Kearny in order to post telegrams and request reinforcements for the beleaguered fort. For citizens of the East, weary of four years of horrific Civil War, the event seemed like a minor incident in a far-off and unimportant land. At first reports were but mere snippets on back pages of newspapers. Even in towns close to the Great Plains frontier, editors seemed more concerned with stories from the Reconstruction South and recent activities of the militant Irish Fenian Brotherhood.[4] Only when the magnitude of the event became known did America thirst for answers. By 1868, the army abandoned the forts along the Bozeman Trail and Fort Phil Kearny was burned to the ground by Little Wolf's Northern Cheyennes. The government closed the Bozeman Trail to emigrant travel by 1867. The politics of the Treaty of 1868 that closed the forts and seemingly favored the Lakotas, especially Red Cloud's Oglalas, would haunt both the federal government and the Lakotas for years to come. The status of William J. Fetterman as a martyr to manifest destiny was almost forgotten after writers made comparison to Custer's defeat in 1876 and because of efforts of the captain's commanding officer, Col. Henry B. Carrington, who cast blame on Fetterman for the defeat in order to absolve himself of the same.

Carrington's obsession with clearing his own name moved quickly. Did Fetterman exercise poor tactical judgment by allowing the Indians to decoy him over Lodge Trail Ridge where he was met by hundreds, even thousands, of waiting warriors? Did he disobey orders because of contempt for his commanding officer as Carrington further alleged? Most of the officers at Fort Phil Kearny despised Carrington, a Yale lawyer and a political military appointee from Ohio who had once served as Washington Irving's secretary during the Mexican-American War. Although the official commander of the 18th Infantry since the Civil War, Carrington had never seen combat during the great rebellion. His defense-mindedness was ineffective against warriors of the plains, his officers claimed, as did his department commander, Gen. Philip St. George Cooke. His command decisions were ineffective, ill timed, and inappropriate, the officers said, while also slamming Cooke for not giving Carrington enough men and effective weapons. Carrington countered by blaming Cooke for the same reasons. He then blamed the dead Fetterman for disobedience and insubordination. As western expansion began once again to take a more prominent stage in American current affairs after the controversial election of 1876, the enigma grew and the Fetterman fight gained notoriety as an event comparable to Little Bighorn. And throughout it all no one considered the statistical probability that if one's command is outnumbered almost twenty-five to one, in all likelihood those forces will be defeated. In the case of the Fetterman fight an analogy may be made to historian Robert Utley's words regarding Little Bighorn in his masterful biography of George Armstrong Custer. His modern sentiments apply equally to the troops at Fort Phil Kearny in 1866: "To ascribe defeat entirely to military failings is to devalue Indian strength and leadership."[5]

Yet in the last decades of the nineteenth century, a time when forces of global imperialism, Social Darwinism, and colonialism held sway as sound and righteous government policy for the industrializing nations of the world, there was little sentiment for ascribing victory to indigenous peoples. The thinking was: the army lost because someone in command authority, at some point in the process, made massive mistakes.

Consequently the Fetterman fight has built up over the years a sense of mystery, like Little Bighorn, because none of the soldiers in the fight lived to tell what happened. Like Little Bighorn the mystery has logically, and sometimes illogically, fostered a body of myth, some of which has endured to this day. Much of the myth from the Indian Wars period has endured because of a lack of belief, or lack of respect, over the years for the accounts of Native American participants. When their stories are told as more than mere sketches of their actions, or more than obligatory generalizations, they are told in works whose separateness occasionally creates confusion for the students of the events in question. The mysteries, like the perceived "right" of an industrializing nation to intrude into Third World environments and societies, are clouded by ethnocentric bias. Therefore the myths that emerged from the events of 1866 became shaped on faulty assumptions. One of the officers at Fort Phil Kearny made massive mistakes. How else could a group of aboriginal peoples standing in the path of manifest destiny obliterate a portion of a veteran unit that had won glory and suffered one of the highest casualty rates of the Civil War among the regulars of the Union army?[6] As a result, this thinking led to an official investigation on the part of the War Department to ascertain what had happened at Fort Phil Kearny and if necessary to fix blame. Accusations spurring the investigation had gone far up the chain of command.[7]

The final report of the Sanborn Commission, as the official investigating committee assigned to investigate the possibility of negligence at Fort Phil Kearny was called, absolved Carrington personally for the deaths of Fetterman and his men. Nevertheless, the government buried the official documents of the Sanborn Commission in Indian Bureau files along with letters of prominent Carrington detractors including the commander of the Department of the Platte, Gen. Philip St. George Cooke, and James Powell, an officer at Fort Phil Kearny. Public opinion remained negative toward Carrington while the eighty-one dead on or near Massacre Ridge momentarily became martyrs to westward expansion. Carrington spent the next twenty years seeking vindication.[8] By the early twentieth century, because of the sheer volume of materials alone, Carrington's version became the *only* story of the fight for the Powder River country and it mostly persists to this day.[9]

In 1908, at the age of eighty-four, Henry Carrington returned to Wyoming with his wife Frances to dedicate a stone monument on Massacre Ridge, the site of the last stand of Fetterman's troops forty-two years previously. Carrington was the keynote speaker and used the opportunity once again to vindicate himself and cast blame on Fetterman. The inscription on the brown stone monument that had actually been in place since 1905 still stands today. The metal plaque reads as follows:

On This Field On The 21st Day of December, 1866, Three
Commissioned Officers And Seventy-Six Privates Of The 18th U.S.
Infantry And Of The 2nd U.S. Cavalry And Four Civilians Under
The Command of Captain, Brevet Lieutenant Colonel William J.
Fetterman Were Killed By An Overwhelming Force of Sioux Under
The Command Of Red Cloud. There Were No Survivors.

The inscription is wrong on several accounts. There were only two civilian casualties, not four. Cheyennes and Arapahos were also present. Red
Cloud, by numerous accounts, did not personally lead the ambush. And, of
course there *were* survivors, perhaps two thousand Indians or more.[10] Today
the Lakotas and Cheyennes remember the fight as a great victory, second
only to Custer's defeat a decade later. Some warriors claimed there were
more Indians in the Fetterman fight than in the Battle of Little Bighorn.
The Lakotas and Cheyennes call the engagement "Where a Hundred Soldiers
Were Killed [or slain]" or "Hundred in the Hand." White writers have often
referred to it as the "Fetterman disaster" or the "Fetterman massacre."[11] It
was not a massacre. Armed soldiers were pursuing Indians with whom they
were at war and whom they intended to engage in combat if possible. No
noncombatants lost their lives on either side that day over Lodge Trail Ridge.
The term "massacre" does not reflect actual events and diminishes the strategic and tactical victory of one of the greatest military accomplishments for
the Plains Indians in their history.

Although the Fetterman fight has always been looked upon as a great
victory by Lakotas loosely under Red Cloud's influence, the Northern
Cheyennes claimed shortly after the battle that the spiritual medicine of the
Cheyenne holy man Crazy Mule, whose gaze could incur dizziness among
the enemy, causing them to become disoriented and fall over, was responsible
for the victory.[12] Cheyenne historian Father Peter John Powell argues that the
battle marked the beginning of the ascendancy of the Northern Cheyenne
Elkhorn Scraper soldier society. The leader of the Elks was Little Wolf, Sweet
Medicine Chief of all Cheyennes, who would win recognition from Indians
and whites alike for his 1,700-mile trek from Indian Territory to homelands
in the Powder River country in 1878–79, the high water mark of Northern
Cheyenne history in the nineteenth century.[13]

The Cheyennes leave us with some of the most vivid accounts of the fight, ones that corroborate tightly the Lakota accounts in terms of the significant events. Most of the Indian testimony, however, is filtered through the notes and writings of white interviewers like George Bird Grinnell, Thomas Marquis, and Walter Campbell. But the Indian testimonies conform remarkably with the forensic evidence and military accounts.[14]

That such a defeat of a unit of the regular U.S. Army could take place at the hands of aboriginal peoples was almost unimaginable during the latter half of the decade of the 1860s. To the Lakotas and their allies, however, the enormity of the event and their huge numbers at the fight, and their intent to annihilate the troops at Fort Phil Kearny (they would try for such total victory again in 1867) need both introspection and a wide vision. To understand the unusual intensity of the Indians' feelings in their hatred of the forts in the Powder River country we cannot limit our focus to the Fetterman fight as an isolated event. The Powder River country, despite its isolation from all but a small segment of Euro-American population in 1866, already had compiled a long, rich history of cultural interactions. It was an important contested land and had been long before Henry Carrington or William Fetterman had probably even heard of it. The region had been fought over not only between Indians and whites but between Indian factions as well and for reasons that had far-reaching consequences. To understand the seminal events of 1866 in the Powder River country, it is necessary to explore the environmental changes throughout the arid West just before the 1860s and the resultant patterns of movement of peoples on the northern plains during these important and turbulent times.

CHAPTER 1

THE SOWING OF THE DRAGON

At last the four year storm of fratricide
Had ceased at Appomattox, and the tide
Of war-bit myriads, like a turning sea's,
Recoiled upon the deep realities
That yields no foam to any squall of change.[1]

ON APRIL 24, 1865, AN EIGHT-YEAR-OLD MIXED-BLOOD GIRL stood on a dusty plain about one and a half miles from Fort Laramie, Wyoming, then a part of the Dakota Territory. She was Susan Bordeaux, the daughter of a post trader, French-American James Bordeaux, and Red Cormorant Woman, a Brulé Lakota of the Red Top Lodge Band. Seventy years later, when Susan Bordeaux Bettelyoun transcribed her memoirs, she still vividly remembered the ghastly scene she had witnessed on that long ago spring day. A Cheyenne warrior had been brought to this place by soldiers of the 11th Ohio Cavalry. The warrior was singing his death song. Soldiers escorted him to a scaffold and placed a heavy chain around his neck. Around his foot was another chain attached to a manacle and a heavy iron ball. He was to be hanged in chains. As the wagon upon which the Cheyenne was standing pulled away he grabbed the chain and pulled himself up to a crosspiece on the scaffold. Some of the soldiers in the execution detail wanted to shoot him but the orders from General Connor stated hanging. A soldier suddenly climbed the scaffold, grabbed the chain, and pulled. Both men came crashing down from the scaffold. The Cheyenne kicked and struggled, slowly suffocating, until his body went limp, dangling by the chain around his neck and the heavy prison ball manacled to his foot. Months later the ghastly figure was still there, hanging, the ball having pulled the decomposed leg completely off where it lay as a warning in the ripe prairie grass below the rotted corpse.[2]

The Cheyenne's name was Big Crow, a war leader of the Elkhorn Scraper soldier society, which was composed mostly of Northern Cheyennes living in the Powder River country. Big Crow had been given the honor by his soldier society of luring troops out of Camp Rankin near Julesburg, Colorado Territory, earlier that year. The action was a raid of revenge allegedly for the Sand Creek Massacre of November 29, 1864. Big Crow had been captured two months earlier and charged with murder. When soldiers of the 11th Ohio returned to Fort Laramie in an angry mood after recent engagements with Indians in the North Platte River country in April, they had dragged Big Crow from the guardhouse and tried to lynch him. Two days later Big Crow met his fate under orders from Gen. Patrick E. Connor, commander of the Military District of the Plains and known to the Indians as "Red Beard." Connor sent a telegram from his headquarters in Denver to Lt. Col. William Balmer, commander of Fort Laramie. Big Crow was to be taken to the spot where a soldier had been recently killed near the fort. "Erect a high gallows," Connor ordered; "hang him in chains and leave the body suspended."[3]

One month later, on May 26, 1865, this form of military due process was repeated again at Fort Laramie. This time the victims were two Oglala Lakota chiefs, Two Face and Black Foot, both leaders of the Spleen band. Once again young Susan Bordeaux witnessed the grisly execution. Two Face had been captured on May 15 by Indian scouts from Fort Laramie, about ten miles east of the post. Two Face's people had with them Mrs. Lucinda Eubank and her small son. They had been captured on the Little Blue River by Cheyennes in August 1864 and traded to the Lakotas. Although the woman had been abused and mistreated, Two Face claimed to be bringing her to Fort Laramie for release. On May 24, Indian scouts also captured Black Foot's band about one hundred miles from the fort.

Col. Thomas Moonlight, commander of the 11th Kansas Volunteer Cavalry, now in charge of the Fort Laramie section of the Subdistrict of the Department of the Plains, determined that Two Face and Big Foot had led raids in Kansas and Nebraska the previous year. Moonlight assumed authority to have the two chiefs hanged on May 26. "Tie them by the neck with trace chains, suspended by a beam of wood," Moonlight declared, "and leave them there without any foothold."[4] The two chiefs went to their deaths boasting they had killed many whites and would continue to do so if they were set free. Although other officers feared retribution from the Lakotas and Cheyennes, the two corpses, like that of Big Crow's, were left hanging as a warning to transgressors. Later that spring, General Conner relieved

Moonlight of his command for incompetence in handling administrative matters and ordered his mustering-out from military service.[5]

"No one dared go near the place" after that, Susan Bordeaux remembered years later. "All the travelers going west could see these bodies hanging there from the scaffold." In August a priest (Susan claimed he was Father DeSmet, but probably not), arrived at Fort Laramie. "He could see the Indian corpses hanging from the scaffold," Susan remembered, "dangling in midair. Every wind that blew just swayed them back and forth." Big Crow's skeleton was still hanging. He "had a large Mexican medallion tied up in his black handkerchief around his neck. As he swung in the wind it shone bright and glistening like a looking glass against the sun." The clergyman had the skeletons cut down for proper burial. "When the Father put on his scapular, with two boys to hold the incense and holy water to perform the requiem mass at the burial," Susan recalled, "all of us children followed in the rear of the procession to the burial. The grave was dug and the skeletons were drug into it. They were covered with new blankets and the earth was piled over them. The hanging of Two Face and Black Foot was not so easily forgotten by the Indians. The sight of [the bodies] incensed [them] to an attitude of revolt."[6] Whites around the fort also questioned Moonlight's decision. Post trader Will H. Young noted in his journal, "All the Indians near the garrison are now in bad humor and persons are rather careful about going too far from the protection of the fort."[7]

Indeed, the hanging of the chiefs at Fort Laramie was part of a violent breakdown of civilization, a result of almost three years of brutal warfare on the plains during the Civil War in which both sides had committed acts of barbarism. For the Lakotas and Cheyennes it became a flashpoint to propel hostilities into the Powder River country north of Fort Laramie during the next year and a half. For the army in the West, these hostilities would result in a number of disappointments and failures in the ensuing years brought about by the Civil War, the effects of that war, and the manpower needs of Reconstruction. One result would be the annihilation of Capt. William J. Fetterman's command in December 1866. Following the firing on Fort Sumter in 1861, most units of the regular army were marched eastward to meet the Confederates.[8] New reorganization laws of Congress divided the army line into three distinct divisions, Regulars, state or territorial Volunteers, and local Militia. Citizens flocked to the volunteer regiments where discipline was lax, at least early in the war, and promotions swift. These volunteer regiments bore much of the brunt of the fighting during the Civil War and reaped most of the glory. Militias were similar to Volunteers but could not serve outside their home state or territory. Militias from the western territories, composed of men who often lived in Indian country, were usually eager, if undisciplined and impetuous, to take advantage of the national conflict in the East to rid the territories of their indigenous inhabitants despite treaties recognizing many Indian lands in the West. Volunteer regiments were a different matter. Enlisting with visions of saving the Union or, to a lesser degree as the war progressed, of a glorious crusade against slavery, largely among African American recruits, some of these regiments, especially those from states on or near the frontier, ended up patrolling overland migration routes and defending their lives from superior numbers of Indians. While other units from their home states campaigned in the great battles of the Civil War, the morale of their "unlucky" kinsman in the West often sagged as they campaigned against Indians. Nonetheless, most did their duty despite their dislike of it.[9]

In 1862, paroled Union soldiers from Minnesota units were released from Confederate prison camps on the condition that they return to Minnesota to defend it during the Dakota conflict. By 1865 the "Galvanized Yankees," Confederate parolees from Union prison camps, were added to this eclectic mix as U.S. volunteer units in the West.[10] That the Lincoln administration appreciated the acute need for these troops in the West between 1861 and 1865 was never in doubt. The allegiance to the Union of western territories was crucial to the war effort; so too was the need to protect western gold and silver reserves and the travel routes leading to them. As a result the Civil War caused hardly a blink in the western migration. The Colorado gold strikes of 1858–59 were dangerously close to Confederate Texas in 1861, and the recent Comstock lode in Nevada needed protection given its remoteness as did the Fraser River rush into lands of the Pacific Northwest. And in 1861 the riches of the upper Missouri brought hordes to newly established Virginia City. By 1864 some thirty thousand gold seekers ensured the creation of Montana Territory that year to complement the giant Dakota Territory (1861). Deserters from both Union and Confederate armies, killing one another one month in the East, panned for gold side by side in the West the next.[11] From the temperate Front Range corridor in Colorado Territory (1861) through the game-rich Powder River country, the quest for gold, despite the Civil War, meant that the federal government would not turn its back on the West despite the great rebellion back East. Contrary to popular myth that the western plains tribes took advantage of the "white man's war" to assert themselves with the withdrawal of the Regulars in 1861, more troops (of all kinds) were in the West by 1865 than there had been in prewar years, with numbers approaching twenty thousand.[12]

The wars of Indian resistance to manifest destiny soon to erupt for more than a decade in the Powder River country had their origins many miles to the east during these years of the Civil War. To understand the conflict in 1866 a brief overview of those causes and the consequent violence that spilled over into the Powder River country is in order.[13] Some of the most momentous military campaigns in Indian country occurred between 1862 and 1865 while the Civil War raged in the East. The first action that would eventually affect events in the Powder River country was the so-called U.S. Dakota Conflict of 1862 in Minnesota. Minnesota's Siouan peoples were mostly Santee or Isanti Sioux ("Sioux" being a French name), commonly referred to, if sometimes incorrectly, as Dakotas. Chippewas and Winnebagos also resided in Minnesota after it attained statehood in 1858. Close by the Missouri River lived the Nakota or Ihanktum peoples ("Middle Sioux"), two groups whose names were anglicized as Yankton and Yanktoni.

By the treaties of Traverse des Sioux Mendota in 1851 and 1858, respectively, the Minnesota Sioux sold their hunting grounds for three million dollars in exchange for a reservation consisting of a strip of land 20 miles wide and 150 miles long on both sides of the upper Minnesota River, later reduced on the river's north side for an additional $266,880. Most of these funds were to be paid in annual installments over fifty years. As white settlers poured into the former Indian lands, many of them German and Scandinavian immigrants, the white population exploded to nearly 200,000 by the Civil War and swept over into the lands west of Minnesota in what would become North and South Dakota.[14] By then the Wahpeton (Leaf Shooters) and Sissetunwan (People of the Marsh) bands of Dakotas were settled on the Upper, or Yellow Medicine, Agency while the Mdewkanunwan (Spirit Lake People) and Wahpekute (Lake Traverse People) bands settled at the Lower, or Redwood, Agency. Fort Ridgley (1853) near the Lower Agency guarded the reservation's six thousand or so Indian people.[15]

The summer of 1861 saw a potato blight and generalized crop failure in the Indians' fields. The winter was cold and snowy. In the spring of 1862 federal food and annuities were late in arriving due to the Civil War. Agency traders stopped extending credit to the Indians until their annual cash annuities arrived. Sioux were starving. One trader, Andrew Myrick, according to the Sioux, became enraged at the Indians' insistence that he distribute food and supplies and told the Dakotas to eat their grass if they were hungry. Agent Thomas Galbraith supported the traders. Meanwhile a St. Cloud newspaper editor, Jane Gray Swisshelm, a vocal abolitionist and activist for women's rights, called for the removal of the Sioux from the state. Soon, because of the deaths of fellow white residents, she would call for their extermination. Young Dakotas began calling for war to drive the settlers from what they considered their hunting grounds in the woodlands.[16]

On August 17, a Dakota hunting party quarreled with some settlers over stolen eggs, resulting in the killing of the settlers. The warriors appealed to Chief Little Crow for protection and in spite of his reluctance persuaded him to lead them in war against the whites. Other Dakota chiefs, notably Wabasha and Waucota, protested violent action. The next day Little Crow's warriors moved on the Lower Agency to clean out the traders. Among the casualties in the attack was the hated Andrew Myrick. Hearing of the attack, forty-five soldiers of the 5th Minnesota Volunteers marched from Fort Ridgley to retake the agency. Ambushed along the way, they hastily retreated back to the fort.

On August 19, the Dakotas attacked the mostly German settlement of New Ulm but were driven off by the immigrants. Settlers all along the upper Minnesota River poured into the New Ulm settlement for protection as the Indians let loose a war born of a year's worth of frustration. The Indians attacked settlers in the communities of Action, Milford, Slaughter Slough, and others. With nine hundred warriors Little Crow attacked Fort Ridgley and then moved on New Ulm for a second time on August 23. Although the town had been reinforced by local militia, the Dakotas forced the evacuation of the town. By late August former Minnesota governor Henry Hastings Sibley amassed a force of 1,500 troops including Minnesota Volunteers paroled from Confederate prisons and moved into western Minnesota against the Dakotas. The war lasted almost six weeks with major battles at Birch Coulee and the decisive fight at Wood Lake. During this time the fighting extended south to Iowa and west to Dakota Territory. Estimated civilian casualties ranged from three hundred to eight hundred with perhaps hundreds more taken into captivity. Many of Little Crow's followers were captured at Wood Lake. Close to four hundred were quickly tried and all but eighty-five were sentenced to death. Ultimately President Lincoln commuted the sentences of all but thirty-eight of them. On the day after Christmas 1862, Minnesotans gathered in Mankato to witness the hanging of these thirty-eight, the largest mass execution in American history. Many of the warriors faced the gallows bravely singing their death songs and a peculiar chant, "I am here." Later in 1863, a group of white hunters discovered Little Crow and shot him along with his son. Following the end of hostilities, Minnesota quickly moved to nullify the treaties with the Dakotas and expel them from the territory. Eventually some wound up in Davenport, Iowa; some went to Crow Creek, South Dakota. Some fled to Canada, and still others mingled with tribes in Nebraska. Many more fled west to the northern plains and the Powder River country, along with some Nakotas, where they would infuse the Lakota ranks in all-out war during 1864 and 1865, actions that would prompt the government to establish forts along the routes to the Montana gold country.[17]

After defeating such a Sioux coalition at Whitestone Hill in September 1863, Gen. Alfred Sully, whose Nebraska and Iowa troops had been supporting Sibley, turned to the Dakota Territory in the summer of 1864. On orders from Gen. John Pope, Sully, commanding a force of some 2,500 men, rendezvoused with columns of the Minnesota Volunteers in July. After establishing Fort Rice near the upper Missouri, Sully struck a Sioux coalition of five thousand to six thousand warriors under Inkpaduta, a Wahpekute, on July 28. Sully made good use of his artillery and scattered the large force of Indians in an ensuing nine-mile running fight. The so-called Battle of Killdeer Mountain was a decisive victory for Sully. Three young warriors who had slain an officer in Sully's command and, in turn, had themselves been killed were ordered beheaded by Sully and their severed heads placed on poles as a warning. As the Sully expedition disbanded in the fall, the need for a military presence in the region had emphasized the importance of the upper Powder River country and Missouri River country as a travel artery. By the end of 1864, in response to the gold discoveries that spawned Virginia City, Montana became a separate territory. The growing need for a military presence in and around the Powder River country had become urgent for the government and was becoming ever more alarming to the Indians.[18]

Meanwhile gold had already spurred a massive rush to the south-central Rockies, resulting in the creation of Colorado Territory in 1861. An all too rapid campaign for statehood was pushed by Territorial Governor John Evans, newspaper editor William N. Byers, and other empire builders in Denver City. The city leaders' ambitious desires to remove Indians from the territory in order to achieve that goal culminated in the infamous Sand Creek Massacre of perhaps as many as two hundred Southern Cheyennes of Black Kettle's followers near Fort Lyon on November 29, 1864. The Sand Creek Massacre has captured most of the subsequent attention for plains warfare in 1864 at the expense of the large offensive campaigns to the north. So too have the massacre's perpetrators, Col. John M. Chivington and the Colorado Volunteers, captured the spotlight from Sully in the north. Soon Cheyennes from the Arkansas to the Powder River country would join Lakotas, Dakotas, and Nakotas from Minnesota, Yanktons, and Arapahos in the greatest loose coalition the plains tribes had yet formed to resist American intrusion of lands recognized as theirs by treaties dating from 1851. Traditional migratory patterns of buffalo and seasonal patterns of movements of Indian peoples would be disrupted. In essence the equestrian economies of the plains tribes from Colorado to Montana were collapsed by the Treaty of 1851 and more so with the mining rushes of the 1860s.[19]

By December, as stories of Sand Creek reached far to the north, some eight to nine hundred lodges—about 1,500 warriors—assembled in a great camp on Cherry Creek in northwest Kansas near the present town of St. Francis. Included were Little Robe, Leg-in-the-Water, and possibly Tall Bull of the Cheyenne Dog Soldiers. Pawnee Killer and Bad Wound of the Oglalas were there as were Spotted Tail and Little Thunder of the Brulés (Sicangus or Burnt Thighs), the latter of whom had tasted bitter defeat in 1855 at the hands of Gen. William S. Harney's forces at the Battle of Blue Water Creek near the Platte road in the one-year-old Nebraska Territory. Arapahos were also present. On January 7, 1865, many of these warriors avenged Sand Creek by attacking Julesburg stage station along the South Platte. Troopers of Capt. Nicholas O'Brien's 7th Iowa Volunteer Cavalry stationed at nearby Camp Rankin could do little to slow the raid. More raids between the North and South Platte kept the central plains aflame throughout 1865. Soon the war spread east to the Little Blue in Nebraska and north to the Platte road as the southern coalition joined forces with brethren in the north already angered by Sully's intrusions of the previous year: Minnesota Sioux and Lakotas, especially Brulés, long seeking revenge for Blue Water Creek or, more important, for two decades of environmental degradation caused by travel along the Platte road. Soon the war raged along the Platte and around Fort Laramie. The battles of Mud Springs, Rush Springs, and Platte Bridge, where the affable Lieutenant Caspar Collins was killed, and the inept actions by the less than competent Colonel Moonlight attested to the intensity of the fighting between the plains tribes and volunteer troops principally from Iowa and Ohio, as coalitions of northern plains and southern plains Indians assembled in significant numbers in all-out war.[20]

In response, Department of the Missouri commander Gen. Grenville M. Dodge ordered a massive offensive against these tribes. The Powder River Expedition, with a total force of 2,500 troops under the command of Gen. Patrick E. Connor and including additional volunteers from Kansas, Michigan, and California regiments, converged in three columns on the Powder River country in late August. Earlier, in January, Connor's California column had destroyed a Northwest Shoshoni village on the Bear River in Idaho, inflicting more casualties than Chivington had at Sand Creek.[21] But the Powder River Indians easily eluded Connor. Except for minor skirmishes with roving war parties the expedition inflicted little damage until August 29. At 7:30 that morning Connor discovered and attacked a large village of Northern Arapahos camped on the Tongue River near modern Ranchester, Wyoming. The band of five hundred under Chief Black Bear outnumbered Connor's column but the soldiers were able to rout the Arapahos by nightfall.

The use of artillery proved the decisive factor as Connor's howitzers raked the village, killing over sixty, including Black Bear's son. According to the Indians Black Bear's band was camped with peaceful intent at the time of the attack. Thus Connor only succeeded in infusing the warring factions in the Powder River country with more reinforcements. Similarly, when the Indians later learned of Connor's order to subordinates Col. Nelson Cole, Lt. Col. Samuel Walker, and Capt. Albert Brown to kill all male Indians over the age of twelve, it only strengthened their resolve to resist. Following this Battle of Tongue River, with his two other columns facing a lack of food and vulnerable to superior numbers of Indians, the expedition straggled back into Fort Laramie, crowning a year of bad judgments and failures for the army.[22]

As 1865 came to a close, state volunteer regiments, some of whom had refused or showed great reluctance to campaign in the West following Robert E. Lee's surrender at Appomattox in April, eagerly mustered out of service and returned to their homes. As Washington reorganized postwar military departments in the West, Congress became alarmed over the expenditures of the 1865 campaigns. Already the costs of the Connor expedition had reached the level of a scandal in Washington. With the fight between the Johnson administration and radical Republicans over the impending Reconstruction Act of 1866, the government saw little incentive to continue massive campaigns in the new year against the plains tribes on the scale of the Connor and Sully expeditions. Troops would be needed in great numbers to administer and patrol the five military districts in the defeated South under the Republican's proposed plan. Spirit for large-scale offensives against the western tribes waned. The major result of these campaigns was actually to increase the number of warriors in the Powder River country in 1866 and to strengthen their resolve to resist as warriors from east of the Missouri, many refugees from the earlier Minnesota fighting, joined the Lakotas, Cheyennes, and Arapahos.[23]

Although Sibley, Sully, and Connor had won tactical victories when they engaged Indians, never did they completely solve the problem of logistics and supply, despite Sully's efforts to establish forts in the upper Missouri River country. Most importantly, during this half-decade before the railroad and with telegraph lines running only east to west, the problem of communication and mobility gave the Indians of the plains an overall strategic advantage. Basically the Indians did not have to achieve decisive victory. Like native peoples worldwide resisting invasion, they simply had to hold their own, applying guerilla tactics sporadically over a lengthy period of time and simply avoiding *decisive* defeat themselves. They did not have to win. But so long as they did not lose they could utilize their balance of power on the plains to maintain their independence. The army, in essence, had failed in 1865 not because it lost battles and skirmishes to Indians, but because of inhospitable terrain, unmapped domains, unpredictable plains weather, and unreliable lines of supply. These elements had always been the allies of indigenous peoples in their struggles on home soil against technologically superior armed invaders. Now, with postwar cutbacks in both money and manpower, the situation could only worsen. Yet the fighting in the West during the Civil War years had demonstrated at least an alluring potential for massive offensives, given adequate manpower, communications, and logistical support. Sibley, Sully, and Connor, not to mention Chivington, had all demonstrated the effective use of artillery—the mobile Prairie and Mountain Howitzer—in demoralizing larger numbers of the enemy.[24]

Unfortunately for the U.S. Army, the problems of logistics could not be solved during the early years of Reconstruction, even though they constructed new forts in Indian country. Inadequate troop strength in the West as compared to the southern Reconstruction districts was still responsible for much of that problem. Additionally, the lesson learned by the volunteers and militia during the war years would have to be relearned all over again by the regular army regiments sent West in 1866. Many would be the voices of western settlers who would push for the recruitment of local militia regiments in expanding states and territories like Kansas and Colorado in the late 1860s. Settlers considered the militiamen more knowledgeable about Indian fighting than the slim regular regiments recently sent to their aid from the East. In regions like Dakota, Montana, and the future Wyoming Territory, regular regiments sent to far-flung lands devoid of white settlers and convenient sources of local supplies would find the task even more daunting. By 1866 a seemingly impossible dilemma took root in western military policy. The high command would expect small numbers of troops to engage Indians in limited offensive operations from fixed military posts to protect the routes of travel over thousands of miles at a time when peacetime budgets prevented sufficient manpower to do the job effectively if at all. In addition the offensives of 1864–65 had, like the great eastern battles themselves, proved the effectiveness of total war at a time when the Indian Bureau favored negotiation to achieve peace.[25]

Yet the Powder River Expedition of 1865 had drawn attention to the northern lands of the Powder River country as a more feasible route of travel to the gold country of Montana, now more important than ever given postwar deficits and the cost of administering the defeated southern states. The new regulars, despite their inadequate numbers, would be expected to build forts and patrol and maintain peaceful travel through some of the most sacred and coveted hunting grounds of the plains tribes, the lands above the North Platte—the Powder River country, lands long contested among the tribes and defended by the Lakotas and Cheyennes effectively against the whites in 1865—lands to be defended in the future at all costs and to the death.[26]

▼▼▼

Today the Powder River Basin looks much the same as it did in 1865. In the vast land between the North Platte and the Yellowstone cool breezes still slide down the mountain peaks of the Bighorns to the west and the Black Hills to the east on quiet summer evenings, billowing the lush grasses as they did in the time of Red Cloud, Crazy Horse, and Little Wolf. Since their arrival along the Platte during the early nineteenth century, Lakotas and their Cheyenne allies recognized the special meaning of the lands north of the two forks of that river. For both peoples the Black Hills on the eastern edge of the region became the most hallowed of all sanctuaries. Here was the land of *Nohavose*, Bear Butte, the sacred mountain of the Cheyennes, the holy resting place of Sweet Medicine, their great culture hero of tradition. Here, long ago, Sweet Medicine had given his people their sacred covenants *Maahotse*, the sacred arrows, and *Esevone*, the sacred buffalo hat. In the Black Hills Sweet Medicine had taught the Cheyennes how to make their way on the plains. *Paha Sapa*, as the Lakotas called the hills, was and still is the spiritual center of their nation. In addition to the religious significance of the Black Hills, the Powder River grasslands represented some of the most coveted hunting and grazing grounds for Indian peoples and white trappers and traders alike, lands worth the sacrifice of incipient wars of expansion and conquest, for when Oglalas and others moved north in the mid-1850s these were the lands of the Crows. Bitter war with the Crows, Shoshonis, and others who controlled these precious resources ensued and Lakotas drove the Crows out from much of the area.[27]

Although Lakota expansion in the last quarter of the eighteenth century brought them into the proximity of the Powder River country, a tentative peace continued there until the late 1850s. The tribes considered the Powder River country a "neutral zone" where rival equestrian peoples often camped and hunted, but not always without risk of attack from enemy tribesmen. Occasionally isolated violence flared between Crows and Lakotas, usually because of personal grievances. The Fort Laramie or Horse Creek Treaty of 1851 recognized the Powder River lands as *Absaroka*, the sovereignty of the Crows. The treaty also ushered in a brief period of true peace between the Crows and some of the Lakota divisions. The chief commissioner at the councils, D. D. Mitchell, urged the tribes to make a true peace with each other as well as with the U.S. government. Negotiations between the Crow chief, Big Robber, and the aging Miniconjou chief, Red Fish, resulted in peace between those factions and are recorded in Miniconjou winter counts for that time.[28]

Throughout most of the decade of the 1850s, Red Fish's son, Lone Horn, worked to keep the peace with the Crows. Both peoples benefited from the tranquility. For the Miniconjous, who had seen the buffalo herds on their hunting grounds east of the Black Hills drastically diminished in previous years, game was the primary advantage of the peace. For the Crows the truce provided a safe passage southward to trading posts on the upper North Platte River. Even factions of the Oglalas, especially the Smoke People, followers of Man Afraid of His Horse, honored the peace with the Crows for a time during the early 1850s. Only the northern Lakota divisions on the Yellowstone and Missouri, the Hunkpapas, and the Siouan Blackfeet were unified in their refusal to honor the peace with the Crows.[29]

The infamous Harney expedition of 1855 that witnessed the rout of Little Thunder's Brulés from the North Platte at Blue Water Creek indirectly upset the peace between the Crows and the Lakotas. Lone Horn, Man Afraid of His Horse, and others whose people lived generally east of the Black Hills tried to remain moderate. But most of the Miniconjous as well as Man Afraid of His Horse's prominent *akicita* (warrior policeman)[30] Red Cloud sought to leave the white man's roads and move north to the game-rich Powder River country. The Smoke People under Man Afraid of His Horse were soon to turn their backs on the Platte also and move north to the Powder River buffalo ranges. Soon Red Cloud's "Bad Face" faction (tiyospaye) vowed to keep both whites and their roads out of the Powder River country. But before they could achieve their goal they needed to seize these prized hunting grounds from the Crows.[31]

Sometime in 1856 war erupted in the Powder River country. By the winter of 1857–58 fighting between the Crows and the northern Lakotas, now infused by Red Cloud's Bad Face Oglalas and the Miniconjous, became, once again, a normal state of affairs between traditional enemies. The brutality of that war was later recorded through the drawings of Oglala Amos Bad Heart Bull. Born in 1869, Bad Heart Bull was not a witness to the Crow War but he meticulously reproduced images of the major engagements from oral testimonies of warriors who did participate in the fighting. The Captive Hill Fight of 1856, the first large engagement of the war, is likewise recorded in the winter counts of several Oglalas for that year.[32] Bad Heart Bull's depictions of the Crow War of 1856–59 are every bit as dramatic and large in scope as his drawing of Little Bighorn in 1876. By 1859 the Crows withdrew into the Bighorn Mountains and then north to the upper Missouri, never again during pre-reservation years to occupy the lands south of the Yellowstone and east of the Bighorn River. Absaroka, the Powder River country so loved by the Crows, had become undisputed Lakota land by conquest, if not by formal treaty with the United States. And for the better part of the next two decades the Lakotas held that land tenaciously.[33]

Why did the Powder River country become so vital to rival Indian peoples during the 1850s and afterward that they would be willing to die for its conquest and possession? Here, the rich country supported vast herds of buffalo. Before the great shock wave of contraction with European contact and as late as 1820 the entire Great Plains held a probable carrying capacity of about twenty-five to thirty million American bison. Environmental historian Dan Flores estimates that the plains north of the Platte held as many as five to six million animals, many of which frequented the Powder River Basin. Subsistence requirements were approximately 6.5 animals per person per year. Given an estimated 42,000 souls among all the equestrian tribes on the northern plains at this time, the subsistence harvest would have been around 275,000 buffalo a year. With an estimated 18 percent natural increase in the herds per year, an annual harvest was necessary. Add to this mix sizeable herds of pronghorn, mule deer, and other game mammals and birds. Food, clothing, and shelter were not a problem until the trading era. By 1825 things began to change rapidly. By the 1840s, as trade reached a zenith, between 85,000 and 100,000 buffalo robes were reaching St. Louis markets annually.[34] Between 1855 and 1865 the entire Great Plains buffalo population had decreased from twenty million to fifteen million in the span of ten years.[35] Meanwhile the Oglala population in the Powder River country and north of the North Platte remained fairly stable during that decade prior to a dramatic "explosion" by the mid-1870s.[36]

Horses, an object of trade since the eighteenth century, rearranged previous ecological balances. By 1800 an estimated two million wild mustangs roamed the lands below the Arkansas River with an unknown number in the north. Even at that early date these exotic introductions were competing with buffalo for grass.[37] As Indian people migrated westward trade drew horses north in exchange for firearms that were trafficked south. The Cheyennes emerged on the northern plains just before the bulk of the Siouan bands that formed the Lakota divisions, and together they reinvented themselves as some of the most adapted equestrian cultures in American history. The Cheyennes became middlemen in the horse commerce, not only capturing wild animals but also breeding their own private herds.[38] In 1846 the previous biomass that had supported all peoples on the plains began to change drastically and radically. That year saw the beginning of a prolonged decade of severe drought and a steady if seemingly subtle rise in temperature, although striking paradoxical extremes still occurred. This overall drop in annual precipitation marked the end of a three-centuries-long cool, moist period in the Northern Hemisphere known as the Little Ice Age. Both buffalo and people with their horses frequented more often now traditionally drought resistant areas like the Powder River Basin, creating at times a kind of traffic jam of natural resource consumers.[39] The end of the Little Ice Age produced increasing drought that ate up buffalo range and moved the herds to the east on the plains where mid-grass prairies provided better habitat. This climate shift would threaten equestrian lifeways in the years to come. The Cheyennes were the first to follow the herds eastward to the edge of expanding settlements in Kansas. During the summer of 1857 some Oglalas including a young, yet untested Crazy Horse temporarily left the war with the Crows and followed Cheyenne friends eastward to the mid-grass buffalo pastures.[40]

But plenty of game still roamed the verdant Powder River country due to the more adequate aquifers in that land. Not only buffalo but pronghorn, elk, and deer proliferated in the region. Although environmental factors contributed to the concentration of game in the Powder River country, so too did human interaction, especially the Crow War. Historian Richard White, in a study of Indian "neutral zones" in the Southeast, found that warfare actually increased populations of game and that conversely, game populations became depleted in times of peace.[41] Dan Flores concluded the same thing for the Great Plains and the far West: "Warfare had to exist actively to keep the

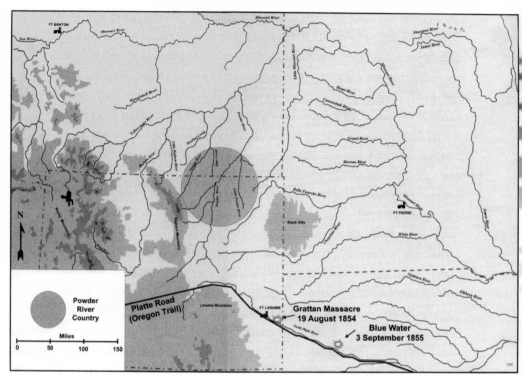

"Lakota Lands and the Powder River Country in 1866." Charles D. Collins Jr., *Atlas of the Sioux Wars*, 2nd ed. (Fort Leavenworth, KS: Combat Studies Institute Press, 2006).

[neutral] zones functioning."[42] With the coming of whites in greater numbers by the mid-1860s continuous warfare would keep the Powder River country functioning through the remainder of the decade. By the Civil War, with the Montana gold strikes and the subsequent intrusion of the military campaigns, the Indians would become all too aware of both the delicate and the not so delicate threats to these precious lands. Societies like those of the Lakotas and Cheyennes had already found it necessary, in the space of two hundred years, to migrate over a thousand miles and to reorganize their social structures several times. Wars, rebellions, and migrations usually solved relatively simple problems that would have life-threatening effects if not dealt with promptly and decisively. The problems were often as simple as securing land containing enough wood resources to survive the winter or sufficient grass for horses after that animal had so dramatically restructured Indian societies. Usually the concerns did not involve finding enough game but rather finding enough

natural vegetation for humans and horses alike to survive, especially in the winter months.[43] By 1847 an estimated 21,000 Siouan peoples lived on both sides of the Missouri River and an estimated 2,500–3,000 Cheyennes were about equally divided on the northern plains and the southern plains between the South Platte and the Arkansas.[44]

By 1866 the Lakotas west of the Missouri had increased somewhat from the influx of refugees from the Dakota conflict of 1862. The size of both Lakota and Cheyenne horse herds, peaking by the early 1850s, were still large in 1866 as the climate became drier and abundant grass was needed. The Indians increasingly made their way into more verdant areas like the Powder River country where they could maintain larger herds of horses through the winter. Although the entire Sioux Nation was expanding during the early to mid-nineteenth century, their natural resources, other than buffalo and other game animals, were actually shrinking. With a decade-long drought during the 1850s and generally drier conditions following the end of the Little Ice Age, the Powder River country took on even more significant meaning to tribes and bands, large and small, all of whom were constricted by the same exacting life-giving requirements of grass, wood, and water. In turn, the availability of these elements determined the size of winter villages, a factor that became critical in times of warfare, especially with whites. A village had to be large enough to afford adequate protection but not so large that resources would be exhausted to a crisis point.[45]

Although a topic rich for research, no meaningful statistical studies exist analyzing wood and grass depletion caused by actual Euro-American emigrant travel on the Oregon/California trail systems during the migration days of the 1840s, '50s, and '60s. But a large number of sources on western trail migration mention the Indians' concern over this specific resource depletion in addition to the disruption of buffalo migration patterns. One need only view the paintings depicting 1850s and 1860s wagon travel on the Platte road by William Henry Jackson, and observe the scarcity of trees at the trail crossings, to understand this fact. The effect of spring floods uncontrolled by man-made reservoirs, fire, and the foraging for new growth along the floodplain by buffalo also help account for the scarcity of firewood in the river basins in the mid-nineteenth century in comparison to the same riparian belts in modern times. Today the lack of forage and flood control dams have created often thick forestation along river courses of the Great Plains.

By the 1860s annual use by migrant campers over the two previous decades only added to the demise. Western empire builders and the U.S. Army in the campaigns of 1864–65 well realized the necessity of these natural resources for the survival of Indian people during the winter and used it to their tactical advantage. Colorado Territorial Governor John Evans had warned Black Kettle of the Southern Cheyennes at the Camp Weld Council in September 1864 that although the Indians' time was "now" (the summer months rich with grass), "his time [the whites'] was coming," the winter, when grass turned brown and the Indians' world physically shrank dramatically as bands went into camps along the wooded stream basins where they could easily be hunted down. Two months hence Chivington's Colorado troops brought death to Black Kettle's people at Sand Creek. On January 27, 1865, troops tried to burn out warring tribesmen by setting fire to the entire countryside on both sides of the Platte road from Nebraska to Wyoming. Days later eyewitnesses reported the fire had spread south with the prevailing north winds, across the Arkansas, two hundred miles, and finally into the Texas Panhandle. During the last two years of the Civil War, natural resource depletion on the central overland migration routes and the intrusion of gold seekers from south to north to the sites of the Montana gold strikes alarmed both Lakotas and Cheyennes as to the possibility of similar degradation of the Powder River hunting grounds.[46]

Here was to be found an overlap of the three most important grass communities necessary for sustaining buffalo and horse herds: bluestem, blue grama, and buffalo grass. Although this overlap extended south from northern Dakota Territory to Texas, the well-watered Powder River Basin created a fairly reliable abundance after 1846, at least more so than in other slightly more arid regions. Drained by the Yellowstone, Powder, and Tongue rivers, the area also contains large shallow head basins underlain by coal or scoria that provide water collection areas. Fire and drought were, and still are, the principal natural disturbance sources, visibly more so after 1846. The comparative environmental integrity of the region as it existed in 1866 was one that necessitated protection and defense from whites by the native peoples, who had surely noticed the natural changes of the past decade.[47]

Grass and water were vital. But modern studies suggest scarcity of firewood most often prompted villages to move.[48] Lakotas and Cheyennes did not measure firewood by Euro-American standards but the needs were enormous, especially during a northern plains winter. Based on clear-cut timber methods with saws and axes, the cutting of wood by whites was more exhaustive than Indian methods. Still, when the two races overlapped in lands of semi-aridity, wood became scarce for both societies. Anthropologist John H. Moore calculated that about 1.5 tons or fifteen acres of wood were needed per hundred native peoples per year as compared to 3.6 tons or thirty acres needed for every one hundred soldiers annually at an army fort on the Great Plains who used clear-cutting methods.[49] By 1880 firewood was totally eliminated within a twelve-mile radius of Fort Dodge, Kansas. During the fighting of 1864–65 a thirty-mile trip was necessary to acquire firewood for civilian and military activities at Julesburg and Fort (Camp) Rankin on the Platte road. A seven-mile trip was necessary by that time to supply six-year-old Fort Larned.[50] Warring Indians were well aware of the whites' need for firewood to provision fixed army posts and towns. They made good use of the tactic of attacking woodcutting parties, especially in winter. Capt. Eugene Ware recounted numerous skirmishes between the tribesmen and woodcutting details during the campaigns of 1864 and 1865. Certainly the attack on Fort Phil Kearny's woodcutting parties during the fall and winter of 1866, so memorable because of the Fetterman fight, was nothing new indeed, although it became a distinguishing feature of the Fort Phil Kearny story.[51]

Although statistical records do not exist for the Powder River country for 1866, we may argue that with convergence of Indian peoples, Montana-bound gold seekers, and supply contractors in the region combined with a decade and a half of drought following the climate shift beginning in 1846, a decline of wood resources may very well have been noticeable to the eyes of Indian people by 1866. As the Civil War armies made their way back to hearth and home by 1866, the decision to provision and protect the northern travel route pioneered by John Bozeman and others with three new military forts through the prime Lakota and Cheyenne hunting grounds in the Powder River country was pivotal. For the Indians, who had just seen the volunteers vacate the area, the arrival of new regular army soldiers intent on establishing a permanent presence was simply too much of a violation of prized, hard-won lands for some of the Lakota and Cheyenne chiefs and their followers to swallow.[52]

One Indian leader who certainly recognized the growing resource depletion in his lands in 1866 was the Bad Face Oglala Lakota warrior

Red Cloud, a rising star among his people. Most historians contend that Red Cloud was born in May 1821 on Blue Water Creek, in what would become the Nebraska Territory, and only about fifteen miles from the site of Harney's punitive fight with Little Thunder's Brulé Lakotas in 1855. The future warrior and chief grew to manhood in the days before extensive traffic on the nearby Platte road. By the time he turned forty, however, he had witnessed extensive depletion of wood and grass along the great overland artery caused by the hungry rush for lands in Oregon and the scramble for California gold.[53]

By 1866 Red Cloud was an honored warrior, a *blotahunka* and a "Shirt Wearer." His aggressive demeanor indicates he was not about to allow the same abuse to be repeated in the guarded Powder River country. Even in that land the winter of 1865–66 had been unusually cold and dry. Buffalo uncharacteristically wintered elsewhere and other wild game was critically scarce. Almost destitute, many Oglalas joined the so-called loafer bands, mostly Brulés who camped for months close to Fort Laramie and who were fed by the government. These bands preferred a life of complacency to hunting on the open plains, a result in part of the economic collapse created by the provisions of the Treaty of 1851 and tribal migration in the wake of the gold rushes of the 1850s and 1860s. On May 30, 1866, a federal commission under the leadership of E. B. Taylor arrived at Fort Laramie to talk peace as part of the government's new "olive branch" policy and to negotiate permission for whites to travel the Bozeman Trail to the Montana gold country. Confident in their mission, Taylor and his commissioners had not counted on Red Cloud's protective determination to keep whites out of the Powder River country altogether. Red Cloud was adamant. He would not permit travel north through the region. According to eyewitness William Murphy, whose account was later recalled by Frances Grummond Carrington, Red Cloud gave an impassioned speech before he bolted from the peace talks with Man Afraid of His Horse and others. He told the commissioners that his people had been pushed farther north and now game was scarce even in the rich lands between the White and Powder rivers. Women and children faced starvation. Grass was scarce and wood diminishing. Intrusion by whites would surely stretch more resources and scatter the buffalo. He urged his people to fight rather than starve or submit to the federal government's wishes to allow travel through those fragile lands.[54]

Similarly, young Black Elk, cousin of Crazy Horse, although only four years old in 1866, remembered stories told to him by his grandfather of the Oglalas' fears of desecrating the wildness of the Powder River country, especially the effects of displacing buffalo herds. "Up on the Madison Fork [of the Yellowstone] the *Wasichus* [white men][55] had found much of the yellow metal that they worship and that makes them crazy," Black Elk stated years later, "and they wanted to have a road up through our country to the place where the yellow metal was; but my people did not want the road. It would scare the bison and make them go away, and also it would let other Wasichus come in like a river."[56] With memories still fresh of the Lakota and Cheyenne corpses hanging in chains at Fort Laramie and the thought of new troops coming to the northern plains, troops that had not yet learned the hard lessons of Sully and Connor, the tribesmen grew bolder. Most important, these new soldiers were fewer in number than those involved in the great military offensives of 1865. Many were new recruits. Red Cloud and many others were confident the Indians could prevail. But these regular army soldiers were determined to establish a permanent presence in the Powder River country with the construction of new forts. As the grasses turned green across the prairie and high plateaus of the northern plains in the spring of 1866, once again war loomed ominously for the Lakotas and Cheyennes.

CHAPTER 2

THIS LAND IS INDIAN

Now rising to a shout
The voice of Red Cloud towered, crushing out
The wonder-hum that ran from band to band:
"These white men here have begged our hunting land."[1]

A CONSIDERATION OF THE PERSONALITIES AND BACKGROUNDS of the principal antagonists who converged in the Powder River country during the spring of 1866 goes a long way in explaining the events that transpired there that year. While the snows still covered the ground the Indian Bureau sent the so-called Taylor Commission to Fort Laramie to conclude a new treaty with the Lakotas and Northern Cheyennes. E. B. Taylor, the head of the Northern Superintendency, headed the commission. He was assisted by Col. Henry Maynadier and Col. R. N. McLaren of Minnesota, and Thomas Wistar of Pennsylvania.[2] Red Cloud's reportedly militant, and possibly flamboyant, stance at these Fort Laramie peace talks in June 1866, whether exaggerated or not, set him on the road to historical immortality. Although historians often emphasize his later life as a great statesman and spokesman for his people, conflicting stories shadow Red Cloud's experiences prior to 1866. But there is little about his early life that we know about that would destine him for such historical immortality.

Makhpiya-luta, or Makhpia-sha, Red Cloud was considered by the Oglalas to be a respected warrior during his youth. Born to an important family, his nephew, He Dog, stated years later that Red Cloud's father was Lone Man, a Brulé chief. His mother was Walks-as-She-Thinks, a member of the Saone or Bad Face clan and a daughter of the band's chief, Old Smoke. Others contend Red Cloud's father was also named Red Cloud and was a man of importance. What Red Cloud's name was in early life, before he took his adult name according to Lakota custom, is unknown.[3] In any event, he grew up an Oglala with his mother's clan, the Smoke People. During Red Cloud's youth petty rivalries among chiefs was not unusual and often encouraged by unscrupulous white traders. Such was the case with two principal chiefs, Bull Bear and Old Smoke, the chief of the band that included Red Cloud and his mother. Apparently Bull Bear was a tyrannical chief whose feud with Old Smoke was long and ongoing. One day Bull Bear challenged Old Smoke to come out of his lodge and fight him. But Old Smoke sat in the lodge with his arms folded, refusing to fight. Bull Bear stormed away, stabbing to death Old Smoke's favorite horse while leaving the camp. Some of Old Smoke's followers including Red Cloud plotted revenge. When the Smoke band was camped on the Chugwater River in present-day Wyoming in 1841, Old Smoke and some of his followers came upon the camp. A fight broke out in which Smoke Band warriors shot Bull Bear when he came out of his lodge, ostensibly to stop the fight. According to some accounts, Red Cloud may have fired the fatal shot and alcohol supplied by traders may have stirred anger, an accusation borne out by at least one winter count (*waniyetu wowapi*).[4]

Red Cloud's involvement in the killing of Bull Bear in 1841 did not bring shame to him among his mother's people. To the contrary, the slaying after a long period of bad blood between the bands may have relieved tensions. But the killing fractured the Oglalas between northern and southern clans or *tiyospayes*.[5] The northerners, the Smoke People, gained strength by assimilating various mixed smaller groups. Red Cloud, about twenty years old when Bull Bear was killed, followed the son of Old Smoke, a Bad Face Oglala, and would soon gain followers among that group although he was not yet a chief. By 1866, however, the Itesicas (Bad Face Oglalas) would be considered by the whites as "Red Cloud's band."[6]

After 1841 Red Cloud gained a strong reputation among all Lakotas as a man with whom to be reckoned. Another story, if true, tells of a young Red Cloud's rescuing a Ute warrior who had fallen from his horse in a river. After dragging him to shore, Red Cloud promptly killed and scalped the Ute.[7] Red Cloud's scalp shirt, housed in the Buffalo Bill Historical Center in Cody, Wyoming, allegedly contains some eighty scalps.[8]

Certainly the Bad Faces prized the Powder River country when they came north from the Platte with others following Harney's brutal campaign in 1855. They took part in warring against the Crows to drive them from that country. Following the Horse Creek Treaty of 1851 designed to protect the Oregon/California Trail, the Bad Faces, who still camped along the North Platte until the mid-1850s, came to disdain the so-called Laramie Loafers, a band of

Oglalas that camped with southern Brulés and Corn Band Brulés, followers of Spotted Tail, who remained close to Fort Laramie taking handouts and abandoning old ways of the hunting culture. The roots of dependency of these Loafer bands on the federal government emerged with the annuity structure of the Horse Creek or Fort Laramie Treaty of 1851. By 1866 the conditions of the treaty had fractured the Oglalas and Brulés and led to a partial disruption and collapse of the traditional equestrian political structure. Still, among the strongly traditional equestrian groups like Red Cloud's tiyospaye, Lakotas were continuing to expand their domain against other tribes, especially the Crows. During the war of expansion against the Crows, Red Cloud certainly gained many of his early laurels while the Bad Faces in general gained a reputation at Fort Laramie as "warlike Indians" who were to be regarded in the vernacular of the age as "hostiles." Although tales exist that the Bad Faces installed Red Cloud as their chief around 1855, biographer Robert W. Larson discounts them. During the early to mid-1860s, Larson asserts, after Old Smoke's death one of his sons became the formal chief, or *itancan*, of the Bad Faces. By the time of the Fort Laramie/Taylor Commission talks in 1866, Lakotas considered Red Cloud to be an important war leader or blotahunka, who would lead warriors into battle using his influence, example, charisma, and sense of élan. With memories of the environmental degradation that befell his boyhood lands in the Platte Valley, this passion for the integrity of the Powder River country may well have enraged Red Cloud to utter the inflammatory oratory ascribed to him at Fort Laramie.[9]

With only white accounts to refer to at this time in his life, and not understanding Lakota hierarchical customs, whites at Fort Laramie assumed Red Cloud was a chief of high status among many or all Lakota people. And this is where some of the legend regarding his role in the war of 1866–68 may have started. Technically Man Afraid of His Horse and Old Smoke were the itancans over most of the Oglalas during the 1850s. But by the mid-sixties Red Cloud had gained his prominence as a war leader of the Bad Faces following the death of Old Smoke, while Old Smoke's son remained the recognized itancan. Essentially the Oglalas were fractured by 1866, a more moderate peace faction leaning toward the pacifist views of the Brulés under Spotted Tail, once a renowned warrior but one who had been "convinced" of the path of peace following the Harney campaign in 1855 and his brief imprisonment at Fort Leavenworth, Kansas.[10]

Again scholars are uncertain as to exactly when Red Cloud first started fighting the whites. James C. Olson asserts that Red Cloud was one of those who strongly supported war against the volunteers during 1865, although few specifics are known. Both George F. Hyde and J. W. Vaughn, using the testimony of George Bent, a mixed-blood Southern Cheyenne, claimed that Red Cloud and Young Man Afraid of His Horse, son and heir apparent to Man Afraid of His Horse, were present at the May 1865 war councils of Sioux and Cheyenne militants on Tongue River and that both participated in the Platte Bridge fight of July 25–26, 1865, in which Lieutenant Caspar Collins was killed. George B. Grinnell, however, who relied heavily on Bent, does not place Red Cloud at either event.[11] Most of the early sources agree that Red Cloud also was present during the harassment of the survey party of James A. Sawyers near Pumpkin Buttes in 1865. Sawyers's men were surveying a route through the Powder River country to Virginia City, Montana, from the Niobrara River above the Platte in present-day Wyoming. Olson states it was Red Cloud who allowed the party to continue after exacting a bribe of food and tobacco.[12]

In any event, by the spring of 1866 Red Cloud was well known to the whites, regarded as "warlike," and along with the peace chief Spotted Tail, Red Cloud was considered (incorrectly) a major chief over all Lakotas. Col. Henry E. Maynadier, who took over at Fort Laramie after the Civil War, first as post commander and then as commander of the west subdistrict of Nebraska with headquarters at Fort Laramie, reported in March 1866 that in regard to Spotted Tail and Red Cloud, "they two rule the [Sioux] Nation."[13] Essentially, by summer 1866, while Man Afraid of His Horse tried to remain moderate, Red Cloud gathered his own following of kinsmen and followers (tiyospaye) and their families who camped and moved together and favored resistance to white intrusion into the Powder River country. Regardless of the specific circumstances, Red Cloud's determination to defend the Powder River country likely began during the campaigns of 1865, the real start of Indian awareness of danger to the ecosystems of the Powder River country, rather than during 1866 when Red Cloud expressed outrage at the Taylor Commission hearings over the intentions of Col. Henry B. Carrington to build additional forts in the region.[14]

Already one fort was operative near the south end of the Bozeman Trail. On August 14, 1865, Gen. Patrick E. Connor officially established a crude fort that bore his name on a shelf of land about fifty feet above the Powder River and about twenty-two miles from the present community of Kaycee, Wyoming, in Johnson County. The post served as a supply base above Fort Laramie for Connor's military activities of that year. But after that failed campaign and the exodus of troop strength, the army dismantled the crude shacks that served the earlier cantonment and renamed the installation Fort Reno on November 11, 1865, to honor Major Jesse Reno, killed in 1862 at the Battle of South Mountain. Now elements of the 2nd Battalion of the 18th Infantry under Col. Henry B. Carrington would assume garrison of the post. Carrington wished to dismantle the post and relocate it farther north on the Bozeman Trail. But due to the obvious Indian activity in the region he changed his mind. He would leave one company (Lieutenant Kirtland's B Company) at Fort Reno under Capt. Joshua Proctor to escort wagon trains north. Carrington dubbed the decrepit little post "Reno Station" but most officers and men continued to refer to it as Fort Reno. The remainder of the command, including Carrington himself, would then proceed north up the Powder River to establish two additional garrisons that became Fort Phil Kearny on Piney Creek (Buffalo Creek to the Indians) and, the northernmost, Fort C. F. Smith on the Bighorn River in Montana Territory.[15]

No one ever recorded any official transcriptions at the Taylor peace talks that summer at Fort Laramie, so sources are a bit suspect, but we know from eyewitnesses that E. B. Taylor, the head of the Northern Superintendency of the Indian Bureau, was thrilled over the prospect for a new treaty of peace with the northern tribes as early as March when chiefs began to gather. On March 8 Spotted Tail buried his daughter, Brings Water (Mini-Aku), on a scaffold above Fort Laramie. The teenage girl, whom he revered, had died of disease, some say of a broken heart due to an infatuation with a young officer at Fort Laramie, perhaps Capt. Eugene F. Ware. Colonel Maynadier considered the burial a gesture of peace as had been the nearby burial of Chief Old Smoke two years before.[16] On the thirteenth Red Cloud arrived at the fort. Man Afraid of His Horse came in at about the same time and eventually Dull Knife, a significant chief of the Council of Forty-Four of the Cheyennes. Taylor himself finally arrived on May 30, after much delay due to weather, and not without some frustration on the part of the Indians. Accounts differ on what happened next. At first Taylor was elated that he had assembled chiefs and warriors who really mattered, not just the ubiquitous and insignificant Laramie Loafers. According to Larson's research Red Cloud had gone to the headwaters of the White River to gather more participants for the talks. Along the way he met up with Carrington, who was marching his troops up the North Platte toward Powder River. Inquiring why he was there, Carrington, ignorant of Indians and never suspecting there would be trouble from them, told Red Cloud of his intentions to build new forts in the Powder River country. Red Cloud returned to Fort Laramie on June 13 (Hyde places it on the sixteenth), when the peace talks resumed. Red Cloud was furious and outraged over the proposal to construct the new forts and bolted from the conference with other militants.[17]

Hyde has it that Carrington met a friendly Brulé chief, probably Standing Elk, a day out from Fort Laramie. With a man named Jack Snead as interpreter, Standing Elk asked Carrington why he had come. Upon his reply regarding the construction of new forts in the Powder River country, Standing Elk told Carrington, "The fighting men in that country have not come to Laramie and you will have to fight them." When Carrington told Standing Elk that he hoped the presence of the forts would prevent fighting, he was being naïve. His force was much smaller than the ones that had been on Powder River the previous year. According to Hyde, the Brulé chief immediately left and informed the militants of Carrington's mission.[18]

Carrington's first wife, Margaret, who was at the council, infers that Red Cloud was previously aware of her husband's purpose when she wrote in 1868, "The [young] Man Afraid of His Horse and Red Cloud made no secret of their opposition, and the latter with all his fighting men withdrew from all association with the treaty-makers, and in a very few days quite decidedly developed his hate and his schemes of mischief."[19] But in 1904, Cyrus Townsend Brady, who obtained his information from Henry Carrington in 1903, inferred that Red Cloud did not meet up with Carrington until after he arrived at the fort and the talks had resumed. When Carrington was introduced to the delegation, "Red Cloud," according to Brady, "noticing his [colonel's] shoulder straps, hotly denounced him as 'White Eagle' who had come to steal the road before the Indians said yes or no. In full view of the mass of Indians who occupied the parade ground he sprang from the platform under the shelter of the pine boughs, struck his tepees and went on the warpath."[20]

Brady's source, which sounds somewhat sensational, is probably an embellishment of what Carrington had told him the previous year. Yet in 1903 Carrington had an "agenda" to restore his good name from blame for Fetterman's defeat. If this version of the story is Carrington's, he certainly demonstrated a sense of self-importance if his version of the meeting was indeed his first encounter with Red Cloud. But his memories of the parley support Carrington's assertion in his reports of 1867 that he had informed Standing Elk of his plans. How could Red Cloud have known for certain of Carrington's intent on the basis of first introductions unless he had possessed Standing Elk's information? In any case the Brady/Carrington rhetoric is an embellishment of Margaret Carrington's early account in her book *Ab-sa-ra-ka: Home of the Crows*. Why not? The book was somewhat of a best-seller and has been published many times to the present day. Colonel Carrington's second wife, Frances, who in 1866 was Mrs. Frances Grummond, married to one of Carrington's subordinate officers and not present at the peace talks, embellished the Margaret Carrington and Henry Carrington/Brady version of the peace talks even further when she wrote in 1910,

> Red Cloud himself, it is *officially reported* [By whom? Emphasis mine], when he saw Colonel Carrington at his visit to the council, upon his arrival threw his blanket around himself, refused an introduction, and left with his announcement of his views, pointing to the officer who had just arrived, "The Great Father sends us presents and wants us to sell him the road before The Indians say yes or no."[21]

The most melodramatic account was written in 1928 by Doane Robinson of the South Dakota State Historical Society. Robinson asserts that Red Cloud "leaped from the platform, caught up his rifle, saying, 'In this and the Great Spirit I trust for the right.'"[22] The least sensational account is that of William Murphy, a soldier in the 18th Infantry. Murphy was present at the peace talks, although his account shows up much later in Frances Carrington's 1910 book, *My Army Life*. Of course Frances was not present that day to record Murphy verbatim. Still, if we can believe Murphy's story second-hand, the soldier described a lengthy and impassioned speech by Red Cloud, appealing not to the commissioners, but to fellow Lakotas present at the gathering.

"The powwow continued for some time," Murphy is reported by Frances Carrington to have said, "until finally the hostile Sioux under Red Cloud withdrew, refusing to have any further counsel or to accept any presents."[23] Did Red Cloud meet Carrington before the formal introductions at Fort Laramie in mid-June? Had he been briefed already by Standing Elk, or did he simply make a big show of things upon seeing a new officer on the scene with the rank of colonel other than Maynadier, the subdistrict commander at Fort Laramie? This demonstration too would not have been out of character for Red Cloud. Whichever version one chooses to accept, and perhaps all have *some* validity or perhaps very little, Cyrus Townsend Brady was quite correct when he wrote in 1904 that about the week of June 13, 1865, Red Cloud "struck his tepees and went on the warpath."[24]

The chiefs who were left behind to sign the treaty were mostly Loafer sycophants or leaders genuinely committed to peace with the whites. The Lakota chiefs who signed the 1866 treaty are as follows:

Brulés
Spotted Tail, Southern Brulé
Swift Bear, Corn Band
Dog Hawk, Orphan Band
Hawk Thunder (band unknown)
Standing Elk, Corn Band
Tall Mandan (an Akicita), Corn Band
Brave Heart, Lower Brulé
White Tail, Wazhazha Band

Oglalas
Big Mouth, Loafer Band
Walks Underground, Southern Oglala
Black Warbonnet, Southern Oglala
Standing Cloud, Southern Oglala
Blue Horse, Loafer Band
Big Head, Southern Oglala[25]

Dull Knife, whose people called future northwest Nebraska home, reputedly signed for the Northern Cheyennes but at a later date, probably in October

1866. Little Wolf, who about the time of the Fetterman fight or shortly thereafter was elevated by the Council of Forty-Four to head, or Sweet Medicine
Chief of all Cheyennes, did not sign and would later suffer personal loss
in Fetterman's defeat. On June 29, an equally sycophantic Taylor wired his
boss, the commissioner of Indian Affairs, C. N. Cooley, and rationalized,
"Satisfactory treaty concluded with the Sioux and Cheyennes. Large repre-
sentations; Most cordial feeling prevails."[26] Of course these particular chiefs
were perfectly willing to sell rights of passage in the Powder River country
if the government paid them for it. They did not live there. Accordingly the
treaty stipulated that the Lakota peace chiefs would receive seventy thousand
dollars a year for twenty years while Dull Knife's Cheyennes, a much smaller
group, would receive fifteen thousand dollars a year for twenty years.[27] What
the treaty basically came down to, according to Olson, was that those chiefs
who had no stake in the Powder River country because they did not live
there, mainly the Brulés, were quite willing to sign a treaty permitting a road
through it while those like Red Cloud and Little Wolf, who lived there and
cherished the country, refused to sign.[28]

Taylor's promise to the Indians that the whites would only be permitted
to travel the road *through* the Powder River Basin and would not be allowed
to shoot the game fell on deaf ears and for good reason. It was patronizing,
and Red Cloud and the other militants knew better. They had heard such talk
before. In December, in the wake of the Fetterman fight, Congress sent an
official named E. B. Chandler to Fort Phil Kearny to investigate the "Indian
problems." Chandler later charged in a letter to Washington that Taylor's
promise to the Indians to keep whites from shooting the game was impossible
to enforce to begin with, and "well calculated, and . . . designed to deceive
the Indians."[29] But Taylor's varied deceptions became the official face of federal government rhetoric when conveying news to the public. Even by the
first week of December 1866, following numerous encounters that made the
road through the Powder River country unsafe for whites, President Andrew
Johnson told the nation in his annual State of the Union address that all the
Indians of the plains had "unconditionally submitted to our authority and
manifested an earnest desire for a renewal of friendly relations."[30] As Olson
pointed out, "A little more than a fortnight later, these same Indians inflicted
upon Colonel Carrington's command the worst defeat the army had yet suffered in the West in Indian warfare."[31]

By late 1866 Red Cloud's tiyospaye had gained a reputation among the whites as *the* most recalcitrant of the warring factions to the point that the Powder River War of 1866–68 has forevermore been called Red Cloud's War. Certainly today, among the Lakotas, the title is one of esteem and honor. But among whites of the nineteenth century it ascribed the aura of savagery to the great warrior and led to the perception that Red Cloud must have been a man capable of centralizing leadership, that he was the *one* who conceived and evolved universal strategy and tactical maneuvers, and implemented them through his powerful authority over hundreds, perhaps thousands of Indians. Undoubtedly much of this ascription by the whites came from whatever dramatic presence he allegedly fostered at the Taylor peace conference in June 1866, and it has followed him all his life and throughout history to the present day.

▼▼▼

Individuals present in the Powder River country have expressed various opinions regarding the effects of the convergence of the distinct personalities assembled in the region during the summer and fall of that fateful year, both Indian and white. They have debated how the ambitions of these men and their differences over what roles they played determined outcomes in the field. Perhaps none other than William J. Fetterman, who will be considered in a later chapter, has received so much attention as Red Cloud's chief antagonist at the Taylor peace talks, Col. Henry B. Carrington. Never would either man take the time to understand one another, for after June 1866 they were at war. Henry Beebe Carrington (1824–1912) hailed from Wallingford, Connecticut, where he grew up in an educated, well-to-do family that included a Protestant minister and a sea captain. Ancestors had fought in the Revolution. Carrington attended Yale, where he received an AB in 1845 and a law degree in 1847. He taught briefly at the Irving Institute in Tarrytown, New York, and served as Washington Irving's personal secretary at the outbreak of the Mexican-American War. In 1848 he moved to family land in Columbus, Ohio, to practice law. There he befriended William Dennison, who became an influential Ohio governor during the Civil War. An abolitionist, Carrington met many influential men in Ohio, particularly Salmon P. Chase, who was destined to become Lincoln's secretary of the treasury. In 1851

Carrington married Margaret Irwin McDowell Sullivant, who hailed from a prominent family. The couple bore six children, only one of whom, James, would reach adulthood. But among his friends and acquaintances, Henry B. Carrington was indeed "well connected."[32]

Carrington led the Republican Party organization in Ohio and served as adjutant general of the Ohio militia just before the Civil War. He was Lincoln's personal bodyguard when the president-elect's disguised train steamed through Ohio. As such Carrington received a "political" appointment to the regular army as the colonel of the 18th Infantry. But Carrington was not to serve in the field during the Civil War. Due to his apparent organizational skills Governor Oliver P. Morton of Indiana secured him out of harm's way, assigning him instead to recruit, organize, equip, and transport volunteers from Indiana and Ohio during the course of the war. By 1865 Carrington was responsible for the recruitment and assignment of more than 200,000 volunteers. Although he mustered out of service in 1865, the army reassigned him as commander of the 18th Infantry the following year. Gen. Philip St. George Cooke ordered him to relieve Fort Reno and build two additional forts (three were initially projected) in the Powder River country and along the Bighorn River, an assignment that he was well suited for insofar as planning, organizing, and establishing the new garrisons. Unfortunately Carrington was ill-prepared in his past experience for a war in the field, especially one with independent bands of Plains Indians, the likes of which he probably had never seen until his appearance on the Platte during the winter of 1865–66. Carrington reasoned the Indians would cause no trouble the following spring.[33]

A privileged man like Henry Carrington, who had escaped the horrors of Civil War battlefields and prison camps, was naturally quite likely to suffer both unspoken and spoken resentment by junior officers who had been under fire in a unit that suffered the highest casualty rate of the Civil War among regular army units and who had received few accolades in comparison to the hometown glories accorded the volunteer regiments. Junior officers of the 18th Infantry too had become career soldiers with ambitions. But those ambitions had to be advanced on the battlefield and not through political connections, of which they had few or none. This budding jealousy that evolved to outright disrespect became one of Carrington's biggest problems in the Powder River country in 1866.

Another major problem Carrington would face at Fort Phil Kearny came not from the officers below him but from those above, especially his immediate superior, Gen. Philip St. George Cooke, commander of the Department of the Platte. Unlike Carrington, Cooke was a rough-and-tumble campaigner in the West. He was fifty-seven in 1866 and had forty years of service as a dragoon. Cooke was not fond of the defensive strategic master plan implemented by the federal government after the large offensives of 1865, a plan to which Carrington remained loyal given his sparse equipage, rations, and manpower. As a southerner (and father-in-law of Confederate Gen. J. E. B. Stuart) who had remained a Unionist, Cooke's advocacy of more troop strength for the West might possibly have been motivated to some degree by the harshness of Radical Reconstruction in the defeated southern military districts in 1866 following the passage of the Reconstruction Act. If Cooke could show the need for large offensives against the Indians in the West, perhaps life would be made easier for fellow southerners, a position the abolitionist Carrington could not have agreed with philosophically. Then again, Cooke had family problems, with the estrangement of his daughter caused by her southern loyalties to her famous deceased husband. Carrington, by contrast, had an adoring wife and two sons who came with him to Dakota Territory as a close-knit family. During the war Carrington had also crushed budding pacifist movements in Indiana and Ohio. In essence, Cooke and Carrington did not especially like each other. But just how this personal dislike carried over to Cooke's perceptions of Carrington's leadership abilities in 1866 must remain speculative. Perhaps had there been peace on the plains following the farcical Treaty of 1866 Carrington's star as an organizer, builder, and administrator would have shone brightly. But there was not peace in the Powder River country that year, and Henry B. Carrington faced a formidable, if not impossible, task, not only because of the Indians, but because of his fellow officers both above and below him.[34]

In essence, Red Cloud and his allies formulated well-defined war aims and a passionate desire to defend the newly won Powder River from the white invaders in 1866. Sometimes against the odds, given the squabbling among the Oglala bands during previous years, in 1866 they would work together with other Lakotas to successfully achieve those war aims. The 2nd Battalion of the 18th Infantry (2/18th) had no such passionate war aims. Their charge was simply to defend hundreds of miles of indefensible road with precious few soldiers and obsolete weaponry. Compounded by the resentment of the commanding officer for his lack of combat experience, arguably this "Fabian strategy" the army delegated to Col. Henry Carrington and the 2/18th Infantry was doomed to failure from the start. By the end of 1866 the only feasible "war aim" of the 2nd Battalion would be their very survival.[35]

CHAPTER 3

THE OVERLAND CIRCUS

The 18th Infantry Enters the Powder River Country

> Serenely now the ghost of summer dreamed
> On Powder River. 'Twas the brooding time,
> With nights of starlight glinting on the rime
> That cured the curly grass for winter feed,
> And days of blue and gold when scarce a
> reed
> Might stir along the runnels, lean with
> Drought.[1]

BY MARCH 1866, FOLLOWING A COLD NEBRASKA WINTER, Col. Henry Carrington collected his thoughts at Fort Kearney along with his skeleton command of the 2/18th Infantry. Armed with obsolete muzzle-loading Springfield rifles and only about one-quarter normal strength at 220 men, the regiment received orders from General Cooke on the twenty-eighth to relieve Fort Reno (old Fort Connor) with haste. As such Carrington would command a new subdepartment of the Military Department of the Platte called the Mountain District. After mustering out volunteer units at Fort Reno, Carrington would then move up the Bozeman Trail and build two to three new posts in the Powder River country and the Bighorn/Yellowstone country. Carrington leaves no indication in his writings that he knew in the spring of 1866 that the Powder River country had only been controlled by Lakotas and Cheyennes for less than a decade. According to the provisions of the Treaty of 1851, the Powder River country was still the land of the Crows. But by that time the Lakotas had pushed the Crows west of the Bighorn River. The ensuing treaty ostensibly would nullify Crow claims to the Powder River country as the old Treaty of 1851 expired in 1866 anyway. Still the Crows considered these precious lands to be theirs by both treaty and tradition. In essence, to paraphrase historian Robert Utley, Carrington's soldiers were going to steal a land from the Lakotas that the Lakotas had just very recently stolen from the Crows.[2]

But others too had recognized the importance of the Powder River country long before 1866. As a neutral zone the region had a rich history of cultural interaction not only among the tribes but among whites as well. As far back as the beginning of the nineteenth century whites had frequented the region, often traveling north along the route that would bear John Bozeman's name after 1863. Indeed the region had been rife with Euro-American presence before 1866. The French-Canadian trapper François Antoine Larocque, whose Northwest Trade Company sought commerce with the Crows, camped on or very near the future spot of Fort Phil Kearny in 1805. Manuel Lisa's trading post, Fort Raymond (1807), sprang up at the mouth of Bighorn Canyon where the Bozeman Trail would one day cross at the site of Fort C. F. Smith. John Coulter, George Drouillard, Jed Smith, Joe Meek, Jim Bridger, Thomas Fitzpatrick, James Beckwourth, and others traveled through the area during the fur trade era long before John Bozeman had ever seen it or Henry Carrington had ever heard of it.[3] Meek described the region in 1830 as a "hunter's paradise" with huge masses of buffalo east of the Bighorns.[4] Jim Bridger, who would figure into the Fort Phil Kearny story, guided the flamboyant Irish lord George Gore on an appalling pleasure hunt through the Powder River country from 1855 to 1857. When Gore mercifully went back to Ireland in 1857 he claimed to have slaughtered during his sojourn of six thousand miles more than 2,000 buffalo, 1,600 deer and elk, and 105 bears. Considering these were years of conquest of the Powder River country by the Lakotas, Gore's campaign of eradication against the region's big game might have been viewed by the Indians as a wake-up call. What might happen to their resources if whites were allowed to remain in the area in significant numbers?[5] Finally, the Connor campaign and Sawyers expedition of 1865 called attention to the Bozeman Trail route to Montana and thus portended even greater calamity for the Indians.

For soldiers of the 18th Infantry and their wives, however, the march to the Powder River country seemed like an expedition into terra incognita, a strange and alien environment that contrasted dramatically with the eastern fields and woodlands they had known so intimately during previous years. Although several officers and men remembered the arduous trek along the

Platte road from Fort Kearney, Nebraska, to Fort Laramie and beyond to the Powder River country, the trip is best chronicled by Margaret Carrington.[6] To many she may not seem to be the type of woman to accompany soldiers into a potential war zone on a far-flung frontier during the high Victorian era, seven hundred miles from the nearest railroad and far from safety. But that image is more the product of recent gender-role prescription. Born in Danville, Kentucky, on May 10, 1831, Margaret Irwin McDowell Sullivant hailed from a distinguished family and grew to womanhood among the privileged classes of the burgeoning Midwest. She received a good education at Oakland Female Seminary in Hillsboro, Ohio. Her grandfather had founded the community that became Columbus, Ohio, while her father, Joseph Sullivant, founded Ohio State University. Margaret's cousin, Gen. Irwin McDowell, as commander of the Army of the Potomac, suffered defeat at First Bull Run in 1861 at the hands of Johnston's and Jackson's Confederates. Her family was related to Thomas Jefferson and Supreme Court Chief Justice John Marshall, while she and her husband had lately been casually acquainted with President Abraham Lincoln.[7]

Although infrequent today, it was not uncommon during the nineteenth century for such a woman to reliantly accompany a military officer husband on campaign. Army wives on the frontier were expected to be models of gentility, morality, fortitude, grace, and above all symbols and examples of advancing American civilization against so-called savagery. Margaret Carrington and other officers' wives of her generation assumed the roles of making the process of conquest seem more just and proper. Only twenty when she was married in 1851 and thirty-five when she made the journey to the Powder River country, Margaret had already given birth to six children, only two of whom, young Jimmy and Harry, survived early childhood. These two boys accompanied the Carringtons to Fort Phil Kearny, accepting, like their mother, whatever hardships might be in store for them.[8] Still a handsome woman in her prime, Margaret suffered from tuberculosis that may have influenced the Carringtons' decision for her to journey to the dry climate of the Rocky Mountain West. In 1870 the disease would prematurely take her life. But during the two years before her death Margaret Carrington would leave one of the most thorough accounts of that historic and arduous trek into the Powder River country and of the Fetterman fight as well. More significantly, her writings, in later years, would help fix blame and cast controversy over the events of December 21, 1866, that mythologize the Fetterman fight to the present day.[9]

While in winter quarters at Fort Kearney, Nebraska, during 1865–66, Margaret entertained at a dinner party the recently appointed commander of the Division of the Missouri, Gen. William Tecumseh Sherman. Particularly jovial despite the recent reduction of military forces in the West, Sherman suggested that officers' wives should keep journals of their experiences during the ensuing spring and summer. Margaret took Sherman's words to heart and her journal, *Ab-sa-ra-ka: Home of the Crows*, published in 1868, became a classic of Indian Wars history from the army viewpoint. In many respects her writings are typical of countless women's travel journals composed during this period, focusing upon the juxtapositions of wild scenery and immense natural beauty. "The nights in Absaraka," she wrote, "were peculiarly beautiful when cloudless. The rarity of the atmosphere gave full play to the star-beams, and it seemed as if there were twice as many as in any firmament elsewhere."[10]

Like other army wives of the period, Margaret Carrington held misconceived notions about Indians. Almost Byronian in outlook, her impressions are born of schoolroom stereotypes steeped in the Puritan captivity myths and James Fenimore Cooper mythology—a fearsome contradiction: the noble savage and the proud warrior, yet always vengeful and dangerous like the wild western landscape. "In ambush and decoy, splendid," she exhorted; "in horsemanship, perfect; in strategy, cunning; in battle, wary and careful of life; in victory, jubilant; and in vengeance, fiendish and terrible."[11] Typical also was her sentiment for what was then perceived to be the inevitable disappearance of Indians against the onslaught of civilization. "These same Indians have read the book of fate," she wrote. "There comes the inevitable sentiment of pity and even of sympathy with the bold warrior in his great struggle."[12]

Indeed, Margaret's words support the statistical reality that women heading west were among the most ubiquitous chroniclers of the U.S. settlement movement. Her expressions of individuality, however, would be twofold. Margaret Carrington was not one to complain about the hardships or write about them to family in the East, although the claim by some historians that women's complaints regarding their new environment were somewhat universal may be overblown. In all sense of the word Margaret was ambitious to advance her husband's career and viewed such endeavors as a mark of personal achievement. To her the West became a personal challenge to overcome as assuredly it was for the men of the 18th Infantry. "Any life on the plains is a good school," she wrote, "and its practical suggestions take all the starch and false pride . . . out of the human creature . . . The triplet of 'I never could, I never would, and I never will,' became almost obsolete; and in their place was these other impulses, . . . 'I could, I can, and I *do*!'" Margaret Carrington was above all else a dutiful nineteenth-century army wife.[13]

Aside from Margaret's frequent stoicism, most of the adults' accounts of their experiences in the Platte and Powder River countries are filled with fear and monotony. For the few children who accompanied the battalion, however, memories were those of a grand adventure. Vividly recalling the trek more than sixty years later, James Carrington, Margaret and Henry's son, reminisced,

> Looking back over the many years that have gone, it seems to me that we children thought chiefly of the good times we were having; to us it was a wonderful and glorious adventure. Little did we appreciate the ever-present anxiety that filled the minds of our mothers, the downright hardships and privations they endured, the wearing responsibilities that bore so heavily upon the shoulders of the commander . . . To us it was mostly *wash-ta-la*, good, but to our elders it was *wau-nee-chee*, very bad.[14]

Like his mother, Jimmy Carrington was most impressed by the beauty of the plains and especially the wildlife. He leaves us with impressions both familiar to modern travelers on the plains and others long since eclipsed from the prairie environment, and a military frontier now lost in memory and vague in the pages of history. "Nightly we heard the weird and mournful howling of wolves," he remembered in 1928, "sometimes the deep rumble of a stampeded herd of buffalo, that fairly shook the earth . . . Never a day without the sight of leaping antelopes, an occasional sneaking coyote . . . and the ever expanse of sage covered plains, blinding dust, the big skies stretching to the blue horizon, distant mountains, gorgeous sunsets, and in the heat of some days a shimmering mirage that looked like a great sea . . . And all through the dark, at regular intervals, the reassuring calls of the sentinel on watch."[15]

The complement of 220 veterans that set out along the Platte in May toward Fort Laramie and the Mountain District had recently been reinforced by the 3/18th Infantry and Company F, 1/18th Infantry, and included many raw recruits to be distributed among all regimental companies. They swelled the numbers to about 2,000 men. Most would guard the Platte road and thence the route to Salt Lake City. Only eight companies of the 2/18th would make the trek north to the Powder River country in the Mountain District. A twenty-five-piece military band under Bandmaster Sergeant Samuel Curry accompanied the expedition to relieve the monotony. Carrington had armed them with seven-shot Spencers while the other infantrymen still carried Civil War–issue single-shot muzzle-loading Springfields. While en route to Fort Laramie with two hundred wagons and awkward construction machinery, adjutant Lieutenant William Bisbee later recalled that "some one had given [the expedition] the name of 'Carrington's Overland Circus.'"[16] Officers of the 2/18th who made their way to Fort Laramie that spring included in addition to Colonel Carrington, adjutant Lt. William H. Bisbee, quartermaster Lt. Frederick Brown, and captains Tenador Ten Eyck, Joshua L. Proctor, Nathaniel C. Kinney, and Thomas B. Burrowes. Other lieutenants included John I. Adair, Isaac D'Isay, Frederick Phisterer, and Thaddeus Kirtland, a cousin of Henry Carrington.[17] Several officers' and enlisted men's wives were with the command. Although women and children rode in ambulances, young Jimmy and Harry Carrington acquired a small Indian pony at Fort Kearney. They named it Calico. "We would take turns riding him," James wrote years later, "to get relief from the monotony and cramped quarters of the ambulance."[18] Guides and scouts for the expedition included sixty-two-year-old Jim Bridger, as well acquainted with the Powder River country as any man, and Henry Williams, both of whom had been with Connor during the previous year. Bisbee remembered Bridger in that year as "a plain, farmer-like looking man, five feet ten or eleven in height. He dressed in the customary 'store clothes,' low crowned, soft felt hat, never affecting . . . long hair or showy buckskin suits."[19] Carrington hired Jack Snead, who had lived with the Pawnees, as official interpreter. Reputedly the Bad Face Oglalas hated Snead and had placed a bounty on his head.[20]

The command brought with them an almost burdensome amount of equipment including hay cutting machines and a sawmill that would be used to build the intended forts. They would pick up more at Fort Laramie. The trek from Fort Kearney to Fort Laramie was typical of travel along the Oregon/California Trail before the railroad. Encounters with insects, dust, and rain were frequent. The battalion survived a particularly harrowing crossing of the North Platte. The command was excited at seeing Court House Rock, Chimney Rock, and Scott's Bluff. Anxiety increased with Carrington's tightening of security once Lakota and Cheyenne country was reached. There were also the minor joys of reaching "civilization" at Julesburg and Fort Sedgwick where needed provisions were either obtained or found to be in too short supply—the stuff of countless pioneer travel journals.[21]

During the crossing of the North Platte near Scott's Bluff an eight-yoke ox team stampeded down the bank to the river with two wagonloads of equipment including parts for a sawmill. "I do not believe any of these steers were alive when they got to the bottom of the hill," Pvt. William Murphy of Company A remembered years later. "This saw-mill was intended for Fort Phil Kearney [sic] and arrived a month or six weeks later. This of course delayed us some in building the Fort."[22] As May gave way to June the 18th Infantry made its way to Fort Laramie. Carrington had his parley with Standing Elk and witnessed the anger of Red Cloud, Man Afraid of His Horse, and other Lakotas at the Taylor peace talks. To Carrington's horror, 100,000 rounds of ammunition that General Cooke had promised would await him at Fort Laramie had not arrived. Carrington squeezed only 1,000 rounds from Colonel Maynadier. Promised horses were likewise nonexistent at Fort Laramie. Rations too were in bad condition, musty and caked flour, hardtack too hard to chew, and moldy bacon was all he could procure for his continued journey north. Carrington was finding that the problem of logistics and supply over long distances was a common condition for the army in the West before the railroad. He was experiencing many of the same difficulties that had plagued Connor the previous year.[23]

Carrington did add two scouts to his command at Fort Laramie: James J. Brannan, who had scouted with one of Connor's detachments in 1865, and the almost legendary, now elderly mulatto mountain man James P. Beckwourth, who had married into the Crow tribe and who might gain useful knowledge from the Crows if it came to trouble. While at Fort Laramie Carrington almost picked up a photographer for his expedition, an affluent Quaker from Philadelphia with long blonde hair named Ridgeway Glover. The photographer quickly befriended the Carringtons. Already Glover had developed a number of stereoscopes of Indians and Indian villages. Glover hoped to trap furs during the fall and then "spend the winter in Virginia City, Montana, and secure some winter Rocky Mountain scenery." Carrington wished Glover to accompany his command into the Powder River country, but the army's departure was too soon for Glover's plans that summer. He would join another wagon train later and travel north.[24] After Carrington sent two urgent telegrams to Omaha for ammunition and supplies, about seven hundred men of the 2/18th marched out of Fort Laramie on June 17, 1866, about five hundred of whom were raw recruits, along with four officers and officers' families, a couple of family servants, and a few enlisted men's wives and civilian contractors with their families. They were "splendidly furnished," wrote one chronicler, "with everything except arms, ammunition, and horses." Carrington deployed the remaining 1,300 men of the 18th Infantry along the overland route to Salt Lake City.[25]

Out from Fort Laramie the command crossed the North Platte once again at Bridger's Ferry on June 20. Now they were in country where they suspected Red Cloud's warriors might be. Carrington ordered pickets stationed outside the guarded perimeters of every campsite for the remainder of the journey. They learned from an operator of a road "ranch" named Mills that Indians, reputed by a Lakota employee to be Bad Faces of Red Cloud's tiyospaye, had stolen some stock from the ranch on the previous day.[26] Shortly before reaching Fort Reno the women in the party purchased merchandise at another road ranch, one run by Louis Gazeau, whom locals affectionately called "French Pete," his Lakota wife, Mary, and several children. French Pete gave Dr. Horton's wife an antelope that, for months after the construction of Fort Phil Kearny, would scamper around the parade ground until one day it drank a bucket of paint and died.[27] On July 28 the command reached the ramshackle collection of partially collapsed and unwalled adobe structures that passed for Fort Reno and were soon engulfed in a torrential storm, the hailstones from which Private Murphy described as being as "large as pullets' eggs."[28]

Located on a dry shelf about fifty feet above the left bank of Powder River, the complement of the 2/18th found Fort Reno to be inhospitable. "Absolute sterility excludes all elements of vegetable beauty or production," Margaret Carrington wrote in 1868. "The same old sage brush and cactus persistently monopolize the soil for miles, and Powder River itself . . . is muddy and so strongly alkaline as to be prejudicial to both man and beast."[29] Lieutenant Bisbee remembered Fort Reno as "presenting sufficient ugliness and barrenness to warrant gladness that we were not to remain there long."[30]

Fort Reno was garrisoned by two companies of the 5th U.S. Volunteers, "galvanized Yankees," who were eagerly awaiting the arrival of the regulars so they could be mustered out of the army. A party of Winnebagos had been at the fort and met Carrington along the trail. Enemies of all Sioux, they wanted to stay and scout for the 18th Infantry, but having no authority to employ them Carrington dismissed them, a decision that could easily have haunted his dreams for years to come. The 2/18th spent ten days at Fort Reno, while the temperature rose above 100 degrees in the shade. Carrington arranged for the battalion's assignments in the Powder River country; he mustered out the 5th Volunteers and loaded provisions from the storehouses for use at the new forts. Private Murphy was detailed to load the wagons. "We loaded up some sacks of bacon," he wrote. "I do not know how old it was, but the fat had commenced to sluff off from the lean and it was from three to five inches thick. There was a lot of flour in the store rooms and the mice had tunneled through it and the bacon, evidently for some time."[31] Independence Day was spent somberly for the women but an army paymaster had arrived on July 3 and the men had received four months' back pay. Post sutler A. C. Leighton did a lively holiday business. Private Murphy witnessed the punishment of a drunken soldier. It was "one of the worst cases of cruelty I saw in the Army," he remembered. "At the guard tent four stakes were driven into the ground and the drunken soldier was stretched at full length and tied to them. This was called the 'Spread Eagle.' The sun was beating down on him when I saw him, and I thought he was dead. Flies were eating him up and were running in and out of his mouth, ears and nose."[32]

Shortly after their arrival a party of Indians, probably southern Brulés, ran off the sutler's horses from the post. A party of eighty troopers including Lieutenant Adair pursued them for seventy miles to near Pumpkin Buttes without being able to recapture the horses. The men did, however, bring in a stray Indian pony laden with merchandise presumably, Margaret Carrington thought, from the Fort Laramie peace talks.[33] Consequently Carrington decided not to abandon Fort Reno completely, figuring travelers would need a secure place between Bridger's Ferry and the proposed site of New Fort Reno to be located to the south. Dubbing the old post Reno Station, Carrington ordered Lieutenant Kirtland's Company B to remain there with twenty-two horses that would serve as mounts for about one-third of his men and would be used for messenger and escort duty. Capt. Joshua

Proctor would command the station that most of the men continued to call Fort Reno. Under his direction Fort Reno was greatly enlarged with new structures slightly north of Reno Station. "New Fort Reno" (Cantonment Reno) would not be established until 1874. Cantonment Reno lasted until 1877, when it was abandoned and Fort McKinney was built fifty miles north. Five companies under Carrington and Captain Ten Eyck would then move north to establish what would be the middle fort in the chain. The name of the new northern fort would be Fort Phil Kearny to honor Gen. Philip Kearny, who was killed at the Battle of Chantilly, Virginia, in 1862. Capt. Nathaniel Coates Kinney and two companies would then move up the road from Fort Phil Kearny to build and staff Fort C. F. Smith at some future designated site on the Bighorn River. Carrington hoped to establish another post on the Yellowstone as well but already his lines were growing too thin. The expanded Fort Reno served as temporary headquarters of the Mountain District while Carrington designated Fort Phil Kearny battalion headquarters of the 2/18th.[34] On June 30 Carrington had issued instructions for the protection of wagon trains. All trains large and small were to stop at Fort Reno. They could only proceed when there were thirty armed men in the train, including a military escort detail, and all trains were to move in compact formation and not scatter along the trail.[35]

On July 9 seven companies of the 2/18th, including three officers' wives, left Fort Reno to points unknown along the upper Powder River where a site for Fort Phil Kearny would be selected. The weather was sweltering and the dust choking. At 113 degrees July 9 was the hottest day of the year. The command was now moving up to lands unfamiliar to them and devoid of any amenities of white civilization. "The march which [had] brought us to Fort Reno closed up all possibility of meeting any resident traders," Margaret Carrington remembered. "[T]here was [now] not a resident white man between Bridger's Ferry and Bozeman City, Montana."[36] By the time the command left Fort Reno they had been traveling the southwesterly section of the Bozeman Trail for some time since the route had left the Platte road in the vicinity of modern Douglas, Wyoming. Called by many "the Montana Road" on its northern course, the trail would continue northwest, skirting the east side of the Bighorn Mountains. It then crossed tributaries of the Bighorn River to the Bighorn proper in Montana Territory where Fort C. F. Smith would be built. The trail then passed around the

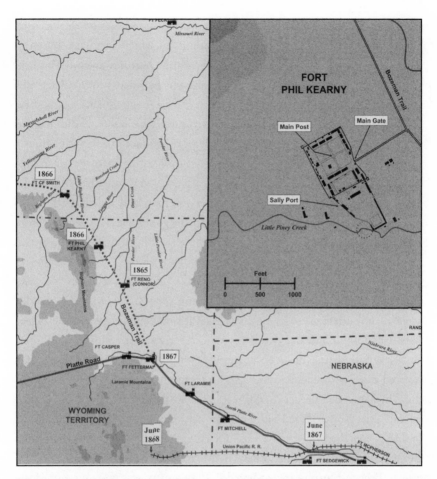

"The Bozeman Trail Forts, 1866–68." Charles D. Collins Jr., *Atlas of the Sioux Wars*, 2nd ed. (Fort Leavenworth, KS: Combat Studies Institute Press, 2006).

northernmost outcroppings of the Bighorn and Pryor mountains, crossed the Clark's Fork River and other streams, and swung around the Beartooth Mountains, eventually reaching the main Yellowstone River near modern Livingston, Montana. From there it crossed Bozeman Pass and gained the Gallatin Valley and on to Virginia City.[37]

Although whites had traversed the region numerous times, it was John Bozeman, a Georgian and veteran of the Colorado gold rush, along with John Jacobs who made the route well known to gold seekers. The pair were entrepreneurs who wished to popularize the route and draw traffic away from the Platte road system with the lure of a shortcut. They intended to make quick cash guiding emigrants and to strengthen the flow of settlers into the Gallatin Valley, thus boosting land values to holdings in which they had invested. They also hoped to strengthen their mercantile ventures around Virginia City.[38] With a population of over ten thousand by 1864, Virginia City had eclipsed earlier Bannock to become the territorial capital of Montana. The mining camps around Alder Gulch were so numerous residents dubbed the place "Fourteen-mile City." The gold rush there produced the largest amount of placer gold in the Northwest, about $120 million. By 1866 the gulch had produced $30 million in just the past three years. No wonder the region was important to the wartime and postwar economies, and that it offered the lure of a shortcut from the East, no less so for gold seekers. A sense of *mission* surely encompassed Henry Carrington as he diligently plodded onward through the Powder River country.[39]

The first camp north from Fort Reno was made on Crazy Woman Creek, twenty-six miles above that post, a watering spot that would soon be the scene of ambush for unwary travelers. As if it were foreboding of a bad place, Mrs. Carrington and the two other officers' wives, Mrs. Horton and Mrs. Bisbee, while sitting in camp chairs watching a sunset, looked down and noticed three rattlesnakes lounging with them under their chairs. An orderly quickly dispatched the reptiles. On July 12, the command grew even smaller when Carrington assigned more men to help in the expansion of Fort Reno and they marched off to join Captain Proctor.[40] On July 13 the command came to Buffalo Wallow, another "bad place," as it turned out, for Indian attack, Private Murphy remembered.[41] The country was growing more lush now, the grasses high, the sagebrush giving way to what appeared to be green pastures. Game was sighted. These were the select lands of the Powder River country. At 11:00 AM on July 13, the command passed Lake De Smet and camped on the banks of the Big Piney about four miles from the Bighorn Mountains near modern Story, Wyoming. "At last, we had the prospect of finding a home," Margaret Carrington remembered years later, "and Cloud Peak seemed to look down upon us with a cheerful face as the sunlight made his features glow and glisten."[42]

On July 14 Carrington, along with lieutenants Phister and Brown, Captain Ten Eyck, scouts Brannan and Stead, and an armed escort of enlisted men, rode out on a seventy-mile reconnaissance to determine what spot was best suited for the construction of Fort Phil Kearny. Although Jim Bridger had urged Carrington to proceed on to Tongue River the officers determined that the Tongue was too far from a good source of timber and too far from the Powder River and the principal travel route of the Bozeman Trail. The Tongue River site would also have left the Indians in control of the forks of Piney and Peno Creeks and have given them a well-sheltered avenue to the Tongue River. Soon the Lakotas would congregate along the Tongue themselves, followed sometime later by Miniconjous and factions of the Cheyennes and Arapahos. Carrington decided the plateau where the battalion was camped was best suited for the site of the new fort. It was six miles or so from abundant timber, well watered by Big and Little Piney Creeks where sawmills could operate, and had abundant grass for grazing.[43] "A more ideal spot for a fort could not be imagined," Sergeant Fessenden remembered. But Private Murphy thought differently. "For some reason they picked out a location about seven miles from the timber," he wrote in 1930, "and from five to eight miles from any hay bottom."[44]

Through the years historians and others have criticized the location of Fort Phil Kearny. The location was, however, closer to timber and hay than what was found on the Tongue. Possibly the reason for such criticism is that the far side of Lodge Trail Ridge to the northeast where Fetterman's troops were killed was out of sight of the fort. Indeed the country is broken around Fort Phil Kearny. Sullivant Hills slightly to the northwest, which Colonel Carrington named after his wife's family, along with the vegetation on the banks of the Piney forks, presented obstruction for the soldiers and hiding places for the Indians. To the south the only obstructed view from the fort is a knob of land the soldiers called "Pilot Hill." From that summit, however, a sentry who was most always present had a good view of the surrounding countryside, including the wagon route along the Bozeman Trail and the route to the timber-cutting operations.[45]

Colonel Carrington wasted little time. On July 15 he began preparations to lay out the fort and assigned specific duties to the men. "Engineer J. B. Gregory was soon at work trying to put in shape and operation a horse-power saw-mill," Margaret remembered, "until the steam mills [that had fallen into the North Platte near Scott's Bluff] should arrive, the whole garrison was broken into details for ditching, chopping, hauling, hewing, and such other varied duty as loomed up as a vast burden, to be overcome before winter should overtake us."[46]

The men laid out the fort so that it faced the Bozeman Trail with Piney Creek below. Civilian contractors with mowing machines planed the grass into a parade ground and soldiers set up tents along new-mown "streets." Soon the garrison would construct log structures to replace the canvas ones. Margaret Carrington recorded best the results of the construction of Fort Phil Kearny that summer:

> The Fort proper is six hundred feet by eight hundred, situated upon a natural plateau, so that there is a gradual shift slope from the front and rear, falling off nearly sixty feet in a few rods, thus affording a natural glacis, and giving to the position a positive strength, independent of other defenses. A rectangle, two hundred by six hundred feet, is occupied by warehouses, cavalry stables, laundress quarters and the non-commissioned staff.
>
> About the parade-ground, already referred to, are officers' and men's quarters, offices, guardhouse, sutler's and band building.
>
> The stockade is made of heavy pine trunks eleven feet long, hewn to a touching surface of four inches so as to join closely, being pointed and loop-holed, and firmly imbedded in the ground for three feet. Block-houses are at two diagonal corners, and massive gates of plank with small wickets, all having substantial locks, are on three fronts, and on the fourth or southern front, back of the officer's quarters, is a small gate for sallies, or for officer's use.[47]

A platform surrounded the interior walls at every port-hole, "so that in case of attack," Sergeant Fessenden remembered, "a man could fire, then step aside and reload while another man took his place for a shot."[48] Fessenden remembered the company buildings as being "very nice for log structures," with the bark side of the logs being turned to the outside. "The roof," he recalled, "was of poles about four inches thick, put close together, then covered with corn sacks or grass, with about six inches of earth over this for 'shingles.' Such a roof seldom leaked."[49] At the "pineries," about six miles from the fort where woodcutting details would labor daily, the men constructed two blockhouses some distance from each other, "we having what was known as the upper and lower cuttings," Fessenden remembered. "Every morning twenty wagons were sent out for this purpose. About half a mile

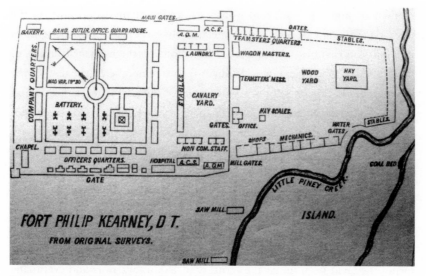

Layout of Fort Phil Kearny from Original Survey Drawing. Margaret Carrington preserved for prosperity the layout of Fort Phil Kearny in her book *Ab-sa-ra-ka, Home of the Crows*, 1868.

before reaching the timber, the road forked at an angle of about forty-five degrees, one road running to each cutting. Here we found trees that were ninety feet to the first limb, and as straight as an arrow."[50]

Although soldiers and contractors applied finishing touches to Fort Phil Kearny well into January 1867, the stockade proper, 2,800 feet in circumference, and the interior buildings were completed by October 1866. On August 3, captains Kinney and Burrowes departed with companies C and D to establish Fort C. F. Smith on the Bighorn. Jim Bridger guided them with instructions to return to Fort Phil Kearny as soon as possible while Jim Beckwourth left to reconnoiter with the Crows as to the disposition of the Lakotas and Cheyennes. Kinney officially established Fort C. F. Smith at the mouth of Bighorn Canyon in Montana Territory on August 12 while Carrington abandoned plans to establish the fourth proposed post because of insufficient numbers of troops.[51] With the installation of the flagstaff Carrington declared a holiday on October 31 to celebrate the completion of the post. A formal ceremony accompanied the first official raising of the Stars and Stripes over a garrison in the upper Powder River country.[52]

Perhaps the flag raising was the last joyous celebration held at Fort Phil Kearny. Soon winter set in and the moods of soldier and civilian alike turned somber. At night people heard wolves scratching at the wood posts of the stockade. For some of the garrison melancholy was offset set by the sense of stoic mission that often accompanied battalions on the military frontiers of the American West. Lieutenant William Bisbee remembered the days of the Indian Wars as "a waste of twenty-five years of our earthly existence," paraphrasing a fellow officer, "an oblivion apart from civilizing participations or influence . . . oftimes lapses of months without newsprints or in touch with the outside world [nothing but the] monotonous, humdrum daily rotations of life in tents, or small log house garrison with furnishings limited to one room, bedstead, table, chair and candlestick . . . My only answer could be, we did it for Civilization."[53]

By the fall of 1866 melancholia was the least of the worries for the garrison at Fort Phil Kearny. Ever since they had left Fort Laramie in the spring they had been under the scrutiny of Lakota warriors and eventually Cheyennes and Arapahos as well. After they turned north from Fort Reno that scrutiny had increased. Jim Bridger surmised the Indians were counting troops. According to almost all those who left records to history, by the time the 2/18th reached their destination at the site of Fort Phil Kearny hardly a day passed without sighting Indians or seeing evidence of their presence. If soldiers like Lt. William Bisbee felt a sense of isolation far from "civilization," such was the opposite for Red Cloud's followers. As they moved comfortably in familiar surroundings, their "civilization" was already present along the Powder River, the civilization of the Lakotas and Cheyennes. Proud of their recent expulsion of the Crows and defiant in their determination to defend what they perceived to be not a raw wilderness, but rather a rich economic storehouse, the Indian peoples who surrounded Fort Phil Kearny that autumn would not tolerate what they considered an invasion of recently conquered territory, hard won from Crow enemies. For them the raising of the Stars and Stripes over Fort Phil Kearny represented an intention on the part of the whites to permanently colonize coveted Indian property. So it was that the Powder River country during the summer and fall of 1866 became once again a blooded and contested land.

CHAPTER 4

LAKOTAS STRIKE TO DEFEND THE POWDER RIVER COUNTRY

The Powder River gathering of the Sioux?
And lo, at one far end the day was young;
Noon saw the other! Up along the Tongue
Big villages were dancing! Everywhere
The buzzing wasp of war was in the air.[1]

RED CLOUD AND OTHER LAKOTAS WOULD NOT TOLERATE a permanent occupation of the Powder River country by white soldiers, symbols as they were of American authority over Indians and their land. Allowing travel north over the Bozeman Trail was one thing, and a number of emigrants had little trouble before July 1866. But forts represented a permanent military presence and a signal of conquest. The presence of the forts was a far greater immediate and emotional cause for war in 1866 than the long-range threats to game and other natural resources. Until the Connor campaign the previous year, Lakotas had let travelers pass to the Montana gold country. Occasionally they warned the emigrants along the North Platte to continue westward and go north by the longer route through Utah. But the essence of permanent forts was the last straw for the war factions. Oglalas set a deadline at Crazy Woman Creek in the southern reaches of the Powder River country. They would do everything in their power to stop traffic north of that point on the Bozeman Trail.[2] As such both soldiers and civilians would feel the Indians' wrath during the summer of 1866. Historians will probably always disagree regarding the amount, if any, of centralized authority exercised by either Red Cloud personally or any particular coalition of chiefs and warriors in general among the lodges and villages that collected in the valleys of the Tongue, Rosebud, and Powder rivers that summer and fall, eager to resist white encroachment. The label of "Red Cloud's War," as the fighting of 1866–68 came to be called, has always suggested in the non-Indian mind a high degree of centralized leadership under the war's namesake. The Bad Face warrior George Sword (Hunts the Enemy), who was in both the Fetterman fight and the Wagon Box fight, remembered that "[i]n those days they were not looking up to chiefs . . . these were young men thirsting for the fray . . . There was no one person in charge of the Indians."[3] The actions by the Indians in the summer of 1866 in the Powder River country took on elements of an "insurgency" comprising mostly independent guerilla actions and demonstrations in defiance of a smaller but technologically superior occupation force. By late fall the Indians would become better organized.

Whatever organizational leadership that did or did not exist in the summer among specific Indian leaders, and at what level, is secondary, however, to the emergent strategy that proved superlative and to tactics that, for the most part, were effective by fall. By December the garrison at Fort Phil Kearny was frustrated, angry, and for many soldiers and civilians alike emotionally drained in their tight confinement during a bitter cold winter. Veteran officers and enlisted men who had seen service on the battlefields of the Civil War found themselves bewildered by the hit-and-run guerilla tactics of the Indians, who refused to fight in any semblance of conventional closed-order formation. Often it was difficult to tell peaceful bands of Indians from those resisting, a situation of confusion and uncertainty that was ultimately conducive to rash actions.[4]

With a couple of exceptions, however, a certain pattern emerged to the Indian attacks during the summer and fall of 1866. During July, following a successful assault on the Fort Phil Kearny mule herd, the Indians focused their attacks on both soldiers and emigrants near Fort Reno in order to threaten travel northward on the Bozeman Trail and to hopefully discourage the building of Fort Phil Kearny along the Piney, a stream the Lakotas and Cheyennes called Buffalo Creek. Later in the summer and on into fall the Indians' focus shifted north again to Fort Phil Kearny once its presence was felt. For the most part, until summer 1867, the Lakotas would simply try to cut off Fort C. F. Smith from supplies moving north by concentrating on Fort Phil Kearny in the middle of the chain. But Fort C. F. Smith received supplies from the Montana gold camps and survived the winter of 1866–67 better than Fort Phil Kearny. The Bighorn River lands farther north on the Bozeman Trail were also the domain of the Northern Cheyennes, Hunkpapas, and Blackfeet, who could eventually deal with Fort C. F. Smith if they wished, once the time was right. But in the end it would once again be the Oglalas who dealt with Fort C. F. Smith in 1867. Efforts during the summer of 1866 centered on running off precious livestock, cattle, mules, and horses, but any soldier or emigrant who strayed too far from military columns or wagon trains ran the risk of imminent attack and equally imminent death. For the Lakotas the theft of livestock not only reduced subsistence at the forts but proved profitable in trade.[5]

With the approach of the cold season warriors initiated the tactic of assaulting hay-cutting and woodcutting details at Fort Phil Kearny. The "pineries," as the stands of timber being cut were commonly called, had to be fortified, and large escorts of troops were necessary. Any thought of a direct attack on a fortified perimeter like Fort Phil Kearny, Fort Reno, or Fort C. F. Smith, however, was wisely out of the question. But as numbers of Indians favoring war grew through autumn they developed tactics to lure soldiers from Fort Phil Kearny to their destruction once Indian numerical superiority became sufficient. They would engage the same tactics in 1867 against Fort C. F. Smith. The gathering of war factions in the Powder River country that summer and fall tended to disrupt somewhat normal patterns of movement of previous years. Peace factions like those of Dull Knife's Cheyennes moved south into the Republican River country and the Platte Valley to escape the war, while some Brulés congregated northward with the Miniconjou war advocates.[6]

All summer and into fall scattered bands of warriors and their families slowly gathered in the Powder River country, determined to drive whites from these lands. Black Elk, cousin of Crazy Horse, was only three years old in 1866 but years later he recalled a story told by his father, also named Black Elk and whose leg was shattered in the Fetterman fight. He alludes to the possibility of *some* level of organized leadership or influence once the Wasichus (the whites) established their permanent forts along the Bozeman Trail. "And so when the soldiers came and built themselves a town of logs there on the Piney Fork of the Powder," Black Elk recalled, "my people knew they meant to have their road and take our country and maybe kill us all when they were strong enough. Crazy Horse was only about nineteen years old then, and Red Cloud was still our great chief. In the moon of the Changing Season (October) he called together all the scattered bands of the Lakota for a big council on the Powder River, and [by late fall] a [man on] horseback could ride through our villages from sunrise until the day was above his head, so far did our camp stretch along the valley of the river; for many of our friends, the Shyela [Cheyennes] and the Blue Clouds [Arapahos], had come to help us fight."[7] Black Elk's words rang true among the Indians. They came to view and fear the forts not as temporary "bases" to protect the narrowly snaking confines of traffic along the trail, but as the first steps in taking all of the Powder River country from them. This belief would transcend the 1860s and influence even the Great Sioux War of the next decade. Black Elk's assertions convey that by the fall of 1866 Red Cloud's influence in fostering resistance was enormous, an influence that was certainly recognized by the whites at the time.[8]

The Bad Face Oglalas were united for war and would soon be joined by Miniconjous, other Lakotas, northern groups of Arapahos, and even some Minnesota Sioux by late fall. But the war clouds that gathered over the Powder River country earlier in the summer fractionalized the Northern Cheyennes. Many of these people revered the Elk River and Bighorn valley to the north and the area east of the Powder River near the Black Hills close to Nohavose, the Sacred Mountain. Long ago, near Nohavose the Cheyenne culture hero Sweet Medicine had instructed his people in the ways of the plains and given to them their precious covenants, Maahotse, the sacred arrows, and Esevone, the sacred buffalo hat.[9] Most were camped near Nohavose in the spring of 1866. When chiefs Little Wolf, Old Bear, Box Elder, and others received word that Carrington was proceeding north to build forts in the Powder River country, some became furious. They directed their anger at other chiefs like Dull Knife, whose given name was Morning Star, for favoring the peace treaty that he indeed signed in October. As dissention grew, about 176 lodges—at least 600 people—who supported the peace treaty broke camp and left Little Wolf's villages. Among them were Dull Knife, Black Horse, White Head, and Lame White Man of Little Wolf's Elkhorn Scraper warrior society. Many of these who left were older chiefs and warriors, Dull Knife being in his fifties in 1866. Earlier, followers of Turkey Leg including the esteemed Crooked Lance warrior Roman Nose had gone south to fight alongside the Dog Soldiers. Soon they would be a reckoning force against the advancing Union Pacific and Union Pacific Eastern Division (Kansas Pacific) railroads. Interestingly, the treaty faction headed north and camped along the Tongue and Goose Creek in June, only a short distance above Red Cloud's Bad Faces who favored war.

Close by were the camps of Man Afraid of His Horse. This mixture of "treaty Indians" and militants would compound a volatile situation for whites and Indians alike as individuals from one faction mixed with the other.[10]

Sometime in early July Black Horse and his peaceful band of Cheyennes left their Tongue River camp and rode south to trade with the whites. Seven miles north of Fort Phil Kearny, Pierre "French Pete" Gazeau and his partner, Henry Arrison, traveled north and set up a road ranch to capitalize on trade with emigrants headed to the gold camps. They had arrived at their destination even before Carrington's "circus" had arrived at the Piney forks. At Fort Reno four more white men joined their company, including Joe Donaldson, who had worked as a contractor for Carrington's quartermaster when the 2/18th was at Fort Reno. French Pete had his Lakota wife, Mary, and his four (some say five) mixed-blood children with him. He felt perfectly safe. Black Horse's people camped nearby and traded with French Pete for several days.[11] During this time several Oglala messengers brought word to Black Horse that a patrol of soldiers was moving up the trail. On July 14, Black Horse met up with Lt. John Adair, whom Carrington had dispatched to track down nine deserters who were now headed north for the gold country. Black Horse asked Joe Donaldson through Gazeau, acting as interpreter, to return to the Fort Phil Kearny construction site with the message "We wish to know does the white chief want war or peace. Tell him [Carrington] to come to me with the black white man."[12] The individual in question was Carrington's official interpreter, Jack Snead, an African American who was married to a Lakota woman or had been so in the past. Donaldson rode off with Adair, who apparently gave up the chase for the deserters. Carrington detained Donaldson at Fort Phil Kearny for a day. This delay alarmed Black Horse so that he and his band headed back for their camps along the Tongue River.[13] Carrington, Donaldson, and Snead caught up with Black Horse on the sixteenth. Carrington invited the Indians to his encampment on the Piney for a council. Carrington wrote a message for Black Horse informing him that "I [Carrington] tell all the white men that go on the [Bozeman Trail] that if they hurt Indians or steal their ponies I will follow and catch them and punish them. I will not let white men do hurt to the Indians who wish peace."[14]

Other chiefs present at this ensuing council were Dull Knife, Wolf That Lies Down, Jumping Rabbit, Red Arm, and Little Man, as were warrior society headmen Lame White Man, Pretty Bear, and others. Jim Bridger came in and was there with Jack Snead to interpret. Black Horse told Carrington that his people represented 176 lodges along the Tongue and Goose Creek and that although they wished peace with the whites they were displeased that soldiers had come into their country to build new forts. The chiefs informed Carrington that the Bad Faces and their allies were under the influence of Red Cloud and had five hundred warriors. Black Horse claimed the Oglalas had tried to persuade his band and that of Dull Knife to join them but that they had refused. Black Horse declared that Red Cloud had told him that if Carrington's soldiers would return to Fort Reno there would be peace but that any new forts along the road would not be tolerated. When Carrington informed the chiefs that the soldiers would not be leaving the Piney forks, Black Horse promised him that his people would not travel in harm's way along the Bozeman Trail. In return Carrington promised these Cheyennes they could always go to Fort Laramie for food and he gave Black Horse and others letters of safe passage stipulating that they be "treated kindly, and in no way be molested in hunting while they remain at peace. When any Indian is seen who holds up this paper," Carrington wrote, "he is to be treated kindly." Black Horse also offered to provide Carrington with one hundred warriors to help him fight the Oglalas. Carrington declined. For a second time Carrington refused the offer of Indian allies.[15]

On the return to Tongue River from the council Black Horse, Dull Knife, and others stopped at French Pete Gazeau's camp to talk and trade. Gazeau had moved his operation to the valley of Peno Creek north of Lodge Trail Ridge. That evening a number of Oglalas visited the Cheyenne camp not far from French Pete's. Red Cloud may have been among them. They asked the Cheyenne chiefs what Carrington had told them. Was he going back to Fort Reno or was he going to stay? The Oglalas grew angry when they heard the answer. When Black Horse informed them that Carrington had given them food and promised them shelter and protection the Oglalas became furious. Black Horse said Carrington had urged them to persuade the war factions to come into Fort Laramie and sign the new treaty. When the Lakotas heard this they lost their temper. Drawing their bows they struck the Cheyenne chiefs on their backs and faces, shouting "Coup. Coup!" as if they were counting coup on an enemy in battle. Black Horse, Dull Knife, and the others suffered this humiliation in silence, but by late July these peace chiefs had gone south to the North Platte, driven from the rich Powder River country by the mounting war.[16] Before they left for their Tongue River camps the friendly Cheyenne chiefs warned Pierre Gazeau that he should move his operation to the site where Carrington was preparing to construct Fort Phil Kearny. French Pete did not take their advice.

War Begins

For all practical purposes "Red Cloud's War" began for the 2/18th about 5:00 AM, July 17, 1866. The previous day Capt. Henry Haymond had arrived with four companies that had remained behind on Crazy Woman Creek to repair wagons. They camped between the forks of the Piney a short distance from Carrington's construction site. Oglala warriors struck early the next morning. Several young men sneaked into the camp past the picket and cut the rope of a bell mare. Jumping on its back, a warrior galloped off through the camp at a dead run. The remainder of the herd—some horses and many more army mules—stampeded after the mare, some 174 of them. Haymond's soldiers started out after the animals but the Oglalas were too fast for their pursuers. The Indians decoyed Haymond's command into broken hills where his mounted infantry, not riding in any disciplined formation, bunched into small groups. About three hundred warriors awaited them, shooting at scattered soldiers wherever they found them.

Meanwhile some of the Indians herded the livestock about fifteen miles from the 2/18th encampment. Soon Haymond's troops were vulnerably bunched and isolated. The Lakotas surrounded them. Warriors charged back and forth against the small groups until Haymond risked sending a courier back to the fort construction site for reinforcements. A relief party of fifty mounted men and two infantry companies under Lt. William Bisbee enabled Haymond to restore order and continue the pursuit that Bisbee later described as a running fight of fifteen miles. But it was no use. The soldiers only recovered four slow animals. Two infantrymen lay dead and three were wounded, including Pvt. John Donovan of William Murphy's company who Murphy remembered was wounded twice, once with an arrow and once with a bullet. "The odds were against us," Bisbee remembered, "and we lost the mules as Red Cloud had promised."[17]

Falling back to the Bozeman Trail in their return to the encampment, Haymond and Bisbee came upon a ghastly sight. They discovered several wagons destroyed, covers torn to shreds, and plunder strewn on the ground. Around the wagons Bisbee's men found the remains of five dead civilians and one man mortally wounded. "It was a terrible sight," remembered Pvt. John Ryan. "The victims had been mutilated in the most horrible manner and it gave us all a most convincing lesson."[18] Bisbee had come across the camp of trader Pierre Gazeau, who had given Mrs. Wands a pet antelope back at Fort Reno and who had recently been trading with the Cheyenne peace chiefs. French Pete had three bullet wounds and two arrow wounds, one in his groin. The body of partner Henry Arrison was shot to pieces. A teamster, Thomas Burns, had his throat cut as did a man named Moss. A man named Dowaire was similarly shot up along with an unidentified man.[19]

The soldiers buried the bodies of Gazeau, Dowaire, Moss, and the unidentified man where they lay. They brought back the remains of Arrison and Thomas Burns, who became among the first, but by no means the last, to be interred in the new Fort Phil Kearny cemetery. The Indians spared Mary Gazeau and her children because Mary was Lakota. Soldiers found them hiding in nearby bushes. Mary told Capt. Frederick Phisterer back at Fort Phil Kearny that over three hundred Oglalas had attacked her husband's camp. She stated that "over a thousand Indians" were by then gathered on the Tongue and that they had threatened to steal all the livestock from the fort, kill all the Americans, and end all travel on the trail within a month.[20] Mary's children later filed a depredation claim with the federal government, but apparently no action was taken to compensate her for her husband's property, possibly because she was an Indian.[21] On August 3, 1866, an emigrant named William K. Thomas passed the mass grave of Gazeau and the others buried along the trail. "As I passed the grave," he recalled, "I saw that wolves had made an opening to the inmates and had torn flesh from the bodies and left their ribs exposed." Red Cloud's warriors had given the whites around Fort Phil Kearny only a small taste of things to come. Even traveler William K. Thomas who commented on the condition of Gazeau's grave would ultimately suffer the Indians' wrath.[22]

Although Little Wolf and other Cheyenne chiefs who did not favor the peace treaty tried to remain moderate for a while, as did Oglala itancan Man Afraid of His Horse, many of their warriors left the Cheyenne camps to join the Lakotas. One of the Cheyennes who would join the war factions in December was Two Moon, a rising Kit Fox warrior who would gain renown in his people's wars with the United States. By late July Carrington sent a detachment of soldiers under Capt. T. B. Burrowes with eighty wagons back to Fort Reno for more supplies. On July 22 Lakota and Cheyenne warriors struck the road to test the strength at both Fort Reno and Fort Phil Kearny. Groups of warriors feinted several times in small groups at the Fort Phil Kearny encampment and were successful in running away four horses and several mules from a wagon train camped nearby.[23] Other groups likewise feinted at Fort Reno on the same day and drove off an army mule. Also on the twenty-second at Buffalo Springs, about seventeen miles from Fort Reno, a group of warriors attacked an emigrant train, killing one man and wounding another.[24]

By the twenty-third Indian numbers multiplied around Fort Reno in an attempt to halt wagon traffic moving north. At the Dry Fork of the Cheyenne River they attacked a wagon train and killed two men. Farther north, on their way down to Fort Reno, Captain Burrowes's supply train was shadowed by warriors along the trail north of Dry Creek. As the soldiers went into camp on Clear Creek a messenger from a nearby wagon train rode in with a message from the wagon master, Thomas Dillon. Dillon had met up with Black Horse earlier, who had warned him of many Indians in the immediate vicinity of the trail. Dillon's message stated that his ox train was pinned down as was another wagon train of a Mr. Kirkendall three miles from Dillon's. Burrowes did not have sufficient force to come to the rescue of either. Instead the captain sent a courier off immediately to Carrington on the Piney for reinforcements as the "Sioux were very numerous."[25]

The courier reached Fort Phil Kearny safely. Carrington responded immediately, dispatching sixty infantrymen under Capt. Nathaniel C. Kinney to support Burrowes. Part of the equipage that the 2/18th had brought up the trail to Fort Phil Kearny were as many as four Mountain howitzers, the "gun that exploded twice" as it was called by some of the Indians.[26] Kinney had one of the artillery pieces with him. The sight of the gun dispersed the Indians to higher ground as the combined commands moved down the trail toward Fort Reno to rescue the wagon trains, but an unwise soldier in Burrowes's detail was discovered dead along the road during the march. The soldier had left the safety of the command the previous day to chase buffalo and had been fallen upon by the Indians.[27] The soldier was Corporal Terrance Callery of Company G, 2/18th. Kinney buried him on Crazy Woman Creek; soon

Kinney would reach yet another train under fire, that of his fellow comrades in the 2/18th.[28]

The Fight on Crazy Woman Creek
July 20, 1866

Knowing that the crossing of the Bozeman Trail at Crazy Woman Creek was a favorite camping spot and a watering hole for horses and oxen, a large body of warriors remained nearby to await travel north from Fort Reno. On July 20 they found more than they had hoped for. The previous day a train of some thirty-two military personnel had left Fort Reno for Fort Phil Kearny. They were under the command of Lt. George Templeton, a compassionate officer, judging from his writings. Two years later Templeton would lead a detail to relieve the beleaguered scouts under Major George "Sandy" Forsyth following the Battle of Beecher Island in Colorado Territory. Templeton was en route to Fort Phil Kearny and then to a command at Fort C. F. Smith, the site of which he would help select on August 10. Several other officers bound for Fort Phil Kearny were in Templeton's party, including lieutenants James H. Bradley, Napoleon Daniels, Henry H. Link, Prescott M. Skinner, and Alexander Wands and his wife, who had recently been at Fort Reno. Chaplain White and Surgeon Hines were with the party as was band sergeant Frank Fessenden, his wife, and his infant daughter. Fessenden's wife had recently given birth to a baby girl at Fort Sedgwick in Colorado Territory and named her "Sedgwick," reputedly at the suggestion of Capt. William J. Fetterman, who was present at the fort during the time of the birth. The Fessendens had with them an African American servant. The Philadelphia photographer Ridgeway Glover was likewise with the party. According to Frances Grummond, who was not there, one of the enlisted men, S. S. Peters, later told her that he had a premonition of doom as the caravan approached Crazy Woman Creek. Indeed Peters's fears were not unfounded if his claim is true, for Lieutenant Daniels would never reach his posting at Fort Phil Kearny.[29]

As Templeton's command reached Dry Creek hoping to find water, Peters claimed that they discovered the mutilated remains of a dead soldier, scalped and filled with arrows, probably a courier from Fort Reno. His tattered blue shirt identified him as a soldier.[30] This incident is not mentioned in any of the principal officer's official reports, however, and could well be a figment of

Peters's aging imagination when he wrote his account in 1908. In any event the command pushed on to the Crazy Woman, arriving there about 9:00 AM on the twentieth. Needing feed for their stock, lieutenants Templeton and Daniels crossed a dry creek bed funneling into Crazy Woman Creek and rode off, looking for a grassy resting spot to spend the morning. Templeton and Daniels were ignorant of Indians. As commander, Templeton's first mistake would cost Lieutenant Daniels his life. When five of the wagons bogged down in the deep sand of the dry creek bottom the warriors attacked. Instantly Lieutenant Bradley's infantrymen jumped from the wagons, formed a line, and advanced under heavy fire toward the embankment of Crazy Woman Creek proper. Other soldiers quickly dragged the wagons together for protection, again under a heavy storm of arrows. Soon a wild-eyed riderless horse raced back toward the wagons, its saddle slipping under its stomach. The horse's neck and flank were filled with arrows. It was Lieutenant Daniels's mount. Right behind it was Templeton, riding for his life. Templeton ordered the wagons corralled as about a hundred warriors descended upon them. After a detail secured water from the creek, the command made a dash for a more defensible knoll about a half-mile away. They were under fire in a running fight the entire time. When they arrived at the knoll some of the Indians had already beat them to the high ground but the soldiers fought them off, partially due to the effectiveness of Lt. A. H. Wands's sixteen-shot Henry rifle.[31] Above them, the Indians had left the body of Lieutenant Daniels lying near the road. They had filled him with arrows and bullets, scalped him, and cut his body to pieces.[32]

According to Lieutenant Wands, "Templeton was closely pursued by several mounted Indians. One of them so close that he had his spear drawn, ready to thrust as he past . . . the train [which] was surrounded by about one hundred Indians, most of whom were mounted. They fought us in this corral [*sic*] about three quarters of an hour during which time [they] were so near the wagon covers were filled with arrows as well as bullets."[33] The musician Sgt. Frank Fessenden described the fight at the lower corral as hot with "only twenty one of our party capable of fighting. We had formed the wagons into a hollow square, placing the women and children inside for protection."[34] Fessenden accompanied 2nd Lt. Henry Link to a spot where Link shot with his Henry rifle a warrior who appeared to be leading the attack, upon which the Indians dispersed into some nearby timber. When the command moved to the higher knoll Fessenden remembered the Indians coming "out of the timber, with loud yells, and again attacked us. We reached the foot of [the knoll where] we saw they had [occupied] the timber . . . It was suggested we make a rush up this hill and form for defense. After some sharp skirmishing, we accomplished this, reaching the top of the hill, where we again formed a hollow square. Some of the men began to hastily dig rifle pits," he recalled. "We had a hot skirmish with the Indians here, and it looked for awhile as it were all off with our little party."[35]

When dusk arrived Chaplain White and an enlisted man escaped the fighting and carried word back to Fort Reno that help was needed. The fight continued until about 7:00 PM when suddenly dust was sighted in the distance. It was Captain Burrowes's command, which was coming to the rescue of the civilian wagon trains but had run into Templeton's besieged troops instead. By the morning of the twenty-first the Indians dispersed and the command located Lieutenant Daniels's body, pierced by twenty-two arrows and three bullets.[36] "I have yet one of those arrows in my possession which went through the lieutenant's body," Sergeant Fessenden remembered years later, "also an arrow that was shot at me, and which narrowly missed me."[37] The *Leslie's* photographer, Ridgeway Glover, whom Templeton described in his diary as a "queer genius," was likewise on the firing line.[38] Recklessly fearless (or foolish), Glover was restrained from setting up his camera to photograph the attack, according to Peters. Battle-action photojournalism except for images of the dead was far from accepted practice in 1866. Peters's version of the fight, however, which Dee Brown accepts in lengthy detail, is far more sensationalized than the reports of Wands and Burrowes and Fessenden's later account. Peters describes several men wounded and a warrior whooping in the distance wearing Lieutenant Daniels's uniform. Peters further states that the Indian was killed and that his body was found the next day. No such finding is mentioned in any of the other reports, again making Peters's sensationalized 1908 account—given to Frances Grummond who thus wrote it secondhand—highly suspect.[39]

Besides Daniels and Callery, "no other loss occurred to our force in that fight," Wands reported. The "Indian loss was not known—several were dismounted and blood, robes, and moccasins, were found the next morning showing they must have suffered some."[40] Lieutenant Wands was bitter after the fight on Crazy Woman Creek. "The Commanding Officer at Fort Laramie

[Maynadier]," he remembered, "was well aware of the strength of our party, and stated to us there was no danger on the road, as a satisfactory treaty had just been concluded." When Templeton's command left Fort Reno that post's commander, Captain Proctor, did not realize the danger that was just getting started during this fateful week in July 1866.[41]

Captain Burrowes, being the ranking officer, took command upon his arrival at Crazy Woman Creek. Soon the soldiers were joined by Lt. T. S. Kirtland and thirteen mounted infantrymen from Fort Reno that Proctor had dispatched in response to Chaplain White's urgent message. Burrowes ordered the combined command back to Fort Reno to regroup and resupply. Along the way the command caught up with a contractor supply train of thirty-nine wagons bound for Fort Reno. The train was being escorted by only a corporal and eight privates so Burrowes ordered them back with his command. They arrived at Fort Reno on July 21 at 3:00 PM. The next day, a Sunday, they buried Lieutenant Daniels's body with full military honors, Chaplain White officiating.[42] That evening about five o'clock a party of warriors attempted unsuccessfully to stampede the mule herd at Fort Reno. The following day, Monday, July 23, Burrowes's command headed back north toward Crazy Woman Creek and Fort Phil Kearny to find the civilian wagon trains of Kirkendall and Dillon that had previously sent a message for assistance.[43]

Emigrants

The popular image of travel along the road to Montana has it that civilian wagons were under an almost constant state of assault from Lakota, Arapaho, and Cheyenne raiders to the extent that the trail took on the rather awe-inspiring epithet "The Bloody Bozeman."[44] Such popular imagery does not stand up very well to historical scrutiny. Certainly during the conflict in 1863 and 1864 the possibility of danger existed, but travel was light and wagons traveled in large groups. In 1865 the army completely closed the trail to civilian travel during the Connor campaign. The early months of the travel season of 1866 as well as the weeks following July 26 of that year were likewise mostly safe between Fort Reno and Fort Phil Kearny. Indeed the time of extreme danger for civilians along the trail involved those unfortunate souls who traveled between Fort Reno and Fort Phil Kearny between July 17, when French Pete Gazeau was killed, and July 26, when the raids suddenly stopped, a period of only nine days. The psychological effects of these nine days, however, would have implications that reached far into the future. To this day we have no idea who the Indians were who perpetuated the carnage among both soldiers and civilians during this short time for none of the participants was ever interviewed nor did any others offer any insight into their identity or to which bands they belonged. *Presumably* the warriors who struck close to Fort Phil Kearny were from the Tongue River camps and consisted of Bad Face Oglalas and perhaps some Cheyennes. Those warriors who struck closer to the North Platte and Fort Reno may have been from the Southern Brulé war faction under Two Strike, a leader of the influential Miwatani soldier society.[45] But individual names will never be known. Consequently, virtually all accounts from the time of the fight on Crazy Woman Creek to July 26 are white accounts.

The historian who has studied emigrant travel on the Bozeman Trail most extensively is Susan Badger Doyle. In her exhaustive study of emigrant diaries and demographics Doyle estimates that about 2,000 civilians went over the trail in 1866 in 1,200 wagons, a far higher number than in 1864. By 1866 a vast majority of the citizens traveling to Montana were opportunists eager to provide business and service to the mining communities rather than placer miners themselves. A significant proportion of these were freighters and contractors hauling supplies to both the towns and the forts along the trail rather than nuclear families. A good number of these emigrants, especially the men and especially the freighters, were veterans of frontier life. Farther south in growing regions like Kansas, Nebraska, and Colorado Territory, it would be family homesteaders that would soon suffer the brunt of Indian raids in response to the expanding railroads. Women caught near their houses on the open prairie, without the advantage of the comparatively safe confines of a corralled wagon train, especially would suffer as captives as they had in 1864 and 1865. But such was not the case on the Bozeman Trail. Because civilian records are scarce from that remote country in the 1860s the number of actual emigrant deaths at the hands of Indians is impossible to estimate. But presumably almost all victims were men. There are no documented deaths of women and only one child died, with nobody taken into captivity along the trail in 1866.

In essence the ratio of people to wagons was lower than in 1864, 1.667 per wagon in 1866 as opposed to 3.333 per wagon in 1864. The number of wagons, however, was greater in 1866. Doyle likewise demonstrates that travel over the trail in 1866 occurred over a longer period of time than in individual previous years. Still, she estimates that the ratio of 80 percent men to 20 percent women and children was about the same in 1866 as it was in 1864. Her findings illustrate that the gold frontiers of the West were always largely male propositions for at least half a decade following any gold strike. Increased numbers of wagons in 1866 hauling loads of freight including military supplies over a longer period of time created a perception among the Indians of impending permanent white occupation of the Powder River country.[46]

During the middle week of July, the initial attacks around Fort Phil Kearny and to the north were followed by a shift to the south around Fort Reno the following week. Following French Pete's demise on the seventeenth, a different party of warriors, perhaps Hunkpapas, struck a freighter's train north on the Bighorn River. There is some evidence warriors harassed another train a week before in the same vicinity, but no details remain. The train on the eighteenth belonged to Craniums Beers and consisted of ten four-mule-team wagons. At daybreak the Lakotas drove off six of Beers's mules, then returned the following day and drove off nine more. The freighters were stranded at the Bighorn crossing for a month during which time they corralled their wagons and operated a ferry service charging ten dollars a wagon to cross the river. When the 18th Infantry established Fort C. F. Smith at the crossing in early August the sutler, A. C. Leighton, took over the ferry service and reduced the price to five dollars per wagon.[47]

Back near Crazy Woman Creek on July 23, Burrowes's command consolidated with freighter Kirkendall's train. Kirkendall's operation consisted of forty-three mule wagons under wagon master George McGee and another company, Toole and Leach, of twenty-four ox wagons led by wagon master Thomas Dillon. The combined military-civilian train consisted of over two hundred wagons. The following day, July 24, as they headed north toward Fort Phil Kearny the wagons were stretched out over six miles. Dillon's and Burrowes's command went into camp on Clear Creek with Dillon going into camp three miles behind and Kirkendall bringing up the rear three miles behind Dillon. The triple separation was a recipe for disaster. Indians appeared near Burrowes's camp but the captain soon ascertained these were peace-faction Cheyennes from the band of Black Horse who presented their letters of safe passage from Carrington and warned of danger among the Lakotas to the south. Soon another band of Cheyennes, possibly under Dull Knife, came in. Burrowes gave them a few rations and they moved off.[48]

Soon after Kirkendall's train corralled, a party of about twenty-five warriors descended on them and unsuccessfully tried to drive off their mules. Meanwhile Dillon and five of his men unwisely rode back on the trail to see where Kirkendall was situated at the time. Suddenly a war party of Lakotas jumped his little group. The men put up a defense around a small perimeter they set up with their saddles, killing at least two Lakotas. During the fighting the attackers fatally wounded Dillon. When the Indians withdrew the following morning, Wednesday, July 25, the survivors brought Dillon's body back to the train. Also that morning Capt. A. C. Kinney found Burrowes's command. Kinney had sixty mounted infantrymen and the Mountain howitzer. The sight of the artillery piece dispersed the Indians. Kinney assumed command of the "expedition," consolidated the train, and brought it into Fort Phil Kearny about 2:00 PM. The next day soldiers buried Dillon in the expanding post cemetery.[49]

Attacks on the southern end of the trail began in earnest on July 22. That morning twenty-three-year-old Perry A. Burgess witnessed the shooting of his uncles, Mansel and Lewis Cheney, near the Dry Fork of Powder River above Pumpkin Buttes, about twenty miles east of Fort Reno. Burgess, riding with several other men some distance behind his uncles, watched as nine warriors descended from nearby hills toward the two men. The group fell behind and became separated from their train. The Indians "rode up to them [the Cheneys]," Burgess wrote in his diary, "apparently very friendly and commenced shaking hands with them, when one . . . suddenly drew a pistol from beneath his blanket and fired at Mansel who fell from his horse dead. Lewis' horse jumped and ran toward us . . . We recovered from our surprise, however, in a moment and drawing our pistols, charged at the Indians, fired a few shots at them, and drove them off."[50] When Burgess, Lewis, and the others returned to recover Mansel's body they found that the Indians had stripped and mutilated him, plundered their wagon, and shot arrows into some of their livestock. The men buried Mansel Cheney about seven miles east of the Powder River crossing of the trail.[51]

On the same day a party of warriors approached a train ahead of Burgess's asking for food. After they were given something to eat they asked for ammunition but were refused. As they rode away they shot a man on herd duty.[52] In another incident on the same day warriors tried to drive off a herd from a train about twenty-five miles from where Mansel Cheney was killed. About the same time a train of freighters several miles south was camped for their noon stop on the Dry Fork of the Cheyenne River. A war party tried to drive away their livestock and during the ensuing melee two men and five oxen were killed and several more oxen wounded. Another train not far away came upon the scene. Samuel Finley Blythe wrote that "the two men killed were buried by moonlight. The funeral services were conducted by a minister belonging to our train. The unfortunate men's names were [L. C.] Moore and [George W.] Carr. Both men were from Illinois."[53] On the twenty-third, the same day Kirkendall's train was under fire to the north, Indians again tried to run off stock from a train to the south camped along Antelope Creek. Lakotas attacked Blythe's train the same day but the civilians drove off the warriors. Also on the twenty-third Indians attacked freighter E. R. Horner's train along the Dry Fork of the Powder River. Two men were killed and five mules captured.[54]

The next day, July 24, warriors attacked a rather large train of emigrants and freight wagons between Brown Springs Creek and the Dry Fork of the Cheyenne River. The captain of one of the consolidated trains, Nathan Floyd, had ridden ahead to look for water and was shot and killed. Hearing the firing, thirteen men from the train rode ahead to find Floyd. They found Indians instead. Outnumbered, eight were killed and the remaining five wounded. A military freight train discovered them the next day and sent out a detachment to recover the bodies. The soldiers discovered Floyd riddled with arrows, decapitated, with his severed head several hundred yards away from the body. Two of the remaining eight had been so severely chopped to pieces the soldiers buried their body parts in a common grave on a nearby hill. They brought the remaining bodies back to the train and buried them inside the wagon corral.[55]

As Doyle points out, "As abruptly as the raids began, they ended."[56] By the end of July Carrington ordered all trains heavily consolidated. Detained at the forts, at least two trains had to move together, sometimes more depending on size. Also fewer people rode alone away from the trains for any purpose, and tight controls ensured that wagons did not fall behind or get ahead of the main body. There exists no estimate of Indian casualties during the times of these attacks. The exact number of non-Indian civilian deaths along the trail at this time is likewise uncertain as previously stated. Captain Proctor at Fort Reno estimated in excess of thirty but that figure may be slightly exaggerated. Sensationalized too were reports by frontier newspapers, notorious examples of commonly flawed nineteenth-century journalistic sources. The *Omaha Weekly Republican*, for example, stated that in the fight on Crazy Woman Creek on July 20, "five soldiers were killed and a large number wounded . . . All the wounded that fell into the hands of the savages were scalped, and tortured in the most barbarous manner."[57] But only Lieutenant Daniels and Corporal Callery had been killed. The chief effect of these raids in mid-July was psychological. Fear struck the hearts and minds of emigrants who traveled the trail after that time. Certainly newspaper accounts augmented these fears. Diaries from 1866 usually note the passing of one or more graves of victims. Emigrants and soldiers alike have left accounts of feelings of foreboding while traveling the Bozeman Trail. S. S. Peters told Frances Grummond that he had a feeling of doom as he approached Crazy Woman Creek on July 20.[58]

For some hardened frontiersmen like James A. Sawyers, who had helped pioneer parts of the trail at the time of the Connor expedition and was doing so again in 1866, the threat of Indians was a given condition of travel in the Powder River country. Knowing how to take precautions, Sawyers's train encamped near Fort Phil Kearny on July 20. The men dug rifle pits to protect their livestock. "Just at dusk," Sawyers wrote matter-of-factly, "the Indians made a dash at the herd, but the shots from the . . . pits prevented them from getting anything—Course northwest, parallel with the mountains."[59]

The mood of inexperienced emigrants from the East was often not so nonchalant. Perhaps the most poignant story of anyone traveling the Bozeman Trail during the last week of July is that of William K. Thomas and his young son, Charley. Articulate and from an affluent Illinois family, Thomas and his son had made it through the troubles with Kirkendall's and Dillon's trains on the twenty-fourth unscathed. But the psychological effects on Thomas were profound. Perhaps this had been the first time in his life he had looked death in the face. Feelings of melancholia accompanied him through the remainder of his journey. His diary entries became more reflective of his surroundings, especially the sight of roadside graves. Readers might have the impression that he was witnessing the beauty of God's creation for the last time and suddenly facing the reality of his own mortality. Any forebodings he might have had during July would come to fruition in August. Thomas and his son Charley arrived at emerging Fort Phil Kearny on July 25. "This is the most beautiful place for a fort that I have seen west of Fort Leavenworth," Thomas wrote in his diary; "its mountain scenery is most striking and majestic with its beautiful range of hills on either side north and south as [if] it were throwing their arms around and clasping in their bosom."[60] Thomas remained at Fort Phil Kearny for a week waiting for permission to proceed north. On August 2 he departed with a train of 110 wagons, 171 men, 6 women, and 5 children. He commented in his diary the next day on the sight of French Pete's disturbed grave. On August 7, Thomas wrote,

> Just before we cross[ed Twin] Creek to the left of the road is a lone grave the inmate was deposited in July last. [We] could not make out his name part of the head board being gone . . . [He] was killed here by the Indians. The poor fellow's remains had not been left in peace to molder away into dust—but as his life had been taken by merciless Savages—so had his body been disturbed by the wild and insatiable wolves. They had dug down until they had left the inmate half covered and [g]nawed the flesh from his face—we could see that he had been scalped.[61]

August 22 was the last entry in Thomas's diary. By then he had crossed the Bighorn River and was approaching the Yellowstone. Some wagons from the large train had gone their separate ways in the previous days and Thomas, apparently thinking he was now safe from Indian attack, trudged on along Sawyer's cutoff while other emigrants waited behind for a large freight train with which they were traveling while its men made repairs to several wagons. Besides son Charley, a man named Joseph Schultz was in the single wagon with Thomas. On August 23 they camped on the banks of the Yellowstone. The next day the emigrants that had stayed behind at the previous camp with the freighters came up and found their bodies. They discovered William Thomas riddled with thirteen arrows and young Charley with three. They found Schultz's body on the riverbank along with a fishing rod nearby. Indians had scalped all three men.[62] The arrows and one of Charley's boots that the emigrants found at the site are now in the possession of the Montana Historical Society Museum. They buried all three along the side of the trail. Today a sign marks the grave near Greycliff, Montana, along old U.S. Highway 10, now a frontage road on the north side of I-90.[63] Thomas's diary is likewise housed at the Montana Historical Society. The last words in it are an undated entry titled simply "Random Thoughts." Perhaps they were William Thomas's last thoughts. Writing of Fort Phil Kearny and the Powder River country, his words surely reflected the impressions of that land by other emigrants, Lakotas, Cheyennes, and Crows alike: "What shall I say of the mountain scenery around most beautiful to behold too majestic to describe too lovely to define too picturesque [to] imitate. It is a picture of nature drawing by the finger of God inimitable, one hill rises above another until lost in a grand range of mountains among the kingly heads crowned with snow."[64]

By August the war shifted north. The Indians harassed a few trains near the Bighorn in mid-July before Captain Kinney's arrival with two companies of the 2/18th on August 4 to build Fort C. F. Smith. But by late summer and on into fall the Indian coalitions turned their attention mostly away from travelers near Fort Reno and toward Fort Phil Kearny in the middle of the chain of trail defenses. As construction proceeded toward completion it became obvious that Fort Phil Kearny was not going to go away as Red Cloud had demanded earlier in the summer. By focusing on that post Fort C. F. Smith could be virtually cut off from supplies moving up the Bozeman Trail while Fort Reno, with its communication link to Fort Laramie along the Platte road, could be severed from communications safely moving south and east along the road. On August 2, 1866, a wagon train that included emigrant George Fox from Council Bluffs via Ohio pulled into Fort Phil Kearny. "We are the first train to come through without being attacked by Indians," he wrote in his diary.[65]

The week before another emigrant, Davis Willson from Ohio, while waiting at Fort Reno to proceed, learned of the death of Charles Barton, one of eight killed in a train behind Willson's. Barton had traveled with Willson on an earlier leg of the journey. Emigrants found Barton with twenty arrows in his body and a knife sticking in his side. Warriors had scalped his head and whiskers and stabbed him in several places around his eyes.[66] "He sleeps the cold sleep of death," Willson reflected in his diary, "and his bones lie in mournful solitude upon the broad desolation of the wild prairie."[67] By the last week in July Davis Willson understood only too well the determination of Red Cloud and his followers to protect the Powder River country. "They are on the 'warpath,'" he wrote, "and are determined to keep the whites from the upper country."[68]

When the last wagon train reached the gold camps in the Gallatin Valley in the fall of 1866, at the end of the travel season, the Bozeman Trail was finished. By early 1867 the government determined the road to be unsafe for civilian travel and it was closed forever as an emigrant road. Henceforth it was a military corridor with supply trains moving under heavy army escort. By the time the cold season set in, soldiers of the 2/18th were too preoccupied protecting their positions and fighting for their very lives, let alone their presence in the Powder River country, to safely and effectively protect civilian travel on an extended road. Indeed the defensive "Fabian" strategy of the Reconstruction army's limited war policy in the West had failed miserably. Avoiding pitched battles and trying to wear down Indian resistance from permanent fortifications with limited numbers of troops, in the end, proved mostly futile. The Lakotas and Cheyennes had successfully halted civilian travel into their lands hard won from the Crows and decisively defended those lands from the whites through aggressive insurgent tactics during the first phase of "Red Cloud's War" in 1866.[69]

CHAPTER 5

AUTUMN OF TRIAL

The Army View of the Powder River War in 1866

By now they saw their forces cut in two,
First Fort Reno Post upon the Powder, then
Fort C. F. Smith upon the Bighorn needing men;
And here the center of the brewing storm
Would rage[1]

BY SEPTEMBER, AFTER A FEW SCATTERED and probably uncoordinated ser-endipitous raids on Fort Reno in late August to drive away livestock, the emerging strategy of the Lakotas and their allies became evident to Colonel Carrington and the men of the 2/18th. Lakotas and eventually Cheyennes made Fort Phil Kearny the center of activity in order to keep Forts Reno and C. F. Smith fairly disconnected from reliable communications and supplies coming north or south from the center of the chain on the Piney Forks. While continuing their opportunistic raids on livestock, the Indians began to focus also on woodcutting and hay-mowing details whose efforts were so vital to winter survival in the Powder River country. By this time Jim Bridger, Bill Williams, and Jim Beckwourth, from their reconnaissance among the Crows to the north, had obtained disconcerting news. During the summer the Lakotas had attempted to gain the support of their old enemies the Crows to help them drive out the whites. A few of the younger Crow warriors were in favor of joining the insurgency in exchange for the return of some of their old hunting grounds in the Powder River country. From the Crows and friendly Cheyennes, Bridger ascertained that the camps of Red Cloud and Man Afraid of His Horse along the Tongue were growing larger, continuously being rein-forced by Cheyenne war factions. In addition Buffalo Tongue's Lakota camp on the Powder was now active, probably accounting for some of the small raids around Fort Reno. Medicine Man, whose Arapahos, along with Black Bear's, had encountered General Connor the previous year, had also joined the fray with twenty-five lodges. Bridger reported in excess of 500 lodges in all, perhaps 1,000–1,500 fighting men with many Miniconjous yet to come. Brulé chief Iron Shell, who had earlier favored peace but who had become angered by the building of the forts, was present also as were a smattering of Hunkpapas from the north and a few Minnesota Sioux.[2]

Bridger also asserted that the war factions were *planning* [emphasis mine] two attacks that they spoke of as "Pine Woods" (near Fort Phil Kearny) and "Bighorn" (near Fort C. F. Smith). If true, the reconnaissance gained by Bridger's party supports the idea that a major attempt to lure many soldiers from the forts was already being discussed and planned months before the fateful day of December 21, 1866.[3] Assuming that Carrington was well aware of the situation, his actions were unbelievably contradictory. While continually requesting reinforcements and additional officers from General Cooke, Carrington certainly did not help his argument when he wrote in the same message that no women or children had been captured, that all trains were cared for to their satisfaction, and that the newspaper accounts of superior numbers of Indians at war in the Powder River country were "gross exaggerations."[4]

Back on August 9 Oglalas had made their first attack on a timber-cutting train from Fort Phil Kearny, capturing four mules. The pattern would continue. Troops heavily guarded the wood trains, which were usually composed of twenty-four to forty wagons moving together in two parallel lines with pickets riding beside on either flank. A picket stood on duty at all times on Pilot Hill using signal flag messages to relay impending danger along the road in both directions. The Indians struck a wood train on August 13 but were driven off with two casualties. Meanwhile several sporadic stock-raiding parties were active around Fort Reno throughout the latter half of August.[5]

On September 1 the first snow of the season fell in the Bighorn Mountains above Fort Phil Kearny. Both the civilian hay cutters along Goose Creek and woodcutters at the pineries were working hard now preparing for winter. Well aware of the dependency of the garrison on these resources, the Indians watched in the hills above the fort before making their move against both contingents by the middle of the month. Until then they had continued to focus on the third essential for the garrison: livestock. During a blinding wind and rain storm on September 8, warriors struck a large herd that had come up on the fourth from Fort Reno. Although Frederick Brown and Lieutenant Adair raced out of the fort with men in pursuit, the Indians were too fast for them and made off with twenty prime horses. Two days later Lakotas and Arapahos of Medicine Man's band swept down from the hills on a mule herd owned by one of the civilian contractors. Again they led Lieutenant Adair on a merry chase. At the same time a second party of fighting men struck the military horse herds a mile from the fort, driving off thirty-three horses and seventy-eight mules. Then on the twelfth a war party attacked the hay cutters on Goose Creek. They charged in several times against the eighty whites, killing three and wounding several others. Finally the hay cutters corralled their wagons on a hill and watched while the Indians smashed to pieces six mowing machines and burned the nearby haystacks. Later in the day a number of these warriors attacked the beef herd grazing in sight of the fort by stampeding a buffalo herd among the cattle and using them for cover as they cut out some two hundred of the steers. Only on the following morning was a party from the fort able to relieve the hay cutters.[6]

The entire middle week of September was a horrific one for the garrison at Fort Phil Kearny. On the thirteenth the Indians struck a horse herd close to the fort and exchanged shots with two of the pickets, wounding one with an arrow in the hip and the other with a bullet in his side.[7] The very next day a patrol of soldiers found the bloody uniform of a private, probably a deserter, who had been missing for four days. On September 26 warriors killed a soldier riding out as a flanker for hay-cutting wagons returning from Lake DeSmet. The soldier, Pvt. Peter Johnson, was attacked by a single warrior charging out of a ravine. Although the private tried to outrun the Indian, the warrior gained on him; Johnson panicked and dismounted but was ridden over and killed. Private Johnson's body was never found.[8] On the same day the somewhat eccentric *Leslie's* photographer, Ridgeway Glover, encountered the Indians. Somewhat of a loner, Glover made his headquarters in a cabin with the woodchoppers at the upper pinery. For reasons unknown he decided to make a journey alone, on foot, to the fort. It was Sunday and woodchoppers warned Glover there would be no woodcutting detail going to the fort that day to protect him and that he should wait until Monday. Glover had long blonde hair and Sgt. Frank Fessenden once joked to him that the "Indians would delight to clip that hair for him some day."[9] Oblivious to danger Glover set out for the fort anyway. According to post chaplain David White, Glover was "careless of life, traveling frequently by himself—one time to the snow[y] range of the Bighorn Mountains—with nothing but a butcher knife."[10] Soldiers discovered Glover's body about two miles from the fort the next day. The Indians had mutilated the corpse badly. "The head was found a few yards off," Pvt. Samuel Peters wrote, "completely severed from the trunk, scalped. The body was disemboweled, and then fire placed in the cavity. His remains, horribly mutilated, were decently interred, and a search made for his apparatus [camera?], but it could not be found."[11] Thus ended any hope of preserving for history any original photographic record of Fort Phil Kearny and the Powder River country in 1866. Lieutenant William Bisbee remembered the incident differently years later. His detail had discovered the corpse, and according to Bisbee's recollection, Glover's body was "naked, laying face down across the road with a tomahawk cleft in his back [but apparently with his head intact], a sign that he had not been brave" in his last moments, Bisbee surmised.[12]

The seventeenth was indeed a frustrating day for the garrison at Fort Phil Kearny. Not only had Glover's body been found but a large party of warriors, perhaps those that had killed Glover, came charging out of a ravine near the junction of the pineries and attacked pickets on the east lookout guarding the last of the fort's cattle herd. The Indians exchanged shots with the pickets and drove off forty-eight head of cattle. Frustrated and infuriated, Carrington personally fired a round from one of the howitzers at the fleeing warriors. The shell exploded in their midst and knocked one warrior from his horse. The Indians fled in panic across the hills, abandoning the stolen cattle. A second attack at the same time in front of the fort by some fifty warriors had similar results. Two howitzer rounds exploded above the warriors, knocking one man from his horse. His companions recovered his body and fled into the terrain.[13] Col. Henry Carrington had quite serendipitously discovered a defensive weapon the Indians feared more than pursuing mounted infantry. But despite Carrington's frequent pleas for additional ammunition including howitzer rounds, the use of artillery was only minimally used defensively. Had he possessed additional cannon, his position at the Piney forks might have seen less harassment. The offensive potential of his artillery was barely used even to a limited extent as cannon had been used by the volunteer regiments in 1864–65 at places like Tongue River. A third party of warriors in great numbers showed themselves in front of the fort later on the seventeenth.

Carrington dispatched a patrol to rout them. The Indians casually watched the soldiers leave the fort before they slowly and arrogantly sauntered off and scattered into the hills, apparently fearless of any abilities of the 2/18th despite the howitzer actions earlier in the day.[14]

By early autumn the tactics of the Lakotas and their allies had been successful in harassing communication and supply lines along the Bozeman Trail. For a time it looked as if their attempts to reduce the livestock at Fort Phil Kearny would prove to be devastating for the whites while providing an economic boon to the Indians. Given the enormous problems of logistical support to frontier posts before the railroads, it is a wonder that the forts on the Bozeman Trail were not reduced to the point of functional obsolescence. Miraculously, however, despite the danger and the nuisance of the raids the most dramatic results may have been psychological. Supplies continued to arrive at Fort Phil Kearny. Farther north merchants and contractors from the Gallatin Valley mining communities in Montana supplied Fort C. F. Smith during the winter months of 1866–67. Fort Reno, due to its proximity to the Platte road and Fort Laramie, was in less dire straits during Red Cloud's War. On September 17, almost as if to balance the raids and killings, a contracted supply train arrived at Fort Phil Kearny. The train carried sixty thousand rounds of ammunition for Springfield rifles. Some corn for the hungry horses also arrived in the wagons. On the same day a mail escort arrived with an ambulance wagon for the garrison. Colonel Carrington immediately wrote dispatches from his quarters. Although communications continued they were maddeningly slow and were usually unreflective of the rapidly changing events by the time they reached their destination. Carrington requested an additional 100,000 rounds of ammunition in addition to side arms and either Spencer repeating rifles or carbines for the mounted troops because the long Springfield muzzle-loaders, which he complained were in too short supply anyhow, were practically useless for mounted troops. Recognizing the potential of his artillery during the actions of the previous days, Carrington requested ammunition be released from Fort Laramie for his twelve-pound howitzers.[15]

As always, Carrington requested reinforcements, the effective garrison at the fort being only 341 officers and men. Since August three enlisted men and five contract civilians had been killed and one enlisted man had deserted.[16] Carrington especially needed cavalry if Sherman and Cooke expected him to conduct any kind of offensive operations, which indeed, both did expect of the commander at Fort Phil Kearny but then later changed their minds. Second only to the Indians the biggest problem for Colonel Carrington and the garrison during the previous months had been the slowness and ambivalence of the high command in responding promptly to logistical needs. This reality would continuously hamper the effectiveness of the frontier army during the years between 1866 and the mid-1870s when Reconstruction monopolization of federal troops and supplies in the defeated South held priority. Earlier in the summer Sherman and Cooke had approved the transfer of two companies of cavalry and one company of infantry to Fort Phil Kearny. Back on August 27 the assistant inspector for the Department of the Platte, Col. William Hazen, arrived at Fort Phil Kearny, escorted by a company from Fort Reno under Lieutenant Kirtland. Hazen reported that Fort Phil Kearny was "[t]he best stockade I have seen excepting one in British America built by Hudson Bay Company."[17] But no reinforcements arrived with the inspector as Carrington had expected. Hazen could not explain the delay. True cavalry would not arrive at Fort Phil Kearny until November, and then only one company of the 2nd Cavalry, not two as promised.

Indeed, after his three-day stay Hazen ordered Carrington to provide him with twenty-six of his best men and Lt. James Bradley to serve as his escort to inspect Fort C. F. Smith. Also in the mail that day were letters from General Cooke complaining about the depredations inflicted on civilians along the trail in July. The mail courier also brought a letter from the adjutant general's office in Washington complaining that the office had not received any post returns for June (the fort was not established until July 14; there were no post returns for June), and a letter from General Sherman written at Fort Laramie at the end of August informing Carrington that he would order General Cooke to reinforce Fort Phil Kearny so that the garrison could conduct aggressive offensive operations. Carrington had been under the impression that Cooke had been ordered weeks before to send reinforcements quickly to Fort Phil Kearny. The dispatches that day clearly illustrated the major problem facing the frontier army of the 1860s, not only ineffective logistics but a lack of resources as well.[18]

With the mail escort on September 17 came an officer and his pregnant young wife who were destined to become two of the most intriguing and important characters to play out roles in the drama of events in the

Powder River country in 1866. The garrison considered thirty-two-year-old 2nd Lt. George Washington Grummond and twenty-one-year-old Frances Courtney Grummond to be the most romantic and charming couple at Fort Phil Kearny, having scarcely been married a year. But under the surface Lieutenant Grummond was not what he appeared to be. On balance he would prove to be a most dangerous catalyst for the events that led to the annihilation of Capt. William J. Fetterman's command on Lodge Trail Ridge on December 21, 1866. Descended from a long line of merchant sailors, Grummond served in the 1st and 14th Michigan infantry regiments during the Civil War, rising to the rank of lieutenant colonel of volunteers. He saw action at Kennesaw Mountain and Bentonville. Although his promotions would suggest an admirable Civil War record, such was not the case. A penchant for the bottle and a mean temper engendered a hatred of Grummond among junior officers of the 14th Michigan. In 1864 those officers petitioned the adjutant general of the Army of the Cumberland to investigate Grummond's fitness to command. Among their allegations were numerous occasions of drunkenness in the face of the enemy, shooting at a fellow officer while the officer was carrying out an order, pistol-whipping a sergeant, beating a private, and shooting an aged unarmed civilian to whom he then refused to give medical attention. In 1864 while intoxicated, Grummond ordered a suicidal charge on the heights of Kennesaw Mountain. Corporal Patrick Walsh climbed above Grummond on a trench and pelted his commander with stones, convincing the drunken Grummond that the stones were actually enemy bullets.[19]

Grummond appeared before a general court martial, which found him guilty of shooting the junior officer and the unarmed civilian. He was given a public reprimand. On another occasion Grummond engaged in battle with Confederates before other units were in place. Confederates cut off his command and Grummond's men had to be rescued by a relief unit.[20] At the end of the Civil War his first wife, Delia, sued for divorce on the grounds of gross negligence to provide for her during his absence during the war. She won her case and was awarded two thousand dollars in alimony to be paid within a year. During his stay at Fort Phil Kearny, Grummond continually borrowed money from enlisted men, perhaps to defray the costs of the court order. During 1864 Grummond met Frances Courtney in Tennessee. The two were married on August 3, 1865, twenty days before his divorce from

Delia was made final. Frances did not find out this information until after she left Fort Phil Kearny and returned to Tennessee in 1867. At least one historian has described George Washington Grummond as possibly psychotic.[21] Nevertheless, the army gave him an honorable discharge on July 18, 1865. Grummond then applied for commission in the regular army, received it, and was assigned to the 2/18th on May 7, 1866. Grummond's propensity for rash action would of course be compounded at Fort Phil Kearny by his total ignorance of Indians. Hailing from Michigan, he probably had never seen an Indian before arriving on the plains. Such a combination of personality flaws would prove disastrous for Grummond and the lives of those around him.[22]

By contrast Frances Courtney, a fairly religious young lady, was apparently seduced by the charm that Grummond could exude. Frances hailed from an affluent family in Franklin, Tennessee, that had remained loyal Unionists during the Civil War. She was educated in local schools. Following the bloody Battle of Franklin on November 30, 1864, Frances nursed Union wounded in the Courtney home. Sometime during this period she met Grummond. The couple was married in the Courtney home in Franklin.[23] Certainly George Grummond could not have told her of his past transgressions or that his divorce from his first wife was not yet final. Was twenty-one-year-old Frances infatuated but highly naïve? Frances's memoir, *My Army Life: A Soldier's Wife at Fort Phil Kearny* (1910), is considered to be one of the primary sources on the history of that post and the Fetterman fight. Published in 1910, forty-two years after Margaret Carrington's memoir, *My Army Life* in some respects is simply a rewrite of Margaret's book. Frances's narrative of events before September 17, 1866, are not eyewitness accounts of hers, but of others. Some of her assertions conflict with those of other sources. Still her personal experiences present a vivid portrait of what life was like for an officer's wife at Fort Phil Kearny in 1866.[24]

The Grummonds arrived at Fort Phil Kearny on one of the most active days since its inception. Approaching the fort and spotting the picket on Pilot Hill who halted them, Frances "looked eagerly for the occasion of the delay. It almost took my breath away, for a strong feeling of apprehension came over me," she remembered years later. "We had halted to give passage to a wagon, escorted by a guard from the wood train coming from the opposite direction. In that wagon was the scalped and naked body of one of their comrades [Glover?], scarcely cold, who had been murdered so near the fort." Once within the safety of the gates, Frances admitted, "That strange feeling of apprehension never left me."[25] On the close of that busy day a train of forty miners came into Fort Phil Kearny. They had been unsuccessful in the Montana gold fields. The men reported they had had a sharp fight with Indians the previous day, losing two of their own but inflicting a number of casualties among the warriors. The party was captained by William Bailey, who informed Carrington that he and some of his men had previously been scouts in the West. Carrington offered them employment at the fort for the winter. The party accepted and set up quarters just outside the stockade. One of their numbers was John "Portugee" Phillips, destined to play an important role at Fort Phil Kearny that winter. Carrington had gained the equivalent of a company of cavalry. With Bailey's train was a messenger from Fort C. F. Smith bringing news from Jim Bridger of his talks with the Crows and that five hundred lodges of warring Lakotas and Cheyennes were assembled along Tongue River. According to Dee Brown, the messenger also reported that rumors among the Crows suggested that a few white men were living among the Arapahos, probably married to Arapaho women, and that they had joined the war factions along the Tongue.[26]

That night the first measurable snows of autumn blanketed Fort Phil Kearny, portending an early winter. The Grummonds slept in an army tent and awoke to snow on their bedding. Soon the couple would take up quarters in a small log room where Frances would readily accept army food, such as it was, being a self-professed miserable cook. Her first hours and days were filled with the sense of foreboding she had experienced upon arriving at the fort on the seventeenth. Of her first night: "The snow drifted in [to the tent], covered my face," she wrote over forty years later, "and there melting down my cheeks until if I had shed tears they would have been indistinguishable . . . When I arose from fitful slumber," she discovered that "pillows, bedding, and even the stove and the ground within the tent were also covered."[27] Frances reflected philosophically on the peculiar isolation and role of a garrison of the American nation so far-flung on a frontier unfamiliar to her kind. Although ethnocentric, in one of her more enduring and far-reaching passages in her memoir she wrote with logical understanding, "I often wondered why a post so isolated was not swept away by a rush of mighty numbers of the surrounding savages, to avenge in one vast holocaust the invasion of their finest hunting grounds."[28] Frances Grummond was a long way from the comforts of Franklin, Tennessee.

Perhaps the most fateful encounter of September 17 was not between Indians and whites. About the time the Grummonds arrived at Fort Phil Kearny, Lt. Frederick Brown returned with the cattle he had recovered from the raid earlier that day. Brown and Grummond had never met. Yet they soon found they had much in common. The most visible common denominator in the garrison's response to the raids near the fort to that point had been Lt. Frederick Brown. Originally hailing from New York, where he was born about 1831, Brown had joined the 18th Infantry almost from the time of its inception. As a second lieutenant in 1861 he was appointed regimental quartermaster, a job he continued to have at Fort Phil Kearny in 1866. Brown received a brevet to captain for the Atlanta campaign. He served on recruiting duty right after the war, as did his friend from the Civil War William J. Fetterman. Brown joined the 2/18th, once again as quartermaster, at Fort Kearney, Nebraska, in 1865 when Carrington was preparing to occupy the Mountain District. Thus Brown was with Carrington from the beginning of the battalion's march to the Powder River country. In April 1866 Carrington appointed him chief quartermaster of the Mountain District.[29]

Like his friend Fetterman and his new acquaintance of September 1866, Lt. George Grummond, Brown had a charming personality and was described by Margaret Carrington as a genial and good-humored bachelor.[30] Like the other officers of the 2/18th and indeed most of the officers of the frontier army of the 1860s, Brown had a patronizing view of Indians at best, an illusion that at times translated to outright disdain. This latter trait led to extreme ethnocentric misconceptions regarding the martial abilities of Indians. Yet perhaps these views were also shaped in part by the frustration that mounted in Frederick Brown's behavior between July and December 1866. Back at Fort Kearney, Nebraska, in 1865, his friend Lt. William Bisbee painted the picture of a more humorous, happy-go-lucky Brown, but a Brown still grossly patronizing of Indians. According to Bisbee, Brown's quarters at Fort Kearney were "separated by a thin partition from mine. His chief joy was to pack the room with Pawnee Indians, fill them with 'chow,' in return for which they gave gruesome and noisy exhibitions of scalping, war dances, and buffalo hunts."[31]

Unlike Grummond, however, Brown was not an alcoholic with a mean streak. But like Grummond, Brown became irrational during his service at

Fort Phil Kearny. As a professional soldier he took his quartermaster duties as the officer responsible for the fort's livestock very seriously, as well he should have given the isolation of the post. More often than not Brown was in the vanguard of pursuing troops, usually out the gate in pursuit without awaiting orders, whenever Indians drove away livestock. Occasionally he was successful in recovering some of the stolen animals, as he had been on September 17, but usually he was unsuccessful. According to Margaret Carrington, Brown had a melancholy demeanor regarding the universally slow promotions in the regular army. This despite the fact that he had been made chief district quartermaster and promoted to captain of regulars in October 1866, a rank he had held only as a brevet during the Civil War. Still, believing that he had often been unfairly passed over for promotion, he acquired the attitude common among frontier officers that advancement would only come through notable deeds of combat.[32]

Brown became impetuous, even reckless, in prompting action with Indians, and verbalized his obsession with the idea of "taking scalps." He once boasted that in a fight he could conceivably take twelve scalps by himself. With his promotion to captain, Frederick Brown was transferred to Fort Laramie in the fall of 1866. But he tarried, waiting for one last action in which he could excel, and he often asserted that he could not leave Fort Phil Kearny without personally taking "Red Cloud's scalp." Most likely Brown's deteriorating attitude at Fort Phil Kearny was due to his seemingly daily frustration of losing horses, mules, and cattle to an enemy he often visualized as being inferior. He was anxious to prove otherwise, perhaps not so much to the promotion board that had already rewarded him as to himself.[33]

On September 19 a sizeable party of warriors made a demonstration on a hill near Fort Phil Kearny, shaking their bows and lances in defiance. Then some of the Indians proceeded to attack the miners' camp outside the stockade. Bailey rallied his men and put up a stiff defense, dropping six of the warriors and about twelve of their horses. The soldiers in the fort aided the cause by firing the howitzers into the hills, once again successfully dispersing the attackers.[34] Indians attacked the miners for a second time the next day, although the warriors only made a half-hearted assault on their perimeter. But on the twenty-first the Indians made a strong attack on the hay mowers working near Goose Creek under contractor Levi Carter. Carrington dispatched forty soldiers under Lt. Winfield S. Matson to the aid of the hay cutters but the overwhelming number of warriors kept them pinned down for over six hours. As the Indians, whom Carrington reported as being "Sioux and Arapahos," slipped away, a white man dressed in Indian clothing rode up to Matson. The man had several fingers missing from one of his hands. He said his name was "Captain" Bob North. Just what his business was Matson never found out. One of Matson's men rode up to report the discovery of the bodies of a contractor named Grull and two of his men. All had been killed and scalped. The civilians had been returning from Fort C. F. Smith when they were attacked. During this revelation the strange character who called himself Bob North slipped away. Apparently Jim Bridger's assertion from the Crows that one or more white men were with the war factions on the Tongue had some validity.[35]

That truth was confirmed the following day, September 23. In the cold gray dawn a sizeable war party descended on a cattle herd grazing outside the fort and cut out ninety-four head. This time the eager Lt. Frederick Brown was prepared. He came dashing out the gates of the fort with a body of troops in hot pursuit. A number of Bailey's miners came with him, anxious to mix it up with the Indians. The warriors gained no great distance due to Brown's particular vigilance that morning. The cattle slowed the Indians down and soon Brown's men caught up with them. The warriors turned the cattle loose and scattered, and then turned to face the soldiers. Brown ordered his mounted infantrymen to dismount and move forward in skirmish order. But the scattered warriors quickly reassembled and charged the dismounted troops. Brown's men repulsed them. They charged in a second time and Brown noticed a white man among them swearing profusely in English. Again a hard volley repulsed the attackers but they thundered in for a third time and this time the strange white man fell from his horse. The Indians had had enough. They quickly swept up their dead and wounded and withdrew from the field. The Indians may have lost as many as eight dead with five more mortally wounded and many more slightly wounded in this fight. Brown suffered only one man slightly wounded. The soldiers and miners returned triumphant with some of the recovered cattle herd. In his report of the fight, Carrington stated that the white man who was killed was Bob North.[36]

Later Carrington considered that the fight of September 23 was the first decisive victory his men had inflicted on Red Cloud's followers.[37] Decisive or not, the ambitious and excitable Frederick H. Brown made the most of it. The skirmish most likely contributed to his promotion to captain in October. His boasting about the fight of "the 23rd of September was frequent," wrote Margaret Carrington, and "he [wrote] up its history, [in] which he said 'showed [the] one good fight he had with the rascals.'"[38] Despite Brown's victory, Sgt. Frank Fessenden remembered Carrington's new orders of this time that "none of our men should ever go out of the fort alone." Fessenden had often left the fort to tend a milk cow that he had purchased from Chaplain White. "I used to arm myself and go out hunting for that cow," he remembered years later. "I presume the Indians also wanted her for they ultimately got her anyhow." Orders by then were "so strict that I did not dare go outside the stockade."[39]

Other bands of warriors, possibly Arapahos, renewed raiding around Fort Reno during the week of September 17, 1866. Mostly these were small raids on livestock herds, but on September 21 a contractor's train was hit on the Dry Fork of Cheyenne River, eight miles from Fort Reno. Two whites were wounded in a sharp skirmish. There were no Indian casualties.[40] Meanwhile, Fort C. F. Smith had seen relatively few incidents, supporting the strategic notion that if the Indians could cut off supplies moving that far north, the fort would soon have to be abandoned. According to Little Moon, Jumping Rabbit, and Wolf That Lies Down, all peaceful Cheyennes who conferred with Carrington, some Gros Ventres and some lodges of Sans Arcs and Two Kettle Lakotas were camping along the Bighorn below the new post. Having made a temporary peace with the Crows, they were now ready to join the cause of Red Cloud and the other war factions. Sometime during September a group of these warriors demonstrated outside of Fort C. F. Smith. Jim Beckwourth came out to council with them but did not believe they were peaceful. No provisions were given to them as they had requested. In response the Indians killed a woodcutter returning to the fort and scalped him in sight of the garrison.[41]

Back at Fort Phil Kearny the actions of September 23 did not endure for long. On the cold morning of September 27 the Indians struck again. By now their pattern was predictable. Never entertaining any foolish notions of trying to assault the fort itself, the warriors concentrated either on grazing cattle outside the stockade, the lookout post on Pilot Hill, or the woodcutting activities at the pineries. By this time Carrington had suspended hay cutting on Goose Creek for the time being if not for the season. About fifteen war-riors moved among the thick trees on Piney Island that morning looking for woodcutters who had become separated from their companions while cut-ting down trees. They found one. Pvt. Patrick Smith suffered a most horrible death. The Indians filled him with arrows and scalped him while he was still alive. Private Smith began crawling to the timber cutters' blockhouse about a half-mile away. He broke off the arrow shafts so they would not drag across the rough terrain as he crawled. He reached the blockhouse covered with dirt and his face covered in his own blood. Loose skin hung from his forehead where he had been scalped. Although a detachment was sent back to the fort for one of the surgeons, it was no use. Private Smith died the next day after suffering twenty-four hours of agony. On the same day Smith was mortally wounded, another war party of warriors, one hundred strong, charged out of the woods and killed two civilian woodcutters while they were chopping down trees.[42]

Later that same morning assaults were made on all sides of Fort Phil Kearny but not on the post itself. Seven warriors burst from a thicket and headed for the sentries on Pilot Hill. While this diversion was going on another band of fifty warriors attacked the livestock herd of Bailey's miners on the north side near the post. Then a party came riding in from the west while a larger party demonstrated across the top of Lodge Trail Ridge. The soldiers noticed the warrior parties were signaling one another with mirrors, indicating an element of coordinated action. This turned into a defensive artillery battle. Fire from the post's howitzers dispersed the Indians, knocking a couple to the ground. The howitzers were proving their worth for the whites once again in defensive action.[43]

During the melee Lieutenant Brown, assisted by Lieutenant Adair and twenty mounted men, burst forth from the fort in hot pursuit. While chasing a group of warriors up a ridge Brown noticed that the warriors stopped for a minute to confer with another band of Indians who were not fleeing. Brown continued to pursue the retreating warriors for some time. Upon his return he found the second group still on the ridge holding up papers. They were peace faction Northern Cheyennes under Little Moon, Jumping Rabbit, and Wolf That Lies Down. The Northern Cheyennes came into the fort with Brown. Carrington welcomed them and told them to camp along the Piney where he would council with them the next morning.[44]

That night an event occurred that could have made conditions at Fort Phil Kearny much worse than they would become. By now the news of Private Smith's horrible death was being heard by the enlisted men. Anger slowly festered to the breaking point. After all, the warriors camped outside the fort were still Indians. They could be lying. They could be treacherous. Stressful emotions of the past three months engulfed some of the men. Late that night a number of them slipped out of the stockade and quietly sneaked toward the peaceful Cheyenne camp. The soldiers were armed. Some had their guns cocked. Fortunately Chaplain White, who had overheard some of the men plotting an attack, warned Carrington. The colonel ordered Capt. Tenador Ten Eyck to stop the soldiers. Ten Eyck shouted after them to stop. Soon Carrington appeared, yelling for the men to return to the fort. Many scrambled through the darkness to reach the stockade before being halted. A shot from Colonel Carrington's revolver halted some as others fled to their quarters. An embarrassing massacre had been averted.[45]

The next morning Carrington conferred with the Cheyennes. Little Moon was their spokesman.[46] Little Moon told Carrington that the assembled Cheyennes were old Black Horse's people but that Black Horse was very ill and would soon die. The chiefs confirmed what the Crows had stated earlier about the growing numbers, around five hundred lodges, of Indians along the Tongue. He told Carrington that they had not found many buffalo near the Platte road and asked his permission to hunt in the Powder River country since fall was the time of the annual buffalo hunt. They were willing to suffer the wrath of Red Cloud and the Bad Face Oglalas to do so. They likewise inferred that Red Cloud and Man Afraid of His Horse were the principal influences over the war factions in the Tongue Valley while Buffalo Tongue was dominant in the south. Carrington fed them and granted them permission to hunt.[47] By early October a number of Northern Cheyenne chiefs rode into Fort Laramie ostensibly to sign the treaty; Dull Knife was among them. By late fall most of these people were hunting buffalo in the Republican River country of Kansas and Nebraska.[48] Dull Knife headed north to the Rosebud Valley that he frequented but might not have been very welcome in during the autumn of 1866. His actions after that time are not clear.[49] By the end of the month, for the soldiers at Fort Phil Kearny, the future looked uncertain. On the last day of the month a supply train arrived from Fort Reno bringing tons of corn and grain for the now emaciated horses and mules. But the people of the garrison were not so fortunate. By September 30 the post had lost between six hundred and seven hundred head of cattle, mostly to Indian raids. Fresh meat for the winter months was in doubt. Early fall at Fort Phil Kearny had been bleak indeed.[50]

By October the intense raids around Fort Phil Kearny fell off a little. As the prairie grasses turned brown and cured in the long rays of the autumn sun the Lakotas and Cheyennes prepared for the annual buffalo hunt. By the 1860s the Oglalas established their winter camps at the forks of the Tongue each year.[51] But during October, November, and into December of 1866 the camps grew larger than normal, taxing natural resources. In addition to the villages of the Bad Face Oglalas and the other Lakotas and Arapahos along the Tongue, the Northern Cheyennes camped together at the forks of Muddy Creek in the Rosebud country. Little Wolf was there, determined to fight. Likely Dull Knife and his followers were there also, determined to stay out of the fighting. Other Northern Cheyennes remained for the winter in the Republican River Valley far to the south. With Red Cloud's Oglalas now below the mouth of Hanging Woman Creek on Tongue River were the bands of five prominent Miniconjou chiefs: Brave Bear, Makes Room, White Hollow Horn, Black Shield, and One Horn. Although some Miniconjous had participated in the raids during the summer and fall, they now, perhaps more than any other group, for the first time called for a great winter raid on the stockade itself at Fort Phil Kearny. This idea had been scoffed at by chiefs during the past summer. It was at this time, October, that old Black Elk remembered the Lakota villages stretched for miles along the Tongue and that a man on horseback "could ride through our villages from sunrise until the day was above head, so far did our camp stretch along the valley of the river."[52] Black Elk also asserted that it was in October that Red Cloud himself had held council with many chiefs to persuade them to join the camps along the Tongue for a winter campaign against what the Indians now called the Buffalo Creek fort. Black Elk's testimony lends support to the notion that by fall 1866 Red Cloud's influence among the warring factions was growing.[53]

For Col. Henry Carrington and the 2/18th, October and early November continued to be a time of trial for several reasons. The only significant action came on October 6 when a party of one hundred Oglalas attacked the wood-cutting detail of about twenty men working at the pinery. The soldiers fought their way to the blockhouse but the Indians charged the loopholes. When the warriors broke off the engagement and the woodcutters returned to work, they were continuously shot at by snipers concealed in the woods. In the action privates John Wasser and Christian Oberly of Company A were killed and another man was wounded. A messenger reached the fort and Carrington with a thirty-man detail brought up one of the howitzers and shelled the woods. The little cannon's offensive effectiveness and mobility finally proved itself, if in a limited engagement, in the pine forests of the West as it had in the muddy thick eastern woodlands of the Civil War. Carrington left the artillery piece along with a gunnery detail at the pinery blockhouse, the result being that the Indians gave the woodcutters very little trouble from that time until late December.[54]

Two other freighter's trains arrived with enough hay and oats to sustain livestock for the winter. Later other trains would arrive with enough provisions and medical supplies to sustain the garrison. The Indian coalitions had failed to completely cut off supplies to Fort Phil Kearny. But in other ways trouble and discontent were starting to brew. Frustrations among junior officers, enlisted men, and even civilians started to show. Carrington thought better of punishing the men involved in the thwarted raid on Little Moon's peaceful Northern Cheyenne contingent camped outside the fort in late September. Meanwhile at Fort Reno Captain Proctor relieved Lieutenant Kirtland of his duties for the loss of all the livestock there during the past months. But Carrington supported Kirtland and cited Proctor as unfit for command. At the same time some of the freighters who had brought hay to the post that month deserted the train and decided to accept an offer from Captain Ten Eyck of employment at the fort, unbeknownst to Carrington. Later in the month an historic cattle drive of perhaps six or seven hundred head under Nelson Story arrived at the post on their way to Montana following a sharp fight with a Lakota war party. Carrington refused to allow them to proceed until another train came along to join them. Furious at the prospect of spending the winter at the fort, Story left anyway in the middle of the night without selling any of his beef to the army at low government prices as Carrington had requested.[55]

Carrington was losing command control. In an attempt to counter matters he abruptly made them worse with some unpopular orders for reorganization. On October 7 he issued an order relieving Captain Ten Eyck of his duties as post commander. Carrington assumed that responsibility in addition to his major role as commander of the Mountain District. He reassigned Ten Eyck to command the captain's old Company H as well as making him the titular commander of the 2nd Battalion. Lieutenant Bisbee replaced Lieutenant Adair as adjutant, upon which Adair resigned his commission pending the return of Lieutenant Bradley from escort duty with General Hazen at Fort C. F. Smith. Lieutenant Wands was placed temporarily under Brown as assistant quartermaster, as Brown's captain's promotion had come through with reassignment to Fort Laramie. In addition, every officer, soldier, and civilian was assigned a loophole on the stockade line in case of attack so that each could be accounted for.[56]

If these orders were not enough to challenge Carrington's leadership abilities, problems of uncertainty and ambivalence from the high command did. Major James Van Voast, successor to Maynadier as commander at Fort Laramie, had ideas of his own. By late October or early November of 1866 he was planning a winter offensive against the Lakotas. Van Voast had twelve companies at Fort Laramie. Gen. Philip St. George Cooke at first gave tentative approval but then rescinded it, claiming his force would be in too much danger due to its size. Unbelievably, Cooke thought Carrington, who had a far smaller force at Fort Phil Kearny, could handle winter offensive operations.[57] Cooke had informed Carrington as such in early September.[58] But then Cooke changed his mind, stating that winter operations would prove impossible unless he could "surprise Red Cloud in his winter camp" by using two to three hundred infantry with much suffering.[59] Perhaps Cooke was influenced by General Hazen's dispatch to him when he had left Fort Phil Kearny for Fort C. F. Smith in August. "Indian depredations, so far, have been of a desultory, thieving nature," Hazen wrote. "With care, nothing should have occurred, and the whole character of affairs here have been greatly exaggerated . . . Col. Carrington appearing to think only of building his post."[60]

Cooke was losing patience with Carrington and his whining pleas for reinforcements. Then when he received Carrington's dispatches of September he changed his mind again regarding offensive operations after learning of the depredations along the road that summer. He accused Carrington of not communicating with departmental headquarters. Of course this was a problem of slow mails in a frontier region, not of indifference on Carrington's part, something Cooke should have realized from his previous service in the West. On October 13, Cooke abolished the Mountain District, a paper change to be sure, but probably a subtle, unstated reprimand of Carrington. On November 12, 1866, Cooke reminded Carrington that there were "large arrears" to be reconciled.[61] By now Carrington was balancing press reports of the forts' being in a virtual state of siege with Hazen's assertions, as well as his own, that hostilities were "greatly exaggerated" in order to counter Cooke's growing antipathy. But back at the end of August Cooke had not known where Carrington stood on the matter. He accepted what Carrington had told him earlier, that the Indians' only interest was "plunder" and that there was no possibility of an "Indian alliance."[62]

By October and November, of course, Carrington knew better, but still he had little fear of the general insurgency. "Red Cloud," he told Cooke, "does not comprehend the idea of a year's supplies, nor that we are now prepared to not only pass the winter, but next spring and summer, even if he takes the offensive."[63] Even Van Voast at Fort Laramie, perhaps envious that Carrington might get the glory he sought in action against the Indians, supported the idea that hostilities were exaggerated. He openly discounted Jim Bridger's reconnaissance report regarding the idea of an alliance. "I do not believe much of what Mr. Bridger says," he wrote. "He exaggerates about Indians." Bridger later denounced the accusation. If the events of July had not convinced Carrington that the Indians had seriously taken "the offensive," then the events of September surely would have convinced him.[64]

Carrington and Van Voast were trying to preserve their reputations. Cooke's understanding of the situation became confused by conflicting reports of exaggeration on the one hand and requests for reinforcements, carbines, and ammunition on the other. But his actions appeared on the surface to be ones of indifference rather than confusion in a time of limited resources and budget restraint. Cooke's reputation too was on the line. When in doubt do nothing. And Cooke did just that. After all, during 1866 Cooke had many personal problems in addition to his administrative ones. The estrangement of his son, who had fought for the Confederacy, and the absence of his daughter-in-law, living in poverty in the ruins of Richmond, Virginia, following the death of her husband, Confederate Gen. J. E. B. Stuart, surely plagued his mind. But Carrington's and Van Voast's rhetoric of the autumn of 1866 sealed Carrington's hopes of receiving reinforcements of two companies of cavalry and one of infantry that he had requested. Carrington would be fortunate to obtain one company of the 2nd Cavalry in November. Indeed, by then Cooke was suggesting that Carrington send horses back to Fort Laramie for redistribution.[65]

On October 27 General Hazen returned along with Lieutenant Bradley and his contingent of mounted infantry. One man from the detachment, a scout named Jim Brannan, had been killed and three privates had deserted for the gold camps. On the last day of October Carrington declared a holiday to celebrate the symbolic completion of Fort Phil Kearny, although some finishing touches would be put on during the next couple of months. The women of the post prepared food and treats for the children. Carrington gave a moving patriotic speech reminding the whites of their manifest destiny. A howitzer was fired several times to celebrate the occasion. The explosion attracted a group of Indians around Sullivant Hills who quickly vanished into the terrain.[66] Back in Omaha, General Cooke's seeming lack of concern reached higher levels. General Sherman, who had urged officers to take their wives along, still viewed the situation in the Powder River country as insignificant. In Washington, General of the Army Ulysses S. Grant felt the same. Later he would write in a letter to Secretary of War Stanton, which reached western newspapers, that "[a] standing army could not prevent occasional Indian outrages, no matter what its magnitude." Col. Henry Carrington, as he watched "Old Glory" ascend the new flagpole at Fort Phil Kearny, probably had no conception that his position in the Powder River country was hanging by a thread. During the following two months the thread would break.[67]

CHAPTER 6

WAU-NEE-CHEE

Lakotas Unite for War/Fetterman Arrives at Fort Phil Kearny

Attest the treaty signed! So said the mail;
But those who brought it up the Bozeman Trail
Two hundred miles, could tell of running
     fights,
Of playing tag with Terror in the nights
To hide by day. If peace was anywhere,
It favored most the growing graveyard there
Across the Piney under Pilot Hill.[1]

AS THE SEASONAL CHANGES OF AUTUMN took hold in the Powder River country, and the Lakota and Cheyenne camps along the Tongue River and Rosebud Creek gathered more warriors, life at Fort Phil Kearny tried to approximate some semblance of order. Indian summer weather lingered along the Bighorns. But for the garrison at the fort the rituals were an illusion of normalcy broken often by attacks at the pineries and the incessant livestock raids. Perhaps most of all the growing number of graves in the post cemetery gave a constant witness that the garrison was in unremitting danger and far from Euro-American civilization. The feelings of vulnerability, of being vastly outmanned by an enemy whose multitudes grew weekly, surely were obvious for many, if unspoken. In July 1867, an attorney, J. B. Weston, who had wintered at Fort Phil Kearny the previous year, testified before the investigating committee into the Fetterman "massacre." Weston admonished the high command for their lack of insight into the seriousness of the war as it had progressed during the fall of 1866. "The War Department has failed to appreciate its extent and magnitude," Weston stated; "has sent a military force into this country so small, inadequate, and insufficient in numbers, arms and supplies, that instead of conquering a peace, it has aggravated and augmented the troubles."[2]

But morale remained average. By November, with the practical completion of the fort, "we now began to feel safer," Sgt. Frank Fessenden remembered. "We were well aware, however, that it behooved us to be on our guard every minute of our time . . . [But] we began to have some few enjoyments. We had church services, which were well attended every Sunday." The garrison conducted dress parades each afternoon. The soldiers would have worn Civil War–era uniforms, either sack coats or high-collared shell jackets for the company of 2nd Cavalry once it arrived at the post. Kepis were still worn in the field as standard headgear, while some officers and enlisted men probably sported dashing Ostrich-plumed "Hardee" or "Jeff Davis" hats, in use on the frontier in the 1860s as they had been during the late war. Sergeant Fessenden's band gave concerts frequently. There was even an officious guard mount ceremony each morning. "All this served to help break the awful monotony of our lives in that desolate country," Sergeant Fessenden remembered.[3]

Yet too the people of the garrison were always aware of the mounting number of graves in the cemetery, still modest, but fairly consistent enough in its growth to elicit frightening memories many years later of that wild Wyoming country. "I do not remember that we buried but one man here who was not killed by the Indians," Fessenden recalled, "and that man was our band leader [who died of disease]. The night he died I well remember how the wolves howled and made the night hideous, and we could hear them scratch at the stockade posts. When we buried the body we had to dig very deep . . . to prevent the wolves from digging the body out."[4]

Not until later into the fall and winter, with the coming cold, did everyone in the garrison finally accept the grim reality that the Lakotas and Cheyennes had singled out Fort Phil Kearny as the locus of their activities. "We did not hear from Fort C. F. Smith for three months," Lt. William Bisbee wrote, "and fearing disaster to their two companies, Sergeant Grant and a companion volunteered to make an attempt to go through the hostile country, a distance of 90 miles . . . The garrison was found safe." Neither had there been any troubles "at the lower stations, Reno and Laramie," Bisbee recalled, "Phil Kearny was the point of special hostilities."[5] Indeed, Captain Templeton reported from Fort C. F. Smith on November 30 that "[t]he Indians have committed no depredations during the month." At the end of

December Templeton wrote, "No hostile Indians have made their appearance."[6] But at Fort Phil Kearny, "Conditions were becoming more alarming every day," Sergeant Fessenden remembered. "The Indians were becoming more numerous than ever in every direction, and they also were desperate . . . We kept fifty horses constantly saddled, there were now no idle moments, but plenty of anxiety."[7]

Few Indian participants in Red Cloud's War have left to the outside public any specific testimonies as to their individual activities during the fall before December 21, 1866, although their numbers were constantly growing along the Tongue. High Backbone of the Miniconjous had come in along the Tongue during the early fall. By November his people were beginning to infuse the Oglala camps. By December almost one hundred Miniconjou lodges stood a half-day's ride from Fort Phil Kearny.[8] Indeed, attacks at this time were not as intense as earlier although the Indian presence was still felt at Fort Phil Kearny almost daily. On the first day of November following Carrington's October 31 holiday to celebrate the completion of the fort, a war party fired on citizen hay contractors in the night, wounding three, one of whom later died. Another man lost his leg. About the same time warriors lit fires on the hill, half a mile from the fort, and attacked a group of civilian herders about a mile away. Captain Brown went out with twenty-five men to recover the stock after troops shelled the Indians with several rounds from the Mountain howitzers. Civilian contractor John Bratt claimed many years later that he talked to Oglalas who had been on the hill that night. According to Bratt, they were planning a feint on the fort that very evening but the artillery was the thing that convinced them otherwise.[9] On November 7 warriors attacked a wood escort but the soldiers drove the Indians off. On the twenty-first the Indians made an unsuccessful assault on a cattle herd in the night. Two days later, November 23, they captured a mule herd. Once again, Captain Brown pursued the raiders with thirty men without success. Again, on November 25, warriors stampeded a cattle herd and this time Colonel Carrington himself with seventy-five men pursued them, recovering many of the cattle, but the Indians killed four steers to prevent their recovery. By this time some of the raiders were Miniconjous.[10]

As in previous weeks, by November the main catalyst for the 2/18th in these pursuits, most of them futile, was Capt. Frederick Brown. That Brown's frustrations were mounting was obvious and his actions surely contributed in part to either the causes or the effects of the declining discipline and spirit of the men of the 2/18th during this time. But testimonies are conflicting. Pvt. George B. Mackey later testified that discipline was "[v]ery good as I was able to judge, among the enlisted men . . . There was ill feeling among the officers, but the reason for it I know nothing of."[11] But Capt. James W. Powell testified about the same time that discipline among "the company officers was good, with an effort on their part to discharge their duties to the best of their abilities. With the enlisted men it was chaotic." When asked his opinion regarding the cause of poor discipline among the enlisted men Powell stated it was due to a "want of proper support, officially and personally, by the company commanders, [and] from the commanding officer." Powell's statements were later challenged by Carrington in a written rebuttal.[12]

The feeling among some officers and enlisted men was that discipline and morale at Fort Phil Kearny had become a problem by late fall 1866. Certainly the commanding officer Col. Henry Carrington carried that responsibility. But the reasons are less clear. Jealousy among veteran combat officers of Carrington's rank and position, untested in the Civil War, was a factor. This perception as well as Carrington's reluctance to commence any type of offensive operations have often been cited as reasons for the frustrations and morale problems at Fort Phil Kearny. But Carrington's reluctance to commit troops to the offensive amounted to common sense as his force was hopelessly outnumbered in the Powder River country during 1866. More likely, no officer from Carrington on down to company commanders and lieutenants quite knew what they were doing during this time. None had experience with the plains Indians. The necessity of swift pursuit of raiders was the most severe problem and no one seems to have worked out an efficient systematic method of dealing with that particular problem. Surprise attacks by the Indians seemed always to create disorganized confusion. "Previous to the 6th of December," infantryman George Mackey testified, "the troops went out in a loose manner, each man that chose to go, saddling up his horse and going without any ranks being formed, and each one on his own hook. Captain Brown usually went out with them."[13] Capt. James W. Powell, who arrived at Fort Phil Kearny in early November, likewise seemed to allude to the concept of loosely organized chaos in pursuing Indians after a surprise raid. "I must say," Powell testified at the Sanborn investigative hearings in 1867, "that there *seemed to be a system of volunteering* [emphasis mine]; officers going out in charge of men [without direct orders] from the number of about 40 to about 60, which *custom* seemed to have been tolerated by the post commander." But when asked who took command of the mounted infantry in the midst of alleged chaos, Powell replied, "Capt. F. H. Brown."[14]

Most of the reasons why many of these pursuits were unsuccessful before the arrival of a company of 2nd Cavalry at Fort Phil Kearny are easily ascertained. If a lack of organization and discipline *appeared* to be a standard factor, much of that can be attributed to lack of experience in fighting Indians by both officers and enlisted men. Perhaps more important, there was an almost total lack of experience in horsemanship by *infantry* soldiers of all ranks. Although "mounted infantry" existed in the army during the nineteenth century, these were specialized troops trained in horsemanship. The 2/18th were not mounted infantry; rather they were infantry *trying* to ride horses without any training in how to do so. As Pvt. William Murphy wrote, "Some reports stated that we had a mounted infantry, but that was a mistake. They were about thirty men who were detailed out of the infantry company at the fort [with no training]."[15] Lieutenant Wands, who had seen service in the last Seminole War, described the futility of this effort when questioned about the tactical effectiveness of these improvised horse soldiers. "They would not reserve their fire," he stated, "but would fire at long range, and waste their ammunition in that manner. Most of the engagements with the Indians were running fights."[16] Certainly the ineffectiveness of inexperienced infantry with obsolete weapons, mounted on horseback, attempting to catch warriors mounted on swift Indian ponies exacerbated the frustration of officers like Capt. Frederick Brown. It likewise had a demoralizing effect on the enlisted men at Fort Phil Kearny. But help was close at hand, or so Brown and his fellow officers believed.

On November 3, 1866, one of the two companies of cavalry promised to Carrington arrived at Fort Phil Kearny. Company C, 2nd U.S. Cavalry, consisted of sixty-three men, many new to the service. They were armed with all the wrong equipment: obsolete Enfield rifles, Springfield muzzle loaders, and Starr carbines, hardly weapons that could easily be used by horse soldiers. Company C was commanded by Lieutenant Horatio S. Bingham, a native Minnesotan. Bingham was an experienced soldier who had seen service in the Civil War from First Bull Run to Antietam, where he was wounded. As a member of the 2nd Minnesota Volunteer Cavalry he had some experience with his unit's involvement in the Dakota War albeit mostly administrative. But given where he hailed from, Bingham was not one to take Indians lightly.[17] Frances and George Grummond immediately took a liking to the Midwesterner, "a fine young fellow," Frances remembered years later. The Grummonds often invited Bingham to dinner in their quarters at Fort Phil Kearny.[18]

Capt. James W. Powell arrived with the cavalry and took over Company C, 2/18th Infantry, in relief of Lieutenant Adair, who retained the duties of regimental adjutant. Powell, who would later create much trouble for Carrington at the Sanborn hearings, was a veteran soldier in the regular army. He had seen dragoon service before the Civil War. During the war he fought in some of the bloodiest campaigns in the western theater. For the remainder of his life he carried two balls in his body received at the Battle of Jonesboro in 1864. Occasionally suffering from the effects of his wounds, Powell would see little action around Fort Phil Kearny in 1866 although the next year he became the consensus hero of the renowned Wagon Box fight. Many years later Carrington would attribute to Powell's wounds a declining stability in his mental health that possibly shaped his negative opinions regarding Carrington's leadership abilities. But according to writer Sterling Fenn, "Captain James Powell may have possessed the most battle-disciplined experience, judgement [*sic*] and respect for Indian fighting prowess of the entire officer corps" at Fort Phil Kearny in 1866. The paymaster, Major Henry Almstedt, likewise arrived with the column.[19]

But the most fateful figure to arrive with Bingham's cavalry on November 3, 1866, was Capt. William J. Fetterman, fresh from recruiting duty, which Margaret Carrington admitted he excelled at, due no doubt to his charming demeanor. Margaret described Fetterman as "commanding esteem by his refinement, gentlemanly manners and adaptation to social life." His return to the regiment, she wrote, "had been sought, and no less looked for with glad anticipation, as officers were so few, and his social and professional character alike made him a favorite . . . he was a gentleman."[20] Fetterman was reunited with comrades Capt. Frederick Brown and Lt. William Bisbee, who described Fetterman as "intelligently disciplined" as a combat officer.[21] The other member of the famous trio who would die on Massacre Ridge before the next month was out, Lt. George W. Grummond, had either never met Fetterman or knew him only briefly from casual encounters earlier in the year.[22]

Fetterman arrived at Fort Phil Kearny fresh and optimistic. General Cooke had informed him that soon, under the Army Reorganization Act, the 2/18th would become the nucleus of the new 27th Infantry while Carrington would retain command of the 1st Battalion as a nucleus for a revamped 18th Infantry. That Fetterman was an ambitious young officer who might finally be realizing some laurels that he had hoped for during the Civil War is obvious for many. So too it was for Frederick Brown, George Grummond, and most officers at Fort Phil Kearny and on the postwar frontier of 1866. That he was impatient to finally punish the Lakotas and Cheyennes in the Powder River country is certain, despite his nonexistent experience with fighting Indians. But Fetterman was no more determined to punish the Indians than were Brown and the other officers at Fort Phil Kearny. After all, as line officers that was their job, and using sound military judgment in executing those responsibilities was also their job.

Given his social graces, and sensing the frustration among the families of the garrison by November 1866, Fetterman made a rhetorical comment to lift their spirits: "A company of regulars could whip a thousand, and a regiment could whip a whole array of hostile tribes," attributed to him by Margaret Carrington and reaffirmed almost verbatim many years later by Frances Grummond Carrington.[23] But Frances remembered that Fetterman's boasts were "seconded" by Captain Brown and Lieutenant Grummond. None of these officers was unique in his parlor rhetoric. Chauvinism toward Indians was commonplace among officers on the frontier. The belief of the ultimate superiority of the victorious Union army, so soon after the war, in comparison to overall aboriginal martial abilities, was perhaps even close to being universal among the officer corps in the West at that time. As late as 1876, was it not a general officer, Alfred Terry, who wrote to General Sheridan on May 16, 1876, as his Dakota column of six hundred strong (including George Custer and the 7th Cavalry) confidently marched out of Fort Lincoln, Dakota Territory, asserting, "I have no doubt of the ability of my column to whip all the Sioux whom we can find"?[24] Yet the epithets made by William Fetterman, or imagined by his contemporaries, that November have reshaped his character in death and throughout history unfairly because history interprets them as somehow being *unique*, which they were not, rather than obviously and simply *untrue*, in respect to the military capabilities of Indians. On balance the ethnocentric and contemptuous statements made about Indians by white soldiers who were at war with them constituted acceptable and expected parlor conversation during the 1860s. Fetterman's contemporaneous social graces, which were obviously memorable to Margaret Carrington, were surely articulated in a fashionable manner by the young captain in this regard.[25]

Little in Fetterman's military service either during the Civil War or at Fort Phil Kearny suggests that he was disobedient of authority or unusually arrogant (although chauvinistic to be certain like most junior officers serving in Indian country), or that he warranted the epithet of "fire-eater" as he is still being portrayed in the popular literature.[26] Born in April 1835 to a military family in Connecticut, Fetterman's mother died while he was an infant, and his father, Lieutenant George Fetterman, 3rd Artillery, died nine years later in 1844. The young Fetterman, orphaned at an early age, was then raised by an uncle, William Bethel, who like Fetterman's father was a West Point graduate. It would be natural that young Fetterman would covet a chance for an education at the U.S. military academy. While serving as a bank teller in Rochester, New York, in 1853 his petition to West Point was turned down for reasons unknown. Although some modern writers have stated that Fetterman was a West Point graduate, he never attended the academy.[27] Lacking the necessary political connections he faded from the picture until the Civil War, when he was rescued from oblivion. On May 14, 1861, while residing in Washington, Delaware, Fetterman wangled a commission in the 18th U.S. Infantry, a regiment created only a week and a half earlier by President Lincoln, ultimately under Carrington's titular command. He reported for duty on July 6, 1861, in Columbus, Ohio. The 18th Infantry was an element of the Army of the Ohio, which included the able Gen. George H. Thomas, who would earn the title "The Rock of Chickamauga."[28]

The popular literature in current times almost universally ascribes to Fetterman a distinguished and impressive record of combat service during the Civil War. Promoted to captain, he received two brevets to the rank of brevet lieutenant colonel. He participated in several battles including the siege of Corinth (1862), Chaplain Hill (1862), Stone's River (1863), and Jonesboro/Atlanta after the 18th had been reassigned to the 2nd Brigade, 1st Division, 14th Corps of the Army of the Cumberland.[29]

But historian Mark W. Johnson in his recent exhaustive study of the regular army regiments in the Civil War and afterward disputes the inflation of Fetterman's Civil War exploits following the notoriety he gained with his death in 1866. "Actually, Fetterman's Civil War service was extensive," Johnson wrote, "but not notably spectacular." He points out that a multitude of officers in the Civil War had records exceeding Fetterman's and that such records as Fetterman compiled were fairly commonplace. In fact Fetterman is not often mentioned in reports of other officers until after his death, and then mostly by his close friend William Bisbee. The few reports recall how Fetterman simply came to the support of other units already engaged, an honorable trait to be sure, but one to be expected of any officer in combat. His role in support of troops already engaged figured significantly in his actions and perhaps his reactions at Fort Phil Kearny. However, "he was not cited for gallantry at Stone's River" as some assert, Johnson wrote, and "he commanded the 2/18th during the Atlanta Campaign only because he was the battalion's ranking officer present for duty that week, not as a reward for supposed heroics" as has been asserted. Fetterman never served on the staff of the XIV Corps to which the 18th had been recently assigned, a claim that has been attributed to him. In a letter to a friend, Oliver Sheperd, in 1866, Fetterman himself states that the Atlanta brevet was a "blanket" award given to many officers who participated in the fall of Atlanta. And the Stone's River brevet was not even submitted to the U.S. Senate until five months before his death, July 26, 1866. Indeed Fetterman seems to have received quite a bit of recruiting and other staff assignments between campaigns, duties, Johnson contends, he may have been better adept for than the reckless form of élan that characterized his successor in martyrdom to manifest destiny, George Custer.[30]

In fact, Fetterman's arrival at Fort Phil Kearny in November 1866 followed his most recent stint at recruiting duty. Despite attempts by modern writers to ascribe the same vainglorious characteristics to both Fetterman and Custer as a form of comparative history, Custer, who was a very different personality from Fetterman, easily wins that contest. It's not even close. Yet the accolades to Fetterman by Dee Brown and others of glorious service rendered, and his reputed arrogance and boastfulness, have cast him in the light of a Custer and helped set up a remarkable historical irony that haunts his death on Massacre Ridge almost a century and a half later.[31]

These modern portraits of Fetterman do not stand up to original source scrutiny when one considers what little is actually known of his life. Margaret Carrington described him as a gentleman.[32] So too did his close friend Lieutenant William Bisbee, who described Fetterman as an officer with great respect for orders. Apparently so too did enlisted men at Fort Phil Kearny take kindly to Fetterman. Wrote Charles Wilson of H Company: Captain Fetterman was "always looking out for them [the enlisted men] seeing to their needs, and saving all unnecessary sufferings." Only a year later Custer would order deserters pursued and shot. Capt. William J. Fetterman was certainly chauvinistic in his views of Indians, but "arrogant" and a "fire-eater" no more so and probably less so than many other officers in the West at that time.[33]

Although not detailed in the official records, Fetterman apparently came in person to Colonel Carrington on November 5, two days after his arrival, to set a trap for Indian livestock marauders. Carrington approved the plan. Fetterman took a detachment of volunteers into a cottonwood thicket along Big Piney Creek that night. The moon was bright so that Indians in the vicinity could easily see. The soldiers hobbled some mules near the trees as bait. The soldiers hid in the trees until sunrise but the Indians did not fall for the trap. As the soldiers returned to the fort in the morning a party of warriors struck instead a mile away and ran off a cattle herd belonging to civilian contractor James Wheatley.[34]

Two days later, on November 7, Fetterman, in the company of Capt. Tenador Ten Eyck and lieutenants William Bisbee and H. H. Link along with a small escort, were riding toward the pineries ahead of the enlisted men to inspect the timber-cutting operations when they were ambushed by about twenty warriors. Shots were exchanged. A messenger returned to the post and Colonel Carrington brought out a relief party; no casualties were claimed. The exchange of volleys in such skirmishes as Fetterman first encountered most often resulted in no casualties. If he gained a contemptuous perspective of the Indian's small arms accuracy rate, it must be pointed out that neither did Fetterman's soldiers inflict any casualties among the Indians in these incidents. Indeed in his report, Captain Ten Eyck did not consider the incident particularly significant. He noted simply, "The officers in advance of the escort, were fired upon by about 20 Indians in ambush. The officers afterwards united with the escort and scoured the woods for Indians but found none and returned to the Post."[35]

Fetterman's next encounter with the Indians is confused in the literature. On November 21 Captain Powell drove off a war party attempting to steal cattle in the night. Again on the twenty-third Indians drove off nine mules and Brown and Bisbee pursued them without success. On the twenty-fifth

(Dee Brown places the incident on the twenty-third) another war party ran off eighteen head of cattle belonging to civilians Weston and Saunders. According to Ten Eyck, Colonel Carrington and seventy-five mounted men pursued the warriors and recovered eight head while the Indians managed to kill eight steers to prevent their recovery. Although Ten Eyck's report and other original accounts do not place Fetterman at the scene, Lieutenant William Bisbee, writing about it decades later, places Fetterman there although Bisbee confuses some of the elements of the events with the skirmish of November 7, making no mention of the cattle or Carrington's pursuit. Dee Brown, among others, likewise compounded Bisbee's failing memory by frequently combining the two incidents. Bisbee makes mention of one warrior's trying to decoy himself, Fetterman, Ten Eyck, and Link into an ambush in the woods. The Indian was "plainly a decoy," Bisbee wrote, "tempting us to a trap. It was not accepted, but in temptation to see what the young brave was really made of I charged him. Zip, zip came several shots from concealed Indians in the woods." Returning to the fort Bisbee noticed the flag at half-mast. According to Frances Grummond a messenger had come into the fort to report that all had been killed. "I recall, as if of yesterday," Frances remembered years later, "the blanched face of Mrs. Bisbee, knowing as she did that her husband was with the wood party, when a little bugler boy dashed up to the door where we were standing with the exciting announcement that 'all were killed.'"[36]

Dee Brown took these composite events to advance his thesis that Captain Fetterman was too inept to understand a decoying maneuver. "From this account it is clear that Bisbee had learned something of Indian fighting," Brown wrote; "he recognized a decoy trap when he saw one. Perhaps he passed a warning to Fetterman on that day, and restrained the overconfident captain from dashing into the woods. But whether he did so or not, Fetterman must have received the lesson with skepticism, or soon forgot it."[37]

But Fetterman did not forget it. The most indisputable evidence that the event of November 25 was indeed a pursuit of stolen cattle and not the pinery incident of November 7 comes from William J. Fetterman himself. Like Ten Eyck, he plays down the incident while acknowledging the ferocity of his enemy. In a recently discovered letter not available to Dee Brown, Fetterman wrote to a friend, Dr. Charles Terry, from Fort Phil Kearny on November 26, the day after the skirmish. Fetterman stated, "The Indians are very hostile and barbarous . . . Yesterday [Nov. 25] with about 30 mounted men [part of Carrington's pursuit] I chased a band of them who had run off some stock. Rode 40 miles and recovered all the cattle but five [actually four], which the Indians had shot to prevent them from falling into our hands." In the following sentence Fetterman confusingly refers to the skirmish near the pinery on November 7: "I with three other officers, while riding out to view the country a few days since [he must mean *previous* since he wrote the letter on the twenty-sixth] I fell into an ambuscade of Indians who fired a volley at us." Thus it seems that Fetterman's first encounter with Lakota decoys was on the seventh, not the twenty-fifth. And by the twenty-sixth he had not easily forgotten the lesson for on that date in his letter to Dr. Terry he wrote, "Our escape was a very narrow one."[38] Eleven days after Fetterman posted his letter, December 6, 1866, he once again would encounter a vivid and harrowing lesson in Indian decoy tactics, a lesson he could not possibly have forgotten, and not the kind of experience that would drive such an officer ignorantly and arrogantly over Lodge Trail Ridge two weeks later.

Yet during William Fetterman's first month at Fort Phil Kearny there is little doubt he added to the tensions resulting in disrespect between some junior officers at the fort and their commanding officer, Col. Henry B. Carrington. In Fetterman's letter to Terry he also added the bold and telling statement "We are afflicted with an incompetent commanding officer viz. Carrington, but shall be relieved of him in the re-organization, he going to the 18th [Infantry] and we [2nd Battalion] becoming the 27th Infantry."[39] The rift between Carrington and some of his junior officers has been speculated upon at two levels, that of Carrington's inaction in promoting offensive operations against the Indians and that of disrespect for a commanding officer with no previous combat experience purporting to understand the critical situation in the Powder River country. As stated earlier, Carrington had become only too aware since July of how greatly his forces were outnumbered in the Powder River country, a situation that was not disputed by scouts like Jim Bridger who understood the situation from experience. Never did Bridger or other old hands try to urge Carrington to take the offensive. Bridger later supported Carrington during the time of the Sanborn investigative hearings with a statement to the press. Fetterman's arrival in November, when he was still ignorant of the situation and eager for action, naturally spurred this fresh officer on the scene to want to take the field. But his early experiences in the failed ambush and his skirmish at the pinery and in the futile attempt to recover livestock on the twenty-fifth surely made impressions on the bright young captain as to the actual situation.

Earlier, Fetterman and Brown had come to Carrington with a request to lead fifty mounted men and fifty civilians on an assault of Indian villages on the Tongue River; Carrington had refused on the grounds there would not be enough horses left at the fort for mail escort or picket duty. He cited the garrison's inability to afford enough protection to fulfill hay contracts for winter and that the Indians were too large in numbers. Their villages could not be successfully attacked and destroyed. Although understandably eager for action Carrington's administrative insight must have made some logical impression on Fetterman as he made no further pleas from that time forward. Fetterman obeyed his orders from that time until December 21 without any complaint or disobedience as referenced by either himself or his fellows at Fort Phil Kearny.[40]

That Carrington himself was willing to initiate offensive action, or at least give voice to it to his commanding officer, Gen. Philip St. George Cooke, is well documented. Carrington simply became frustrated with Cooke's ever-changing orders on the idea. When Cooke ordered offensive operations in November Carrington again responded on the twenty-fifth, trying to impress upon Cooke the need for more men and supplies. "I shall look for another company of cavalry soon," he wrote. He then added, "I will in person, command expeditions, when severe weather confines them [the Indians] to their villages."[41]

Carrington's lack of offensive-mindedness may or may not have fueled discontent and disrespect among his subordinates. But the main source of Fetterman's and other officers' dislike of their commanding officer was also contested on the second level, that Carrington's position of authority was untested in major combat, and perhaps his outward appearance of pomposity. His higher station in life, his affiliation with Yale, his acquaintance with men like Washington Irving and President Lincoln, and a political appointment to a colonelcy, combined with his small, demure stature, could easily have been sources of envy and disrespect among combat-tested junior officers like William J. Fetterman who had held equal rank in brevets won on the battlefield. The fact that by 1866 frontier promotions were slow only added fuel to the fire of discontent. The fire of discontent surfaced again on November 11. On that day two enlisted men, a Sergeant Garrett and

Pvt. John Burke commenced fisticuffs on the parade ground in full view of several officers and women. Whatever the circumstances, profanity flourished, including epithets uttered probably by Lieutenant William Bisbee, although Fetterman has often been blamed by modern historians. Colonel Carrington was appalled by the profane speech, it being a Sunday and while he and Margaret were on their way to religious services. Following services Carrington issued infamous Order No. 38, forbidding swearing and fighting and admonishing officers to enforce this "respect for authority requiring obedience."[42] Within days soldiers were calling the decree "Bully 38" and the order served as the butt of jokes around the fort. Officers began to view Carrington as a pompous ass and a man ignorant of soldiers' propensity to brawl among themselves on frequent occasions, especially in a remote spot where there is no chance of obtaining leave. Such social envy augmented by the recognition that there was no simple, effective way to punish the Indians may well have been the main source of Fetterman's caustic remarks to Dr. Terry in his letter of November 26, 1866.[43]

Despite Fetterman's shared disrespect for Carrington, however, there is simply no evidence whatsoever that his actions in combat from the time of his arrival in November until December 21, 1866, reflected any disobedience or rational breakdown. More than thirty years later when Carrington's version of the Fetterman fight was well entrenched in the public mind, an old soldier, George Webber, formerly of Company C, 2/18th Infantry, wrote in a newspaper article that Fetterman and other officers came to be inspired with a "mad determination to pursue the redskins whenever [they] could regardless of numbers."[44] Webber was speaking of Capt. Frederick Brown as well as Captain Fetterman, and in the case of the former officer his words ring true, although by December even Brown had learned something of caution as demonstrated by his personal actions during the fight on December 6, but for Fetterman Webber's rhetoric falls far short. Indeed Fetterman's actions in November and early December do not reflect to the slightest degree any personality traits suggestive of anything as extreme as "mad" incompetent determination. Fetterman would get his next chance to advance his newly acquired, if limited, skills at Indian fighting on December 6, 1866. Once again he would demonstrate restraint and composure, although such cannot be said for some of the other officers who participated in that skirmish.

The Discomfited Fight of December Sixth

The action near Lodge Trail Ridge on December 6, 1866, has often been portrayed as an ominous portent of the Fetterman fight two weeks later. Although there are similarities, writers have often used this earlier fight to further cast William J. Fetterman as an unstable personality, obsessed with vengeance against the Lakotas and Cheyennes, who did not learn the lessons of his limited combat with Indians effectively.[45] If the results of this confused fight demonstrated anything at all it is that the exact opposite is likely true. The writer who has scrutinized the site of this action the most extensively is J. W. Vaughn.[46] Until the mid-twentieth century the exact location of the fight was not precisely known due to inaccurately sketched maps drawn by Colonel Carrington. Using metal detectors Vaughn and his companion L. C. Bishop uncovered a pattern of artifacts by the early 1960s that likely identify the location. Aerial surveys supported their conclusions. The "scientific" accuracy of this amateur archaeology project is, of course, arguable among professionals, but still quite logical and thus *probable* given the nature of the terrain and the records of the fight. According to Vaughn, most of the action on December 6 took place in the broken area west of Massacre Ridge and the Bozeman Trail.[47]

Most likely the Lakotas approached the fort from their villages along the Tongue by riding westward past the Bozeman Trail and circling around in the valley between the Bighorn Mountains and Lodge Trail Ridge. After crossing the north and south tributary forks of the Piney they arrived near the woodcutting pineries from the north. This route concealed them from the fort and sentries on Pilot Hill. As such, they could make surprise attacks on parties coming out from the fort toward the pineries by riding down over the west end of Sullivant Hill from the north.[48] Vaughn contends the Indians likely used this approach to attack a wood train returning from the mountains on December 6 about four miles west of the fort. George Hyde asserts that by this time the attacks by the Indians had some semblance of coordination using signal mirrors and that on the sixth Red Cloud himself was "seen on a hill directing the movements of the warriors by signals."[49] Regardless of Hyde's largely unsubstantiated claim, the action that day appears to be another of the ubiquitous attacks on a woodcutting detail to which the garrison at Fort Phil Kearny responded in their usual haphazard fashion. Vaughn suggests, however, that the maneuvers by the soldiers that day took on an offensive dimension as planned by Carrington in an attempt to respond to the demands by General Cooke for aggressive action. The idea, asserts Vaughn, was to send one column of soldiers west along the wood road to relieve the train as usual, while another element of troops would march north over the east end of Lodge Trail Ridge and then descend to the valley of Peno Creek and surprise and cut off the Indians who used the shelter of the valley as a route of retreat. Then the column along the wood road would push the warriors northeast and force them into a pincer.[50]

Certainly the maneuvers on December 6 began to unfold in this fashion although the events as they developed would taint the plan and tarnish the outcome. In addition, the maneuver, by circumstance, was spontaneous, in response to an attack on a wood train. Thus it took on the usual dimensions of a defensive response to a raid rather than a well-developed and cautiously executed "offensive" against the Indians when they might least expect one, which is what General Cooke would have had in mind when he ordered offensive operations. Still, a semblance of disciplined order was more efficiently organized at the time of this attack. Following a messenger's alarm that the wood train had been attacked by about one hundred or more Indians, Colonel Carrington ordered every horse mounted.[51] According to Pvt. George B. Mackey, on this day the troops did not leave the fort in an unorganized "loose manner," as he later testified they had done before December 6. "There was a regular detail made," he remembered. "The detail was formed on the parade ground, and the officers detailed took command of them in regular order."[52] Carrington ordered thirty to thirty-five troopers of Company C, 2nd Cavalry, under the immediate command of Lieutenant Horatio Bingham and seventeen mounted infantrymen from Company A, 2/18th Infantry, to move west along the wood road, relieve the train, and then turn about-face and push the Indians back over Lodge Trail Ridge where another wing of troops would cut off their escape northward. Carrington placed this "left flank" or western wing, including Bingham's cavalry and the seventeen mounted infantrymen, under the command of Capt. William J. Fetterman, who was now the ranking field captain and commander of Company A. Meanwhile Carrington would personally take charge of the "right flank" or eastern wing of about twenty-four mounted infantrymen along with Lieutenant Grummond and ride northeast around the eastern end of Lodge Trail Ridge and into the Peno Valley to block the Indians' retreat.[53]

Never one to miss a fight, Frederick Brown had already ridden out of the fort, possibly without direct orders, along with two infantrymen, and ascended Pilot Hill to ascertain the extent of the attack. When he saw Fetterman moving out, he rode swiftly back to where the train was corralled and thus was already on the spot as a "volunteer" when Fetterman arrived at the train. Fetterman's column was soon joined by Lieutenant Wands, who had a repeating Henry rifle. Wands was supposed to accompany Carrington but was delayed by changing his saddle to a horse he preferred. When he asked a sentinel outside the fort which way Carrington had gone the picket pointed west, and thus Wands wound up with Fetterman's column, not Carrington's.[54] Fetterman obeyed his orders to the letter and executed them perfectly according to the overall plan. The Indians retreated when they saw the approach of the cavalry and Fetterman pursued them hotly northeastward and stayed on their trail.[55]

Meanwhile Carrington and Grummond proceeded north around the eastern end of Lodge Trail Ridge just west of the Bozeman Trail as planned after breaking through ice at the spot where the Bozeman Trail crossed the Big Piney. Descending to what is now called Massacre Ridge, Carrington spotted about one hundred Indians crossing the Piney just below the north and south tributary forks, followed in hot pursuit by Captain Fetterman, who was executing the maneuver in textbook fashion. Moving north along the ridge to a high point, Carrington spotted thirty-two warriors hidden in the ravines below him. Turning around slightly to the west on the ridge, these Indians fell back before his advance. Carrington then continued north to a crest of the ridge. From that vantage point Carrington looked into the valley and spotted Indians waiting along the west bank of Peno Creek. Fetterman was still in pursuit of the original group of warriors about five miles from where he had begun the chase. These Lakota warriors and their allies were being reinforced either from groups of fighting men hiding in the ravines near Peno Creek or from additional warriors coming upon the scene from the north or east. The Indians in the valley halted, turned, and prepared to make a stand on the west bank of Peno Creek against Fetterman's dogged advance. But when they saw Carrington approaching in their rear from the east they easily envisioned an unfolding envelopment. Quickly they retreated slightly northeastward. Fetterman was now in the valley of Peno Creek.[56]

But Carrington was unable to carry out the plan to attack their rear and complete the envelopment. Although he tried to keep his men together, many of his mounted infantrymen, inexperienced in horsemanship, were strung out along the ridge. The descent into the valley was too slow. Carrington was unable to close on the Indians' rear when they suddenly turned on their attackers approaching from the west. Emboldened by Carrington's failure to complete the envelopment, and perhaps gaining confidence from their numerical superiority, the Indians had turned to attack Fetterman's wing. They made their assault in front of a low hill near Peno Creek. Fetterman later estimated there were about a hundred warriors that came around in a circle from the north and surrounded his command on three sides, probably on the north, west, and south in what Lt. Alfred H. Wands later described as an elongated horseshoe. Used to such combat situations, Fetterman knew, after skirmishing a few moments at this spot, that he would have to try to join Carrington's wing since he was greatly outnumbered by the oncoming warriors. But after moving slightly eastward in an attempt to reach Carrington and the Bozeman Trail, Fetterman, from his next actions, apparently found the task too risky. He ordered his column to halt, dismount, form up in a perimeter, and fight on foot.[57]

At that point things began to go terribly wrong. Instead of halting, dismounting, and fighting on foot, about three-fourths of Lieutenant Bingham's cavalry suddenly and inexplicably bolted away eastward toward the Bozeman Trail. With perhaps what was extremely good fortune in the face of foolishness Bingham's men became scattered below Carrington's position on the ridge. Stunned by Bingham's unexpected action, Fetterman, Brown, and Wands compelled a few of the 2nd Cavalry men to dismount by threatening to shoot them if they disobeyed. "We were then surrounded by about one hundred and fifty Indians," Wands remembered, who "fought us for about three quarters of an hour."[58] "In the most unaccountable manner the cavalry turned and commenced a retreat," Fetterman later reported . . . [With] the Indians corralling and closing in around us, it was plain the retreat [actually a sideward advance to join Carrington's wing], if continued, would be a rout and massacre . . . Lieutenant Bingham while retiring, my party of about fourteen men was left to oppose a hundred Indians."[59] But without panic, Fetterman formed what defensive perimeter he could put together and with Brown and Wands, with his repeating Henry rifle, the officers kept the small body of soldiers focused. By reserving fire until the

Indians came into range Fetterman made sure the little force maintained tactical cohesion and he was thus able to save them from being overrun and destroyed.[60]

Fortunately too for Fetterman the warriors spotted Carrington's column descending the valley, presumably to support Fetterman, and finally broke off the fight. But Fetterman had been unable to push the warriors toward Carrington's column with his small force, which was probably under continuous fire. Carrington spotted Bingham's retreating cavalry and, assuming it was Fetterman's whole command, rushed to the rescue, actually veering slightly south from Fetterman's true position (which he could not see due to the terrain) by about a mile, leaving the little fourteen-man force still stranded. According to Lieutenant Wands, "At the place where the junction was made with Lieutenant Bingham's detachment, we could not be seen. The Indians, seeing the party pass on their right, returned and fought us about fifteen minutes longer, wounding one man and three horses. They then retired."[61] While Fetterman was thus engaged, Carrington was having a time of it himself. Once he had seen Fetterman's party first attacked he had ordered his command down the rough slope of the ridge to attack the Indians and squeeze them between the two forces as planned. But as he descended the slope toward the upper branches of Peno Creek he discovered fifteen of Bingham's frightened cavalrymen dismounted and huddled together in a ravine and without an officer. He angrily ordered them to mount and follow him at a gallop. Most did not, remaining in the ravine, thoroughly demoralized. By now Carrington's force was so strung out on the ridge that a large force of warriors attacked him in attempt to cut off his forces from Fetterman below. Carrington and six men found themselves cut off from the rest of the column. A young 2nd Cavalry bugler, Adolph Metzger, who had linked up with Carrington presumably from Bingham's bolting troopers, informed the commander that Lieutenant Bingham and several of his men had gone around a hill to the east, to the left of Carrington's men. Suddenly the Indians met the head of Carrington's column and charged it. Private McGuire fell wounded with his horse on top of him. Carrington dismounted his little force, still slightly separated from the bulk of the column, and kept up a hot fire on the Indians. Carrington personally claimed he emptied a saddle of one Indian "with a single shot."[62]

At this juncture the stragglers appeared and united with Carrington's column, and the Indians, about one hundred in number, broke off the engagement and rode northeastward down the valley. But Carrington's inept horsemen could not get around them and force them back upon Fetterman's little detachment. Even if he could have turned them, with the defection of Bingham's cavalry, Fetterman's fourteen-man force would have been inadequate to check the warriors. So the Indians escaped northeast and rode back toward their camps. This ended the only offensive combat action of Col. Henry Carrington's military career. He had not brought about disaster to his command but he had not achieved envelopment. It is highly likely that he would not have been able to do so even if Bingham's cavalry had held their position with Fetterman because of his slow-moving mounted infantrymen. Carrington's scattered wing reassembled west of the Bozeman Trail and about twenty minutes later Fetterman came up and joined him. But Lieutenant Bingham and a few of his cavalrymen were nowhere to be found. The joint columns immediately started off to find Bingham and what troopers remained with him.[63]

Soon Bingham came in sight down the road seemingly to join Carrington and some of his men closed ranks with the column. But Bingham himself and several other troopers did not. Without reporting to Carrington, Lieutenant Bingham beckoned to Lieutenant Grummond to break ranks and join his small group in a chase of a small group of warriors that appeared to be retreating. Without asking permission of his commanding officer, Grummond alone bolted the column and joined Bingham. Carrington shouted for him to return, then sent an orderly to bring him back, but the soldier could not catch up to Grummond as he and Bingham galloped off toward a body of retreating warriors. The two officers with about three or four men pursued the retreating Indians and Bingham wounded the horse of one. This lone warrior took to his heels and Bingham and Grummond chased after him. According to Dr. C. M. Hines, Bingham and Grummond were armed only with revolvers. Bingham, after losing one pistol in the chase, "and after firing the other, so excited did he become that he threw it away," a seemingly unwise move until we consider that, according to Pvt. George B. Mackey, both Bingham and Grummond had foolishly left the fort with no ammunition other than the loads in their revolvers.[64] Suddenly the little group saw two large parties of warriors flanking them on both sides in precision fashion. Clearly the initial group of retreating Indians had been decoys.

According to Hines, Grummond and the cavalry troopers drew their sabers and "laid about them right and left."[65]

But the warriors closed in and tried to pull the soldiers off their horses by lassoing them with their bows. Later Grummond told Sergeant Fessenden that in the hand-to-hand combat he "shut his eyes and literally slashed his way out, as did others. Grummond said he could hear his saber 'click' every time he cleaved an Indian's skull."[66] "Lieutenant Grummond ran [directly] against the Indians," Dr. Hines remembered Grummond's telling him, "and [by] cutting right and left with his sword, got through with the balance. After a while they were surrounded again by a large[r] number of Indians . . . they halted, and Lieutenant Grummond then told the rest to follow him."[67] All made it through save two. Sgt. Gideon Bowers turned to fire at his pursuers. As his horse slowed, the Indians overtook him and put an arrow in him and then split open his skull above the eyes. He lived in agony for a short time but eventually died. Pvt. John Donovan, armed with a Colt revolver, was able to escape a close call at the last moment by shooting two warriors who attempted to pull him from his horse.[68] One other was missing, Lt. Horatio Bingham. Later Grummond would explain that while he and the men were slashing their way through the Indians, Bingham had been cut off from the others and killed.[69]

As Carrington and Fetterman rode northeastward to find Bingham, Grummond, and the other missing men, Lieutenant Grummond and three troopers suddenly came riding up a ravine, still hotly pursued by warriors who broke off as the beleaguered Grummond entered the ranks of the main force. His adrenaline flowing, Grummond was in a rage. Demonstrating behavior bordering on insubordination, Grummond hotly asked his colonel "if he was a fool or a coward to allow his men to be cut to pieces without offering help."[70] Once Grummond cooled off, the command began the search for Bowers and Bingham. They found Bowers first, and although a messenger brought an ambulance from the fort, Bowers did not make it back alive. After an hour of searching the command found the body of Lt. Horatio Bingham a little east of the Bozeman Trail, along a ridge in the brush, a bullet in his brain and "shot with over fifty arrows." The body was lying over an old tree stump.[71] The confused fight of December 6 was finished. Carrington reported the Indians lost about ten warriors dead with many more wounded. The garrison of Fort Phil Kearny had lost Lieutenant Bingham, 2nd Cavalry,

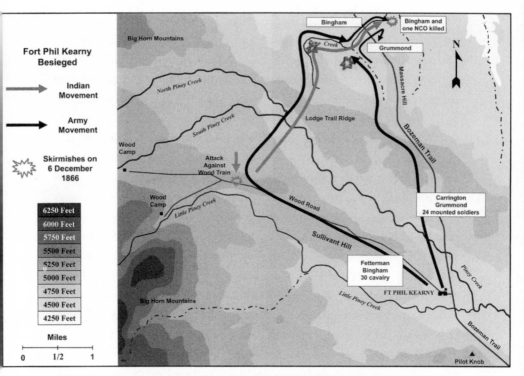

"The Fight of December 6, 1866." Charles D. Collins Jr., *Atlas of the Sioux Wars*, 2nd ed. (Fort Leavenworth, KS: Combat Studies Institute Press, 2006).

and Sergeant Bowers, Company E, 2/18th Infantry, killed; Sergeant Aldridge, 2nd Cavalry, wounded; Private McGuire and three other unnamed privates, wounded. Three horses had been killed and five wounded.[72] According to oral tradition, the man who had led the main attacks on Fetterman and Carrington was the Oglala Yellow Eagle, the son of a tiyospaye headman.[73]

The command reentered the gate of Fort Phil Kearny on that cold December night with their two dead about 7:00 PM after six hours in the field. Apparent to all was that, as an "offensive" maneuver, the fight had resulted in an Indian victory. The two columns had not been able to complete envelopment. The causes for that failure were obvious to many at the time although Carrington's slow-moving column probably would never have been able to close on the rear of the Indians. How could a seasoned combat officer like Lieutenant Bingham, a soldier who had suffered wounds at Antietam—the bloodiest day in American history—do such a thing as to abandon his immediate commander, Captain Fetterman, leaving him with only fourteen men to face more than one hundred warriors, only to reappear a little later and persuade Grummond to break ranks and join him in pursuit of Indians? Fetterman remained relatively composed over the mystery. "I cannot account for this movement on the part of an officer of such unquestionable gallantry as Lieutenant Bingham," he wrote in his report.[74]

Was Bingham's defection due to a lack of experience fighting Indians? Fetterman detractors have likewise used the action to assert that Fetterman was too incompetent a commander to maintain tactical cohesion.[75] Both assessments are too generalized and oversimplified. Regardless of what enemy was at hand, an experienced officer like Horatio Bingham was not likely to take his troopers and desert his immediate commander under heavy fire and leave him to greet the enemy with only fourteen men, certainly not when two others, Wands and Brown, were bravely standing their ground with Fetterman as ordered. One cavalryman offered testimony that at the time the Indians attacked Fetterman's column, the sudden halt caused Bingham's horse to bolt and "run away with him and he could not restrain him [the horse]."[76] His men followed his lead. This possibility is not unlikely. The year before, to relate one of the more famous incidents of this kind, a rambunctious mount had carried Lt. Caspar Collins to his death within the Indian lines at the Battle of Platte Bridge and a decade later another frightened horse would stampede 7th Cavalryman Pvt. James Turley to the same fate at the lower end of the Lakota village during Major Marcos Reno's "valley fight" at the onset of the Battle of Little Bighorn. Another possible scenario is that some of Bingham's raw recruits may have panicked and the lieutenant went with them to lead them away from possible destruction, a possibility preferred by Captain Fetterman himself in his report. "It is presumed that being unable to prevent retreat of his men," Fetterman wrote, "he deemed it most prudent to hold his men in hand as much as possible, and fall back on the mounted infantry [Carrington's wing] who were expected on the road."[77] The likelihood of this event is supported by Wands, whose testimony related how he, Fetterman, and Brown had kept several of Bingham's men from bolting by threatening to shoot them if they did not dismount. In either case the bolting of the cavalry occurred so suddenly and with such surprise that it is to Fetterman's credit that he, Brown, and Wands were even able to restrain *any* of Bingham's troopers from bolting in panic. In any event, in death, Lieutenant

Bingham was never accused of cowardice or deserting his comrades in the face of the enemy by Colonel Carrington or any of the other officers at Fort Phil Kearny, and that judgment is most likely correct.[78]

Even so, despite being outnumbered, the maneuver might have had a better chance of success if Bingham's cavalry had not bolted from their position and been able to take a stand with Fetterman's wing as properly ordered. Could Bingham have rallied his troopers and brought them back to Fetterman's line or was he cut off and felt it more appropriate at that point to find Carrington's wing quickly and bring them into the Indians as Fetterman assumed in his report? We shall never know for certain, but Bingham's failure to do either incurred the wrath of Lt. A. H. Wands, who insisted that because of Bingham's actions the Indians gained the confidence they needed to defeat the entire command at Fort Phil Kearny. "I consider the conduct of the cavalry on that day, disgraceful," he stated to the Sanborn Commission after the Fetterman fight, "and of such character as to induce the belief on the part of the Indians, that they could overcome the garrison or any party from the garrison, in an open fight."[79] Albeit after the fact (Fetterman's annihilation), Wands's assessment of the situation was not far from wrong.

Questions like these had to plague the minds of the officers at Fort Phil Kearny as exhaustion overcame them in their quarters on the night of December 6, 1866, realizing what a close call they had had with the Lakotas that day. Fetterman personally wrote a letter of condolence to Lieutenant Bingham's sister Stella in St. Charles, Minnesota, and spoke of how highly regarded her brother was with the men of the garrison.[80] The battle seemed to have made a sobering impression on Fetterman and even Margaret Carrington noted it as such when he came to the colonel's office to submit his report of the fight. "Captain Fetterman has been in," she wrote, "and says 'he has learned a lesson, and that this Indian war has become a hand-to-hand fight, requiring the utmost caution,' and he wants no more such risks"—certainly not a statement reflecting an impatient, tempestuous, and arrogant officer with no sense of pragmatism as Fetterman has been so often portrayed.[81] Carrington praised Fetterman in his official report, stating that Fetterman "knew little of the country, but carried out his instruction promptly. Captain Brown who accidentally joined him knew the ground, and as a result [it] would have been a good fight if he had retained Lieutenant Bingham's command."[82] That Fetterman obeyed his orders in this fight while others did not is certain despite efforts by modern writers to portray him as impetuous during the action and to conclude that the fight portended similar behavior on December 21. According to historian Charles D. Collins Jr. of the Combat Studies Institute at Fort Leavenworth, "On 6 December 1866 . . . Lieutenants Bingham and Grummond disobeyed orders and pursued Indian decoy parties into an ambush that resulted in the death of Bingham and one noncommissioned officer. Only the stern discipline and timely action taken by Captain Fetterman who advanced toward the sounds of the guns prevented a larger tragedy on that day."[83]

Only the impetuous Capt. Frederick Brown seemed to be unfazed by the fight. Vaughn asserts that with Brown as spokesman, several officers requested of Carrington after the fight to be allowed to take forty mounted infantry and sixty civilians to assault the Indian camps on the Tongue River. Vaughn is likely mistaken. This plan is almost certainly the one made a couple days after Fetterman's arrival at Fort Phil Kearny *before* the fight on December 6. By that date it is reasonable to assume that any and all officers at the fort would have realized the folly of such action.[84] Carrington later testified before the Sanborn Commission that Captain Brown's clerk, H. Shiebe, was willing to testify that Fetterman and Brown had "previously" planned to be out of the fort in considerable force.[85] The reference to "previous" plans to move against the Indians, however, likely referred to earlier talk as no original records support such reckless plans following the sobering realizations Fetterman had experienced with the fight of December 6. Again, Brown's urgent aspiration to take a scalp before he reported to Fort Laramie in accordance with his transfer may have been another matter.

The most interesting behavior of all the officers during and after the fight of December 6 is that of Lt. George Washington Grummond. The only officer in the fight that day that original sources can support both willingly and purposefully violated direct orders during the fight was Grummond. Without authority he bolted Carrington's column to join Bingham and defied attempts to compel him to return to the column when ordered to do so. He, along with Bingham, was pulled into a classic decoy maneuver that cost the lives of Lieutenant Bingham and Sergeant Bowers. Only by fierce hand-to-hand combat was Grummond able to personally escape death. Later he loudly condemned his commanding officer, Colonel Carrington, in front of his troops for not coming to his support at a point in time when the reunited columns of Carrington and Fetterman likely did not even know exactly where he was. Indeed Grummond's irrational behavior on December 6 was in line with such bizarre actions as he had displayed in combat during the Civil War, especially his near lethal orders issued on the heights of Kennesaw Mountain two years previously. That behavior had been just one of the several rash exhibitions that prompted Grummond's court-martial in 1864 along with allegations by his subordinates that he was unfit for command. The impulse to follow his own irresponsible course with almost suicidal consequences, in both the Civil War and on December 6, the ferocity of his saber combat that ultimately saved his life, and his uncontrolled and insubordinate public display of rage at his commander afterward are more suggestive of irrational behavior than anything exhibited that day by Capt. William J. Fetterman.[86]

Like Fetterman, had Grummond "learned a lesson" on December 6? After he returned to his quarters that night Grummond's emotions were still at a high pitch. He related to his wife how he had "abandoned the use of spurs and jammed his sword into [his horse] to urge him to greater effort." He told Frances how he was followed "by the chief [?], in full war dress, with spear at his back so near that but for his good horse he would then and there have met a terrible fate."[87] But soon Grummond grew pensive, reflecting a somber temperament, perhaps just as intense as his aggressive personality, a persona that Margaret Carrington later described as charming but was in actuality more emotionally dysfunctional. George W. Grummond's wife, Frances, remembered:

> I was to learn from my husband['s] own lips, The dreadful story of the experience that nearly cost him his life. How I endured the shock I don't know, but in mercy I seemed to be paralyzed for the time and [then] we both sat for a long time in silence, then mingled our tears in gratitude for the wonderful deliverance.[88]

Lieutenant Bingham and Sergeant Bowers were buried in the post cemetery on December 9. Bingham received full Masonic honors. Captain Brown placed his own Army of the Cumberland badge on Bowers's body. They had fought together in the Civil War. Chaplain White performed the funeral. Then the wooden coffins, lined with metal to protect the corpses from wolves, were lowered into the graves. Margaret Carrington later reflected on the funerals. "Thus our cemetery fills up with only victims of violence!" she wrote. "Sometimes it seems as if nobody cared if we had help or not."[89]

Later that day a mail escort left for Fort Laramie. With the escort were Lieutenant William Bisbee and his wife and son, off to a new assignment with department headquarters in Omaha, an assignment that would later prove fateful for Henry Carrington. He was replaced as post adjutant by Lieutenant Wilbur F. Arnold. The Fort Laramie detail carried a pleading dispatch from Colonel Carrington along with the reports of the fight on December 6. "I need mittens for the men," Carrington wrote. "I need every officer I can get. The cavalry has none. There are but six [officers] for six companies including staff . . . This is all wrong. There is much at stake; I will take my full share, but two officers to a company is small allowance enough, with mercury at zero and active operations on hand." Carrington too had learned a lesson on December 6. He began vigorously drilling his raw troops. Fetterman drilled the infantry while Grummond was given charge of the mounted infantry and cavalry with orders to keep fifty horses saddled and ready at all time from dawn to dusk.[90]

The Lakotas were licking their wounds also. They and their allies were quiet for a time following the fight of December 6. But Carrington had to be worried. Jim Bridger told him he had to train his troops better to fight Indians.[91] The drills intensified. Finally on December 19 another wood train was attacked and Carrington sent Major Powell to relieve it with strict orders to "heed the lessons of the 6th." Powell drove off the Indians without pursuing them over Lodge Trail Ridge. The following evening, December 20, a rather compulsively impatient and ridiculous looking Capt. Frederick Brown visited the Carringtons. "Only the night before the [Fetterman] massacre he [Brown] made a call," Margaret remembered, "with spurs fastened in the button-holes of his coat, leggings wrapped, and two revolvers accessible, declaring, by way of explanation, that he was ready by day and night, and must have one scalp before leaving for [Fort] Laramie, to which place he had been posted."[92] The next morning Brown would have his chance. There is no record suggesting that Carrington was particularly concerned with the well-being of any of his officers that night, or with their abilities to do their duties. But if he were, his concerns would not have been with Capt. William J. Fetterman but rather with Lt. George Washington Grummond.[93]

CHAPTER 7

WHERE A HUNDRED SOLDIERS WERE KILLED

> The horse-chase ended. Once again the wave
> Began to mount the steep on the other side,
> While warriors hailed their fellows and replied:
> Be ready!—We are ready, brothers!
>   Then
> The hillsides bellowed with a surf of men
> Flung crowding on the boulders. 'Twas the end.[1]

SOMETIME DURING THE FRIGID THIRD WEEK OF DECEMBER 1866 three young Northern Cheyenne warriors, White Elk, Plenty Camps, and Rolling Bull, decided to ride west from their villages on Muddy Creek to make a raid on the Shoshonis. White Elk was the youngest of the three friends, then in his late teens. They were determined to travel below Fort Phil Kearny to the head of Powder River and then go into the mountains. But along the way they met four Cheyennes who were returning to camp who warned them to stay away from the fort as they had been mistaken for a war party by the soldiers near there and had been fired upon. The three young men couldn't decide what to do. They made camp and stayed in it for a couple of days. Besides, it was the beginning of the cold season. On the morning of the second day White Elk heard people singing in the distance. Soon four Lakotas rode into sight. Rolling Bull, who could speak Lakota, ascertained their purpose. They were messengers from a large group headed to the Cheyenne camps to ask the Cheyennes to join the Lakotas in trying to draw soldiers from Fort Phil Kearny and destroy them. Soon the entire group of Lakotas, men, women, and children, appeared and White Elk and his companions decided to go to the Cheyenne camps with them. A number of Cheyennes, including White Elk, agreed to join the Lakotas in a proposed decoy maneuver against the soldier fort. The next morning the combined force moved up toward Peno Creek, which the Indians called Crow Standing Off Creek. This was probably December 20 but possibly the nineteenth.[2] White Elk would survive the impending battle to tell its story years later to George Bird Grinnell.

Although Oglalas had been considering the idea for some time, the initial organization and subsequent plan to send a large number of warriors against Fort Phil Kearny in December was basically an inspiration of the Miniconjous. Indeed, the Indians had become better organized since summer. A large number of Miniconjous were camped on Tongue River in December under chiefs Brave Bear, Makes Room, White Hollow Horn, One Horn, and Black Shield, as well as brave war leaders like High Backbone. They had already sent the war pipe to Red Cloud and Man Afraid of His Horse and the Oglalas, many of whom decided to join them, including Blue Horse, Pawnee Killer, American Horse, and possibly the young Crazy Horse and his close friend He Dog. There is no direct evidence that Man Afraid of His Horse or his son personally joined the fray but many of his warriors did.[3] The attack was to be a special one to honor the dying wish of a Miniconjou chief named White Swan who hated the whites because some white men had allegedly once looted his tepee. As White Swan lay dying he had urged these other chiefs to make all-out war on the whites. Some Arapahos under Black Coal and Eagle Head too had pledged to comply with White Swan's dying wish.[4] Although the Northern Cheyennes were still divided, the Sweet Medicine Chief, Little Wolf, along with Two Moon and Box Elder, finally decided for war.[5] Consequently they moved their followers over to the Lakota camps on Tongue River. Dull Knife may have been with them but probably did not participate in the Fetterman fight as he still stood for peace. In preparation for the battle to come the Cheyenne fighting men were inspired by Crazy Mule, a highly respected warrior who demonstrated his bulletproof power by allowing people to shoot at him with bullets and arrows that left him unscathed.[6]

As the Cheyennes joined the Lakotas in their camps the number of fighting men swelled. White Bull remembered years later that "the Miniconjou and Cheyennes were more than a thousand men, and besides these there were the numerous Oglala." Two Moon claimed there were over a thousand Lakotas not counting the Cheyennes and Arapahos and White Elk recalled that there were a good many Cheyennes and Arapahos, with three times as many Lakotas. White Elk claimed there "were more men than in the Custer fight."[7] Among the Cheyennes were warriors of two principal soldier societies. The Crazy Dogs was one of these, led by the bulletproof Crazy Mule. But the Fetterman fight saw the rise of the Elkhorn Scrapers as a famed military unit under the leadership of Little Wolf. Among the Elks were Little Wolf's brother Big Nose, Medicine Wolf, and Wild Hog (Hog), who would gain notoriety in 1878–79 during the great Northern Cheyenne odyssey north from Indian Territory to their homelands in Montana, the seminal event in Northern Cheyenne history.[8]

Finally the great war party leveled out on a plain not far from the forks of Peno Creek where they made camp on December 20. Sometime that day the Lakotas went up the right-hand or north fork of the creek and formed a long line. There near the banks of the frozen water they made their ceremonial preparation for the attack to come the next day. For large military movements the Lakotas sometimes consulted the spiritual power of a w*inkte*, or *berdache*, often called a "half-man half-woman," to hopefully foresee the outcome of the ensuing battle. The Cheyennes too placed faith in the clairvoyant powers of these transgendered persons, calling them *Heemanah*.[9] Soon the winkte pushed out from the Lakota line. He wore a woman's dress and his head was covered by a black cloth. According to White Elk he was riding a sorrel horse and blew on an eagle bone whistle as he zigzagged through the hills seeking a vision. Several times he returned having foreseen various numbers of dead soldiers. White Elk remembered him asking the chiefs on one of his rides back to the line: "I have ten men, five men in each hand. Do you want them?" "No, we do not want them," replied the chiefs. "Look at all these people here. Do you think that ten men are enough to go around?" Several times more the winkte rode into the hills and ravines. Finally he returned, falling off his horse as if from great weight in his hands. "Answer me quickly," he asked the chiefs. "I have a hundred or more." According to White Elk great shouts went up from the warriors and many jumped off their horses and began beating the ground with their coup sticks. And so the ensuing battle would find its name, "Where a hundred soldiers were killed [slain]," or "Hundred in the hand."[10]

During the journey to the place of ambush the Miniconjou White Bull remembered that the weather was very cold. He wore a buffalo robe with the hair turned in that he had fastened around his waist with a belt. He carried a red four-point "Nor'west" blanket. His weapons included a bow and quiver with forty arrows as well as a war lance. His father had made the iron arrow points from a frying pan.[11] Previous raiders around Fort Phil Kearny had constructed shelters along the route from the villages on Tongue River to Peno Creek. White Bull remembered they consisted of willow poles placed in a circle and covered with brush and sometimes horse blankets. A fire could be built in the middle and the crude shelters could sleep ten men and keep them safe from the elements.[12]

The plan the chiefs had outlined a few days before was simple. Warriors would be concealed in the gullies north of Lodge Trail Ridge on both the east and west sides of the Bozeman Trail while about forty warriors would feint on the wood train making its daily run to the pineries and then lure the relief party that would be sent out from the fort northeastward toward Lodge Trail Ridge to intercept them behind the ridge. Ten hand-picked decoys would lead these soldiers over Lodge Trail Ridge and into the hands of the many warriors waiting in ambush on the other side. Most of the Indians carried bows, there being only a few old muzzle-loading rifles among them. The Lakota Wolf Tooth told his grandson years later that during this time his people had strong bows reinforced with parts of buffalo horn tied to each end that gave the bow more range and velocity. Wolf Tooth also claimed that bows were the weapons of choice in the winter because the warriors would not have to handle the cold iron parts of guns with their bare hands.[13] On the night of December 20, according to White Elk, the Lakota chiefs and war leaders (probably High Backbone, Black Leg, and Black Shield) chose ten decoys to spring the trap. There were two Cheyennes, two Arapahos, two Oglalas, two Miniconjous, and two from other Lakota bands.[14]

Only White Elk gives us knowledge of who the decoys may have been for the Northern Cheyennes. He claims that Little Wolf and Wolf Left Hand were chosen from among the Northern Cheyenne contingent. But Little Wolf, eager to make up to his brother Big Nose following a personal squabble among the siblings, rode over to Big Nose and said, "Brother, I have been called to go and attack the post; take my horse and do you go." But Big Nose was still angry with Little Wolf and replied, "Take back your horse; I do not want him." The chief Bull Hump, eager to mediate the bad feeling between the brothers, told Big Nose, "My friend, here are my moccasins and my war clothes. If you have any bad feeling you may have those clothes to lie [be killed] in." Big Nose accepted the war clothes and agreed to go. It was a great honor to be selected as a decoy.[15]

The only Lakota eyewitness account of who their decoys might have been is that of American Horse, who told Eli S. Ricker in 1905 that he was one of the Oglala decoys.[16] George W. Colhoff, a clerk who had once been stationed at Fort Laramie in 1865 as a member of the 5th U.S. Infantry ("Galvanized Yankees"), told Eli S. Ricker in about 1906 that Sword (Sword Owner), son of Oglala Chief Brave Bear, was chosen leader of the decoys. But this claim, of course, is secondhand.[17] Despite a claim by Hyde and imaginative narrative among writers of secondary sources and latter-day oral tradition, there are simply no original Indian accounts that name Crazy Horse as a decoy in the Fetterman fight. White Bull and others simply recorded that Crazy Horse was coming into his own at this time as a war leader of the Oglalas, inferring logically that he was probably in the fight, but no eyewitnesses claim that he was a decoy.[18]

What role Red Cloud may have played in planning the attack is conflicting. Given his influence he may very well have been involved. Support for Red Cloud's presence during the Fetterman fight comes from Hyde and James Cook. "His [Red Cloud's] own band, the Bad Faces, were present," Hyde wrote, "and the old men of his band contend today that Red Cloud was among the leaders."[19] Capt. James H. Cook of Agate Springs, Nebraska, the closest white friend Red Cloud ever had, declared that Red Cloud often spoke to him of being in the Fetterman fight and that "many Oglalas confirmed Red Cloud's statements."[20] The most compelling evidence that Red Cloud was present with Oglalas at the Fetterman fight observing the action in the west ravine is a statement by Big White Horse and White Face in 1903 that they "saw him there" during the battle.[21]

The morning of December 21 dawned bitterly cold but sunny. At daybreak a contingent of between 1,500 and 2,000 warriors assembled near the forks of Peno Creek. According to most accounts the Miniconjous, with their chief, Black Shield, were in charge of the day's activities. The steaming breath of the horses and so many men in the cold December air made for a tremendous sight. As guests of the Lakotas the Cheyennes were given a choice of which side of what is now called Massacre Ridge they would like to hide their warriors. They chose the gullies on the upper or west side of the road. The Arapahos joined them. Most of the Oglalas also chose the west side lower down the ridge. Some were on foot and hid in the brush at the lower (north) end of the ridge where it started to flatten out along Peno Creek. The warriors who were mounted rode southward up the ridge and took their positions. The numerous Miniconjous took positions about a quarter-mile or more from the road and east of the ridge. They hid themselves and their ponies in gullies between two smaller ridges that kept them well concealed from soldiers advancing along the road. As they waited in silence the air grew colder in the early morning hours. Crusted snow clung along the sides of the gullies and was visibly deep in elongated wind-blown drifts on the top of the ridge. The trap was set.[22]

Several Lakota chiefs, probably including Black Shield and Black Leg, positioned themselves high on either Lodge Trail Ridge or Sullivant Hills in view of the fort to await any actions by the soldiers. Little Wolf and Red Cloud possibly positioned themselves nearby to observe while allowing younger warriors the chance to attain war honors. The Indians waited until about 10:00 AM when they saw a wood train leave the fort. The woodcutting detail that morning was under the command of Corporal Legrow of E Company, 2/18th Infantry. Civilian contractors and escort troops together numbered about ninety men. When the watching chiefs saw the detail head west toward the pineries, they sent a party of forty warriors to attack them. About the same time a couple of soldiers in front of the fort saw the chiefs on the hillside and waved at them to go away. The chiefs assumed the soldiers wanted to eat their breakfast in peace. But Lakotas signed back to them in defiance that they would get their bellies full of fighting on this day.[23] By eleven o'clock the lookout on Pilot Hill signaled that the wood train was corralled and under attack. But as was the intention the feint did not last long. The attackers broke off the assault within minutes. The chiefs, wrapped in red blankets, moved closer but still out of rifle range. It was then they sent in four of the decoys on the northeast side of Big Piney Creek. As the Indians heard the sound of bugles two soldiers distinctly heard one of the decoys shout at the garrison in English, "You sons of bitches come out and fight us."[24] Carrington replied with three shots from a twelve-pound howitzer that flushed out a number of warriors from the rocks. The warriors withdrew and took up a position on Lodge Trail Ridge but still in sight of the fort.[25]

Soon the Indians spotted infantry from the fort starting toward the Bozeman Trail leading up Lodge Trail Ridge. The infantry were soon joined by a detachment of cavalry and two civilian riders, eighty-one men in all. The chiefs committed the rest of the decoys. The decoys knew exactly what to do. White Bull, hidden in a draw on the east side of Massacre Ridge with his fellow Miniconjous, heard shots from the top of Lodge Trail Ridge to the southwest as the decoys rode toward the troops at a gallop and then pulled back, taunting the whites all the while to come after them. Soon White Bull spotted the decoys at the top of the ridge scampering back and forth across the Bozeman Trail, shooting at the soldiers as if they were trying to protect the escape of an injured man behind them.[26] On the west side the Northern Cheyenne warrior White Elk also witnessed the antics of the decoys. Years later he remembered seeing Big Nose, astride a black war horse, ride back and forth across the ridge in front of the soldiers, "seeming to fight them, and they were shooting at him as hard as they could. It looked as if Big Nose was trying to fight and hold back the soldiers in order to help someone ahead of him get away," White Elk remembered.[27] Soon the soldiers appeared at the top of the ridge. According to all pertinent Indian sources, the cavalry was out ahead of the infantry on the flanks. As Big Nose started down the ridge the troops stopped and Big Nose "charged back" directly at the soldiers, White Elk remembered, "and seemed to go among the soldiers so that he was lost to sight" over the ridge.[28]

Hiding in the gullies north of Lodge Trail Ridge on either side of the Bozeman Trail perhaps two thousand warriors lay in wait, readying their weapons.[29] A little farther down the road the Oglalas could now see the soldiers advancing over the Lodge Trail Ridge. The Oglala warrior Fire Thunder remembered:

> After a long while we heard a shot up over the hill, and We knew the soldiers were coming. So we held the noses of our ponies so that they might not whinny at the soldiers' horses. Soon we saw our men [decoys] coming back, and some of them were walking and leading their horses, so that the soldiers would think they were worn out. Then the men we had sent ahead came running down the road between us, and the soldiers on horseback followed, shooting.[30]

By the time the soldiers went over the top of Lodge Trail Ridge they were out of sight of Fort Phil Kearny. Summarily, at this point, white eyewitness

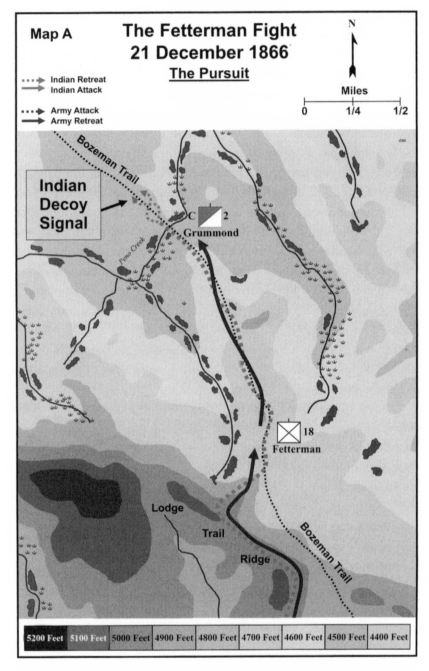

"The Fetterman Fight, 21 December 1866. *The Pursuit*." Charles D. Collins Jr., *Atlas of the Sioux Wars*, 2nd ed. (Fort Leavenworth, KS: Combat Studies Institute Press, 2006).

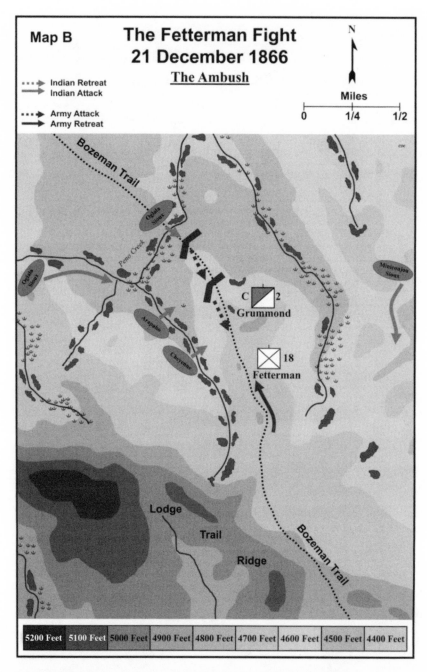

"The Fetterman Fight, 21 December 1866. *The Ambush*." Charles D. Collins Jr., *Atlas of the Sioux Wars*, 2nd ed. (Fort Leavenworth, KS: Combat Studies Institute Press, 2006).

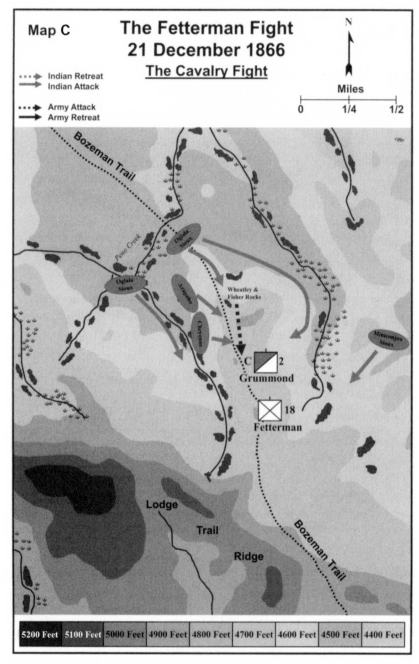

"The Fetterman Fight, 21 December 1866. *The Cavalry Fight*." Charles D. Collins Jr., *Atlas of the Sioux Wars*, 2nd ed. (Fort Leavenworth, KS: Combat Studies Institute Press, 2006).

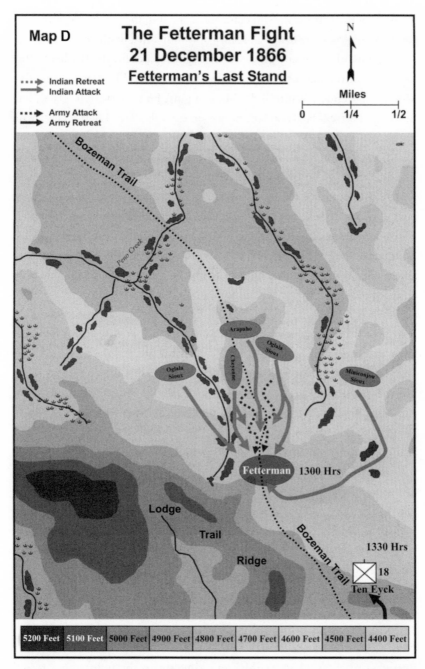

"The Fetterman Fight, 21 December 1866. *Fetterman's Last Stand.*" Charles D. Collins Jr., *Atlas of the Sioux Wars*, 2nd ed. (Fort Leavenworth, KS: Combat Studies Institute Press, 2006).

accounts of the Fetterman fight come to an end. On the north side of the gun smoke along Massacre Ridge all identifiable individual firsthand accounts are Indian, more than for any other western fights except for the Battle of Little Bighorn and the massacre at Wounded Knee. White Elk (Cheyenne), Two Moon (Cheyenne), White Bull (Miniconjou), Fire Thunder (Oglala), and American Horse (Oglala) are primary sources while Black Elk (Oglala), Wolf Tooth (Cheyenne), Wooden Leg (Cheyenne), and Michael Boyer (mixed-blood) while contemporaneous are secondhand accounts as none of these men was actually in the fight. They heard details directly from those who were present. Although the reminiscences of these warriors are filtered through the pens of white ethnologists and chroniclers and latter-day Indian descendants who interviewed them (Grinnell, Bent/Hyde, Campbell, Neihardt, Ricker, Marquis, Stands In Timber/Liberty), all their stories of the fight are remarkably similar as to the major points of action. Slightly different perceptions do arise depending on what geographical point each primary informant personally engaged in along the ridge. But one agreement they all have in common is that the decoy attack on December 21 came together well. It was immaculately executed, and likely constituted the most successful decoy maneuver in the history of Indian military conflict with the United States in the West. The idea persists to this day that the plains Indians always fought individually, as an unorganized group, charging in on the enemy in quick strikes in attempts to achieve individual glory, and then sharply retreating only to once again repeat the maneuver. Certainly once a battle was joined this was often the case. But according to ethnologist E. Adamson Hoebel, who studied Cheyenne ways extensively, "The tactics of attack and battle are carefully planned by the leaders . . . [and] the enterprise is policed; scouts who slip in such a way are beaten [by the police or akicita in the case of the Lakotas] just as though they had broken the rules of the communal hunt. When [the plans] are faithfully carried out [they] often result in a successful clash."[31] Certainly the Fetterman fight is a masterful example of Hoebel's observations.

▼▼▼

But what of the soldiers at this same time up to the point they crossed over Lodge Trail Ridge and out of sight of the fort? Unlike the Indians accounts, the whites' testimonials of what transpired in the few minutes

between the attack on the wood train and Fetterman's disappearance over
Lodge Trail Ridge are somewhat contradictory. Immediately following the
bugle call signaling the attack on the wood train, Colonel Carrington organized a relief party, the largest sent out from the fort to date. Officially he
reported in January 1867 that he gave the task to Capt. James Powell but
that Fetterman claimed the right through seniority. "Upon tendering to . . .
Powell the command of Company C, U.S. Cavalry, then without an officer
[Bingham was dead], but which he had been drilling," Carrington wrote,
"Brevet Lieutenant-Colonel Fetterman claimed, by rank, to go out. I acqui-
esced, giving him the men of his own company [A], that were [fit] for duty,
and a portion of Company C, 2nd Battalion, 18th Infantry."[32] Fetterman
received twenty-one men from Company A, nine from Company C,
six from Company E, and thirteen from Company H, all 2/18th Infantry.
Carrington inspected the men in front of his headquarters and mounted a
guard, appointing Lieutenant Wands the officer of the day.[33]

Carrington's first wife, Margaret, and later his second wife, Frances
Grummond Carrington, writing from their husband's official report and
trying to guard Henry's reputation, supported the assertion that Fetterman
claimed the command role through his seniority. Captain Powell, however,
testified later before the Sanborn Commission that the command was given
directly to Fetterman. Sergeant Fessenden, who probably did not hear the
order, stated in his memoir years later that "Fetterman offered his services."
Lieutenant A. H. Wands, the officer of the day and who surely was present, never mentioned that Carrington originally selected Powell to lead the
detachment.[34] A few minutes later Lieutenant Grummond requested to take
command of the cavalry. "Lieutenant Grummond, who had commanded the
mounted infantry," Carrington reported in 1867, "requested to take out the
cavalry. He did so."[35] Carrington possibly had mixed feelings. Grummond's
insubordination and disobedience at the December 6 fight had embarrassed
him. Why then, if Carrington's assertions are true in his official report of
January 1867, did he offer the *reliable* Powell command of Company C of
the 2nd Cavalry, then after taking that command decision away from him
and giving it to Fetterman with the infantry companies, turn around and
give Company C, 2nd Cavalry to the *unreliable* Grummond? Why not
retain the cavalry with Powell as originally ordered, only under Fetterman's
overall immediate command, and hold Grummond at the fort? Carrington's

assertions in his official report, written when he was under scrutiny by the high command, are somewhat baffling and suspicious.

Carrington stated in his official report that he gave Fetterman explicit orders: "Support the wood train, relieve it, and report to me. Do not engage or pursue Indians at its expense; under no circumstances pursue over the ridge, namely, Lodge Trail Ridge."[36] Both Margaret Carrington and Frances Grummond Carrington meticulously emphasized these orders in their respective books and Frances stated that she was outside her quarters and heard Carrington give these specific orders to Fetterman.[37] Other eyewitnesses made the same claim. Sergeant Fessenden remembered Carrington's simply stating to Fetterman: "go out and bring in the wood train." Captain Powell testified before the Sanborn Commission that he saw Carrington in conversation with Fetterman but did not hear what he had said.[38] In an article written in 2004, historian Shannon Smith Calitri asserts that except for Frances Grummond Carrington's later claim that she was present when Carrington gave the orders no one actually heard what Colonel Carrington said to Fetterman. Still, he had issued the same instructions to Powell two days before and several others at the fort including Surgeon Hines, Lieutenant Wands, Sgt. Alexander Brown (who was standing beside Carrington when Fetterman received the orders), and others at least inferred at a later date that Fetterman disobeyed Carrington's orders.[39] Vaughn suggests that Carrington's instructions to Fetterman were actually to implement a tactical offensive maneuver in accordance with General Cooke's instructions, much like the so-called tactical "offensive" operation that had resulted in the failed actions on December 6. Therefore, according to Vaughn's thesis, no one actually disobeyed orders but Carrington supposedly later covered up this fact because it would have cast responsibility for Fetterman's demise back on him.[40]

Whatever Carrington's orders really were, all sources are in agreement that Fetterman left the post by the wood mill gate with the infantry between about 11:00 and 11:15 AM. All of this organization took only a matter of moments. Grummond's 2nd cavalrymen quickly joined him along with Captain Brown. The men were poorly armed with obsolete Springfield muzzle-loaders but the cavalry had Spencers. The troops headed straight north toward Sullivant Hills and then northeast to Lodge Trail Ridge rather than due west along the road toward the wood train. And Carrington saw nothing wrong at this point! Why? Almost immediately after Fetterman left the fort (about 11:15 AM) the sentry on Pilot Hill signaled that the wood train was no longer under attack and was proceeding toward the pineries. Fetterman, after also seeing the signal that the wood train was safe, obviously went east and north to Lodge Trail Ridge on the Bozeman Trail to cut off the retreating attackers "behind" the ridge. Carrington later wrote that Fetterman was "evidently moving *wisely* [emphasis mine] up the creek and along the slope of Lodge Trail Ridge, with good promise of cutting off the Indians as they should withdraw . . . the course adopted was not an error, unless there was then a purpose to disobey orders." Margaret Carrington later supported the idea that Fetterman was maneuvering to cut off the retreat of the Indians. Carrington also remarked that Fetterman had deployed in a skirmish line. In effect, by this point in time, the situation had suddenly changed and Carrington apparently saw no problem with Fetterman's cutting off the attackers behind Lodge Trail Ridge. Had he been concerned he easily could have sent a messenger out to retrieve Fetterman as he had done with Grummond on December 6. What is critical is that Carrington, Fetterman, or likely anyone else at the fort never envisioned more than about one hundred Indians waiting over the ridge as on December 6. And that is exactly what the Indians hoped the soldiers would do. One hundred warriors possibly waiting in ambush was not a problem for eighty-one soldiers. The possibility of Indian numbers in the thousands surely never entered the minds of anyone at Fort Phil Kearny. At first Carrington thus praised Fetterman for his initiative. Only later, when Carrington was made a scapegoat for the deaths of Fetterman and his command, did he change his mind and focus on Fetterman's disobedience of orders.[41]

If there is a lack of clarity as to what specific orders Carrington actually gave to Fetterman, there is almost universal agreement that several people heard the specific orders given to Lt. George W. Grummond when he took out the cavalry just a few minutes after Fetterman and the infantry had left the fort. The testimony of the officer of the day on December 21, Lt. Alfred H. Wands, is the most compelling:

> Colonel Carrington directed me to inform Lieutenant Grummond
> that his orders were to join Colonel Fetterman's command, report to
> and receive all his orders from Colonel Fetterman . . . I gave those

instructions to Lieutenant Grummond, and while the Corporal of the Guard was unlocking the gate, I returned to Lieutenant Grummond and repeated them, and asked him if he thoroughly understood them. He replied that he did, and would obey them to the letter.

Lieutenant Grummond . . . proceeded about two hundred yards when he was called back by Colonel Carrington who was on the sentinel's platform at the time, and who called out in a loud voice, repeating the same instructions given to Lieutenant Grummond by me, and asking him if he understood them. He replied I do. Lieutenant Grummond's command was seen to join Colonel Fetterman about a mile from the Post.[42]

And Carrington wrote in his official report, "To Lieutenant Grummond I gave orders to 'report to Brevet Lieutenant-Colonel Fetterman, implicitly obey his orders, and not leave him.' Before the command left, I instructed Lieutenant A. H. Wands, my regimental quartermaster and acting adjutant, to repeat these orders. He did so."[43] Margaret Carrington remembered that "[t]he health of Mrs. Grummond was such that Lieutenant Wands and other friends urged him, for his family's sake, to be prudent, and to avoid all rash movements and any pursuit that would draw them over Lodge Trail Ridge."[44] "Everybody knew," she stressed, "why special emphasis was given to these orders." Years later Frances Grummond Carrington repeated Margaret's account almost word for word while adding that she was "filled with dread and horror at the thought that after my husband's hairbreadth escape scarcely three weeks before he could be so eager to fight the Indians again . . . I stood for a time, moments indeed, almost dazed, my heart filled with strange forebodings, then turned, entered my little house, and closed my door."[45]

Given the evidence it is absurd to contend that Carrington had actually instructed Fetterman to execute an offensive maneuver as Vaughn suggests while then emphatically emphasizing to Grummond several times to obey Fetterman's instructions and not proceed over Lodge Trail Ridge. If Carrington had indeed ordered an offensive action he certainly would not be concerned that the impulsive Grummond would disobey these instructions. But once Carrington ascertained that the Indians who had feinted on the wood train were in retreat he at first had shown little concern with the direction Fetterman was moving or with any disobedience of orders, assuming that Fetterman was trying to intercept them and cut off their retreat. Carrington's behavior was in no way unusual in this respect. After all, Capt. Frederick Brown had frequently pursued or tried to cut off retreats of raiding parties for many miles over the summer without any orders at all and without suffering casualties to his hastily assembled mounted infantry. By all indications, judging from Carrington's correspondence up to the twenty-first, the commanding officer at Fort Phil Kearny was nothing short of supportive of Fetterman. Likely, in light of the rapidly changing situation, Carrington still trusted Fetterman to make the right judgment as to an immediate course of action when he saw him ascending Lodge Trail on the twenty-first with eighty men in pursuit of forty retreating Indians who had constituted an attack group and were not obvious decoys. As such, he did not become worried until sometime *after* Fetterman disappeared over the ridge. Again, what Carrington did not know at the time, of course, nor Fetterman, or Grummond, or Brown, or anyone else at Fort Phil Kearny, was that indeed up to two thousand warriors awaited Fetterman's command on the other side of Lodge Trail Ridge. Carrington's only point of reference was the fight on December 6 when no more than 150 Indians had been engaged at any point. The presence of ten decoys on the south side of Lodge Trail Ridge would do nothing to change this belief. As such, one is compelled to accept Lieutenant Wands's testimony that even though Carrington's orders were not to proceed over Lodge Trail Ridge, once he knew the train was safe and the warriors were fleeing, Carrington was not especially concerned if Fetterman took the initiative to go over the ridge. Nothing in Carrington's reports up to this point contradicts the notion that he completely trusted Fetterman's judgment in the heat of the moment of rapidly changing developments.[46]

But there is circumstantial evidence that Carrington did not especially trust Grummond to keep a cool head in a fight. That no one seems to have heard Carrington's orders to Fetterman is in direct contrast to the fact that the same orders were repeated to Grummond three times, twice by Wands and once by Carrington after calling Grummond back from his march out of the fort. From Wands's testimony and the later anguish of both Margaret Carrington and, understandably, Frances Grummond, it seems apparent that, given the results of December 6, the officer who Carrington was most worried might disobey any orders given on December 21 and ride off in a merry chase after the Indians was not Capt. William J. Fetterman but rather Lt. George Washington Grummond.[47]

Lieutenant Grummond with twenty-seven troopers of the 2nd Cavalry left the fort shortly after Fetterman and the infantry and soon caught Fetterman not very far from the post. The cavalrymen were armed with the seven-shot repeating Spencer rifles and/or carbines of various sizes that Carrington had recently procured for them from the regimental band. Two civilian contractors, James S. Wheatley and Isaac Fisher, armed with repeating Henry rifles, volunteered to go out. Ever vigilant, and eager for one last chance to get a Lakota scalp before he departed for his new assignment at Fort Laramie, Capt. Frederick Brown borrowed the pony Calico from Carrington's son Jimmy and rode out of the fort shortly after Lieutenant Grummond and the cavalry, eager to catch up to his friend Captain Fetterman once it became apparent the command was heading toward Lodge Trail Ridge to engage the retreating warriors that had attacked the wood train. They all joined Fetterman easily within sight of the fort.

The exact route Fetterman and Grummond took at this point is controversial, Carrington stating it was west of the Bozeman Trail, the route that he, Carrington, had taken on December 6. J. W. Vaughn collected artifacts during the early 1960s and ascertained that Fetterman and Grummond went over Lodge Trail Ridge *on* the Bozeman Trail or just slightly to the west of it.[48] By most accounts eyewitnesses agree that before the command passed out of sight over the southern knobs of Lodge Trail Ridge Fetterman had deployed the infantry in skirmish order, perhaps as early as the crossing of Big Piney Creek below Lodge Trail Ridge on the south, with the cavalry out on the flanks and slightly ahead of the infantry. Again, by this time Carrington, if he had been concerned with any disobedience of orders, would have had plenty of time to dispatch a rider to bring the command back before it crested the ridge and descended into the Peno Valley. But he did not because he was not bothered by Fetterman's sudden maneuver. His lack of concern at this point is supported by the testimony of Lt. W. F. Arnold before the Sanborn Commission. Arnold was watching from the fort. "Firing was heard from the direction his [Fetterman's] command had taken," he stated, "between, I think eleven and half past eleven o'clock A.M. but it did not alarm anybody as it was the largest force that had ever been sent out from the garrison."[49] Thus it is probable that Carrington could not have been much concerned with what, at that point, was obviously disobedience of his orders.

Quite understandably Fetterman and Grummond after him did not go anywhere near the wood train to the west when they left the fort despite a later statement from Lieutenant Bisbee, who was not present, since it was no longer in danger.[50] As stated earlier, shortly after the command's departure from the fort the picket on Pilot Hill signaled that the wood train was no longer under attack and was headed unimpeded for the pineries. Carrington later stated that when he obtained this news he "entertained no apprehensions of further danger."[51] Pvt. William R. Curtis, Company K, 2/18th Infantry, later told Walter Camp that when forty Indians attacked the train about fifteen soldiers charged them and easily dispersed them. "Fetterman did not come near our train," he wrote. The wagons proceeded on to the pineries, filled the wagons with logs, and returned to the fort, arriving by 4:00 PM. If Lieutenant Arnold is correct in his estimation of the time, Fetterman's detachment pushed over the ridge sometime around 11:30 AM and soon thereafter a few scattered shots were heard. By noon Carrington was sitting atop his sentinel post (Powell states the roof of his quarters) and beginning to have concerns as the firing became steadily more general now that the command was out of sight over the ridge.[52]

▼▼▼

By this time Big Nose, astride his black war horse, Wolf Left Hand, American Horse, and the other decoys were luring soldiers down the ridge toward the Peno forks. From that point forward the only eyewitnesses to what exactly happened are the warriors who survived the battle. As Big Nose and the other decoys taunted the soldiers over Lodge Trail Ridge, at some point in this ruse Grummond and the cavalry went ahead, chasing them downhill on or just west of the Bozeman Trail, as all the pertinent Indian sources assert that the cavalry was ahead of the infantry before the trap was sprung. Two Moon told George Bent that the cavalry was at least a half-mile ahead of the infantry.[53] Mixed-blood scout Michael Boyer, who knew several of the warriors who were in the Fetterman fight, testified before the Sanborn Commission that according to his informants the cavalry was more like a mile ahead of the infantry at the time the Indians sprang the trap.[54]

Some of the more athletic infantrymen grabbed hold of the stirrups of cavalry saddles or the horses' tails as they moved ahead. They did not want to miss the fight. According to White Elk the cavalry pursued the decoys down the ridge to where the land flattens out near Peno Creek and where many Oglalas were hiding in the brush and broken land along the creek bottom near the forks. When the decoys were nearly to the stream they separated into two parties, riding away from each other, and then turned and rode back toward the troopers. The two parties of decoys crossed paths as the cavalry reached flat ground. This was the prearranged signal to spring the trap. Chiefs gave the Northern Cheyenne warrior Little Horse the honor of initiating the attack. When he rose up on his pony, all sprang up and, according to White Elk, the sound of the ponies' many hooves "made a noise like thunder."[55] On the west side of the road White Bull saw the decoys cross paths and cried out, "Come on! We must start!" The Miniconjous sprang up and pressed the attack uphill from east to southwest. On the other side the Oglalas and Northern Cheyennes pressed the attack from the opposite direction. By now, according to White Bull, the trailing infantry were "well within the trap" but less than about a quarter-mile north from the modern monument.[56]

It took the warriors only a matter of moments to complete the envelopment. The Miniconjous swept around Fetterman's rear south, then west, while the Oglalas along Peno Creek rushed the cavalry from the creek bottom north of Massacre Ridge, pushed them back south, and then joined their comrades along with the Cheyennes and Arapahos pressing from the west along and across the ridge. With the initial attack the cavalry began retreating southward up the ridge. But most did not make it very far. Some rejoined the infantry as far south as the modern monument and died there. A few, including the civilians Wheatley and Fisher, knowing it was futile to run, made a stand behind some rocks at the far north end of the battlefield, probably the farthest penetration of the cavalry at the time of the attack. Numerous Henry shell casings were discovered after the fight, indicating the two civilians who fought at what came to be known as Wheatley-Fisher Rocks put up stiff resistance before they died. A member of the relief party, R. J. Smyth, told Walter Mason Camp in 1913 that relief forces found remains of cavalrymen stretched out well over half a mile.[57] I possess two fired Spencer bullets recovered north of this area on private property during the 1950s, indicating that cavalrymen must have been separated by close to a mile from

Fetterman and the infantry. Although White Bull claims the infantry were wiped out first, White Bull was only fighting on the south end, up the slope of the ridge, where the infantry had halted. He could not see the cavalry to the north below his position on the ridge due to the hilly terrain. It is more likely that Grummond's cavalry along with Wheatley and Fisher were the first victims. The Indians asserted that some of the cavalry retreated up the ridge and died with Fetterman and Brown and the infantry where the monument now stands. Vaughn found a few empty Spencer cartridges around Monument Hill supporting this assertion.[58]

It seems more likely that cavalrymen who survived the initial onslaught frantically rode back south, up the ridge toward the infantry position, perhaps even passing some of the infantrymen at first as the infantry retreated to the spot of the monument from the point of their farthest penetration into the valley. "They charged up the hill [south] losing men as they went," Fire Thunder remembered.[59] If some cavalrymen reached the rocks where the monument stands today slightly ahead of the retreating infantry and turned loose their horses, this would explain White Bull's misconception when he saw the infantry join them. He would assume the cavalrymen had reached Monument Hill first as all Indian accounts agree that near the monument the mounted troopers who were still alive released their horses and made their last stand.[60]

Some cavalry troopers who did not make it back up the ridge dismounted and made a stand on a high level area, down the valley from the monument but obscured from the view of the infantry to the south by a hill. Vaughn confirmed the spot, now called Cavalry Hill, through relic recovery and the fact that Lieutenant Grummond's body was found in this vicinity.[61] Wheatley and Fisher were also obscured from sight of both the cavalry position and the infantry position. Thus neither the Indians nor the soldiers could tell what was happening to any of the other two elements during the battle from their points of engagement. This, of course, enabled the warriors to destroy the separated command in detail. Fire Thunder was in the cavalry fight. Years later he remembered:

> When the soldiers started back [the cavalry retreat], I held my sorrel [horse] with one hand and began killing them with [my] six-shooter, for they came close to me. There were many bullets, but there were

more arrows—so many that it was like a cloud of grasshoppers all above and around the soldiers; and our people, shooting across, hit each other. The soldiers were falling all the while they were fighting back up the hill, and their horses got loose. Many of our people chased the horses, but I was not after horses: I was after Wasichus. When the [cavalry] soldiers got on top there were not many of them left and they had no place to hide. They were fighting hard.[62]

White Bull too remembered the furious rain of arrows across the ridge. "All the Indians were shooting, arrows were flying in every direction," he stated. "Some of the Indians were hit by arrows, among them Thunder Hump and King. The ground was so covered with arrows that a warrior did not have to use his own; he could pick one up almost anywhere."[63] The Oglala warrior Standing Bear remembered fighting the U.S. cavalry a decade later. "The white cavalry did not know how to fight," he claimed. "They stuck together and thus made an easy target for us . . . After we were on the ground [fighting on foot] we would jump around and, and it was pretty hard to hit us. We'd zigzag toward them. It was open order fighting. We fought in circles because when we go around them it would scare the soldiers and then we would charge on them at this time. Some would go one way and others would go another way, thus disorganizing the soldiers." The Indians used these same kinds of individualized tactics toward the end of the Fetterman fight.[64]

The Miniconjous were probably the first to strike Fetterman's infantry detail, possibly even from the rear as they charged south and then swung west to envelop the soldiers and cut off any attempt at retreat back to the fort while Oglalas and Cheyennes stopped Fetterman's advance north down Massacre Ridge. According to White Bull, Thunder Hawk was the first to kill and count coup on a soldier. The Miniconjou Eats Meat, eager to display his bravery, rode his horse straight through the infantry ranks. The soldiers let him pass through but then turned and emptied a volley into him. Eats Meat was the first Miniconjou to die in the fight. The Indians attacking the infantry rode around them, hanging on the sides of their horses, loosing arrows at them continually. The infantrymen then shot a warrior named Bull Eagle. But "the fire of the soldiers was so hot," White Bull remembered, "that no one dared to go to his rescue." Bull Eagle had been on foot and was about to club a soldier when he was wounded. White Bull later claimed that he dismounted and crawled to Bull Eagle, grabbed him by the wrists, and dragged him to safety. White Bull returned to his horse but was soon struck by a bullet from a Springfield. He was unhurt but found that the bullet had passed through his red Nor'west blanket just behind his shoulder.[65]

Northern Cheyennes were in the infantry fight in the early stages. White Elk later claimed that shortly after the second Lakota was shot (Bull Eagle?) an order was given to charge the infantry. The soldiers were mixed together in hand-to-hand combat, White Elk remembered, and a Lakota was killed. Then another Lakota was struck by friendly fire, a stray arrow that went through his forehead above his nose and into his brain.[66] The Northern Cheyenne Wolf Tooth ran out of arrows and went to his friend Sap to obtain more. He too had a narrow miss from a stray arrow.[67] And sometime during the fight the Northern Cheyenne warrior named Strong Wind Blowing, older brother of Wooden Leg, was killed.[68]

All the Indian accounts agree that the fight ended on top of the hill where the monument stands today. There the last survivors made it to a rock grouping (some of which are inside the present monument walls) that afforded some protection . . . but not enough. The entire fight lasted about forty minutes and relief forces later counted forty-nine of eighty-one bodies clustered together around the rocks on Monument Hill. By all indications, toward the end of the fight the warriors massed their entire force on the hill against what remained of the infantry and a few cavalry troopers who had made it up the ridge to join the infantrymen. Fetterman was there and so too was the ubiquitous Capt. Frederick Brown. Indian testimony suggests that the cavalry at least attempted to maintain tactical cohesion in their retreat up the ridge. White Bull remembered that the remaining cavalrymen who joined their comrades on the hill "moved [retreated up the ridge] in a compact body, shooting all the time. They were half-hidden in the powder smoke." The teenager White Bull rode in, shot, and counted his first coup on one of these troopers. By this time cold weather had moved in and the temperature plummeted. Blood froze on arms and legs as it flowed from wounds. The top of the hill was covered with patches of snow and the trampling of many feet was turning it to ice, no place for displays of horsemanship.[69]

A warrior who has never been identified called out to the Indians to dismount and crawl up the ravines. White Bull moved slowly forward with his friend Charging-Crow. When the Miniconjous neared the top, close to the soldiers' defensive perimeter, Long Fox stood and yelled, "*Hopo!* Let's go." The Miniconjous rushed forward in battle frenzy. White Bull and Charging-Crow reached the top. Suddenly Charging-Crow fell at his friend's feet, mown down by musketry. White Bull was unscathed. The Indians moved into the soldiers' perimeter fighting hand to hand, scuffling in smoke and dust. White Bull later stated this type of fight was called "Stirring Gravy."[70]

Miniconjous continued coming up the ravines from the east. The Northern Cheyennes and Arapahos and most Oglalas crawled up the western slope of Monument Hill. From his place of concealment White Elk remembered that his friends kept calling to each other, "Be ready. Are you ready?" Others would call back, "We are ready." They began an all-out and final assault on the soldiers' position. Then the warrior Little Horse gave the command and the Cheyennes and Lakotas ran in among the soldiers and engaged them in fierce hand-to-hand combat."[71] The Northern Cheyenne decoy, Big Nose, brother of Little Wolf who had performed so well in luring the soldiers over Lodge Trail Ridge, went after one of the cavalry horses that had been turned loose. When he returned to the final fighting his own black war horse was exhausted. The horse balked and would not move forward. A second later Big Nose was shot off his horse, mortally wounded. His friend White Elk went to his side. "Lift my head up the hill," he said, "and place me where I can breathe the fresh air." Big Nose was shot on the ridge in the first sag northwest of the monument by some large rocks not far from where a lone tree now stands on the battlefield. Little Wolf and Crazy Head later came to the side of Little Wolf's brother Big Nose and placed him on a travois and took him back to the camp on Tongue River where Big Nose died a couple of days later.[72]

"We were told to crawl up on them," Fire Thunder remembered years later. "When we were close, someone yelled, 'Let's go!' This is a good day to die. Think of the helpless ones at home! Then we all cried, 'Hoka hey!' and rushed at them. I was young then and quick on my feet, and I was one of the first to get in among the soldiers. They got up and fought very hard until not one of them was alive."[73] "I killed five or six of these soldiers myself," Fire Thunder remembered, "three with my six-shooter and three with arrows."[74] Fire Thunder was sixteen years old. This was his first battle. Sometime during the action the Oglala American Horse (the younger) breeched the soldier line on his war horse. He saw what appeared to be their leader,

Capt. William J. Fetterman. American Horse rushed the captain and slammed his war club into Fetterman's skull, knocking him down. American Horse then dismounted, took his scalping knife, and cut Fetterman's throat open with a deep gash all the way to the cervical spine.[75] After the fight American Horse selected the Fetterman fight as the mnemonic (pictograph) for 1866/1867 on his winter count. The simple drawing depicts soldiers on Monument Hill completely enveloped.[76] The last to die in the fight was not a soldier but a dog that was discovered by the Indians among the soldiers' bodies. "Do not let even a dog get away," a warrior cried out, reputedly a Cheyenne named Big Rascal. The Indians killed the animal with arrows. It was over.[77]

After the fight the Indians stripped the bodies, cut them to pieces, and shot arrows into the corpses. One soldier was riddled by a hundred arrows. According to White Bull, he believed that the bodies of the soldiers were mutilated because they had put up a stiff fight and killed many Indians. The Indians were determined to show the Americans their fierce determination to defend the Powder River country from white intrusion. According to ethnologist Royal B. Hassrick the Lakotas were ethnocentric people and their warriors vainglorious: To their "exhibitionism was added the aura of violence . . . in severe extremes. To kill an enemy was not enough; often he must be mutilated." The Lakotas "were a people convinced of their superiority." On December 21, 1866, many a warrior's conviction of this belief was bolstered on the frozen slopes of Massacre Ridge.[78]

American Horse remembered that some of the soldiers seemed demoralized, probably the infantry who found it impossible to effectively load their Springfield muskets in a timely fashion. These men, American Horse asserted, did not put up much of a fight and some committed suicide at the end.[79] American Horse's assertion is contradictory to other Indian accounts that claim the soldiers fought courageously. Two Moon remembered in 1913 that the "soldiers made no attempt to run . . . or get away."[80] Among the Northern Cheyennes Little Wolf's Elkhorn Scraper soldier society had played a major role in wiping out Fetterman's troops. As such one of their bravest men, Big Nose, had given his life. The Elks stripped many uniforms from the dead soldiers and put them on. Reputedly one of the Elks shouted, "Now, from this time on, we will call ourselves Blue Soldiers, from this clothing that we are wearing." After that time the Elks rode into battle in formations of twos imitating the soldiers they had helped to annihilate at the Fetterman fight.[81]

Lakotas boasted that it was the vision of their winkte that had created the great victory. But the Northern Cheyennes asserted that it was the powerful medicine of the bulletproof Crazy Mule that brought about the soldiers' defeat. They believed that Crazy Mule's power had caused some of the whites to fall down dead on their own so that the Indians would not have to shoot them.[82] According to the Lakota warrior Rocky Bear, following the fight, Red Cloud received all the war honors.[83]

▼▼▼

Shortly after Fetterman's command had ascended Lodge Trail Ridge Carrington realized that a surgeon had not accompanied the detachment. He ordered Surgeon Hines to do so but Hines soon returned to the fort with the information that there was heavy firing on the far side of the ridge. Both Hines and Captain Ten Eyck later testified that Carrington still did not hurry to send a relief party. Only after soldiers inside the fort heard the shooting begin to subside did Carrington order a relief force under Captain Ten Eyck to ride to Fetterman's rescue. Ten Eyck left the fort within seventeen minutes after being given his orders with about seventy-five men: infantry, civilians, and dismounted cavalry. Dr. Hines went along as did Lieutenant Winfield Scott Matson and several civilian volunteers. The detachment moved at double time until they reached the Big Piney where many of the men had to break through ice and take off their shoes and socks to cross so that their clothing would not freeze.[84]

Ten Eyck ascended the ridge via the Bozeman Trail along the same route Fetterman had taken and then veered eastward from the road to avoid a dangerous defile that could have been a possible point of ambush. He then proceeded to a crest on the ridge where he had a better view of the valley. Later, in attempting to absolve himself from blame, Carrington criticized Ten Eyck's movement eastward, a movement that Ten Eyck had not mentioned in his report. Carrington implied that Ten Eyck could have taken a more direct route over Lodge Trail Ridge and saved time in arriving at the scene of the action. The accusation implied cowardice on Ten Eyck's part. Although Carrington, years later, rescinded any implication of cowardice the damage was done. Ten Eyck's career was ruined. He started drinking heavily and retired from the army.[85]

When Ten Eyck crested the ridge, about 12:45 PM, he saw Indians around Monument Hill and more warriors "extending a distance of a mile or more beyond the furthest point of the ridge." Surgeon Hines later asserted that we "were just in time to see the last man killed."[86] When the troops descended into the valley the Indians dispersed and joined their comrades down the valley, then rode to a distance estimated by Ten Eyck as being about two miles and formed a line. There the Indians taunted Ten Eyck's men and urged them to come down and fight them. Ten Eyck estimated their numbers between 1,500 and 2,000 but Surgeon Hines thought perhaps 3,000, although this is probably an inflated figure.[87] As Ten Eyck's command descended the road toward Monument Hill he soon saw the extent of the horrible carnage. By this time Carrington heard no more firing so he dispatched the remainder of Company C, 2nd Cavalry, to reinforce Ten Eyck. He also sent an ambulance and two wagons loaded with three thousand rounds of Springfield ammunition and two cases of Spencer cartridges. Ten Eyck, at the same time, sent a courier back to the fort, Pvt. Archibald Sample, Carrington's personal orderly. Ten Eyck requested one of the howitzers but there was no serviceable horse at the post to haul it and Carrington wanted to keep the cannon in reserve in case the fort was attacked. Sample stormed into the fort on his horse at full speed. Carrington was waiting in front of his headquarters.[88]

"Captain Ten Eyck says he can see or hear nothing of Captain Fetterman," Sample reported. "The Indians are on the road challenging him to come down . . . The Captain is afraid Fetterman's party is all gone up, sir." Somberly Carrington turned to his quarters and wrote his gloomy dispatches to Fort Laramie.[89] As Private Sample rode back to the ridge to inform Ten Eyck that the howitzer was unavailable, the captain's detachment headed down the ridge and soon spotted the naked bodies of their comrades that the warriors had stripped and mutilated. The Indians moved off westward and out of the bloody Peno Valley. They had seen enough fighting for one day. Coming upon the bodies around what would be named Monument Hill, Ten Eyck's men gazed upon a ghastly scene. Years later Private Murphy of the 2nd Cavalry remembered:

> There was at that time a large stone that had the appearance of having dropped from a great height and thereby split open, leaving a space between the pieces men could pass through, which made a

good protection for a small body of men, I should say for about twenty-five or thirty. Around this rock was where the main body of men lay. There were just a few down on the side of the ridge north of the rock, not more than fifty feet from the main body.[90]

Murphy noticed too that the dead cavalry horses found below the rocks had their heads pointed toward the fort, evidence of a hasty retreat to safety that was never achieved. Ten Eyck found several Spencer cartridges scattered among the rocks, giving additional support to the fact that a few of the horse soldiers had escaped up the ridge only to be killed with Fetterman and the infantry at the end. Many broken arrows littered the ground around the corpses. Private Murphy found one of his comrades of the 2nd Cavalry among the rocks, "scalped, stripped, and mutilated," then filled with "arrows, as they were sticking out of him all over like porcupine quills . . . all the bodies were stripped, scalped, and mutilated with the exception of two," he remembered.[91] Surgeon Hines noted that most of the bodies "were in one heap" and that most were shot with arrows.[92] Private Guthrie discovered the bodies of Fetterman and Brown and noted that Captain Brown's body was "hacked up and had a lot of arrows in him and was scalped."[93] Surgeon Horton later found a wound in Brown's left temple caused by a pistol ball and likely the cause of death. No such wound was found on Fetterman. Apparently Brown had committed suicide, but Fetterman did not, despite Carrington's later assertions that the pair killed themselves at the end.[94]

Ten Eyck's men recovered the frozen remains of forty-nine of their comrades that afternoon. The only living thing they found on the field was a gray 2nd Cavalry horse named Dapple Dan. The horse lay near the boulders riddled with a dozen arrows. Ten Eyck ordered the poor creature put out of its misery.[95] By the time the soldiers loaded the corpses into the wagons the sun was low on the horizon, obscured by ominous clouds of an afternoon cold front moving in that portended snow. The temperature soon turned bitter cold as darkness descended over the mountains about 4:00 PM on that winter solstice of the year 1866. As the wagons turned back toward the fort in the gray dusk Surgeon Hines noted and later testified that "[w]e brought in about fifty [actually 49] in wagons like you see hogs brought to market."[96]

By now the garrison at Fort Phil Kearny had become fully aware of what had befallen Fetterman's command. Colonel Carrington put the fort on full alert. He ordered arms stacked in front of quarters, all men armed, and prisoners released from the guardhouse. Portals were manned around the wall and Carrington ordered all nonmilitary activities halted. Windows and doors were barred except for rifle portals. Men corralled wagons around the ammunition magazine. Carrington fully expected an attack upon the fort in the night. That evening he sent couriers to Fort Laramie for reinforcements. Three-fourths of his garrison was outside the post, spread among Ten Eyck's detachment and a few men at the pineries that he quickly recalled to the fort. But another order was grimmer still. Years later Sergeant Fessenden of the regimental band remembered:

We had ten women and several children with us [and the Carringtons' and Wandses' African American servants]. The colonel gave orders that as soon as the Indians made the expected attack, the children and women should enter the magazine, and the men should hold the fort as long as possible. When they could hold it no longer, they were to get behind the wagons that surrounded the magazine, and when the colonel saw that all was lost, he would himself blow up the magazine and take the lives of all, rather than allow the Indians to capture any of the inmates alive.[97]

"I shall never forget the face of Colonel Carrington as he descended from the lookout as the firing ceased," Frances Grummond remembered. "The howitzers were put in position and loaded . . . [And Colonel Carrington] encouraged all to wait patiently and be ready for the return of the troops. How different was the reality, soon to be realized."[98] The waiting was especially hard on the women of the garrison. When the firing had ceased over the ridge the wives gathered near the headquarters building, their eyes searching the hills to the north. For Frances Grummond, certainly recalling her husband's narrow escape of December 6, "the silence was dreadful."[99]

A shroud of darkness descended over the Bighorns as Ten Eyck's wagons ground in through the gate at Fort Phil Kearny with their gruesome cargo. Sgt. Frank Fessenden was at the gate and never forgot what he saw.

There were "arms and legs in all shapes, divulging the horrible manner in which our brave comrades had died. It was a horrible and sickening sight, and brought tears to every eye, to see those men, many of whom had served four years in the War of the Rebellion, meeting with such an awful death on the western plains. Some of these men had but ten days more to serve, when their enlistment would have expired, and they could have returned to their homes."[100]

Colonel Carrington's young son Jimmy also glimpsed the corpses and parts of corpses as they came into the fort in the wagons. Years later he would still have nightmares. "How many times," he wrote, "I awoke in the dark in terror, to see again the tortured bodies and bloody arrows of that night."[101]

The women had gathered at the Wandses' quarters when the wagons returned to the fort. Soon Frances Grummond learned that her earlier forebodings of the past September upon first setting eyes on Fort Phil Kearny had come true. Margaret Carrington informed her that her husband was not found alive and that his body had not been recovered. "To a woman whose house and heart received the widow as a sister," Margaret later remembered, "and whose office it was to advise her of the facts, the recital of the scenes of that day, even at this late period, is full of pain."[102]

Dawn on December 22 came in gloomy and overcast. The temperature was bitter cold, the mercury hovering around zero. The sky warned of an impending blizzard. Almost no one had slept. Carrington summoned his surviving field officers, captains Ten Eyck and Powell and lieutenants Wands, Arnold, and Matson, to his quarters. Twenty-nine soldiers and two civilians were still missing. Carrington announced that he would personally lead a detail of eighty men with Captain Ten Eyck and Lieutenant Matson to recover the remaining bodies. Margaret Carrington was caring for Frances Grummond that morning in the Carringtons' quarters when the colonel told Frances, "Mrs. Grummond, I shall go in person, and will bring back to you the remains of your husband."[103] According to Dee Brown, Jim Bridger volunteered to join the detail and posted pickets on the ridges to look for activity by the Indians but there is no corroboration of Bridger's presence at the fort on that day or December 21 recorded in any original records.[104] The temperature remained around zero all day. According to Frances Grummond, Colonel Carrington once again issued an order to the officer of the day, Capt. William Powell, to place women and children in the powder and ammunition magazine and blow it up if the fort were taken by the Indians during the detail's absence.[105] Certainly tension spread among the garrison as only about forty effectives remained behind at the fort. "We did not know but the colonel and his command would meet the same fate as their comrades on the previous day," Sergeant Fessenden recalled. But no warriors appeared on the ridges around Fort Phil Kearny on that dreary first full day of winter.[106]

Carrington found the bodies of his soldiers scattered north along the road from Monument Hill for a distance of over half a mile. At the far north end, among a couple of prominent rocks the detail found the bodies of the two civilians, Isaac Fisher and James Wheatley, and a few of the older veteran troopers. They had sold their lives dearly. Numerous Henry cartridge casings were found around them and Carrington counted sixty-five pools of blood along the road.[107] Not far away Carrington discovered the body of his son Jimmy's pony, Calico, that had been given to him and his brother as a gift at Fort Kearney, Nebraska.[108] According to Vaughn the body of 2nd Cavalry bugler Adolph Metzger was found near Wheatley-Fisher Rocks, but most original accounts place his body on Monument Hill with Fetterman's. According to Pvt. John Guthrie, who was with the detail, Metzger's body was never found.[109] But according to teamster Finn Burnett, Metzger died heroically, fighting off Indians at the end using his bugle as a club. His body was not mutilated, Burnett claimed. "His heroism had aroused the admiration of the savages," he wrote; "they covered his corpse with a buffalo robe as a symbol of extreme respect."[110] Metzger became somewhat legendary in the literature of the Fetterman fight, and quite quickly. A newspaper printed a story allegedly obtained from a group of trappers and Crows who had heard the story of Metzger's struggle. Supposedly he was the last survivor, fighting furiously until he was overwhelmed and carried off to the Lakota camps and tortured to death. The story became sensationalized when published in 1867 in the *Army and Navy Journal* even though it likely never happened as reports do not indicate that his body was missing at the time of interment.[111]

About halfway between Monument Hill and Wheatley-Fisher Rocks lay the bodies of Lt. George W. Grummond and Sgt. Augustus Lang. Grummond's head was crushed with a war club and he had almost been decapitated; the Indians had cut off all of his fingers and filled his body with arrows.[112] Apparently Grummond had made it about halfway up Massacre Ridge toward the infantry from his forward position where Wheatley and Fisher made their last stand before he was overwhelmed. Carrington had a lock of Lieutenant Grummond's hair cut off and he presented it to Grummond's widow that night.[113] Also that evening Margaret Carrington, following the duty of the commandant's wife, consoled James Wheatley's nineteen-year-old widow, whom Finn Burnett described as a "beautiful girl . . . and a splendid soldier."[114] Bodies of the cavalry were strung out along the ridge, indicating their flight back toward Fetterman's position.[115]

According to Finn Burnett the ground was sodden with blood, "which frightened the mules until they were well-nigh unmanageable," he remembered. "A man was obliged to hold the head of every animal while other teamsters loaded the naked, mutilated remains like cordwood into the wagon boxes." But soon the mules began to "lurch and kick." A wagon overturned and "the bodies were dumped out . . . It was a terrible sight and a horrible job."[116] Private Guthrie recalled that some of the corpses had crosses cut in their bodies. "We walked on top of their internals," he remembered years later, "and did not know it in the high grass. [We] picked them up, that is their internals, did not know the soldier they belonged to, so you see the cavalry man got an infantry man's gutts [sic] and an infantry man got a cavalry man's gutts."[117]

In his official report Carrington described the condition of his men's naked and mutilated bodies in gruesome detail:

> Eyes torn out and laid on the rocks.
> Noses cut off.
> Ears cut off.
> Chins hewn off.
> Teeth chopped out.
> Joints of fingers cut off.
> Brains taken out and placed on rocks, with members of the body.
> Entrails taken out and exposed.
> Hands cut off.
> Feet cut off.
> Arms taken out from socket.
> Private parts severed, and indecently placed on the person.
> Eyes, ears, mouth, and arms penetrated with spear-heads,
>   sticks, and arrows.

Ribs slashed to separation, with knives; skulls severed in any form,
from chin to crown.
Muscles of calves, thighs, stomach, breast, back, arms,
and cheeks taken out.
Punctures upon every sensitive part of the body, even to the
soles of the feet and palms of the hand.[118]

Surgeon Horton confirmed Carrington's assessment. "All the bodies were more or less mutilated," he testified, "and presented in nearly every instance a horrible sight, never to be forgotten by those who saw them." Most of the men had died from blows by war clubs or from arrows and subsequent mutilations, not more than six from bullet wounds.[119]

It took most of the day to collect the bodies and bring them back to the fort. "Sadness overcame us," Sergeant Fessenden remembered, "when nearing the fort; we saw seven wagons loaded with naked bodies."[120] "We hauled them all in to the Fort," Private Guthrie recalled, "and made the guard house at the Fort a dead house."[121] That night the mercury plunged to twenty degrees below zero and the threatening blizzard hit with all-out fury accompanied by fierce winds that would drift the bleak snow high up the walls of Fort Phil Kearny.

▼▼▼

The casualties of Fetterman's command are among the most memorable and precise in American history. Below is a breakdown. The names of the casualties are listed in appendix A.

*Recapitulation of Soldier and Civilian Casualties
at the Fetterman Fight*[122]

	Officers	*Serg'ts*	*Corp'ls*	*Pvts.*	*Citizens*	*Total*
18th Infantry	3	7	8	34	____	52
2nd Cavalry	0	1	2	24	____	27
Citizens	____	____	____	____	2	2
Total	3	8	10	58	2	81

The Indian casualties in the Fetterman fight, as with most accounts of Indian losses during their wars with the United States, are impossible to ascertain. They range (for killed) anywhere from ten to three hundred. Most of the Indian accounts assert that many warriors died of wounds after they had been returned to the camps on Tongue River. Sergeant Fessenden claimed that after the fight some Indian women trading at the fort (probably peace-faction Cheyennes) told him that over 150 Indians were killed outright with 300 wounded of which one-half later died. Given the rapidity of the destruction of Fetterman's command, the hand-to-hand combat, and the obsolete, slow-to-reload weaponry of the soldiers, Fessenden was mildly skeptical. He admitted, "I do not know if these figures are correct, or if anyone really does know the extent of the Indian loss, but this was told to me by these [women]."[123] Below is a list of the various estimates of Indian casualties as claimed by participants in the fight or their contemporaries. No attempts are made here to list possible casualties claimed by later descendants of the participants either Indian or white. The original Cheyenne sources all agree that Big Nose, brother of Little Wolf and an esteemed Elkhorn society warrior, died in the fight as corroborated by their accounts. Two Moon is the only source to estimate Arapaho casualties. A list of the names of alleged Indian fatalities in the Fetterman fight may be found in appendix B.

Estimated Claims of Indian Casualties
at the Fetterman Fight and Sources

1. Michael Boyer (mixed-blood) (hearsay): 8 Indians killed; 2 mortally wounded, 50 wounded, T=10 killed
2. Two Moon (Cheyenne): 2 Cheyennes; 1 Arapaho; 11 Lakotas; T=14 killed
3. White Bull (Miniconjou): 14 Lakotas; unknown for Cheyennes; T=14 + killed
4. White Elk (Cheyenne): 2 Cheyennes; 50–60 Lakotas; T=52–62 killed
5. Wolf Tooth (Cheyenne): 2–3 Cheyennes; unknown for Lakotas; T=?
6. Wooden Leg (Cheyenne) (hearsay): 2 Cheyennes; unknown for Lakotas; T=?
7. Fire Thunder (Oglala): "Many," but Fire Thunder does not give estimates; T=?
8. Sgt. Fessenden (2/18th Inf.) (hearsay): 150 Indians killed; 150 mortally wounded; 150 wounded but survived; T=300 killed

By synthesizing the Indian accounts of the Fetterman fight with the locations of the soldiers' bodies that were recovered it is possible to ascertain by way of summation what may have occurred along Massacre Ridge on December 21, 1866. By doing so one may logically argue that Carrington quite possibly blamed the wrong officer for the army's disaster. All the significant Indian sources agree that as Fetterman's command crested Lodge Trail Ridge the cavalry, led by Lt. George W. Grummond, was out ahead of the infantry. Surgeon Hines's, Captain Ten Eyck's, and other officers' testimonies agree. The Indian testimonials further state that Fetterman and the infantry hesitated at the top of Lodge Trail Ridge before descending on to Massacre Ridge. Once they reached Massacre Ridge they tried to advance but did not get very far as warriors rose up around them and forced the initial survivors to reassemble on the southern high point of the ridge where the monument now stands. There they either maintained some semblance of tactical cohesion, or bunched, indicating loss of cohesion. Here most of them died in the vicinity of the rocks near the present-day monument.[124]

Fetterman had descended on to Massacre Ridge following Grummond and the cavalry that had uncomfortably separated from the infantry perhaps as early as the cresting of Lodge Trail Ridge. The cavalry wound up far north of the infantry. When they were attacked by overwhelming numbers they tried to maintain tactical cohesion by moving as a body back south up the ridge. This cohesion probably made them easy targets and did them more harm than good although all were eventually doomed. The spot where James Wheatley's and Isaac Fisher's bodies were discovered to the north, at the bottom of the ridge, was the vicinity of the cavalry's farthest advance at the time the trap was sprung. Perhaps they even penetrated a bit farther north and then retreated slightly southward to the rocks where Wheatley and Fisher decided to make their last stand. They were no closer than about a half- to three-quarters of a mile to Fetterman's infantry, and if we can give credence to Michael Boyer's testimony, perhaps as far away as a mile from the infantry early in the action.[125]

Some of the 2nd Cavalrymen were killed in close proximity to one another halfway up the ridge during the course of their retreat, apparently attempting to make a stand on foot, or perhaps bunched in panic, at a high point now known as Cavalry Hill. But few shell casings were found here so they must have quickly been overrun despite their repeating Spencers. The relief party found bodies of men and horses along the ridge all the way up to the infantry position at the site of the future monument where the last few surviving cavalrymen turned loose their horses and made a final stand with the infantry. Possibly all tactical cohesion was lost in this last desperate stampede between Cavalry Hill and Monument Hill by these few survivors and it was every man for himself. But one theory holds that little groups of troopers possibly moved up to Monument Hill leapfrog-fashion, thus providing covering arms fire for one another. In other words, cavalrymen's remains were found all along Massacre Ridge perhaps as far away as a mile north from Monument Hill, indicating that Grummond's mounted troopers had far outrun their infantry support at the time they were attacked.[126]

Meanwhile Wheatley and Fisher, realizing the futility of trying to retreat with the troopers, dismounted and made their stand at the north end of the ridge, conservatively the farthest point of penetration north down the ridge. As Fetterman tried to advance in support of Grummond when the cavalry was first attacked, probably not realizing at that point the large numbers of warriors present, the Indians quickly sprang the trap on Fetterman on the south end of the ridge and enveloped his position almost immediately. With Fetterman unable to support Grummond the Indians easily were able to destroy all three elements in detail even though a few cavalrymen and, amazingly, Capt. Frederick Brown were able to retreat to Fetterman's defensive perimeter where at least some semblance of tactical cohesion apparently was maintained to the end.[127]

But who was to blame for this separation and breakdown? The infantry and cavalry were separated linearly down Massacre Ridge over too far a distance for the foot soldiers to reach the cavalry if necessary. This separation could not have logically been designed or "ordered" as any kind of flanking movement unless they thought the retreating Indians would ride between them. Certainly as the immediate commander of the entire detail of eighty-one men Captain Fetterman officially held responsibility. But could he have prevented it? Did he order such a nonsensical and potentially suicidal linear separation? Whether fighting Indians or Confederates such foolishness could prove disastrous, and Captain Fetterman would have easily known this given his combat experience against Indians and, more so, Confederates. The most interesting and convincing evidence contradicting the traditional views is the so-called time and motion study conducted by J. W. Vaughn in the 1960s. Consulting a tactics expert, Brig. Gen. Charles Roberts, U.S. Army, Retired, in 1963 Vaughn learned that "small bodies of infantry could easily make three miles per hour on open level ground. In snow [not to mention an uphill grade] this speed would be reduced to one or two miles per hour for short distances." In Roberts's opinion "Fetterman and his foot soldiers could hardly have gotten over two miles [from the fort] when the firing was heard from the fort [by noon or shortly before]."[128]

Cavalry, however, Roberts proclaimed, usually marched from four to six miles an hour but could go much faster if engaging in a charge or if in pursuit at a gallop. By calculating distances from the fort, the route over Lodge Trail Ridge, and the distance north down Massacre Ridge, Vaughn and Roberts determined that it would have been impossible for Fetterman's infantry to have advanced farther north than Monument Hill by the time the first general firing was heard from the fort. That firing had to come from Grummond and the cavalry that was now very far ahead of the infantry, which was still standing perhaps as far south as the top of Lodge Trail Ridge.[129]

Vaughn concluded from his time and motion study that at some point the cavalry bolted away from the infantry at a fairly rapid pace to fatally pursue the ten Indian decoys down Massacre Ridge while Fetterman remained on top, never able to advance much farther down from where the monument now stands. Certainly it quickly became impossible for the infantry to reach the cavalry. Circumstances were actually the other way around as surviving cavalry troopers frantically tried to scramble south back up the ridge to Fetterman's position. Vaughn speculates that Fetterman deployed skirmishers in an impossible attempt to support Grummond while leaving a small reserve on Monument Hill to guard the protective rocks as the Sanborn Commission had concluded. His men were then quickly forced back to the rocks on the hill where he formed a perimeter; bodies were found facing outward in a ring indicating that Fetterman's remnant command had been surrounded. Soon the few panicked surviving cavalrymen fought their way through and joined the little group behind the rocks on Monument Hill at the end.[130] The mnemonic for 1866–67 drawn by American Horse suggests the notion that Fetterman formed the ring perimeter or hollow square.[131]

Surgeon Hines's testimony before the Sanborn Commission also supports this postulate. When asked, "Would you judge from the appearance of this ground [Massacre Ridge strewn with bodies], that one of the party had advanced and the other halted on the ground where they were lying

[Monument Hill]?" Hines replied, "My impression is, from viewing the ground, [is] that the cavalry were in advance of the infantry [and] that the Indians decoyed them on, . . . [and] the cavalry dismounted and fought on foot . . . [then] fell back to join the infantry."[132] In 1867 after hearing the testimonies of Ten Eyck and others who recovered the bodies, the Sanborn Commission issued its summation. "Our conclusion," they wrote into the congressional record, "is . . . that [Brevet] Colonel Fetterman formed his advanced lines on the summit of the hill [slightly north of the monument] overlooking the . . . valley, with a reserve near where the large number of bodies lay."[133] Vaughn's findings supported the opinion of the Sanborn Commission. "I will get a lot of argument on this," Vaughn wrote to a friend. "There will be many who will disagree with me but . . . I feel on more secure ground."[134]

Vaughn's apprehension, of course, is reflected in the notion that he was bucking the popular Fetterman stereotype of an arrogant, disobedient officer. Although responsibility had to ultimately rest with the operation commander, Capt. William J. Fetterman, someone else, Vaughn realized, may have been far guiltier in bringing about separation and disaster upon the entire command. That person could only have been one of two officers, Lt. George W. Grummond or Capt. Frederick Brown. At some point Grummond's cavalry bolted ahead of Fetterman and sprang the Indians' trap. Doing so was completely congruent with Grummond's similar, almost fatal action on December 6, and in character with his irrational and manic actions during combat in the Civil War. Historian Charles D. Collins Jr. of the Combat Studies Institute, Fort Leavenworth, Kansas, concurs. "It appears that the mounted troops and the foot infantry became separated," he wrote. "[T]he cavalry . . . moved ahead of the infantry soon after passing over Lodge Trail Ridge . . . Based on his past tendency for impetuous action, Grummond was probably anxious to come to grips with the foe."[135] Captain Fetterman, on the other hand, as he had done on December 6, held most of his infantry together and maintained tactical cohesion, however futile the effort. It is unlikely that Brown could have charged ahead and brought all the cavalry with him without the compliance of the cavalry's immediate commander, Lieutenant Grummond. The recovery detail on December 22 found the body of Brown's mount, Calico, halfway down the ridge, indicating that Brown had possibly gone with Grummond but the troopers likely would have followed the orders of their commander, Grummond. Perhaps, though, both Grummond and Brown were guilty of charging ahead in the same instant. Perhaps Brown dismounted and stayed with his friend Fetterman as he had done on December 6 and Calico ran off northward and was killed down the ridge. The exact truth will probably never be ascertained.[136]

The evidence discussed here suggests that Fetterman made a forlorn attempt to come to Grummond's support but did not get very far, and was forced to retreat back uphill to his reserve position where the monument now stands. According to Indian testimony scrutinized in this chapter the warriors at the top of the ridge wanted to lure the infantry farther into the trap before they showed themselves on the south end. It is almost certain that Fetterman did not realize how many hundreds of warriors were awaiting him when he began his short-lived advance down from Monument Hill to try and support Grummond. When he did so he was quickly overwhelmed and enveloped by Miniconjous, Oglalas, and Cheyennes.[137] Supporting Grummond was certainly an impossible task, but attempting to do so was probably instinctive on the part of tactical commander William J. Fetterman. He had done such during the Civil War with success. When Fetterman saw the utter futility of trying to support Grummond, however, he then wisely fell back and established a perimeter on Monument Hill. His ultimate responsibility at that point was to try to save as many lives of his infantrymen as possible.[138]

But could Fetterman have prevented Grummond's impetuosity? As with Bingham on December 6, when cavalry broke away from its combined tactical element, it would be impossible to "retrieve" them. Certainly Carrington had also been unable to retrieve Grummond, a lone rider, when he bolted Carrington's column on December 6 to join Lieutenant Bingham. Of course there are those who will always argue that it was Fetterman who actually ordered Grummond ahead to pursue the decoys if they had gotten too far ahead. This interpretation will probably never be completely proved or disproved. In all fairness to all the officers concerned on that day, none of them could have conceived of the possibility of up to 1,500 to 2,000 warriors hiding in wait for them as they advanced. None of these officers and their men had previously encountered more than 150 or so warriors. Certainly Fetterman and Grummond were aware of the decoying tactics of plains Indians; Fetterman had confessed as much to Carrington after December 6. And this was the largest force ever dispatched from the fort. Ordering Grummond ahead if the command expected to encounter 1,500 or more Indians is not likely. But still, regardless of how many or how few warriors these officers expected to meet, *impetuousness* in the resulting action is far more in line with the character and past actions of Grummond and Brown, not Fetterman.[139]

The question of course remains: did Fetterman disobey orders, the results being the annihilation of his entire command, regardless of who committed the tactical blunder that sealed the fate of eighty-one men? If we are to assume that Grummond had been instructed not to cross Lodge Trail Ridge, we must assume that Fetterman had the same orders; then, certainly, Fetterman disobeyed orders.

But we know that the situation had suddenly changed immediately after the soldiers had left the fort, and Carrington at first did not seem alarmed that the command was moving north up Lodge Trail Ridge rather than west to the wood train, presumably to cut off the retreat of the forty warriors who had withdrawn from their attack on the train. Surely Carrington suspected Fetterman's command was only pursuing about forty or so retreating warriors with perhaps a hundred or so waiting below, a manageable number of Indians to pursue with eighty-one men. The small, isolated decoy tactics of the Indians on December 6 would have given Carrington no real concern that Fetterman's force could not take care of the situation given the "anticipated" numbers. No previous engagement in the Powder River country that year would lead Carrington or any of the other officers to believe the Indians waiting in ambush would number a thousand or more. And again, Carrington could have easily sent a courier to bring back the command when he saw them heading northward against his orders if he felt they were in real danger. But he did not. He likely trusted Fetterman's instincts and there is no previous behavior on Carrington's part to suggest that he did not trust Fetterman's instincts. Carrington's concerns, given his past behavior, possibly were with Lieutenant Grummond, perhaps even to the extent that Grummond might once again disastrously strike out with only a handful of men as he had done on December 6.[140]

Indeed, the suggestion by Vaughn that Fetterman could not possibly have made it to the site of the attack on the cavalry by the time it began reinforces Carrington's concerns before the cavalry's exit from the stockade about Grummond's possible actions rather than those of Fetterman. The Indians saw the infantry halt at the top of the ridge but not the cavalry. It is entirely possible that Lieutenant Grummond and the cavalry bolted at this point and charged ahead in pursuit of the decoys. Arguably Fetterman would have been grossly derelict in his duties had he not at least made an attempt to support his subordinate officer when he saw his element engaged as far as a mile away down the ridge if he did not believe at that point there were many Indians present. But Fetterman likely had no idea how many Indians there were when he tried to come to Grummond's support since the warriors had not all showed themselves as yet, waiting instead for the infantry to advance a bit farther into the trap as Indian testimony asserts. But once he realized the unprecedented numbers of Indians present he wisely withdrew to Monument Hill and established a perimeter in a futile attempt to try and save his infantry. Had he not withdrawn at *that* point and tried to save his infantry he certainly would have been derelict in his duty.

But someone had to take the blame for what was the worst disaster for the U.S. Army in the West up to that point. At first Carrington heaped no official castigation on Fetterman's actions. The captain was one of his officers who had just been killed in action. But Carrington would soon be removed from command, made the scapegoat for an embarrassing disaster, be castigated by his commanding general, and spend the remainder of his life trying to vindicate himself by casting blame back on the operational commander of the action, the dead Capt. William J. Fetterman, when it well may have been the reckless Grummond who deserves the bulk of the criticism. But in heaping all the blame on Fetterman, Henry B. Carrington and others would, over the years, create a distorted perception and a body of myth that endures to this day based on flimsy circumstantial evidence that could have been cast in one of two, possibly three [not discounting Captain Brown] directions. The making of that myth will be examined in chapter 9. But given the weight of the forensic evidence in reconstructing the fight, and assimilating it for once with the Indians' memories of the sequence of events, there exists a very strong possibility that Col. Henry B. Carrington made a huge mistake by blaming Capt. William J. Fetterman.[141]

Young Man Afraid of His Horse, taken at Pine Ridge in 1891. Along with Red Cloud, Oglala Young Man Afraid of His Horse opposed federal intervention in the Powder River country in 1866, but some of his specific roles following the Fort Laramie council of that year are unclear. Courtesy of Gallery of the Open Frontier, University of Nebraska Press.

Facing page: Red Cloud. Red Cloud was the most vocal proponent of war in 1866 to reduce the forts along the Bozeman Trail. Courtesy of Gallery of the Open Frontier, University of Nebraska Press.

Col. Henry Beebe Carrington as he appeared about 1866. Carrington, who had no combat experience, was a master organizer, planner, and engineer, but he found the tactical operational orders presented to him in 1866 impossible to achieve. Courtesy Wyoming Tales and Trails.

Jim Bridger. Bridger, who guided the 18th Infantry into the Powder River country in 1866, had a fairly ambiguous presence at Fort Phil Kearny by autumn of that year. Courtesy Wyoming Tales and Trails.

Gen. Philip St. George Cooke. Although Cooke had served in the West for some time, his understanding of the logistical problems in the Mountain District of the Department of the Platte was inexplicably almost lacking. Courtesy Digital Library, Virginia Tech.

Margaret Carrington. Officers' wives often accompanied their husbands into combat zones during the nineteenth century. Margaret Carrington left to history one of the most complete memoirs of the war in the Powder River country in 1866. For decades it has shaped modern perceptions of that conflict, often inaccurately, because of her attempts to shed the best light on her husband's actions there. Courtesy American Heritage Center, University of Wyoming.

Capt. Frederick Brown. Captain Brown, often a rather comical and obsessive character, died with Fetterman on December 21, 1866, likely committing suicide when he knew all was hopeless. Cyrus Townsend Brady, *Indian Fights and Fighters*, 1904.

Red Cloud and American Horse in later life. Two principal allies in the Powder River country in 1866, Red Cloud and American Horse lived into the twentieth century. Courtesy Gallery of the Open Frontier, University of Nebraska Press.

Little Wolf, Sweet Medicine Chief of the Cheyennes. An important chief of the Northern Cheyennes, Little Wolf lost his brother, Big Nose, in the Fetterman fight. Little Wolf would later gain recognition for leading his people home from Indian Territory to Montana in 1878–79. Courtesy Gallery of the Open Frontier, University of Nebraska Press.

Two Moon of the Northern Cheyennes. Although Two Moon's accounts of the Fetterman fight are brief, incomplete, and frequently contradictory, he was nevertheless an important war leader against white expansionism during the 1860s and 1870s. Courtesy Gallery of the Open Frontier, University of Nebraska Press.

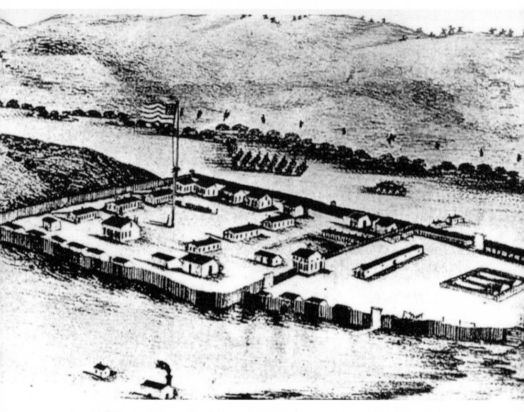

Fort Phil Kearny in 1866: Sketch by Antonio Nicolai. No photographs of Fort Phil
Kearny exist for its short duration. Nicolai's sketch is one of the best renditions left to
history. Courtesy Wyoming Tales and Trails.

Lt. George Washington Grummond. Although well liked by other officers and their wives at Fort Phil Kearny, Grummond's impulsive, possibly manic behavior on December 6 and 21 as well as in the Civil War made him an extreme liability as a junior officer. Arguably Grummond, above all others, contributed the most significantly to the annihilation of eighty-one soldiers and civilians in the Fetterman fight. He was killed in that action. Cyrus Townsend Brady, *Indian Fights and Fighters*, 1904.

Frances Courtney Grummond Carrington as she would have appeared about 1866 while married to Lieutenant Grummond. Frances Grummond Carrington left a memoir of army life at Fort Phil Kearny shortly before her death in 1911. Like Margaret Carrington before her she was concerned with vindication for her second husband, and possibly, if more subtly, her first husband. Courtesy American Heritage Center, University of Wyoming.

Capt. William Judd Fetterman. This is the only known photograph of Fetterman. Although physical appearances make individual impressions, Fetterman was not likely the incompetent "fire-eater" that he has come to be portrayed. Courtesy Gallery of the Open Frontier, University of Nebraska Press.

Looking east from Massacre Ridge to the gullies where the Miniconjou Lakotas waited in ambush. In these ravines the Miniconjou Lakotas lay in wait with their horses for Fetterman's command to descend Lodge Trail Ridge. When they attacked they quickly swung around south in the rear of the soldiers, cutting off any hope of their retreat back to Fort Phil Kearny. Photo by and courtesy of Darren Monnett.

Cavalry Hill looking north from Monument Hill. Here the survivors of the initial attack on the 2nd Cavalry at Peno Creek tried desperately to form a perimeter on high ground. The Indians quickly dispatched all but a few who then struggled their way back south to Fetterman's perimeter where they were killed. Photo by and courtesy of Darren Monnett.

Looking south toward Monument Hill from Massacre Ridge. This would have been the view (without the modern monument) surviving cavalry men would have seen in perhaps their last moments as they struggled to reach Fetterman's position during the final actions of the fight. Photo by and courtesy of Darren Monnett.

The boulders on Monument Hill near where Fetterman and Brown died. Here relief and recovery parties found the human remains of Fetterman's last stand following the fight. Photo by and courtesy of Darren Monnett.

The monument as it would have appeared in 1905. Tourists have been visiting the Fetterman Monument erected in 1905 and dedicated in 1908 for more than a century. Courtesy Gallery of the Open Frontier, University of Nebraska Press.

The Fetterman Monument today. The Fetterman Monument stands today largely unchanged. A stone wall now encloses it and the rocks where Fetterman's men made their last stand. Photo by and courtesy of Darren Monnett.

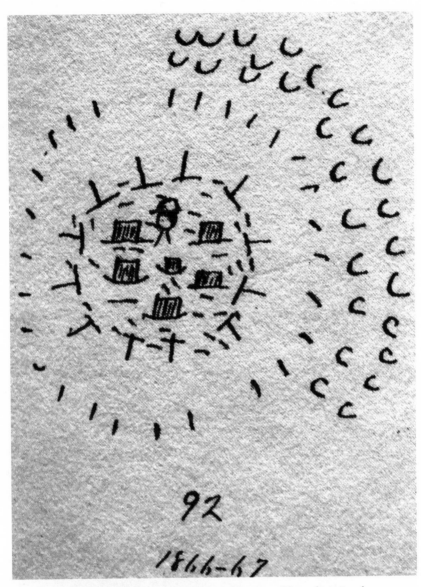

Mnemonic for 1866–67 from the winter count of American Horse depicting the Fetterman fight. American Horse's mnemonic interpretation clearly illustrates an envelopment of soldiers on Massacre Ridge. *Annual Report of the Bureau of American Ethnology, 1888–1898* (Washington, D.C.: Smithsonian, 1894).

Capt. James Powell in later life. Powell, shown here in civilian life, became one of the severest critics of Henry Carrington's leadership abilities and decision making as commander of Fort Phil Kearny. Cyrus Townsend Brady, *Indian Fights and Fighters*, 1904.

Capt. Tenador Ten Eyck. Ten Eyck led a relief force that found the remains of Fetterman's men. Carrington later accused him of taking a detour to the scene of the fight and arriving too late to relieve Fetterman's command. Courtesy Gallery of the Open Frontier, University of Nebraska Press.

Finn Burnett. A civilian contractor at Fort Phil Kearny in 1866, Burnett helped recover the bodies of Fetterman's men and later left history a detailed account of the experience. Courtesy Wyoming Tales and Trails.

John "Portugee" Phillips. Phillips became a local legend in Wyoming for his long winter ride to Fort Laramie to report the death of Fetterman's command. Contrary to that legend he did not make the journey alone. Courtesy Wyoming Tales and Trails.

Monument to John Phillips at Fort Phil Kearny. Phillips's exploit is commemorated at both Fort Phil Kearny and Fort Laramie. Photo by and courtesy of Darren Monnett.

Man Afraid of His Horse (right) smoking the pipe at the Fort Laramie peace council that produced the infamous Treaty of 1868. The second Fort Laramie Treaty in 1868 is one of the most significant in Lakota history as it made the Lakotas reservation Indians. Its ambiguous and confusing provisions helped precipitate the Great Sioux War and still causes legal controversy today. Courtesy Wyoming Tales and Trails.

Lakota chiefs in council at the Fort Laramie peace talks, 1867 or 1868. Red Cloud was among the last to sign the Treaty of 1868. He refused to do so until the forts along the Bozeman Trail were actually abandoned. Courtesy Wyoming Tales and Trails.

Henry and Frances Carrington at the dedication of the Fetterman monument in 1908. Henry and Frances Carrington were among the last surviving whites of the struggle for the Powder River country in 1866. Courtesy Wyoming State Archives.

Disinterment of the remains in the Fort Phil Kearny cemetery for reburial in the Little Bighorn National Cemetery, 1888. Fetterman and his men now rest at Little Bighorn National Cemetery. Courtesy Wyoming State Archives.

The graves of captains Fetterman and Brown at the Little Bighorn National Cemetery. Fetterman and Brown, who did not commit joint suicide, died together on Monument Hill and rest in peace together today. Photo by and courtesy of Darren Monnett.

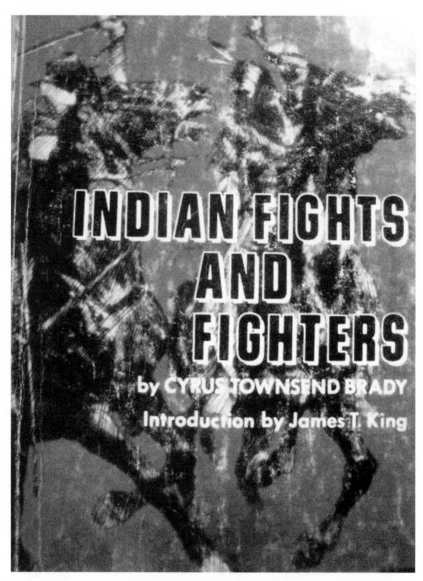

A reprint cover of Cyrus Townsend Brady's *Indian Fights and Fighters*, 1904—the book that started the eighty-man myth. Brady penned a legend in his book by creating an historical irony that has typecast Capt. William J. Fetterman for almost a century and a half. Photo by John H. Monnett. Courtesy University of Nebraska Press.

CHAPTER 8

TIME OF TRIUMPH, TIME OF FEAR

Of night men started from troubled sleep
To think the guards were fighting on the wall
And, roaring over like a waterfall.
The wild hordes pouring in upon the lost.
But 'twas the timber popping in the frost,
The mourning wolves. Nor did the dawn
Bring cheer.
Becandled like a corpse upon a bier
The lifeless sun, from gloom to early gloom,
Stole past,—a white procession to a tomb
Illuminating the general despair.[1]

THE BREATH-STEALING COLD DAYS AFTER DECEMBER 21, 1866, were both a
time of triumph and a time of fear for the Lakotas and Northern Cheyennes.
To be certain, the Bad Face Oglalas had taught the whites at Fort Phil Kearny
a lesson and demonstrated that attempts to seize control of the Powder River
country would be met with unmitigated opposition. For the Miniconjous,
the dying wishes of White Swan had been fulfilled. By keeping Fort Phil
Kearny in danger the Indians knew they had helped isolate Fort C. F. Smith
in the Bighorn country from supplies moving north along the Bozeman Trail.
A few days after the fight the Indians held a victory dance. But the weather
continued to be frigid and soon the people scattered to winter camps. They
did not know if retribution would befall their smaller villages during the cold
time when they were largely immobile and their pony herds were in poor
condition. So the winter of 1866–67 was also a time of great apprehension.
"It must be the fear that I remember most," recalled Black Elk years later, of
that winter when he was a small child. "All this time I was not allowed to play
very far away from our tepee, and my mother would say, 'If you are not good
the Wasichus will get you.'"[2] Black Elk's father broke his leg in the Fetterman
fight and had to be transported on a travois when the Oglalas broke camp.

"I can remember my father lying on a pony drag with bison robes all around him," the boy, now the old man, recalled. "The snow was deep and it was very cold, and I remember sitting in another pony drag beside my father and mother, all wrapped up in fur. We were going away from where the soldiers were." By spring the Oglalas were camped near Cheyenne friends in the valley of the Rosebud.[3]

The winter of 1866–67 was unusually severe in the Powder River country considering this general period of climatic change and many of the Indians could not remember a cold season quite so life-threatening. "It was a hungry winter," Black Elk remembered, "for the deep snow made it hard to find the elk; and also many of the people went snowblind. We wandered a long time, and some of the bands got lost from each other."[4] The focus had turned to survival rather than war. The Indians would not seriously threaten the garrison at Fort Phil Kearny until spring.

For the whites at Fort Phil Kearny the days following the Fetterman fight were filled with anguish, and ultimately for them too a time for survival. Ignorant of the social patterns of plains Indians during the dead of winter, the soldiers and some of the civilians—those new to the West—feared an all-out assault on the fort, a ridiculous notion, given that post returns by the first of the year, 1867, listed eight officers (including medical officers), 320 enlisted men, and 119 civilian contractors.[5] In addition there were at least fifty others wintering at the fort. Many of these civilians, as Wheatley and Fisher had been, were well armed with superior weapons. Because of his earlier pleas, Carrington had enough ammunition for rifles and carbines, and for the howitzers.[6] But so profound was the impact of the Fetterman fight on the imaginations of many at the fort that these numbers did little to reassure them. Unrealistic but stereotypical fears permeated the blistering cold following December 21. "During the nights I would dream of Indians," the newly widowed Frances Grummond remembered, "of being captured and carried away by Red Cloud himself while frantically screaming for help."[7] Sentries were placed at every loophole and relieved frequently through the night because of the intense cold. Snow drifted ten feet up the stockade, and trenches were continuously shoveled out to deny the Indians an easy foothold to get into the fort. The quartermaster's office issued buffalo leggings, wolf robes, muskrat caps, and fur gauntlets reaching to the elbow. "The whole garrison shared the gloom," Margaret Carrington remembered.[8] No one ventured beyond the fort for days except to gather wood. Of these few days of dread following the battle, Frances Grummond would later condescendingly write of Margaret Carrington's African American servant, Dennis, who

> seemed to be actually possessed by a demon, and in his frantic efforts to exorcise the spectre and relieve the tension by efforts of his own he would strike his head with all possible force against the boards of the partition which separated the kitchen from my own room, until they trembled with shock. Finally he continued this mania by butting his head against the stove-pipe and even the stove itself, like a veritable mad man. It was not until the appearance of the colonel with the muzzle of a cocked revolver touching his head that the equilibrium was restored and Dennis became contented to live a while longer and discharge the normal [subservient] functions of his usual employment.[9]

Even in the later days of winter when reinforcements had reached the post the lesson of December 21 tempered any thoughts of conducting offensive operations against the Indians dispersed in winter camps. "The destruction of Fetterman's command within a few miles of the post engendered doubts," Margaret Carrington wrote, "which were freely expressed by the officers, whether the force that could be made available, even after a successful march and surprise, could entirely or singly destroy the villages of Red Cloud." The general consensus "of the whole garrison [was that] the entire plan of destroying the Indians of the Northwest, while the mercury was motionless and the snow was all in motion, was temporarily dropped."[10] As with the Indians, the emphasis of the garrison at Fort Phil Kearny that bleak winter was not on military operations but on survival. Cold and snow tempered their activities while fear gripped their minds. In essence it was not the Lakotas and Cheyennes but rather the garrison at Fort Phil Kearny that, driven by anxiety and the unknown rather than reality, put themselves in a state of psychological siege.

In the hours and days immediately following the Fetterman fight most minds were on the fate of the couriers Carrington had sent out on the night of December 21. Would they make it through alive? If Indians didn't get them the weather might. Would reinforcements arrive soon?

The Ride of John Phillips

About 7:00 PM on December 21 Colonel Carrington had contracted two civilians at the fort to carry his report of the Fetterman fight to the Horseshoe Station telegraph office about 190 miles away in the Platte Valley. The couriers were John Phillips and Daniel Dixon. The temperature was well below zero when the men started out from the fort. Little is known of Dixon at this time, but Phillips became somewhat of a local legend in Wyoming during later years. He was born in the Azores, a colony of Portugal, in 1832, hence his nickname, "Portugee" Phillips. About 1850 he made his way to the California gold rush on a whaling ship and continued prospecting throughout the West until the Montana gold strikes found him wintering at Fort Phil Kearny in 1866, having arrived with the Bailey party in September. That winter Phillips worked for one of the private contractors at the fort.

Both men were paid three hundred dollars for their dangerous mission. Phillips and Dixon arrived at Fort Reno and rested for perhaps ten hours before going on to the Horseshoe Station with additional riders, including a man named Robert Bailey. At Fort Reno Lieutenant Col. Henry Wessells, commanding, gave Phillips additional dispatches for Col. I. N. Palmer, now commanding Fort Laramie. The riders probably rested at Bridger's Crossing before arriving at Horseshoe Station about 10:00 AM on Christmas Day. Now Carrington's news of the Fetterman fight was wired with haste to department headquarters in Omaha and on to Washington. After resting at the telegraph station Phillips continued on alone the forty miles to Fort Laramie to deliver Wessells's dispatches. He arrived there about 11:00 PM on Christmas night.[11]

Phillips rode into Fort Laramie in the snow and a guard took him to see Lt. Col. Palmer, who was attending a dress ball at "Old Bedlam," the officers' quarters at the fort, today the oldest standing building in Wyoming. Lieutenant David Gordon, 2nd Cavalry, stationed at Fort Laramie, remembered:

> It was on Christmas night, 11 p.m. when a full dress ball was progressing and everyone appeared superlatively happy, enjoying the dance, notwithstanding the snow was from ten to fifteen inches deep on the level and the thermometer indicated twenty-five degrees below zero, when a huge form dressed in a buffalo overcoat, pants, gauntlets and cap, accompanied by an orderly, desired to see the

commanding officer. The dress of the man, and at this hour looking for the commanding officer, made a deep impression upon the
officers and others that happened to get a glimpse of him, and consequently, and naturally, too, excited their curiosity as to his mission
in this strange garb, dropping into our full dress garrison ball at this
unseasonable hour.[12]

"In the evening a few ladies and officers assembled to dance," Colonel
Palmer remembered, "but the news of the Massacre at Fort Phil Kearny came
in during the evening, and this created such a gloom over all that the dancing party dispersed early."[13] The next morning Palmer fired off a telegram to
Gen. Philip St. George Cooke asking for reinforcements while giving Cooke
an earful of his assessments of Henry Carrington. "Col. Carrington sends
nothing to me," he stated, "but Wessells begs for reinforcements. Three or
four companies can be spared from here and if Van Voast can have a command would it not be better for him to go? He would go very unwillingly
if he is obliged to be under Col. C[arrington]."[14] Cooke rescheduled troop
movements immediately and ordered four companies of the 1/18th Infantry
and two companies of the 2nd Cavalry to be assembled at Fort Laramie
and move to the relief of Fort Phil Kearny and, if necessary, Fort Reno.
Because of bad weather resulting in poor logistics, reinforcements would
not arrive at Fort Reno until January 11, 1867, nor at Fort Phil Kearny
until January 16.[15]

John Phillips returned to Fort Phil Kearny, worked as a mail courier for
a time, and built a cabin outside the stockade walls as did several civilians.
Soon writers mythologized Phillips in popular literature as they have other
personalities at Fort Phil Kearny down to the present day. One dubious tale
has Carrington giving him the finest thoroughbred in the post stable for his
ride. Upon arrival at Fort Laramie, the poor horse supposedly soon collapsed
and died. Artistic images, both visual and written, often portrayed him riding alone the entire 236 miles to Fort Laramie and pursued most of the way
by Indians. In fact Phillips encountered no Indians along the way. They were
hunkered down against the recent blizzard and the story of the prize horse
and its death at Fort Laramie in front of "Old Bedlam" (officers' quarters)
cannot be substantiated. Yet the myth grew faster even than the aura surrounding William J. Fetterman. Stories have Phillips riding with U. S. Grant

in his carriage while Grant campaigned for the presidency in 1867. Actually Phillips went on to many odd jobs and occupations, including an attempt at ranching. He married a woman named Hattie Bucks in 1869. The couple had several children. Apparently the myth even went to Phillips's head: he allegedly named one of his sons Paul Revere Phillips. John Phillips died of kidney disease on November 18, 1883, in Cheyenne, Wyoming, and is buried there in Lakeview Cemetery.[16]

On that bitter cold and snowy Christmas Day that Phillips made his ride to Fort Laramie, anguish still gripped the garrison at Fort Phil Kearny. They had no idea if either of the riders had made it through or succumbed to the elements—or to Indians. But melancholy and grieving for their own losses occupied their minds even more so because of Christmas. "The holidays were sad as they were cold," Margaret Carrington remembered. "The constant and drifting snow-storms soon so lifted their crests by the west flank of the stockade that officers walked over its trunks . . . The men themselves, who, at the October muster, looked forward to the holidays and December muster with glad anticipations, forbore all demonstrations usual to such a period, and sensibly felt the weight of the great loss incurred . . . The whole garrison shared the gloom. Charades, tableaus, Shakespearian readings, the usual muster evening levee at the colonel's, and all the social reunions which had been anticipated as bringing something pleasant, and in the similitude of civilized life, were dropped as unseasonable and almost unholy."[17]

The day before Christmas was spent making final preparations of the eighty-one bodies that Carrington hoped to bury in a solemn service on Christmas Day. Body parts were laid in place as best they could, arrows were extracted, and some of the soldiers gave their best uniforms to their dead comrades for interment. Frances Grummond remembered. "And the horrors," she wrote, "the making of coffins and the digging in the hard, frozen earth for a burial place, when the cold was so intense that the men worked in fifteen minute reliefs and a guard was constantly on the alert lest Indians should interrupt their service.

"One-half of the headquarters building, which was my temporary home, was unfinished, and this part was utilized by carpenters for making pine cases for the dead. I knew my husband's coffin was being made, and the sound of the hammers and the grating of saws was torture to my sensitive nerves."[18] The bodies, of course, had been kept frozen, thus augmenting the difficulty in preparing them for burial. According to Margaret Carrington the deceased were put in their boxes and placed in lines according to companies along officer's row on Christmas Day so the garrison could pay final respects.[19] Two enlisted men each were placed in a single pine coffin while the three officers had single coffins. All the boxes were numbered and names recorded for future reference. Given the mutilations it is hard to believe that the coffins were open for viewing. But if they were, Capt. Frederick H. Brown must have presented a gruesome sight that Christmas Day. Almost half a century later, one of the men who had helped prepare Brown's solidly frozen body for burial, William R. Curtis, could not escape the memory of the awful sight. "The privates of Capt. Brown were severed and placed in his mouth," Curtis told William Camp, "and considering the extreme cold weather they could not be extricated."[20] Capt. Frederick Hallam Brown, who had so desperately wanted to take a Lakota scalp before reporting to his new duties at Fort Laramie, would be buried in this unfortunate repose. The cold was so intense that the frozen graves were not ready until December 26 when the funeral was held, according to Frances Grummond, "calmly, systematically, and safely."[21] Fetterman's men were interred in a pit fifty feet long, seven feet wide, and seven feet deep and without much ceremony or full military honors due to the severity of the weather.[22]

About the same time the Lakotas and Cheyennes would have taken care of their dead as well. Big Nose, the Northern Cheyenne warrior and decoy at the battle, died a few days after the fight and was laid to rest by the Sweet Medicine chief, his brother Little Wolf. According to all the Indian accounts a number of wounded died at the time of the great blizzard and intense cold. Most likely they were laid to rest among rocks.

As the Indians broke into their winter camps, the garrison at Fort Phil Kearny likewise prepared to hunker down for the winter and to focus mostly on their survival. Reinforcements finally reached them on January 16, 1867, shortly after the first news of the Fetterman fight reached the newspapers of readers sitting at their breakfast tables back East. Indeed the first reports were far-fetched and ethnocentric. The *New York Times* "confirmed" there was a coalition of twelve tribes sent against Fort Phil Kearny with an estimated number of warriors reaching 11,000. "It is thought that the post was captured by treachery," the reporter wrote, "as the force there should have been able to stand a siege, and it seems hardly possible that it could have been captured by Indian assault." The *Times* listed eighty-seven killed under the command of "Brevet Lieut. Col. W. J. Feltman [*sic*]."[23] Although she failed to name the "eastern" newspaper calling into question the credibility of her story, Margaret Carrington wrote of a report that had the fort under attack and Fetterman's command being slaughtered right at the gate of the beleaguered post. The "last band of survivors were driven to the gates of the fort," the newspaper report claimed, wrote Margaret Carrington, "knocking and screaming in vain for admission; when the last cartridge from revolver, carbine, and rifle was expended . . . and when, leaning against the gates, weary and bleeding and all resistance fruitless, all fell in one heap of mangled humanity, unsupported and cared for" while "the commanding officer . . . with two full companies, was looking on, afraid either to fire or open the gates lest the garrison within should be massacred by the infuriated savages and the post should be sacked!"[24]

Although Margaret Carrington did not identify her sources there are enough newspaper accounts to substantiate, especially in the Midwest, that Colonel Carrington was indeed mercilessly attacked in the press. The *Chicago Republican* claimed that Carrington had not allowed pickets on the stockade to carry loaded weapons and to salute all Indians in the spirit of friendship and accused Carrington of "cowardice and treachery."[25] The *Chicago Tribune* asserted that "Carrington [was] sitting beside a barracks stove 'gassing with some of the boys' at 2:30 in the morning following the battle."[26] The *Tribune* was among the most condemning. Of the somber Christmas at Fort Phil Kearny it described how all the officers and men were making merry as if nothing had happened: "Never during our course of human events have we been blessed with the liberty of viewing so much obscenity, debauchery, and drunkenness. The whole garrison was on the 'bust.'"[27] The press, it seems, judged Col. Henry Carrington to be inept, unfit for command, and even treacherous.[28]

Certainly finger-pointing and criticism came quickly from the press and was directed at the fort's commander, Col. Henry B. Carrington, and those above him in the line, especially Gen. Philip St. George Cooke, commander of the Department of the Platte. National media vehicles like *Harper's Weekly* and *Frank Leslie's Illustrated Newspaper*, always quick to criticize federal Indian policy, placed the blame on the shortsightedness of the military. Even in 1866, before the inception of the Grant Peace Policy and the Quaker-led Indian

Reform Movement, the eastern journalistic moguls evoked their criticisms (sometimes naively and condescendingly) about the "military solution" to the so-called Indian problem, while at the same time also showing little sympathy for the Indian Bureau and its everlasting dispute with the army. As early as the January following the Fetterman fight *Leslie's* asserted, "The Indians are, of course, still savage, and consequently not entirely amenable to the rules which govern civilized nations; but all men are naturally affected by justice, and they are not probably an exception to this universal rule. We cannot claim that we are not to blame in many cases where the disputes have arisen, and a want of justice in us is as bad as a massacre is in them."[29]

Many of the criticisms as well as the sympathies were based on faulty assumptions. For example, in a letter written by the commissioner of Indian Affairs, Lewis V. Bogy, to Interior Secretary O. H. Browning, Bogy explained his assessment of the primary causes of the Fetterman fight. Bogy blamed General Cooke for not allowing the Indians in the Powder River country to purchase firearms for hunting. Bogy asserted,

> An order issued by General Cooke, at Omaha, on the 31st day of July last, (herewith sent, marked No. 32) in relation to arms and ammunition, has had a very bad effect. I am satisfied that such orders are not only unwise, but really cruel, and therefore calculated to produce the very worst effect. Indians are men, and when hungry will, like us, resort to any means to obtain food, and as is the case is their only means of subsistence, if you deprive them of the power of procuring it, you certainly produce great dissatisfaction. If it were true that arms and ammunition could be accumulated by them; but this is not the fact. No Indian will buy two guns. One he absolutely needs, and as he has no means of taking care of powder, he will take, if offered to him, but a very limited quantity.

Bogy went on to state that because of the presence of miners in the Powder River country the grass was no longer sufficient to sustain horses and that the Indians had "but few horses," and therefore needed guns to hunt with since hunting with bows and arrows required a sufficient number of horses.[30]

The Indians in the Powder River country had sufficient horses for hunting, if not guns, in 1866. But Bogy's notion is largely discredited by mixed-blood Cheyenne George Bent, who clearly explained in his correspondence with George Hyde that "[a]rrows were always used by the hunters, to avoid quarrels, for each man had his marks on his arrows and he could tell by the arrows which animals belonged to him. If guns had been used there would have been constant squabbling."[31] Bogy knew nothing of Indians. In looking for a scapegoat he singled out Carrington. The "Indians, almost in a state of starvation," Bogy claimed, "were rendered desperate, and resorted to the stratagem which proved too successful. It seems as if the officer commanding could have avoided the catastrophe; and it seems also that men thus armed could have repelled an attack by all the Indians in Western Dakota."[32] The motives for war with the whites in the Powder River country in the summer and fall of 1866 were certainly not for want of weapons for hunting, albeit the winter was one in which game was often hard to find, but rather a dogged determination to drive the whites from this coveted region so recently won by the Lakotas and their allies from the Crows.

The lives of Carrington, Cooke, and even divisional commander William T. Sherman and General of the Army Ulysses S. Grant soon became caught up in the politics of the Fetterman fight. Caught between the continued dispute between the army and the Indian Bureau on the one hand, and the demand for manpower and money to administer the five southern Reconstruction districts and the need to protect settlers, white immigrants, and (beginning in 1867) construction crews of the advancing railroads in the West on the other hand, resources, both financial and human, were simply stretched. The West, especially the military in the West, became a low priority, with the bulk of already insufficient resources earmarked for the West destined for the costliest civil construction project in American history to that point, the Pacific railroad. Activities in such out-of-the-mainstream locations as the Powder River country were almost destined to fail for want of necessary resources. Blunders like the Fetterman fight could be costly and embarrassing to all concerned and thus bring into question the need to spread limited manpower and money so thinly across the continent at a time of financial uncertainty after the Civil War. But the army continued to see the need to protect the Montana gold resources. So when mistakes were made, especially media-intensive ones like the Fetterman fight, and by January 1867 the pragmatic decision to close the Bozeman Trail, someone had to take the hard fall. The *someone* in question was the post commander at Fort Phil Kearny,

Col. Henry B. Carrington, and to an almost equal extent his department commander, Gen. Philip St. George Cooke. The dual blame naturally pitted the general and the colonel at odds, each accusing the other of incompetence and eventually, on Carrington's part at a later time, casting the blame back onto the dead operational commander, Capt. William J. Fetterman.[33]

On December 27, the day after the burial of Fetterman and his men, three new officers reported for duty at Fort Phil Kearny: Capt. George B. Dandy (Brown's replacement), Lt. Thomas J. Gregg (Bingham's replacement), and Lt. Alphonse Borsman. The mail also informed Carrington that the new headquarters for the 18th Infantry would be Fort Casper, where the 1st Battalion would become the core for the reorganized 18th Infantry while the 2nd Battalion at Fort Phil Kearny and Fort C. F. Smith would form the core of the new 27th Infantry. Carrington knew he would soon be leaving the fort he had built. "My duty will be done when I leave, as ordered to my new regimental headquarters, Fort Casper."[34]

The orders for Carrington's transfer became official with the arrival of his replacement, Lt. Col. Henry W. Wessells II on January 16, 1867. It had taken the expedition of reinforcements since New Year's Day to reach Fort Phil Kearny because of storms and heavy snow. With Wessells were the reinforcements ordered out by General Cooke immediately after he had received word of the Fetterman fight. There were four companies of the 1st Battalion of the 18th Infantry under Major James Van Voast with two companies of the 2nd Cavalry under Lieutenant David Gordon. "At last we are saved," Frances Grummond asserted.[35] But since the Lakotas and Cheyennes caused no serious problems for the remainder of the winter these additional troops were not needed and only stretched the resources for both man and beast at Fort Phil Kearny until spring. Cooke had cut Carrington's official transfer orders immediately upon hearing of Fetterman's demise and they were worded very curtly and could only be taken as a reprimand: "Colonel H. B. Carrington, 18th United States Infantry, will be relieved from the command of Fort Philip Kearny by Brevet Brigadier General Wessells, and will proceed immediately to Fort Casper."[36]

During Carrington's tenure at Fort Phil Kearny the losses included, in this phase of Red Cloud's War, five officers, ninety-one enlisted men, and fifty-eight civilians killed, with many more wounded.[37] General Cooke, astutely aware of Carrington's previous incessant pleas for more up-to-date weapons, did whatever he could to divert any attention from his own neglect and culpability in what had transpired at Fort Phil Kearny that fall by directing blame back on Carrington. He wrote a letter to General of the Army Ulysses S. Grant on December 27 asserting that Carrington was "an energetic, industrious man in garrison; but it is too evident that he has not maintained discipline, and that his officers have no confidence in him."[38] Although somewhat correct in his assessment of Carrington, it would do Cooke no good as he too would take the fall. The War Department immediately replaced Cooke as commander of the Department of the Platte and replaced him with Gen. Christopher C. Augur, who took over duties in Omaha on January 23, 1867. Nevertheless, Carrington was bitter over the wording of Cooke's relief orders that seemed to him punishment for Fetterman's demise. It would take three decades for Carrington to forgive Cooke and make his peace with him.[39]

On the same day that General Cooke was relieved of his command, January 23, 1867, Colonel Carrington, his family, and his staff departed Fort Phil Kearny. The temperature was thirty-eight degrees below zero. With the Carringtons was Frances Grummond. With her was the pine coffin containing the frozen body of her husband, Lieutenant G. W. Grummond, that had been exhumed from the post cemetery. She would return the remains to Tennessee for reburial. The little entourage suffered terribly from the arctic cold, taking three days in the snow to cover the sixty-five miles to Fort Reno. Two men had to have fingers amputated at Fort Reno because of severe frostbite.[40] Upon arrival at Fort Reno, Carrington learned that the army had decided to close Fort Casper and switch the headquarters of the reorganized 18th Infantry to Fort McPherson, Nebraska. Near Sage Creek, on the route to Fort McPherson, Carrington accidentally discharged his service revolver and shot himself in the thigh. He was transported back to Fort Laramie for two weeks, then taken by ambulance to Fort McPherson. Soon he would learn of the government's intention to assemble a special commission to investigate what it was now calling the Fetterman "disaster." Thus began Carrington's lifelong ordeal to clear himself personally of any blame for the Fetterman fight. At first his argument was with General Cooke, as too was the concern of the commission. During this time Carrington cast no immediate blame upon Fetterman. But during the dispute between Cooke and Carrington the general suppressed Carrington's official report of the fight. Carrington was unable to override Cooke's animosity. So instead he took a different tack to clear his name from wrongdoing. He cast the blame back on the dead Fetterman by stressing dramatically how Fetterman had disobeyed orders on December 21. Carrington would stand by this defense once the Sanborn investigative committee hearings began. He would stick to the story for the remainder of his life.[41]

The Time of Suffering

Meanwhile the garrison at Fort Phil Kearny, now composed of elements of the new 27th Infantry and the 2nd Cavalry, suffered terribly during the remainder of the winter of 1867 following Carrington's departure. As severe weather and intense cold sealed the Bozeman road from travel in both directions, the fort was, for all practical purposes, cut off from its supply and communication lines for much of the time until March. With temperatures often down to forty below zero this was one of the worst winters many had seen in the Powder River country in years.[42] Morale suffered. One soldier wrote home shortly after the Fetterman fight, "We are fighting a foe that is the devil . . . Pray God to hasten the day when I shall get out of this horrible place."[43] Animals suffered even worse than humans. By early spring, the mules began eating holes through the logs in their stables. Wessells ordered Capt. James Peale to return two companies of the 2nd Cavalry back to Fort Laramie in an attempt to save the horses from starvation but most of the animals died along the trail. The men reached Fort Laramie on foot and the bones of their horses could be seen for years along the Platte road. Scurvy broke out and soldiers complained there was no place to wash clothing or take a bath until spring. As the mules ate bark, "Many [people] lived on [the] mules' corn," Finn Burnett remembered.[44]

In May Wessells reported that two soldiers dressed as Indians had deserted with a party of Crows.[45] By March Wessells had heard nothing from Fort C. F. Smith and he feared the worst. John Bozeman himself, one of the pioneers of the trail that bears his name, was killed, probably by Blackfeet, when he tried to make it through from the Gallatin Valley to see if Fort C. F. Smith needed relief. When a small detail from Fort Phil Kearny got through in March they found the soldiers there had fared better than the garrison at Fort Phil Kearny. A supply of potatoes and cabbage purchased in the fall from merchants in the town of Bozeman had kept down scurvy while the garrison had survived mostly on corn.[46]

With the coming of warmer weather the Lakotas and Cheyennes once again began attacking supply trains, woodcutting details, and hay-cutting crews. "As early as February," General Augur, the new commander of the Department of the Platte, reported, "the Indians commenced a system of attacks upon small parties and trains along the Montana route, and, as the season advanced, extended them to all my lines, and have kept it up during the whole summer."[47] As I stated in the introduction, the purpose of this book is to synthesize past and recent scholarship on the struggle for the Powder River country in 1866 and not to present a comprehensive history of all the years of Red Cloud's War. Nevertheless a brief summation of that war as it continued into 1867 and 1868 is necessary to assess the effects of the Fetterman fight itself. By the summer of 1867 the elements of the 27th Infantry and the 2nd Cavalry distributed among three forts found themselves trying to protect a road that the government had closed to civilian traffic the previous fall. The soldiers from the forts were now only protecting themselves and the lives of the civil contractors trying to provision the troops. The military presence in the Powder River country had thus become a self-defeating cycle of supply and survival with no logical means to define a viable war aim.

From generals Grant and Sherman on down the line there was talk in the spring of 1867 of closing the posts in the Powder River country in favor of reinforcing troop strength to the south along the advancing construction lines of the Union Pacific and Union Pacific Eastern Division (later the Kansas Pacific) railroads. Over the winter a large military campaign was planned by the Division of the Missouri involving, among other units, Custer's 7th Cavalry, newly organized under the Army Reorganization Act of 1866 and under the expeditionary command of the Civil War icon and future Democratic presidential nominee Gen. Winfield Scott Hancock. The purpose of the expedition was to shock and awe the tribes and thus prevent trouble for railroad construction crews. But Hancock's and Custer's maneuvers in Kansas and Nebraska had much the same results in 1867 as Connor's largely ill-fated offensive in 1865 and Carrington's defense of the Bozeman Trail in 1866.[48]

Two fights of notoriety one day apart in August 1867 sealed the fate of the Powder River forts although they were tactical victories for the soldiers. The so-called Hayfield fight near Fort C. F. Smith fought on August 1 and the much studied Wagon Box fight at the pinery area outside Fort Phil Kearny on August 2 proved to be somewhat of a mild tonic for Fetterman's defeat. The twin defensive (on the part of the soldiers) battles, fought almost simultaneously, also raise the possibility that there existed at least some kind of coordinated effort among the Indian "coalition" in the Powder River country during the latter phases of Red Cloud's War. By July at least 1,500 Bad Face Oglalas, Miniconjous, and Northern Cheyennes had gathered in the Rosebud Valley determined to press the war, but apparently they were divided on which fort should be their objective, some wanting to resume pressure on Fort Phil Kearny, while others wanting to harass troops at Fort C. F. Smith on the Bighorn. The Cheyennes too were divided on the matter.[49]

The first war party struck on the Bighorn. On August 1 the garrison at Fort C. F. Smith consisted of approximately 350 officers and men of Companies D, E, G, H, and I of the 27th Infantry. They were under the command of Lt. Col. Luther P. Bradley, who had brought in reinforcements and assumed command of the northern post on July 23. Junior officers who would play an important role in the fight of August 1 were Lt. George H. Palmer, a Medal of Honor recipient from the Civil War and a Prussian immigrant, and Lieutenant Sigismund Sternberg, who served in Company G under Capt. Thomas Burrowes.[50] In July contractor A. C. Leighton accompanied Bradley and scout Jim Bridger first to Fort Phil Kearny and then to Fort C. F. Smith. He brought with him, for the infantrymen at both posts, crates containing .50–70 Allin-modified breech-loading Springfield rifles to replace the old .58-caliber muzzle-loaders that had helped seal Fetterman's fate. The new rifles were converted to breech-loading weapons from the old .58-caliber muzzle-loading weapons—still Civil War surplus but guns that would catch the Lakotas and Cheyennes by surprise.[51]

The warriors would focus their attack on Leighton's hay-cutting operations about three miles from the Fort C. F. Smith stockade. There the soldiers had erected a fortification to protect livestock and men in case the hay mowers were attacked. Logs covered with a latticework of woven willow branches formed a defensive corral. The structure was crude and afforded little protection but was flanked by Warrior Creek and the Bighorn River. Three rifle pits were situated at the corners away from the river. During the later days of July soldiers noticed the presence of Indians daily in the vicinity of the fort and on July 31, Lieutenant Sternberg drove a small party of Lakotas away from the mowing operations. Friendly Crows warned the soldiers that the Lakotas and Cheyennes were planning an attack but the warnings went unheeded.[52]

On the morning of August 1 twenty infantrymen under Lieutenant Sternberg manned the corral as nine civilian hay mowers moved out for their day's chores. About 9:00 AM a shot rang out, and soon the mowers came scurrying back to the makeshift stockade. They were followed by a large party of charging warriors. Throughout the morning the Indians attempted repeated attacks against the corral but were driven off with casualties. Early in the fight Lieutenant Sternberg fell, killed instantly, a bullet through his brain. Sgt. James Horton assumed command after Sternberg was killed but soon received a severe wound himself. He was succeeded by a civilian, D. A. Colvin, whose remark "we will never get out of here alive" did little to instill confidence in the men. With Indian women watching from a nearby hill, ready to come down and strip the bodies of the soldiers, the warriors resumed their attacks in the afternoon. Each time they were repulsed by the .50–70s they had not anticipated, expecting instead to overrun the fortification as the soldiers tried to reload muzzles between volleys.[53]

Meanwhile Lieutenant Palmer, who had been escorting a woodcutting detail, saw the soldiers under attack at the hayfield and estimated the Indians' numbers to be about eight hundred. Palmer reported the situation to Colonel Bradley at the post but for some unknown reason (later branded cowardice by some) Bradley was tardy in sending reinforcements. Meanwhile the Indians tried unsuccessfully to set fire to the corral at the hayfield. Finally twenty mounted infantrymen under Lieutenant Shurly were sent out from the fort to relieve the beleaguered defenders. They came under attack themselves and Company G under Captain Burrowes came out to relieve Shurly and return to the fort. Finally even more soldiers came out from the post under Lieutenant Fenton along with a howitzer and the Indians broke off the attack for good. The hay-cutting detail lost Lieutenant Sternberg and another soldier killed and three soldiers and one civilian wounded. There are no firsthand Indian accounts of the Hayfield fight so Indian casualties are not known except that they were heavy. Bradley reported eight dead and around twenty-five wounded. The body of one warrior was never recovered, and the fatigued, angry soldiers at the corral scalped and beheaded the warrior and placed his severed head on a high pole above the corral as a warning to the Indians.[54]

The very next day, August 2, another large party of warriors, Oglalas under Crazy Horse, Miniconjous under High Backbone, and Northern Cheyennes under the bulletproof Crazy Mule, Ice, and Little Wolf's nephew (Young) Little Wolf, struck the woodcutters near the pinery above Fort Phil Kearny. The Wagon Box fight has gained legendary status over the years as a tumultuous and successful defensive stand by woodcutters and their 27th Infantry escort. White Bull is the main Indian source for this fight. Unlike the accounts of the Fetterman fight, White Bull praises the actions of Crazy Horse at the Wagon Box fight.[55] White Bull places Red Cloud in the vicinity of the field but not leading any of the assaults.[56] Capt. James Powell reported that the "hills in the immediate vicinity [of the fight] were covered with Indians who merely acted as spectators."[57] Throughout July the Indians had intensified their harassment of woodcutting details. On July 5 Col. Jonathan E. Smith assumed command of Fort Phil Kearny, replacing Wessells. His second in command was Maj. Benjamin Smith (no relation). Captains Powell and Ten Eyck remained at the post now as members of the 27th Infantry. But new officers had come to the fort as well. One was Lt. John C. Jenness, a Vermonter and a Civil War veteran who knew nothing of Indians. Jenness was assigned to Powell's C Company.[58]

On July 31 Powell and Jenness moved out of the fort to relieve Company A, which had been protecting the pineries. By this time, as had been done at Fort C. F. Smith, the garrison at Phil Kearny had constructed a protective corral of wagon beds to protect livestock and serve as a defensive position in case of Indian attack. On August 2 they would be most grateful they had done so. In his official report Powell stated that "[a]bout 9 o'clock in the morning [of August 2] two hundred Indians attacked" the herders who were caring for the animals some distance from the corral. An additional five hundred warriors attacked the separated wood train at the edge of the mountains, driving away the men and burning the wagon. Although Powell had fifty-two men under his immediate command only twenty-four enlisted men and six civilians along with Powell and Jenness were able to make it to the corral. Shortly they would face the onslaught of perhaps eight hundred warriors.[59] According to one source a number of the men made preparations to take their own lives if overrun by tying one end of a shoelace to one of their feet and the other end to the trigger of their rifle.[60] The warriors made at least two major assaults on the corral and probably many smaller attacks led by individual warriors

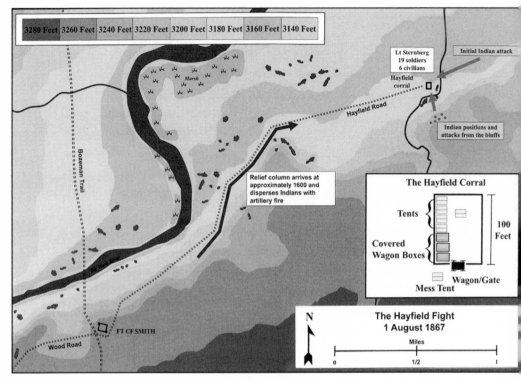

3280 Feet 3260 Feet 3240 Feet 3220 Feet 3200 Feet 3180 Feet 3160 Feet 3140 Feet

Lt Sternberg
19 soldiers
6 civilians

Initial Indian attack

Hayfield corral

Indian positions and attacks from the bluffs

Hayfield Road

Bozeman Trail

Relief column arrives at approximately 1600 and disperses Indians with artillery fire

The Hayfield Corral

Tents

100 Feet

Covered Wagon Boxes

Wagon/Gate

Mess Tent

Big Horn River

FT CF SMITH

Wood Road

N

**The Hayfield Fight
1 August 1867**

Miles

0   1/2   1

"The Hayfield Fight, 1 August 1867." Charles D. Collins Jr., *Atlas of the Sioux Wars*, 2nd ed. (Fort Leavenworth, KS: Combat Studies Institute Press, 2006).

out to win glory. According to Pvt. Sam Gibson, "The whole plain was alive with Indians," he remembered years later, "all mounted and visible in every direction. They were riding madly about, and shooting at us with guns, bows and arrows, first on one side and then on the other."[61]

Others remembered the warriors attacking on foot. That very evening Pvt. Eugene Cummings wrote a letter to his brother stating that "[during] the last two charges they came within 6 yards or so of the muzzles of our guns, and I thought at this time that we were gone up."[62] During the second attack Lieutenant Jenness, who had been fighting behind a wagon in a standing position, was warned to keep down but Jenness did not take heed. "I know how to fight Indians," someone supposedly heard him shout. At that moment a bullet plowed through his forehead from an Indian sniper, killing him instantly. Snipers also claimed the lives of privates Henry Haggerty and Tommy Doyle. But the breechloaders proved their worth. As at the Hayfield fight the previous day the Indians could not advance to overrun the corral because the soldiers could rapidly reload. With the arrival of reinforcements from the fort under Major Smith the Indians finally broke off the attack after several hours of determined fighting. Powell suffered three casualties' dead and two wounded in the corral, and two others killed in the fighting outside the perimeter.[63]

▼▼▼

By all accounts the Indians, however, suffered fairly heavy casualties. "We came on after sunrise," the Oglala Fire Thunder remembered. "There were many, many of us, and we meant to ride right over them and rub them out." But the warriors were soon dismayed and frustrated by the new breech-loading rifles of the soldiers and at least one Henry rifle. "There were not many Wasichus," Fire Thunder stated, "but they were lying behind the [wagon] boxes and they shot faster than they ever shot at us before. We thought it was some new medicine of great power that they had, for they shot so fast that it was like tearing a blanket . . . Our ponies were afraid of the ring of the guns the Wasichus made, and would not go over . . . Then we left our horses in the gulch and charged on foot, but it was like green grass withering in a fire." Fire Thunder, who was one of the informants for the Fetterman fight, claimed the Indians suffered heavy losses. "I do not know how many of our people were killed," he remembered, "but there were very many. It was bad."[64]

White Bull, from his position on the field, claimed one Oglala, a warrior named Only Man, killed and five Miniconjous killed with six more Lakotas wounded, but there were probably many more that White Bull did not see from his position on the field. Captain Powell officially reported sixty Indian casualties. White Bull claimed the fight was intended to be a decoy maneuver to draw soldiers from the fort but that the whites did not fall for it so the attack became a direct assault on the corral. He asserts that in the third charge led by Young Duck, Muskrat-Stands-on-His-Lodge, Dog Tongue, and a warrior with the unusual name of Jipala, along with Young Duck were killed. All of them were Miniconjous. Jipala charged in on foot from the east with a huge buffalo-hide shield, dodging from side to side. "From time to time," White Bull remembered, "he jumped into the air, loosing his arrow[s] from the apex of his leap." During one leap he fell to the ground and moved no

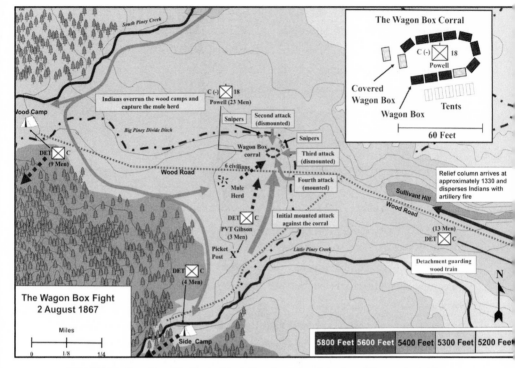

"The Wagon Box Corral." Charles D. Collins Jr., *Atlas of the Sioux Wars*, 2nd ed. (Fort Leavenworth, KS: Combat Studies Institute Press, 2006).

more, shot to pieces by the converted Springfield rifles. The Lakotas could not recover his body.[65] The Northern Cheyennes lost Sun's Road, killed, and an unknown number wounded. Crazy Mule, however, received a scalp wound but survived. According to the warrior Braided Locks, Crazy Mule lost much prestige after the Wagon Box fight as many of the Cheyennes began to question his bulletproof medicine.[66]

Certainly after the loss of Fetterman's command the Hayfield and Wagon Box fights were psychological as well as tactical boosts, albeit defensive victories, for the 27th Infantry in the Powder River country. Conversely, the battles came as somewhat of a shock to the confident coalition of warriors whose strategy assumed two more cases of total victory and possible annihilation of their enemy. They had gone into winter camps in December convinced of their superiority over the whites in the Powder River country. Tactically the twin fights demonstrated that two dimensions are effective in thwarting large numbers of an attacking foe: rapid-firing rifles or carbines and a well-fortified defensive position. Had General Cooke listened to Carrington's pleas and supplied the troops at Fort Phil Kearny with the best available weaponry in 1866, likely Spencer rifles or carbines, things might have turned out differently for Fetterman on December 21, 1866. The importance of both these tactical advantages was demonstrated again the following year, 1868, at Beecher Island and in 1874 at Adobe Walls. Perhaps nowhere was this principle so well illustrated as it was on January 22, 1879, in present-day KwaZulu Natal by British troops of the 24th Foot at Rorke's Drift, who successfully defended their little contingent with Martini-Henry breechloaders while fighting against an overwhelming Zulu army from a hastily built but well-fortified position. The small garrison survived, while only a few miles away at Isandlwana, General Chelmsford's army, with far more troops than the garrison at Rorke's Drift, and armed with the same rifles, suffered one of the greatest defeats in British imperial history when caught in the open by the Zulus. Like the 24th Foot, the battle-tested George Custer and his fatefully doomed companies of the 7th Cavalry, separated like Fetterman, were annihilated in 1876 when caught on open ground while the other companies of the 7th Cavalry under the immediate command of the untested Maj. Marcus Reno, with the help of the experienced Capt. Frederick Benteen, entrenched and thus survived with carbines not that much inferior to some of the Winchesters of the Indians when ability to reload in timely fashion is considered. Again, in 1885, the well-armed and numerically superior forces of Mohammed Ahmad took ten months to reduce by siege Gen. Charles Gordon's hungry but well-fortified garrison with equal weaponry at Khartoum in the Sudan.[67]

But, although defensive victories by imperial forces against indigenous populations make for interesting history, the Hayfield and Wagon Box fights did not bring about immediate peace with the plains Indians any more than did Beecher Island or Adobe Walls or Rorke's Drift with the Zulus. Within a year of Hayfield and Wagon Box, many of the chiefs were willing to listen to peace overtures from the federal government, but only on their terms of 1866, namely the abandonment of the three posts on the Bozeman Trail. By 1867–68, and another winter of financial cost and suffering, the government was willing to listen. The Bozeman Trail was officially closed to all civilian traffic and open only to the military supply contractors. The transcontinental railroad would soon reach Salt Lake City, making that route a safer and faster means to reach the Montana gold country, thus rendering the Bozeman route and its "protective" forts obsolete. In fall 1867 Fort Phil Kearny was under a virtual state of siege and the Indians tried to burn the garrison out. Lt. George P. Belden remembered, while probably dramatically exaggerating the event as he was prone to do:

In the last days of the month [October 1867] the Indians fired the grass all around the post, and for a time we thought we should be burnt up. The slopes of the hills, as far as the eye could reach, were covered with lines of fire, and tall sheets of flame leaped up from the valley or run crackling through the timber. The parade ground of the garrison was lighted up at night so one could see to read, and for a distance of many miles every tree and shrub could be distinctly seen. The crackling of the fire sounded like the discharge of thousands of small arms, and every few moments the bursting of heated stones would resound over the valley, resembling the booming of distant cannon. In all my life I had never seen so grand and imposing a sight, and never expect to witness one like it again. For three days the flames raged over a vast extent of country, and then, having consumed all the grass and dry trees, went out, doing us no harm, owing to the streams around the fort, which completely checked the advance of the destroying element.[68]

Indeed the forts were not by 1868, and arguably not since 1866, protecting anyone but their own garrisons. The lack of any offensive capabilities rendered them not only anachronisms but outright embarrassments to the government. Everyone including the initially reluctant department commander, Gen. C. C. Augur, saw the necessity of closing the forts. This would be a relatively painless concession on the part of the government to Red Cloud and other chiefs.

In addition, as the western railroads pushed into Indian country in 1867 and 1868, many of the warriors of the northern plains refocused their efforts southward. During 1867 and 1868 a number of the northern tribesmen, perhaps emboldened by their victory in the Fetterman fight or eager for revenge following the Wagon Box fight, came south to the Platte and even farther to the Smoky Hill River in Kansas to join their southern brethren in opposing the railroads. Others, like the peace factions of the Northern

Cheyennes, had periodically come south to avoid Red Cloud's War. The esteemed Northern Cheyenne Crooked Lance warrior Roman Nose had already joined the southern Dog Soldiers in 1866, not to escape fighting in the north but to oppose travel on the Smoky Hill Trail. Roman Nose would lose his life fighting at Beecher Island in Colorado Territory on September 17, 1868. Along the Platte and Smoky Hill bloodshed reigned in 1867 and 1868. Making the situation all the more desperate was the spread of the agricultural frontier across Kansas beginning in 1866. Eighteen sixty-seven and 1868 would become the bloodiest years in Kansas history for Indian attacks. Unlike the Powder River country, yet largely unsettled by white agriculturalists, the lives of many civilians including foreign immigrants who had never before seen an Indian would be lost, captured, and abused as a result of raids on homesteaders' farms. Settlers who did suffer from these raids and survived would carry with them for the rest of their lives memories of violence that masked the more complex nature of Indian society and humanity. But for the Indians, the sights of permanent settlers altering the environmental landscape that supported their equestrian bison-based economy and the advancing railroads, an enormous agent of empire, were unnerving. They viewed the settlers as invaders. Homesteads and towns meant permanent conquest of dwindling hunting lands and ultimately the decimation of the buffalo herds by whites, a situation the Indians tried to counter with a determined force in order to discourage or slow up the immense wave of the Euro-American westward movement.

The government was well aware of these developments. But General Sherman disagreed vehemently with Congress in its desire to extend peace overtures to the Lakotas. "The Sioux have not confined their efforts to resist the opening of that single road [the Bozeman Trail]," he wrote. "They have carried war down several hundreds of miles south, and have killed our people, and stolen our horses at Brady's Island, at Ash Hollow, on Lodge Pole, and even south of the Platte. Some of these same Sioux are at this moment at open war, in combination with Cheyennes and Kiowas, as low down as the Smoky Hill, where I believe they never before claimed a right to go."[69]

Sherman's statements of July were as much a result of miscues by the army as they were of Lakotas carrying the war south. Certainly the Southern Cheyennes, Arapahos, and Kiowas as well as some of the Lakotas living along the Platte opposed the extension of the railroad. But back in April the largely botched Hancock Expedition, composed of 1,400 men of the 37th Infantry, 7th Cavalry, and 4th Artillery, designed to impress the tribesmen, had just the opposite effect after Hancock burned a vacated Dog Soldier village on the Red Arm fork of the Arkansas. As part of the Army Reorganization Act of 1866, Congress had authorized the muster of four new regiments of cavalry, the 7th through the 10th, and several of infantry (including the 27th) to help patrol the West. By summer 1867 elements of the 7th Cavalry under Lt. Col. George A. Custer were hopelessly traversing Kansas, Nebraska, and eastern Colorado searching for Indians. West-central Kansas in particular had become a rich zone of cultural interaction among Lakotas and Cheyennes from the north mixing with their southern brethren, Arapahos and Kiowas from south of the Arkansas. In addition to this mix of tribes there were Irish railroad workers and American and Northern European settlers, some of whom could not speak much English and had never encountered an Indian, white cavalry troopers and infantrymen, black cavalry troopers and infantrymen, and Kansas volunteer cavalry eager to rid their state of Indians, and all of whom did not usually get along with each other when they were fighting Indians.[70]

Among the non-Indian elements there was frequent willingness to cast blame on each other, their state governments, or the U.S. Army and Congress. Fights like Prairie Dog Creek bloodied the 10th Cavalry. Fighting extended around Fort Wallace, Kansas, where coalitions of large war parties kept that post, like Fort Phil Kearny, in a virtual state of siege in 1867. Warriors frequently attacked freight depots such as Fossil Creek Station along the Smoky Hill Trail. Custer had a couple of run-ins with the Oglala chief Pawnee Killer, who was in the Fetterman fight and had come south in 1867. Pawnee Killer and his warriors were likely candidates to have wiped out the dispatch party of Lt. Lyman Kidder in July 1867 near today's Goodland, Kansas. Despite the Treaties of Medicine Lodge with the southern tribes in 1867, the Dog Soldiers in particular carried the war into 1868 and 1869, making raids along the Solomon and Saline rivers and Spillman Creek in Kansas, killing settlers and capturing women and children. After Beecher Island in September 1868 the newly appointed commander of the Department of the Missouri, Gen. Philip Sheridan, decided upon a winter campaign in November 1868 in Indian Territory, when the warriors were congregated and largely immobile. But the Washita campaign failed to punish the Dog Soldiers. The whole thing had to be done over again in July 1869 at the decisive Battle of Summit Springs in Colorado Territory where Tall Bull's Dog Soldiers largely met their end. In November 1869 an army supply escort on the way to Fort C. F. Smith under Lt. E. R. P. Shurly was attacked but the warriors were driven off after attempting to capture a howitzer. This was the last engagement of Red Cloud's War.[71] By then peace had come to the Powder River country, where Red Cloud's Bad Face Oglalas and their allies remained militarily undefeated.[72]

The Fort Laramie Treaty of 1868

Following the Treaties of Medicine Lodge with the southern tribes, treaties that did not stop the fighting even by the following spring, the U.S. government sent a "Blue Ribbon Peace Commission" to Fort Laramie to conclude a new treaty with Red Cloud, whom they considered to be the most important chief among the Indians at war in the Powder River country, and with all other chiefs of the northern bands and tribes. The commissioners were generals William T. Sherman, the aged William S. Harney, Alfred H. Terry, C. C. Augur, John B. Sanborn, and politicos Nathaniel G. Taylor, commissioner of Indian Affairs, reform senator John B. Henderson, and Indian agent Samuel F. Tappan. The result was the Treaty of 1868, otherwise known as the Second Treaty of Fort Laramie. Although Dee Brown has contended that Red Cloud and the Indians got everything they asked for and the United States received nothing in return, such was far from the case.[73] In reality the treaty is ambiguous, riddled with legalistic language that the Indians (as well as most history students and history professors) could scarcely understand, and was designed to end the traditional lifeways of the plains tribes. Historian Colin G. Calloway states that the Treaty of 1868 was "one of the most significant and controversial treaties in the history of Indian–U.S. relations. It ended the war, planted the seeds for another war, and provided the legal foundation for Sioux claims to the Black Hills for more than a hundred years."[74]

The treaty was designed not only to end the war by removing the forts on the Bozeman Trail, a measure that had actually become expedient for the government, but to consolidate Indians on reservations and transform their societies. Although the government agreed to close the Bozeman Trail, articles of the treaty gave the government the right to build new roads through hunting grounds. The treaty placed Indians under the jurisdiction of civil courts for individual crimes even though they were not citizens of the

United States. It made provisions to force reeducation of Indian children in the ways of the white man.[75]

Other articles would soon be broken. The Treaty of 1868 created the Great Sioux Reservation, all of present-day South Dakota west of the Missouri River, but ambiguously confirmed the hunting grounds north of the Platte and east of the Bighorns as "unceded territory." But Article 11 stipulated that, at some future time, the Indians "will relinquish all right to occupy permanently the territory outside the reservation."[76] Although the treaty appeared to cede all the northern plains except for Montana to the Lakotas, the government created Wyoming Territory the same year. As soon as 1869, however, Gen. Philip Sheridan issued a general order that all Indians off the reservation, essentially those persons in the unceded territory, "as a rule will be considered hostile." Military historian John Gray contended that the Treaty of 1868 may be viewed as "exclusively a white man's device . . . that it served primarily as an instrument of chicanery and a weapon of aggression" that was designed to obtain from the Indians in peace what the army had been unable to seize in war.[77]

But most of all, the treaty guaranteed to the Lakotas Paha Sapa, the sacred Black Hill, forever. Discovery of gold in the hills, however, would precipitate the Great Sioux War in 1876 and 1877. As a result the government would confiscate the Black Hills in what was the most blatant violation of the Treaty of 1868. Today the legal challenges to get back the Black Hills still dominate federal relations with the Lakotas. Charlotte A. Black Elk, the granddaughter of Nicholas Black Elk, confidant of John G. Neihardt, has dedicated her life and career to this day to a reclamation of the Black Hills by the Lakotas: "It is occupied Territory and it would do the hearts good of every American to give it back to the Lakota people."[78] In essence the Treaty of 1868 created far more problems for both the Indians and the federal government than it solved and became one of the biggest failures of President Grant's so-called peace policy. It cost the government millions and strengthened the Quaker-led Indian reform movement. For the Lakotas it set in motion conditions and infrastructure that would lead directly to renewed war, impoverishment on the reservation, the misguided boarding school experience, disillusionment, the Ghost Dance movement, and the tragic massacre at Wounded Knee in 1890. The Indians did not foresee the long-range provisions of the treaty. Unlike their Dakota cousins in

Minnesota, the Lakotas in 1868 had no previous experience with the reservation system. Bear in the Grass later said, "[T]hese words of the treaty were never explained. It was said that the treaty was for peace and friendship among the whites. When we took hold of the pen they said they would take the troops away so we could raise our children." And Red Cloud, among the last to sign, stated in a speech at Cooper Union, New York, in 1870, "We thought the treaty was [just] to remove the forts and for us to cease from fighting."[79]

The Brulés met with the commissioners in April and Spotted Tail signed the treaty. The easily persuaded "Laramie Loafers" signed in early May. Arapaho chiefs also signed. Little Wolf, Dull Knife, and others signed for the Northern Cheyennes and were allowed to "attach themselves" to the Great Sioux Reservation. Other Northern Cheyennes were furious with Little Wolf for signing the treaty without meeting with the forty-four council chiefs. Many rejected it.[80]

The Oglalas proved to be far more recalcitrant. During deliberations between May 24 and 25, 1868, Oglala chief Kills the Bear stated, "I will sign the treaty provided that the commissioners promise they will remove the posts and give us a big present. I am a rascal, and if the whites don't fulfill this treaty I will show myself [to be] one."[81] American Horse was more specific. "I would like to have my friends here to sign the treaty," he announced. "I will sign, and if there is anything wrong afterwards I will watch the commissioners, and they will be the first one[s] that I will whip."[82] But already, on May 19, General Augur had ordered the abandonment of the posts on the Bozeman Trail. Red Cloud would not come in to Fort Laramie, however, until the forts actually were vacated. "We are on the mountains looking down on the soldiers and the forts," he said. "When we see the soldiers moving away and the forts abandoned, then I will come down and talk."[83]

The forts began to be dismantled in early summer. Sometime between August 18 and 20, 1868, the last wagons rolled out of Fort Phil Kearny. Before the soldiers were even out of sight Little Wolf led a party down from the Bighorn Mountains and burned the fort to the ground, an action for which Little Wolf was later criticized by some Cheyennes who advocated occupying the post.[84] It was not until November 4 that Red Cloud, now recognized as a chief (itancan), came in to Fort Laramie with a contingent of warriors to sign the treaty. Red Cloud's War was over. Red Cloud would keep the treaty but the United States would not. During his long life Red Cloud became a grand statesman fighting for his people's rights as a diplomat. He would travel to Washington, D.C., in 1870 to confer with President Grant. His influence would be felt with the Dawes Committee and the Edmunds Commission. He worked for reform not only between Indian and white but among his own people as well. But throughout his life he continued to believe that he had been tricked by the government with the Treaty of 1868.[85] As ethnologist Raymond J. DeMallie asserts, by the later half of the nineteenth century the Lakotas did not regard their religious and ritual beliefs and practices to be static or monolithic.[86] But Red Cloud never would go to war again.[87] In later years he became a spokesman fighting for his people's rights. Although not as accommodating as other chiefs he became somewhat of a culture broker urging peace and transition to a new life.[88]

Red Cloud did not speak for all of the Lakotas. By the 1870s, many of the younger generation of resisters like Crazy Horse disavowed Red Cloud's posture of peace. Red Cloud was often ridiculed and blamed for what resulted from the new treaty. In the years after 1866 some whites too would point fingers and cast blame, not for the Treaty of 1868 but for the gross embarrassment of the Fetterman fight. They would first hold accountable Col. Henry B. Carrington and Gen. Philip St. George Cooke and pit them against one another. Later they would cast the blame on Capt. William J. Fetterman. Like the Treaty of 1868, that legacy too, while far less important for the lives it has impacted over the years, has lasted to the present day.

CHAPTER 9

THE ACHILLES SYNDROME

An Essay on the Making of the Fetterman Myth

Wherefore stern orders ticked across the land
From Washington to Laramie. Perhaps
No blizzard swept the neat official maps
To nip a tracing finger. Howsoe'er,
Four companies of horse and foot must bear
To Fort Phil Kearny tidings of its shame.[1]

MANY UNANSWERED QUESTIONS AND MYTHS have arisen around the struggle for the Powder River country in 1866 and around the Fetterman fight in particular. These questions rival those surrounding George Custer and the Battle of Little Bighorn in 1876. In both cases soldiers of the U.S. Army were annihilated. Consequently, in the non-Indian mind this has always stimulated controversy and debate. Who was to *blame* for the defeat? For the Indians engaged in both actions the debate over who was to blame is moot. The Indians won. They were to "blame." In both cases, following those actions separated by a decade, the federal government put in place policies designed to speed up Indian assimilation. With the swiftly growing interest in Indian history beginning in the late twentieth century Indian people who do not fully embrace decolonization viewpoints have become more seriously intrigued with *their* history and what role their ancestors might have played in that history. In the twenty-first century both Indian and non-Indian peoples are now seeking answers to questions as to what constitutes a shared history. Both perspectives are necessary for the vigor of the debate. This concluding chapter speculates on two of those interesting and conflicted questions in respect to the struggle for the Powder River country in 1866. For some these questions may ultimately seem trivial in light of current trends and issues. But for others their significance may surpass the trivial and antiquarian. First, considering original-source *Indian* testimony, what role did Crazy Horse actually play in the Fetterman fight? Second, has Capt. William J. Fetterman, because of maneuvering by Col. Henry B. Carrington and because of Fetterman's alleged infamous boast for which he is most remembered ("Give me eighty men and I'll ride through the whole Sioux Nation"), been unfairly and inaccurately stereotyped? Often the answers are not what some wish to hear and may be viewed as detrimental to ethnic and national pride. But varied and debated historical facts and interpretation in no way diminish the significance of, nor the pride taken in, our ancestors and their shared places in the history of all Americans.

The Question of Crazy Horse

Crazy Horse presents historians with a conundrum. As much as we *want* Crazy Horse to be performing feats of daring on the slopes of Lodge Trail Ridge, his participation is unclear. According to popular imagery he is supposed to have played a major role as a member of the decoy party, perhaps even the leader of the decoys that lured Fetterman's command over Lodge Trail Ridge to their deaths. By some recent accounts Crazy Horse bravely played the "wounded quail," dismounting on several occasions to examine the hoof of his seemingly injured pony so that the soldiers could not resist the temptation to pursue him.[2] Of course no military original sources place Crazy Horse on Lodge Trail Ridge because none of the whites at Fort Phil Kearny, with the possible exception of scout Jim Bridger, had heard of him in 1866. Crazy Horse was only in his middle twenties at the time (Black Elk states he was about nineteen) and had not yet gained the reputation among the whites that would shadow him to his death following the campaigns of the 1870s. No known photograph was ever taken of him and no white in the fight who otherwise might have remembered such a figure from the battle lived to tell about it. But what stories do the Indian participants in the fight have to tell? Until the mid-twentieth century the voices of oral tradition were fairly silent on the matter outside Indian country. Among those few Lakota and Cheyenne eyewitnesses to the battle whose stories were told to white journalists and ethnographers at the beginning of the twentieth century, their voices are, perhaps surprisingly, mostly silent as to the role Crazy Horse may have played in the fight, if any.[3]

Although the death of Crazy Horse is well chronicled, the exploits of his early life are more obscure than his exploits at the Battle of Little Bighorn a decade after Fetterman's demise. The scant primary sources merely suggest through inference that Crazy Horse *might have* participated in Fetterman's defeat. But there are no eyewitnesses who claimed specifically that he was in the battle and *no* credible sources offer details that he was a decoy. The testimony of the Miniconjou warrior White Bull, one of the principal informants for the Fetterman fight, is flimsy. White Bull gave his story to Walter S. Campbell (Stanley Vestal) in 1932 and it was published as *Warpath: The True Story of the Fighting Sioux Told in a Biography of Chief White Bull* in 1934. White Bull, who most assuredly was in the Fetterman fight, declares that Red Cloud was not present at the Fetterman fight and that (or is this Campbell's assumption in 1932?) "Crazy Horse led the Oglalas." This ambiguous statement, while ascribing a leadership role to Crazy Horse in 1866, does not place him in any specific part of the action in the Fetterman fight, nor does it ascribe any detailed exploits to him. White Bull goes on to state in the next sentence that "[m]any of the chiefs besides Red Cloud [neither Red Cloud or Crazy Horse were important chiefs or itancans in 1866] led their warriors against the white men in that year of '66." But literally no mention is made by White Bull of Crazy Horse's being a member of the decoy party. Campbell, who like most of his contemporary interviewers in the twenties and thirties was far more interested in which Indian by name personally administered the coup de grace to George Armstrong Custer in 1876, did not offer much additional editorializing about the Fetterman fight. White Bull did tell Campbell that Crazy Horse rode up the Tongue River toward Fort Phil Kearny with He Dog and other Oglalas a few days before the fight, but there is nothing in Campbell's notes that places Crazy Horse in the Fetterman fight.[4]

Another original reference to Crazy Horse at the time of the Fetterman fight is a statement made in 1904 by a warrior named White Bear to Doane Robinson, the secretary of the South Dakota Department of History (SD State Historical Society): "Crazy Horse, though inferior in standing to Man Afraid [Of His Horse], was Red Cloud's principal lieutenant among the Oglalas and Roman Nose from among the Cheyennes." This statement too is ambiguous. In his book *A History of the Dakota or Sioux Indians* (1904), Robinson relates this testimony early in a chapter on the Fetterman fight in context with events occurring before the fight itself. In his narrative of the actual fight Robinson makes no mention of Crazy Horse's presence. White

Bear's claim, while possibly true, still does not identify Crazy Horse as participating in the Fetterman fight directly and certainly does not mention him as being one of the decoys. White Bear's statement regarding Roman Nose as a "chief lieutenant" of Red Cloud's for the Cheyennes is inaccurate. Roman Nose, a prominent Crooked Lance warrior but not a chief, had gone south to Kansas earlier in the year to fight with the Dog Soldiers and was not present in the Powder River country during the fall of 1866.[5]

Wooden Leg, a Northern Cheyenne warrior of Little Wolf's clan, interviewed extensively by physician Thomas B. Marquis in 1922, asserts that in the fall of 1866 Crazy Horse was a principal war leader of the Oglalas. But he does not place him specifically in the battle nor as a member of the decoy party. Wooden Leg was only nine years old at the time of the Fetterman fight and thus did not participate in the action, although his elder brother, Strong Wind Blowing, was killed in the fight.[6] Like Walter Campbell, Marquis was likewise mostly concerned with the Custer story and apparently had no interest in pressing Wooden Leg or other informants about the Fetterman fight. Wooden Leg, like White Bull, spoke of Crazy Horse more than a half-century after the fight, long after Crazy Horse had attained his fame and martyrdom in the 1870s, but his stories, like those of White Bull's regarding Crazy Horse's presence in the Powder River country in 1866, are vague and almost rhetorical.[7]

The most compelling case for Crazy Horse's being at the Fetterman fight is that of frontiersman and scout Frank Grouard. Captured by Hunkpapas about 1870, Grouard later found his way to Crazy Horse's camp in 1873 and befriended him. In his later years Grouard's adventures were recorded by Joe DeBarthe. Grouard was not in the Powder River country in 1866. But DeBarthe relates a secondhand tale of Grouard's, if it can be believed (Grouard tended to be melodramatic at times), of Crazy Horse's coming to the aid of his friend, the mortally wounded Lone Bear, following the Fetterman fight. Lone Bear is a confirmed Oglala casualty of the battle, corroborated by American Horse and White Bull. Lone Bear was a respected warrior. His death is recorded as mnemonics (pictographs) for 1866–67 on at least two winter counts.[8] Of Lone Bear DeBarthe writes, as told to him by Grouard, "His limbs and body were frozen terribly. He died in the arms of Crazy Horse while Hump [High Backbone] stood by, weeping." If Grouard is correct, this account places Crazy Horse on the Fetterman battlefield on December 21, 1866. Grouard, however, mentions nothing of Crazy Horse's being a decoy.[9]

George B. Grinnell was a bit more meticulous. He talked with a number of Cheyennes who were in the battle, most notably White Elk, who took him over the battlefield pointing out the route of the soldiers and where the Indians were hiding, and showing him spots where groups of soldiers fell. White Elk's story is detailed. He relates that Black Shield and Black Leg were the principal leaders of the Lakotas in the fight. He does not mention High Backbone of the Miniconjous. There is no mention of Crazy Horse whatsoever as having been involved in the Fetterman fight although Grinnell discusses his presence numerous times during the 1870s.[10] The other principal Cheyenne account, that of Two Moon (sometimes spelled Two Moons) who claimed to have been in the fight but later denied it, comes to us through the letters of George Bent, who was one of George Hyde's primary informants. Hyde asserts in *Red Cloud's Folk* (1936) that Two Moon claimed in 1912 (Two Moon was an informant of George Bent's) that Crazy Horse led the decoys but offers no elaborate details regarding his specific exploits and cites no sources in his notes. Actually, there is no mention by Bent whatsoever, in any of his letters to Hyde written early in the twentieth century or in *The Life of George Bent Written from His Letters* completed by 1918 but not published until 1968, of *any* participation by Crazy Horse in wiping out Fetterman's command and there is likewise no reference to Two Moon's alleged assertion of 1912 in Hyde's correspondence. Hyde even questions in a footnote the claim that Crazy Horse was a leader. "He Dog, Short Bull, and Black Elk all lived in the same camp with Crazy Horse," Hyde wrote. "If he was the principal leader in this fight, why should these men take the honor from him and give it to a Miniconjou?"[11] Hyde may have confused the 1912 claim with an interview of Two Moon by Walter Mason Camp in 1913. The Camp interview, however, sheds no light on Crazy Horse at the Fetterman fight. Two Moon simply told Camp "the soldiers were decoyed over the ridge." He identifies none of the decoys.[12] Thus Hyde's statement about Crazy Horse's leading the decoys is suspect although it is the earliest source *claiming* Crazy Horse to be a decoy at the fight. But even if one accepts Hyde (Two Moon?), he does not attribute any of the elaborate deeds to Crazy Horse as a decoy that so many modern writers have done.[13]

In *Red Cloud's Folk*, published eighteen years after the Bent material was

shelved in the Denver Public Library and all but forgotten until rescued by
Savoie Lottinville in the 1960s, Hyde also accepts White Bull's 1932 statement that Crazy Horse "led the Oglalas" although not as a principal chief.
But in the earlier 1918 Bent manuscript, completed almost *two decades earlier*,
Hyde had already written Two Moon's version of the Fetterman fight with
no mention of Crazy Horse whatsoever. Two Moon's account that appeared
in Hyde's *Life of George Bent* (1918) was based on a letter from Bent, who
interviewed Two Moon in 1904. Again, there is no mention of Crazy Horse
in this letter. In addition, in 1908 Two Moon denied to George B. Grinnell
that he (Two Moon) was even in the Fetterman fight. Hyde asserts in 1918 in
the Bent manuscript that Crazy Horse gained his reputation as a warrior in
the 1870s. Hyde thus must have based his premise of Crazy Horse's presence
on Lodge Trail Ridge as described in *Red Cloud's Folk* (1936) on White Bull's
and Campbell's short ambiguous 1932 statement with no elaboration and
he offers no verified substantiation in that book of Two Moon's alleged 1912
claim that Crazy Horse was a decoy.[14]

Even with the extensive interviews of Lakotas who knew Crazy Horse
intimately in the wake of his dramatic death at Fort Robinson, the great
Oglala warrior cannot definitely be placed at the Fetterman fight. His close
friend from the time of boyhood, Chips (Horn Chips), was interviewed by
Eli S. Ricker in 1907. Ricker states, "Chips was in the Fetterman Massacre
. . . He says fourteen Indians were killed there. American Horse was there.
American Horse did not lead the decoy party. Chips says he wants to tell
the truth." If Chips did tell the truth as he knew it he certainly did not
place his close boyhood friend Crazy Horse in the fight, let alone the decoy
party. In fact Chips does not even mention Crazy Horse in relation to
activities in the Powder River country in 1866 at all.[15] Neither did George
Sword (Hunts the Enemy) (Owns Sword), the brother of Sword (Sword
Owner) and son of Oglala Chief Brave Bear. George Sword was in the
Fetterman fight while his brother, also named Sword (Sword Owner), was, by
George W. Colhoff's account at least (albeit a secondhand account), a
decoy in the Fetterman fight and possibly its leader. Ricker also interviewed
American Horse, who told him that he (American Horse) was a decoy.
George Sword and American Horse make no mention in their testimonies
to Ricker of their fellow Oglala warrior Crazy Horse being one of the decoys
or even that Crazy Horse was in the fight. Then again by the time of Crazy

Horse's death in 1877, he and American Horse had become estranged by political currents on the reservation.[16]

The cornerstones of original source material on Crazy Horse are the so-called Hinman interviews conducted by Eleanor H. Hinman and her assistant at the Nebraska State Historical Society, Mari Sandoz, in 1930. The two women interviewed several of the old "Long Hairs," as Black Elk referred to the aged warriors from the days of resistance, still living three decades into the twentieth century at Rosebud and Pine Ridge. The two women were specifically interested in the life of Crazy Horse, particularly the circumstances of his death. None of the old warriors they interviewed, including Crazy Horse's close friend He Dog, mentions Crazy Horse as having participated in the Fetterman fight. Then again He Dog had a reputation for keeping mum when it came to sensitive topics.[17]

Yet based on three short ambiguous phrases that may be acknowledged as original narrative testimony by White Bear in Robinson (1904) ("Crazy Horse . . . was Red Cloud's principal lieutenant among the Oglalas"), White Bull in Campbell (1932–34) ("Crazy Horse was the leader of the Oglala"), and an unsupported assertion by Hyde in 1936 that Two Moon had claimed back in 1912 that "Crazy Horse led the decoy party," an ever-expanding fanciful role for Crazy Horse as being a principal decoy on Lodge Trail Ridge has found its way with much vivid embellishment time and again into well-read secondary literature since the middle of the twentieth century.[18]

Charles A. Eastman, a Santee Sioux born in 1858 and later attending Dartmouth, published an anthology of Indian heroes and chiefs in 1918. Some of the individuals he wrote about he knew personally. Eastman was eight years old at the time of the Fetterman fight and spent most of his early years in Canada. He probably never met Crazy Horse. But in his chapter on Crazy Horse Eastman makes no assertion that Crazy Horse led the decoys on Lodge Trail Ridge. Rather he claims that Crazy Horse led the forty warriors who made the feint on the woodcutting detail some few miles west of Fort Phil Kearny, thus drawing Fetterman and his men out of the fort. But Fetterman proceeded in the opposite direction from the wood train, following ten decoys over Lodge Trail Ridge. Eastman cited no sources for his information on Crazy Horse. But if Eastman is to be believed, it is highly unlikely that Crazy Horse would have had the time to make the feint on the wood train several miles in the opposite direction in convincing fashion, then ride to

Lodge Trail Ridge and join and perhaps organize the decoys. Still, Eastman's claim found its way into secondary accounts of the 1920s.[19]

Reputable historians, not so-reputable historians, popular writers, and filmmakers, one of the most recent depictions being Stephen Spielberg's television miniseries *Into the West* on the Turner Network, have dramatized Crazy Horse's dismounting, rubbing his pony's hoof as if it were injured, and in the case of Spielberg, standing on the ridge within pistol range as Captain Fetterman himself personally took potshots at him.[20]

Much of this supposition comes to us from the marvelously entertaining tour de force but historically flawed semifictional biography *Crazy Horse: Strange Man of the Oglalas*, written by Mari Sandoz in 1942.[21] As Eleanor Hinman's transcriber for the Crazy Horse interviews twelve years previously, Sandoz did not garner any information from He Dog or the others that would place Crazy Horse in such elaborate detail, and in such a daring role, on the slopes of Lodge Trail Ridge on December 21, 1866. Sandoz, who visited Lodge Trail Ridge in winter with her typed manuscript in hand for inspiration, wrote, "Several times Crazy Horse had to get off [his horse], once pretending to tie his war rope closer . . . Once when they [the other decoys] had all stopped to turn back he sat down behind a bush as though hurt or worn out and built a little fire, the others going on, leaving him behind. Shots began to splatter around him." Eleanor Hinman, who relinquished her desire to write a biography of the great Oglala to Sandoz, had acquired no knowledge of these kinds of events as none of her interviews comes close to supporting such melodrama. There is nothing in the extensive notes of Mari Sandoz that points to any original testimonies attributing such daring exploits to Crazy Horse as a decoy. Some of her detailed supposition may have come from the Cheyenne White Elk's testimony given to Grinnell regarding the actions of Big Nose and the other decoys in general in feinting on the soldiers as if trying to protect a wounded comrade.[22] Neither is there any revealing information in Grace Hebard's material on the Bozeman Trail that Sandoz acknowledges using for *Crazy Horse, Strange Man of the Oglalas*. In Hebard's book with E. A. Brininstool, *The Bozeman Trail*, volume 1, she makes no mention whatsoever of the decoy maneuver in her narrative of the Fetterman fight.[23]

Yet the "wounded quail" scenario has played out ever since Sandoz published *Crazy Horse* in 1942. Dee Brown echoed Sandoz in *Fort Phil Kearny: An American Saga* (1962), later retitled *The Fetterman Massacre* over Brown's objections. "Crazy Horse won a great name for himself that day with his acts of defiance," Brown wrote, "sometimes dismounting within rifle range and pretending to ignore the presence of the soldiers and the screams of their bullets."[24] Stephen Ambrose in his lengthy trade-edition biography, *Crazy Horse and Custer: The Parallel Lives of Two American Warriors* (1975), goes further than Brown in embellishing Sandoz, having Crazy Horse waving his blanket and whooping, feigning a general retreat of the decoys before Fetterman's onslaught: "The ambush was working," Ambrose wrote. "Crazy Horse took one look at the advancing soldiers, checked his own pony, and turned back toward Lodge Trail Ridge, using the old trick of pretending to beat the horse with one hand while actually holding it back with the other." Ambrose goes on to assert in his endnotes that his material for Crazy Horse's role at Fort Phil Kearny is taken from statements by White Bear given to the secretary of the South Dakota Historical Society Department of History, Doane Robinson, in his book *A History of the Dakota* (1904), page 361. Of course Ambrose is mistaken. White Bear only claims that Crazy Horse was a "chief lieutenant of Red Cloud's" and offers no such elaborate details in Robinson's book. Ambrose's extrapolated drama, like that of Mari Sandoz, is creative but imaginary.[25]

Others have been more brief and cautious from the surveys of the literature in ascribing specific actions to Crazy Horse, including Cheyenne historian Father Peter John Powell, who still places Crazy Horse in a simple sentence or two as a decoy but without an endnote to support it.[26] Less assertive too is Larry McMurtry in his short-form biography of Crazy Horse. While paraphrasing Dee Brown as to Crazy Horse's presence at the fight, McMurtry simply states, "his reputation was enhanced."[27] Although not the most illuminating modern biography of Crazy Horse, Mike Sajna's *Crazy Horse: The Life Behind the Legend* (2000) is perhaps the most honest. Sajna wrote, "Many writers have Crazy Horse leading the decoy party, but that is difficult to support from primary sources. As the leader of the Oglala warriors [as White Bull claims] it seems more likely that he would have stayed back with the main force."[28] Unfortunately these misperceptions have been perpetuated to the present day. Joseph Marshall's inspirationally written *The Journey of Crazy Horse: A Lakota History* (2004) lists as his sources storytellers from the Rosebud and Pine Ridge Reservations. Unfortunately the book has no endnotes to correlate these oral sources with Marshall's narrative.

His description of Crazy Horse's exploits as a decoy at the Fetterman fight strongly echo Sandoz as does other modern oral tradition.[29] In what is overall the best biography of Crazy Horse to date, Kingsley Bray's *Crazy Horse: A Lakota Life* (2006) the same flaws persist, naming Crazy Horse as a decoy and ascribing personal individual actions to him on the slope of Lodge Trail Ridge. Unfortunately Bray's endnotes do not support these specific exploits and he offers no new illuminating sources, not even modern oral histories, to support his detailed narrative ascriptions to Crazy Horse as a decoy.[30]

What we may conclude of Crazy Horse's presence on or over Lodge Trail Ridge on December 21, 1866, is that, based on specific eyewitness testimony, he *may* or *may not* have been there even though his inspirational presence is heavily felt in the secondary literature and modern oral tradition. There is enough circumstantial evidence to conclude that Crazy Horse was an up-and-coming warrior in 1866, a brave and caring man who had earned the honor of "shirt wearer," and perhaps indeed a primary "lieutenant" of Red Cloud's by that date. Likely Crazy Horse and He Dog rode up the Tongue River to the Oglala camps a few days before the fight. Therefore it is difficult to imagine Crazy Horse's not being in the battle at all. And scholars and readers alike want him to be there. Certainly given his devotion to defending the lands of the Oglalas—the Powder River country and the Black Hills—it would have by no means been out of character for him to have been in the thick of the action. Neither is it illogical to assume that he would have enthusiastically led a decoy party or even engaged in daring acts while doing so.

But although we are probably on safe ground in assuming there exists at least a possibility he was *somewhere* in or around the fight, the facts remain, at the very least, that virtually none of the specific daring and dramatic actions and deeds directly attributed to Crazy Horse as a leader or a member of the decoy party can be substantiated by *any* identifiable original sources, save Hyde's short paraphrased comment of Two Moon's (1936) that is highly suspect given his 1918 account. In conclusion, there is no definitive credible evidence that places Crazy Horse as one of the decoys at the Fetterman fight. These dramatic exploits first appear in print in Sandoz's *Crazy Horse* (1942) and have been repeated, embellished, and written into the secondary histories ever since.[31] Given the weight of evidence it is reasonable to suppose that the detailed actions so many writers have attributed to Crazy

Horse as a decoy at the Fetterman fight originate with Sandoz. There are simply no detailed stories of his specific exploits at the Fetterman fight before the publication of *Crazy Horse* in 1942. Unfortunately the absence of valid Lakota family histories generations old available to the general public that might paint a different picture of Crazy Horse's specific actions from those of Sandoz leads to these conclusions. That Crazy Horse "distinguished himself that day" remains to be proven. Many warriors who have gone unnamed in the eyewitness accounts, perhaps even Crazy Horse, *distinguished themselves that day*. Their individual stories simply were never told, made public, or corroborated by eyewitness testimony.

The absolute truth undoubtedly died with Crazy Horse at Fort Robinson in September 1877 and possibly with White Bull, who died seventy years after the battle, a converted Christian in 1947 at the age of ninety-eight and one of the last surviving Lakota warriors to have fought against the United States. But the failure to prove the specific actions of Crazy Horse on December 21, 1866, in no way diminishes his iconic stature for all and his revered reputation as a leader of resistance and a source of spiritual enlightenment for his people in the past and present. The legendary acts attributed to Crazy Horse and the Indians' great victory in the Powder River country in 1866 commingle with the disputes as to who was to blame for the dramatic defeat of the soldiers at Fort Phil Kearny, thereby adding vigor to the mystique of and the debate over the Fetterman fight.[32]

Historical Irony and the Question of Capt. William J. Fetterman

Fort McPherson, Nebraska, was four years old in 1867, a typical dull frontier post situated just above the confluence of the North and South Platte rivers. It had been so-named in January 1866 in honor of Brig. Gen. James B. McPherson, killed near Atlanta on July 22, 1864.[33] Assembled there in late March was a "special commission" appointed by President Andrew Johnson to "ascertain all the facts" concerning the Fetterman fight. The commission that gathered in Omaha on February 23 for their journey to Fort McPherson was composed of four high-ranking army officers, generals John B. Sanborn, Alfred Sully, N. B. Buford, and Col. Eli S. Parker. Two civilians served on the commission, G. P. Beauvais, an Indian trader among the Lakotas, and J. T. Kinney, a former sutler at Fort Phil Kearny. Generally known as the Sanborn

Commission, this group reflected military interests, and, as far as most of them were concerned, was there to preempt any special congressional worries. One month before the convening of the Sanborn Commission the U.S. Senate passed a joint resolution requesting that the secretaries of the Interior and War furnish them all documents pertaining to what was now being called the "Fetterman disaster."[34] Meanwhile General Sherman persuaded Grant to launch a separate court of inquiry to fix blame for the Fetterman disaster. Carrington had to face both commissions. But the court of inquiry was inexplicably suspended in June 1867, probably to deflect criticism of the high command's possible negligence in the Fetterman affair. Thus the Sanborn report constitutes the significant historical document.

The Sanborn Commission arrived at Fort McPherson to take testimony from post commander Henry B. Carrington. The public, the government, and the army wanted answers. Every faction had an "agenda" that spring. The convolution of Reconstruction-era politics in 1867, vexed alongside the continuous monotonous struggle between the Indian Bureau and the War Department for control of Indian affairs, loomed over the hearings. But Colonel Carrington perhaps had the biggest agenda of all. For the first time Carrington had a chance to present his side of the story and clear his name from accusations of wrongdoing. He was sworn in knowing that his chief antagonist would be Gen. Philip St. George Cooke, formerly the commander of the Department of the Platte.

Carrington's purpose was obvious: to absolve himself of any blame for the destruction of Fetterman's command. He came prepared with every bit of correspondence, sent and received, since he had been appointed commander of the Mountain District/Department of the Platte including an official report of his dated January 3, 1867, that blamed Fetterman for tactical error, as well as carefully planned statements meticulously organized in accordance with his adept administrative skills. The government would suppress his January 3 report as part of his testimony for years to come. Carrington mostly reiterated his ubiquitous concerns of the previous year: the lack of officers and troops and the need for superior weaponry, notably his requests for repeating Spencer rifles. As such, Carrington's major issues were with the high command and thus with his commanding officer in 1866, Gen. Philip St. George Cooke. But Carrington also cast blame on erroneous newspaper reports supplied by disgruntled contractors and other disappointed job seekers at Fort Phil Kearny.[35] Early in his statements he eulogized the three officers killed on Massacre Ridge, but especially Capt. William J. Fetterman. In a supporting document dated January 1, 1867, Carrington wrote, "His character was pure and without blemish, he was a refined gentleman and had distinguished his regimental record and honored his own name by duty well done."[36] He was less praiseworthy about Brown: "If he unwisely despised his foe, he fought to the last." And paying respect to Frances Grummond, his comments were rather nondescript of her husband, simply stating where the lieutenant's body had been found and that Lieutenant Grummond had fought bravely.[37]

Never since the fight of December 21, 1866, had Carrington spoken ill of Fetterman in public or insinuated that he might be solely responsible for the "disaster"—until now. Sensing that the commission might be trying to find a scapegoat to satisfy public opinion, Carrington began casting blame on the dead Fetterman, without mentioning his name, in a grand summary climax to his "Statement" before the commission. "Gross disobedience of orders sacrificed nearly eighty of the choice men of my command," he stated. "At least one of the officers sacrificed deliberately determined, whenever obtaining a separate command, to pursue the Indians after independent honor . . . Life was the forfeit. In the grave I bury disobedience."[38] Carrington went on to assert that John Edwards, a clerk at his headquarters at Fort Phil Kearny, and perhaps others had heard his orders given to Fetterman and were willing to testify to that effect. Also ready to testify was Capt. Frederick Brown's clerk, who had allegedly heard Brown and Fetterman agree that they would "move actively upon the Indians" when they were outside the fort with sufficient men. Carrington contended there was strong discipline at the fort but that some of the officers simply disagreed with *his* kind of discipline.[39]

An argument may be advanced that Carrington misread the commission. They seemed unconcerned with Fetterman's alleged misconduct. Essentially, most of their questions for Carrington were concerned with organization of and troop strength within the Mountain District, the number of "friendly" Indians in the region, and orders from above garrison level. Did the commission have bigger game in mind? Was Cooke their target? Had they already decided to brand Carrington? Or were they aiming higher still? They called none of Carrington's supporting witnesses. Soon they moved on to Fort Laramie and then to Fort Phil Kearny to take testimony from others.[40]

Meanwhile Jim Bridger advanced Carrington's cause with a statement he had given to the *Army and Navy Journal* on May 4, 1867. Bridger, who knew the Indians' traits probably better than anyone at Fort Phil Kearny in 1866, also gave support to the idea that some kind of a tribal coalition had indeed allied against the forts in the Powder River country. "Every person that knows anything of affairs in this country," Bridger stated, "knows very well that the massacre at Fort Philip Kearny was planned weeks before, and that the Sioux, Cheyennes and Arapahos had been collecting together in preparation for it on Tongue River . . . The only way to settle the question is to send out a sufficient number of troops to completely whip the hostile Sioux."[41] But apparently sensing that Carrington was interested in casting blame away from himself by condemning Fetterman, a number of Fetterman's friends and fellow officers testified before the commission that the blame should rest with Carrington. Lieutenant William Bisbee (who had already left Fort Phil Kearny by December 21, 1866) gave the most graphic condemnation, when he stated that many of the officers at Fort Phil Kearny felt nothing but "disgust" toward their commanding officer.[42]

But Capt. James Powell's statements were the most damning. He testified before the Sanborn Commission on July 24, a week before he would gain fame at the Wagon Box fight. Powell's statements regarding lack of discipline at the fort were effusive. Powell stated that Carrington waited for more than an hour after firing was heard over Lodge Trail Ridge before he did anything about it. He also insinuated that Carrington made him (Powell) "Executive Officer" of the post at that point and turned the matter of what to do over to him. As such the reinforcements under Captain Ten Eyck were not sent out from the fort until too late.[43] Carrington was so incensed by Powell's statements that he wrote a lengthy rebuttal to the allegations on November 5, 1867, to Secretary of the Interior O. H. Browning.[44]

Carrington then went so far as to visit General Grant in Washington, where he accused Powell of perjury and told Grant that he wished to prefer charges. But Powell had just become somewhat of a hero at the Wagon Box fight and Grant refused. At this point Carrington began to think his superiors were stacking the odds against him.[45] Powell and Carrington did not speak to one another for years afterward. Carrington even insinuated that

Powell suffered from mental illness acquired from a wound that Powell had received during the Civil War. In old age the two finally met and Powell, suffering from clinical dementia, admitted to not remembering much about the conflict.[46]

General Cooke too cast blame at Carrington. Regarding the fight on December 6: "Colonel Carrington's report to me . . . convinced me of great want of discipline and management, to say the least, on the part of Colonel Carrington," Cooke testified. "He was out on this occasion [December 6, 1866], and the circumstances, as detailed to me, indicated misconduct." Regarding the news of the Fetterman fight, Cooke explained how he had ordered reinforcements to relieve Fort Phil Kearny and ordered "Colonel Carrington to turn over the command [to Henry Wessells], and proceed at once to Fort Casper."[47]

But the Sanborn Commission, it appears, was even more interested in Cooke's conduct. When told that the commissioner of Indian Affairs traced all the Indian "difficulties" to the order of General Cooke of July 31, 1866, forbidding the traders from selling Indians arms and ammunition for hunting, Cooke gave a lengthy explanation of how he was simply following directives from generals Grant and Sherman.[48] In the end the Sanborn Commission may have surprised Carrington. When testimony concluded, the commission stated that Fetterman had formed a skirmish line on Lodge Trail Ridge and had advanced slightly, and that his command had become separated and overwhelmed. The commission cast no blame on Fetterman. As for Carrington, he too was apparently off the hook. "In a nutshell," General Sanborn stated, the problem "was that the commanding officer of the district [Carrington] was furnished no more troops or supplies for this state of war than had been provided and furnished him in a state of profound peace, as at Laramie in November, where twelve companies were stationed, while in regions where all was war, as at Fort Phil Kearny, there were only five companies allowed."[49]

Cooke had taken the fall as far as the Sanborn Commission was concerned. He returned to staff duty and eventually to Reconstruction duty in West Virginia, Kentucky, and Tennessee. He retired from the army in 1873 after forty-six years of active service.[50] According to his biographer, the Fetterman fight was one of the biggest disasters of Cooke's career, and the "disaster" may be traced "directly to his carelessness."[51] Cooke had blamed

Carrington, Carrington had blamed Cooke, and many of Carrington's officers tried to protect Fetterman by siding with Cooke. In actuality Cooke was grossly ignorant of the specific circumstances in the Powder River country in 1866. Cooke's initial correspondence regarding Carrington's alleged incompetence was largely drawn from letters written to him by Capt. James Powell and Lt. William Bisbee, the latter of whom was now Cooke's aide in Omaha. In 1890 Cooke realized his mistakes and apologized to Carrington for his reports up the line of command that alleged Carrington to be incompetent. The apology came twenty-four years after the fact. "The country was greatly excited, and the government, very urgent," Cooke told Carrington, "so I endorsed the papers for transmission by one of my staff. I do not remember which. I can do nothing more than to express my deep pain at what transpired. My memory recalls nothing of the details, except that it was hurried off to Genl. Sherman, and you must take my regrets as sincere, and my congratulations, that in the end you were finally vindicated."[52]

Writers have placed blame for Red Cloud's War and the Fetterman annihilation on command decisions at the departmental level and with good cause. But close scrutiny of the Sanborn report can reveal other agendas. Indeed members of the commission, Cooke, Carrington, and Fetterman's supporters were all proceeding in different directions, and for different reasons, under the umbrella of fixing blame or seeking absolution from the same. Rightly, Carrington's claims that he needed far more troops and efficient weapons than he had at Fort Phil Kearny were justified. But he could not shake the aura of jealousy and dislike by his combat-tested junior officers that translated to their perception of a commander who did not possess the necessary disciplinary management skills in time of war. Carrington incurred blame not only from above but from the echelon below him in the line. William J. Fetterman's friends came forth to rescue his memory and good reputation. Sorting out the events from the politics was difficult to impossible at the time. But the players were reacting on three different levels in their attempts to affix responsibility for the biggest embarrassment the U.S. Army in the West had suffered up to that time. Carrington sought to ensure his vindication at two levels, the strategic and the tactical. Strategically, Carrington accurately lamented the lack of sufficient resources to get the job done. But when it came to specific actions on December 21, 1866, he blamed Fetterman of gross tactical error by disobeying orders and passing over Lodge Trail Ridge and into a trap. Powell mostly took the tactical approach by accusing Carrington of *fiddling while Rome burned* and accusing him of lax discipline in maintaining order at the fort. Cooke's testimony only supported that image for reasons of his own rather than for any support of Fetterman. The Sanborn commissioners, however, were a bit more elusive in revealing their motives. For the most part they were utterly unconcerned with affixing tactical blame and hence with pinning the affair on Fetterman. The only one to raise the question of Fetterman's culpability was Carrington.[53]

While the commission sought a strategic explanation, it seems likely they did so for reasons that were elevated to a third level, that of policy. Most of these commissioners were generals and one a colonel. The other two commissioners made their livings to some degree off the presence of military posts in the West. All had vested interests in committing more troops and supplies to the West and away from the Reconstruction South. General Sherman became a powerful force in advancing this cause in his many communiqués to presidential cabinet members. As General of the Army, Grant tried to mediate all sides and would continue to do so after his election to the presidency in 1868. As such, in early 1867 Grant was knocking heads with Secretary of War Edwin M. Stanton, a cabinet member hostile to President Johnson and sympathetic to the "Radical-controlled" Congress. Stanton's agendas were presidential impeachment and punishing the defeated South, not great military offensives against Indians on the plains.[54]

As a consequence the power struggle for control of Indian affairs between the War Department and the Interior became intense in 1867. The Fetterman "disaster" became fuel for both sides to advance their respective causes. The army needed more troops in the West to conduct offensives and they got them after 1867. The civil government forces saw the Fetterman fight, among others, as an obvious need for negotiation and for new treaties by extending what they liked to call "the olive branch of peace." The concern of the "Radical Republican" Reconstruction Congress was to keep troops in the five southern military districts until the South had been sufficiently "punished" for secession and Civil War. So too a host of potential government contractors, carpetbaggers, and scalawags were all eager to appropriate their share of the federal pork for their respective activities within the Reconstruction districts. All these contenders got their way too, to some extent, either directly or indirectly, with the Treaties of Medicine Lodge and the Treaty of 1868. "To some extent" is the operative phrase as the desires of all factions would be based more on hope than reality as the treaties would only spawn further bloodshed on the plains during the period of the so-called Grant Peace Policy. Caught in the middle of these intense and convoluted Reconstruction-era politics were the comparatively miniscule and unimportant reputations of Henry B. Carrington and William J. Fetterman, an enigma that, in some ways, would far outlast in popular memory some of the substance of Reconstruction politics that were certainly more important at the time.[55]

Henry Carrington would have been unimpressed. There were still innuendos and insinuations. Despite his mild vindication by the Sanborn Commission, Carrington received no immediate public exoneration. The War Department suppressed Carrington's testimony and supporting documents for the next twenty years. Carrington felt Grant and Sherman suppressed his version of the fight to protect themselves. Perhaps they felt any more controversy over the army's ineptitude in the Powder River country would bode poorly for Grant's political fight with the government, including Stanton's War Department, and perhaps eventually the general's presidential aspirations. Protecting the recently brevetted Major Powell may also have been a minor reason. No wonder Carrington felt insecure. But if there was a logical reason for the suppression of Carrington's testimony, it probably had little to do with him personally.[56]

But clearing his good name once and for all, an imperative for a man of Carrington's social status during the Gilded Age, was from his point of view of foremost personal concern. He sought other avenues to get his version of the story to the public. In doing so can be found the genesis of the Fetterman myth. Carrington turned to his wife, Margaret, who had kept a journal of her experiences at Fort Phil Kearny. Carrington's former law partner William Dennison suggested that Margaret revise her journal and write a book about her experiences. In 1868 she authored *Ab-sa-ra-ka: Home of the Crows*, published by J. B. Lippincott and Company of Philadelphia. The book sold well enough to bring out a second edition in 1869. Although Margaret died in 1870, Henry Carrington over the years brought out a total of seven editions of her book, changing text occasionally, to make his role in 1866 look noble.[57] The volume has become a classic source on the struggle for the Powder River country in 1866 from the white perspective and remains in print today.[58] The historian who has studied the Carrington wives and their writings the most extensively is Shannon D. Smith, formerly Shannon Smith Calitri. In a recent article she writes,

> In *Ab-sa-ra-ka*, the Carringtons took advantage of Victorian-era middle-class gender roles to get their version of the Fetterman incident into the public eye. Margaret portrayed Fetterman as an honorable and chivalrous gentleman, but also characterized him as inexperienced in Indian warfare and as an officer whose zeal for recognition caused him to disobey explicit orders. In a politically astute move, she dedicated the book to Sherman [for originally encouraging her to keep a journal], who, bound by honor, sent his approval in a gracious and complementary letter.[59]

Smith argues that gender roles of the era prohibited anyone of the officer corps of the army to criticize a lady of the regiment and was honor bound to protect her good name. Margaret's untimely death in 1870 only added poignancy to her book rather than making her writing a target for Fetterman's supporters.[60]

In Margaret's book we find the first statement for public consumption of a boast made by Fetterman: "a company of regulars could whip a thousand, and a regiment could whip the whole array of hostile tribes."[61] Margaret gave readers no image of a "brash," incompetent Fetterman that his actions before December 21, 1866, would contradict. Instead she eulogized him as an officer who possessed "refinement, gentlemanly manners, and adaptation to social life . . . In life," she wrote, "he was a gentleman. In death he was mourned and honored."[62] Yet *Ab-sa-ra-ka* gave the public the impression that the "disaster" was caused by Fetterman's disobedience of orders. The public never forgot it. That Margaret actually pinned much of the blame, if not the command responsibility, on Capt. Frederick Brown has often gone unnoticed. "That his [Brown's] impulses *led* [emphasis mine] Brevet Lieutenant-Colonel Fetterman to disobey orders on the 21st of December," she wrote, "at the sacrifice of the whole detachment, is not questioned."[63]

But of Lt. George W. Grummond, whose widow had become her close friend, Margaret reveals much that evidence simply does not support. "[T]he sketch of the Fetterman's massacre shows how closely he obeyed his orders to remain with Captain Fetterman." But in the very next sentence (correctly if inadvertently) Margaret contradicts her own assertion by stating that Grummond's body was found a quarter-mile from Fetterman's. She explained the separation of the cavalry from the infantry by inferring that Grummond was "gallantly" covering a retreat of cavalrymen who had likely bolted from the skirmish formation.[64]

But neither Margaret nor Henry Carrington would ever criticize Lieutenant Grummond for his widow's sake. Margaret Sullivant Carrington died prematurely on May 11, 1870, one day after her thirty-ninth birthday. She succumbed to tuberculosis, which people always blamed on her harsh life on the frontier but which she probably contracted earlier in her life from her husband, who was an inactive carrier of the disease.[65] But *Ab-sa-ra-ka* would not be forgotten. Henry Carrington would continue to republish it throughout the rest of the nineteenth century. The third edition in 1879 contained an expanded appendix, "Indian Affairs on the Plains," and official documents and reports putting himself in a good light. In 1884 Carrington authored *The Indian Question* that, in later editions, included his official report of the Fetterman fight. But Carrington was most concerned of all with his attempts to have the testimony he had given before the Sanborn Commission in 1867 released to the public. Finally in 1887 Senator Henry L. Dawes of Massachusetts, sponsor of the infamous Indian allotment act of the same year, secured passage of a bill that provided for the Sanborn reports to be published by the government. Carrington, however, must have been horrified when he found that the published reports also contained the damning testimonies of Captain Powell and General Cooke. The struggle to clear his name was not over.[66]

But back in 1871 Carrington had hedged his bet. In Franklin, Tennessee, in 1870 Frances Grummond learned of Margaret's death. She had remained in Franklin since burying her husband's body there on her return in 1867, escorted from Fort Laramie by her brother. Shortly after she arrived in Tennessee Frances Grummond gave birth to a son, William Wands Grummond. Then she applied for her husband's military pension that she was entitled to as a result of his death. It was then she learned the truth. George Grummond's first wife, Delia, had already filed for Grummond's pension. The courts finally ruled in favor of Frances as being Lieutenant Grummond's wife at the time of his death. Frances quite possibly did not know that Grummond had been previously married. Certainly she did not realize that she had married Grummond twenty days before his divorce from Delia had become final in the courts.[67] Perhaps with memories of the past Frances Grummond sent Henry Carrington a letter of condolence. Carrington had just resigned from the army at age forty-six to take a professorship of military science at Wabash College in Crawfordsville, Indiana. The two began a written correspondence between Indiana and Tennessee. Eleven months later, on April 3, 1871, they married. Henry Carrington legally adopted Frances's young son, "Willie," after their marriage.[68]

Of course it is irresistible to speculate on the Carrington/Grummond marriage. But speculate only is what we can do because the eleven-month-long letter correspondence between Henry and Frances has never surfaced and was probably destroyed. But was it a marriage of love? Certainly Margaret Carrington and Frances Grummond became friends at Fort Phil Kearny, and by every indication Henry Carrington felt extreme empathy for Frances's loss, promising to personally retrieve her husband's remains following the Fetterman fight. But Carrington's repeated orders to Lt. George Grummond on December 21, 1866, give rise to a suspicion that Carrington recognized only too well Grummond's impulsiveness in combat and that it could potentially bring about disaster. At the Sanborn hearings Carrington cast blame back on Fetterman without involving Grummond or even Brown. But who, in his mind, did he really suspect of prompting Fetterman over Lodge Trail Ridge? Of the three officers present—Fetterman, Grummond, and Brown—only the latter two had actually demonstrated any penchant for impulsive behavior or, in Grummond's case, outright insubordination and disobedience during the fight on December 6.[69]

One year after Carrington's testimony, Margaret Carrington in *Ab-sa-ra-ka*, while stating that Fetterman's contempt for the Indians drove him to "hopeless ruin," specifically asserted that Brown's "impulsiveness led . . . Fetterman to disobey orders . . . at the sacrifice of the whole detachment, is *not questioned*" [emphases mine].[70] Were Margaret and Henry Carrington in 1868, out of respect for Grummond's widow, Frances, trying to direct all blame away from Lieutenant Grummond, despite the colonel's obvious concerns about Grummond on December 21, and to direct *all* the blame on Fetterman and Brown? Margaret eulogizes George Grummond without criticism in the "Memoriam" in *Ab-sa-ra-ka*.[71] Was Carrington's marriage to Frances designed to protect the reputation of Henry as well as of the dead George Grummond? Certainly we will never know the truth. Henry and Frances were together for forty-one years, more than double the time Carrington had been married to Margaret Sullivant. And, most assuredly, *conspiracy theory*, while exercising the mind, usually ends up making for poor scholarly history in the absence of at least *some* compelling evidence and logic based on that evidence.[72]

During Henry and Frances's four decades together they continued to do what could be done to restore Henry Carrington's good name. On July 3, 1908, a handful of white survivors of the two years at Fort Phil Kearny (there were only a few) assembled on the hill to dedicate a monument where Fetterman and Brown had made their last stand. The state of Wyoming had previously placed the stone monolith at the site in 1905 to commemorate the soldiers of the Fetterman fight. The Carringtons were to be part of an Independence Day celebration of the fortieth anniversary of the "Opening of Wyoming." The monument stands today, itself a more than century-old historic landmark. Pvt. William Murphy, who had helped recover the bodies on December 22, 1866, was present. So too was Sam Gibson, a veteran of the Wagon Box fight. Frances and Henry Carrington were named the guests of honor. The old colonel, thin and white-bearded, wore his old uniform and presented a picture typical of almost any aged Grand Army of the Republic veteran taken in the early years of the twentieth century. Frances was present by her husband's side. Dee Brown described her best from the few old photographs of the occasion that still exist: "She sat in the seat of a buggy drawn up near the small stone monument, a sturdy little old lady in a starched white shirtwaist and a dark ruffled skirt. Her hat—a sort of toque with a magnificent plume—was set at a jaunty angle."[73] That day old Henry Carrington (he was eighty-four, Frances, sixty-three) delivered a stirring speech in which he, once again, defended his actions at Fort Phil Kearny and cast blame on William J. Fetterman for disobedience. At the behest of Capt. Tenador Ten Eyck's daughter he also vindicated the actions of Ten Eyck, who Carrington had previously suggested was negligently tardy in coming to Fetterman's rescue by taking a lengthy route over Lodge Trail Ridge.[74]

Two years later, in 1910, forty-five years following the Fetterman fight, Frances Grummond Carrington published her own book, *My Army Life and the Fort Phil Kearny Massacre with An Account of the Celebration of "Wyoming*

Opened," based on her experiences in the Powder River country. The book reads like a slightly edited version of Margaret Carrington's *Ab-sa-ra-ka*. In some cases she repeats sentences and phrases from *Ab-sa-ra-ka*, most noticeably Fetterman's boast. A "single company of Regulars could whip a thousand Indians," Frances wrote, "and that a full regiment, officially announced from headquarters to be on the way to reinforce the troops, could whip the entire array of hostile tribes."[75] Some of this wording was almost identical to what Margaret had written in 1868.[76] Frances Grummond Carrington died within a year of the publication of her book, on October 17, 1911. Henry Carrington passed away a year later on October 26, 1912. They are both buried in Fairview Cemetery, Hyde Park, Massachusetts. Frances's book also contained the speech the colonel made in Sheridan, Wyoming, in 1908. Like Margaret before her, Frances did not use the currently ubiquitous "eighty-man" reference although Henry Carrington did in his speech in Sheridan. This was the first time he asserted it in a public forum. According to Carrington, Fetterman said, "'I can take eighty men and go to Tongue River.' To this boast my Chief Guide, the veteran James Bridger, replied in my presence, 'Your men who fought down South are crazy! They don't know anything about fighting Indians.'"[77]

But the Carrington wives were not solely responsible for shaping the Fetterman myth—perhaps not even the most important. So where did the most memorable rhetoric of the Fetterman story—"Give me eighty men and I'll ride through the whole Sioux Nation"—originate? Henry not only depended on his wives and himself to tell his version of the Fetterman fight; he ensured that other authors did the same. C. G. Coutant's *The History of Wyoming* (1896) contained a chapter about Fort Phil Kearny and the Fetterman fight approved by Carrington.[78] The colonel was indeed prolific in shaping the tale for later writers. The only counter to his version of the fight was an account by William Bisbee, filed with the Order of the Indian Wars, the veteran's organization for soldiers who served on the western frontier. The paper was not read until 1928, after all the Carringtons had died. Bisbee stated emphatically that his friend William J. Fetterman was too honorable and duty-bound a soldier to have intentionally been disobedient. After all, Fetterman had only a short time left under Carrington in the 18th Infantry before the captain moved to the 27th. Why would he be so irresponsible as to risk a stain on his record at that time even though he held no respect for his commanding officer? Bisbee repeated his favorable assessment of Fetterman in his book *Through Four American Wars*.[79]

But Carrington's version of Fetterman's actions *was* the version that would endure. In fact, the genesis of the "Give me eighty men and I'll ride through the whole Sioux Nation" epithet had actually come to public attention four years *before* Carrington's speech in Sheridan in 1908. In 1903 Carrington sought out author Cyrus Townsend Brady, who was compiling firsthand accounts of the Indian Wars of the West. Carrington gave Brady most of his past material advancing his version of the Fetterman fight. Of course Brady also had access to Margaret Carrington's book. Carrington wanted Brady to include a document regarding Maj. James Powell's duplicitous testimony but Brady refused as he planned to write a chapter on the Wagon Box fight as well as the Fetterman fight. Still, Brady told the story of the Fetterman fight chiefly from meeting with Carrington and from Carrington's notes and documents and he told it faithfully from Carrington's point of view. Carrington was appreciative to Brady for helping to restore his reputation.[80]

A former itinerant missionary and Episcopal priest on the Great Plains, Brady wrote a number of books and novels. His *Recollections of a Missionary in the Great West* is a melodramatic, sensationalized, anecdotal "tear-jerker" recalling his experiences, both real and not so real, as a clergyman on the plains. Some of his stories, especially his heart-wrenching Christmas yarns, are far more folklore than they are history in their specific details. He wrote for such magazines as *Pearson's*, *Munsey's*, and *Ladies' Home Journal*. Although Brady did not by any means achieve wealth from his writing, his *Indian Fights and Fighters*, published by McClure and Philips in 1904, became a minor classic and still makes its way into serious bibliographies today. The book was drawn in large part from firsthand accounts of aging officers, a number of whom, besides Carrington, had divisive "issues" with other officers over their respective experiences in the Indian campaigns. As such, there are a number of biases and errors in the book, Carrington's story being no exception. *Indian Fights and Fighters* is a monumental example of why historians must look for corroboration among original sources and check those sources against more recent scholarship. Brady's chapter on the Fetterman fight is strictly through Carrington's eyes. The story also appeared in *Pearson's* the same year, 1904, as part of a serialized version of the book. Here we have the first alleged statement by Fetterman specifically using the words "eighty men" and "riding through the whole Sioux Nation," thirty-eight years after the fact! The claim specifically included Capt. Frederick Brown. "Fetterman and Brown," Brady wrote, "'offered with eighty men to ride through the whole Sioux Nation'!"[81]

In summarizing the result of the battle on a later page Brady reemphasized the ubiquitously quoted cliché of the Fetterman fight once again: "The total force, therefore, including officers and citizens, under Fetterman's command, was eighty-one—just the number with which he had agreed to ride through the Sioux Nation." We shall never know if the phrase was suggested by Carrington or was a creation of Brady's in his final revisions (Brady allowed Carrington to read and correct the final version), but the tone of the prose smacks of Brady's style, not Carrington's, and Brady knew how to employ attention-grabbing literary devices in his prose. Most important, it has endured to this day as the most often quoted, and remembered, *essential* of William J. Fetterman and his demise. Brady penned a legacy.[82]

Since 1904, most serious histories as well as most not-so-serious histories of the Fetterman fight and fictionalized accounts have used the alleged "quote" to portray an unfavorable image of William J. Fetterman along with such supplemental adjectives as "arrogant," "impulsive," "rash," "brash," "incompetent," "pompous," "insane," "imperious," "fire-eater," and so forth. Modern writers in the past century have painted this picture of Fetterman, his character, his temperament, and his abilities as an officer that simply does not conform to original descriptions or actions of the man garnered from official reports before Carrington's assertions before the Sanborn Commission.[83] What Brady did was to simply create, with the eighty-man number, a striking historical irony that was nothing short of an explosive attention-getter for readers. It would become the most remembered sentence in his book in regards to Fetterman and came to stereotype the Fetterman fight as one of the most "ironic" tragedies in the history of the West. Of course because it *was* ironic it had to be a result of arrogance and incompetence if the image was to be effective. If Fetterman had successfully ridden euphemistically through the "Sioux Nation" with eighty men it would have been remembered not so much as arrogance as it would have been cast as assured confidence. Fetterman and his legacy would have been remembered differently. Such powerful ironies receive attention and they are almost impossible to ignore or forget during the passage of years and even centuries. One would think that well-educated Margaret Carrington would have certainly been struck by this irony if Fetterman had actually made this statement, and she would have utilized it in 1868 rather than the one she did use. Certainly someone would have noticed this illuminating irony during the thirty-eight years between the fight in 1866 and Brady's writings in 1904. But they did not.

One obscure account on first glance lends questionable support to the number "eighty" in the alleged Fetterman boast. Philip Faribault Wells, a half-Santee/half-white former guide for the army at Wounded Knee in 1890, sent a handwritten manuscript to Doane Robinson, by this time a South Dakota supreme court justice as well as an official of the South Dakota Historical Society. Wells claimed that in a Denver saloon in 1872, he heard Jim Bridger state that he (Bridger) had personally heard Fetterman utter the eighty-man boast at Fort Phil Kearny back in 1866. Robinson was puzzled and wrote back to Wells, asking him to clarify. Wells responded in a letter. "I probably mislead you in regard to a talk with Jim Bridger," Wells wrote. "I never had a personal talk with Jim Bridger in regard to this matter. In the spring of 1872, in the hotel in Denver, I heard him telling some men about this. It seems that before Captain Fetterman's death he had been criticizing other military officers about their way of conducting their Indian fighting and said 'if he were given eighty (80) men, he could subdue the whole Sioux tribe.'"[84] Wells then wrote that he heard Bridger say he had told Fetterman, 'If you ever get into an Indian fight with you in command, it will be your first fight and your last one.'" Wells went on to explain to Robinson that his claims regarding the Fetterman fight were based on what he had heard Bridger say in 1872 and on what "Nicki Jonis, Bat Pourrier (commonly known as Big Bat), & Louis Bordeaux told me." "I put it together to make my story and I'm not quite sure I got all exactly as it happened," he wrote.[85]

About the same time Wells sent Robinson a handwritten account of an interview he had in 1887 with Red Cloud. Wells stated that Fetterman and Brown committed joint suicide, a claim that Surgeon Horton's forensics and the assertions of American Horse had already disproved. Wells was eighty-three at this time. His claim of overhearing Bridger's conversation is flawed. By 1872 Jim Bridger was almost blind, suffering from goiter, and engaged in a legal battle with the army to gain title to old Fort Bridger. He had been living on his farm in New Santa Fe, Missouri, since at least 1868 and was in no physical condition to travel anywhere near Denver, let alone to a hotel saloon. But the most fatal flaw in Wells manuscript as a reliable source of evidence that Fetterman used the ironic number eighty in his boast is evidenced by the fact that Wells's manuscripts and his correspondence to Robinson were written in 1933, almost thirty years after Brady's *Indian Fights and Fighters* had become a widely read and accepted version of the Fetterman fight! Wells's correspondence and his manuscripts sound too much like the rhetoric of the Carringtons and Cyrus Townsend Brady to be taken seriously and they cannot be corroborated.[86]

But the eighty-man boast lives on, and is today taken as the essential ingredient of the Fetterman fight. The Brady version is simply more intriguing in its irony than Margaret Carrington's, and later Frances Carrington's, descriptions of William J. Fetterman's rhetoric. And irony often outlasts historical fact. Most middle-school children are familiar with the myth of the invincible Achilles and his vulnerable heel, ironically the spot where he was shot and killed by Prince Paris. But how familiar are these same children with the particulars of the Trojan War, or even whether or not the city of Troy, or for that matter Achilles, ever really existed? The Achilles syndrome endures the millennia, like the ironic biblical allegory of David and Goliath. Philosopher Robert W. Witkin wrote, "We might argue that history develops in a continuous alternation between periods of irony and periods in which there is little disjunction between the form and content of experience."[87]

The colonial experience of western nations during the Victorian era of the nineteenth century was of irony often portrayed in the sentimentalized pathos of the literature and history of the era. Much of this trend actually had a genesis with the popularization of Greek myths in the late eighteenth century. That "white" soldiers could be killed in large numbers at all by indigenous peoples in far-off lands was, in and of itself, *ironic*, during Kipling's age of the "White Man's Burden." When annihilation or near annihilation is added to the mix, the irony and myth become even more profound and enduring; Thermopylae, Balaklava, Isandlwana, the Sudan, Little Bighorn, Kabul, still retain interest in the public imagination. States military historian Alan D. Zimm, U.S. Navy, Retired: "In the vast reach of history, examples of annihilation are mercifully few. Such battles are the stuff of epics, and like epics, they are rare."[88] Witkin argues that "[t]hrough historicizing the abolition of the historical in the ironic vision of modern culture . . . the text [ironic myth] *defiantly* [emphasis mine] proclaims the historical. But then again . . . Irony can shape our view of history . . . often incorrectly."[89]

Later writers could not resist the eighty-man irony and finally it became "actual fact" that defined the "lessons" of the Fetterman fight—boastfulness, arrogance, and recklessness lead to disaster.[90] The annihilation of Fetterman's command, its mystery, and its controversy have fused with contrived ironic elements to create an epic story that often obfuscates reality. As the fictional newspaper reporter Maxwell Scott said to Ransom Stoddard when Stoddard asked him if he were going to print the true version of his life's story in the cinema epic *The Man Who Shot Liberty Valance*, "'This is the West, sir,' Scott replied. 'When legend becomes fact, print the legend'."[91]

Summary

But what are the arguably more mundane facts? It appears recklessness played a significant part indeed in the destruction of Fetterman's command. But has that accusation of recklessness been cast upon the wrong man? What can be garnered from the Fetterman fight? Considering his lifelong obsession to restore his reputation following the Fetterman fight, Col. Henry B. Carrington surmised that he was not to blame for the fate of Fetterman's command on December 21, 1866. Essentially Carrington was hamstrung by forces above him and below him in the chain of command that were beyond his control. Attempts to blame him were based in part on the disrespect for him by junior officers who were combat veterans of the Civil War as Carrington was not.[92] Gen. Philip St. George Cooke certainly did not provide Carrington and the Mountain District's military installations with sufficient resources and manpower before January 1867 to conduct any reasonable offensive operations. That the loss of civilian life during the dangerous summer months of 1866 was as low as it was is somewhat amazing given these limited resources. Given that Indian casualties were also fairly low is understandable given their swift hit-and-run tactics. The heavy loss of livestock by the garrison at Fort Phil Kearny is likewise understandable for the same reason. Cooke perceived Carrington as an inexperienced whiner who exaggerated the situation in the Powder River country. His initial orders to Carrington to conduct offensive operations against the Indian camps were based on this general belief. Cooke was mistaken and possibly, despite his experience in the West, naïve.[93]

But Cooke too was hamstrung from above. The Platte corridor and the initial planning, engineering, and constructing of the Union Pacific and Union Pacific Eastern Division (Kansas Pacific) railroads were a higher priority than the Powder River country, and indeed would soon make the Bozeman Trail obsolete. If Cooke had concentrated most of his manpower and resources in the Powder River country at the expense of the Platte road he would have created arguably more significant problems overall within the Department of the Platte. Cooke's problems were augmented by the politics of Reconstruction and the perceived need on the part of the War Department to retain large numbers of troops in the defeated South. The forts of the Mountain District were left to their own devices, to hold on, perhaps draw Indians northward and thus become sacrificial lambs for the protection of the advancing railroads to the south.[94]

Although the Fetterman fight and Red Cloud's war in general convinced the army of the need to send more troops to the West, especially cavalry, to conduct offensives against the plains tribes, Connor's and Sully's failures of 1865 were apparently forgotten in that regard. It would be almost two years before such offensives would become effective at Washita (November 1868) and Summit Springs (July 1869) on the central and southern plains. It would take longer north of the Platte. Not until late 1876 would manpower on the northern plains be sufficient to decisively defeat the Lakotas. The advent of the Great Sioux War would once again make protection of routes to the northern gold regions essential. Old portions of the Bozeman Trail would once again be used by military expedition forces. By the 1870s railroads across the plains would play a crucial role in timely troop deployment and supply movements along the previous dirt trails and roads as they had in the East during the Civil War, a crucial ingredient of successful campaigning that was not available to Cooke and Carrington in 1866.[95] On the "navigable" Missouri and Yellowstone rivers, steamboats augmented the efforts of the railroads to the south. As such the Great Sioux War became one of attrition now that the Lakotas and Cheyennes no longer held the balance of power in numbers or ability to reduce the subsistence requirements of soldiers operating far from supply depots.[96]

In summary, as to Fetterman's culpability, the man has been unfairly singled out and maligned by history either as the sole or main contributor to the annihilation of his command. It is almost certain that Fetterman (and/or Brown) never uttered the statement "Give me eighty men and I'll ride through the whole Sioux Nation." What Margaret Carrington claimed that Fetterman uttered was "a company of regulars could whip a thousand, and a regiment could whip the whole array of hostile tribes," a chauvinistic statement to be certain, but a feeling quite common among army officers on the frontier.[97]

The genesis of the eighty-man oath is surely a contrivance of Cyrus Townsend Brady in 1904, perhaps with the support and approval of Henry Carrington. Since Fetterman died with exactly eighty men at the hands of what was apparently a sizeable portion of the "Sioux Nation," Brady's statement established a powerful historical irony, and historical ironies are seldom ignored and die hard. They are literary bombshells that get and hold reader attention. Yet the fabled oath has stereotyped Fetterman as a brash, incompetent "fire-eater" personally responsible for the deaths of eighty-one men through his inexplicable disobedience of orders in the minds of people to this very day. Historical ironies can be misleading.

To infer that the demise of Fetterman's troops was only caused by sheer recklessness on the part of the U.S. Army participants also reduces the magnitude of the Indian victory. For the first and only time in the Indian Wars of the West, the Indians of the plains flawlessly executed a decoy maneuver with a large number of warriors in a major fight. No young man out for individual glory acted prematurely and thus exposed the ambush. No horse sounded the alarm or bolted away too soon. The use of the geographical features of the terrain in which to hide, given the Indians' large contingent, was superb. For all the misguided belief in Fabian defensive strategy the army placed on the role of the forts on the Bozeman Trail, and for all the ineffectual tactics executed by the garrison at Fort Phil Kearny, the opposite was true for the Lakotas, Cheyennes, and Arapahos who wiped out Fetterman's troops. Scholars and history buffs may argue endlessly regarding the degree of strategic organizational skills of the plains warriors and the penchant to fight individually. But a well-orchestrated attack *was* executed on December 21, 1866.[98]

For the Lakotas, Cheyennes, and Arapahos there is no controversy regarding the Fetterman fight, no mystery, and no irony. They remember the battle with pride in the warrior exploits of their ancestors and count the battle Where a Hundred Soldiers Were Killed as a seminal moment in their history. They tell stories of their relatives who, they claim through oral tradition, were in the fight. The late Bill Tall Bull (Wolf Feathers) of the Cheyennes, a former member of the Board of the Fort Phil Kearny/Bozeman Trail Association, told stories of his grandparents who were in the Tongue River camps in 1866. "My grandmother would say many years later," Bill Tall Bull wrote, "that no one ever had a good nights rest in this camp. The women were in constant readiness to flee with the children because of the possibility of attack on the camp." His grandparents told of the great victory celebration after the fight. "Brave deeds were told over and over," they told their grandson, "and would become part of the tribal history."[99] Younger generations of Northern Cheyennes write the stories of their tribal ancestors through the Little Wolf Writing and History Center at Chief Dull Knife College in Lame Deer, Montana. There is also the realization that although the Lakotas and Cheyennes and Arapahos may have won the struggle for the Powder River country on the battlefield, they ultimately lost the peace. The Treaty of 1868 that concluded Red Cloud's War was also the first step toward ending their independence by making them reservation Indians.[100]

So why study the Fetterman fight or the struggle for the Powder River country at all? What can it teach us that is pertinent to the present time? Many western historians question the importance of studying the military aspects of five hundred years of Indian resistance in the Western Hemisphere in the twenty-first century. As mentioned earlier, military historians will probably always quibble over whether or not Fetterman actually ordered Grummond's advance and separation down Massacre Ridge. Ultimately it is relatively unimportant who was to blame for the separation, except, perhaps, to quibbling military historians. But the results would have been the same whether Grummond bolted or Fetterman ordered him to advance. What the military aspects of the event can reveal, however, is how untrained, naïve, and arrogant America's frontier army often was in understanding the nature of effective guerilla warfare against a militarily skilled indigenous foe determined not to relinquish its homeland. Whichever officer, if any, made fatal errors is ultimately irrelevant in the overall effects of the conflict. According to historian Robert Utley, American officers and soldiers have traditionally been trained for conventional warfare against enemies possessing equal manpower and technology. Yet more time has been spent in the nation's history engaging unconventional enemies who make effective use of more primitive technology through adaptable strategy and tactics suited to the lands where they are fighting. This mentality has persisted in a strategic sense in military training from the early years of the Republic to Operation Iraqi Freedom, often with disastrous results, and direct comparisons can be made to the imperial experiences of other nations as well as to contemporary events.[101] In the Fetterman fight, the Lakotas, Cheyennes, and Arapahos took advantage of their superior numbers by fighting on home soil to defeat a force of conventionally trained soldiers, mostly with primitive weapons that proved more effective even than the 2nd Cavalry's repeating Spencer rifles. But ultimately more advanced technology leveled the field at the Hayfield and Wagon Box fights. In the end the invading soldiers left the region but finally humbled the Indians, not with force of arms, but through the legal chicanery of the Treaty of 1868. Methods of conquest were indeed varied. So it is meaningful, as military historian James McPherson would argue, to study a battle to determine why one side lost while the other side won. Such analysis *can* be pertinent in today's world. In the case of the struggle for the Powder River country we might add it is also meaningful to determine which side actually *did* lose once the diplomats took over and the gunfire ceased along the Bighorns.

Additionally, the Fetterman fight speaks volumes to the staunch determination of indigenous peoples to resist conquest and colonization by societies with larger populations and advanced technologies. The pride inculcated in the culture of indigenous societies is and should continue to be remembered with honor for these societies' heroes of the past rather than forgotten in decolonization movements. Finally, the Fetterman fight is one of the major episodes in American history that can teach us of the power and perhaps even the potential dangers inherent in historical myth and irony in imagining and shaping our collective history and modern political perspectives. Yet it is that same myth and irony that keep interest sparked in such events as the Fetterman fight where the attraction of the unknown and possibly the unanswerable will endure far longer than the importance of the event.

Today the options for those wishing to ponder the Fetterman mysteries are many. One may peruse official military reports of the fight and testimonies before the Sanborn Commission online,[102] participate in a discussion of the fight on a History Channel–sponsored Internet discussion forum,[103] or, thanks to Bob Reece of Friends of the Little Bighorn Battlefield Association, take a virtual tour of the Fetterman battlefield.[104] But the most illuminating experience is to walk the actual ground that was hallowed with blood on December 21, 1866. The wonderful job of restoration over the years with the support of the Fort Phil Kearny/Bozeman Trail Association has preserved the essence of the fort itself. A fine little museum interprets the history of the fort and the Fetterman and Wagon Box fights. You may walk Massacre Ridge, even on the cold anniversaries of the battle, December 21, regardless of the weather (it was cold in 1866) and retrace the steps of Fetterman and his men. You may locate the hiding places of the warriors and see the rocks where Lakotas and Cheyennes overwhelmed Fetterman and Brown. You may also find offerings left by Lakotas, Cheyennes, or Arapahos honoring their ancestors, especially around a tree and a marker near where the mortally wounded Big Nose, brother of Little Wolf, was taken to rest before he died. The soldier's graves are gone. In 1888 the remains were removed to the Little Bighorn battlefield and reinterred near the 7th Cavalry monument and mass grave on Custer Hill. In 1930 Fetterman, Brown, and their soldiers were moved again, down the hill to the new national cemetery to join other U.S. military frontier veterans near *their* graves. In 2003 arm bones and other bone fragments of Fetterman's soldiers were discovered during excavation of the new Indian memorial at Little Bighorn National Monument and were removed to the national cemetery in the park. Fetterman's men all arrived at their final resting places at the dawn of the twenty-first century.[105]

Indeed, for the scholars, students, and buffs who still consider the military frontiers of the West an important subject of inquiry, the Fetterman story lives on in the public imagination and probably will for decades to come. Historical irony created with the eighty-man myth has cast a false portrait of who William J. Fetterman actually was, but just as ironically that false portrait has kept the story alive and fascinating. The story of the Fetterman fight has likewise helped to shape the tales of Lakota and Cheyenne heroes and their proud records of resistance. One finds it difficult today to gaze at the century-old monument standing among the rocks near where Fetterman fell and brave warriors gained combat honors and not be struck by the idea on the monument's plaque, that in numerous ways the inscription does not state a sentiment of finality when it proclaims "there were no survivors."

APPENDIX A

List of Men Killed in Action near Fort Philip Kearny, Dakota Territory, on the 21st day of December, 1866

(Source: Margaret Carrington, Ab-sa-ra-ka: Home of the Crows, 282–84)

No. Name	Rank	Company	Battalion and Regiment
1. Augustus Lang	1st Sgt.A	2/18th Inf.	
2. Hugh Murphy	Sgt.	"	"
3. Robert Lennon	Crpl.	"	"
4. William Dule	"	"	"
5. Frederick Acherman	Pvt.	"	"
6. William Betzler	"	"	"
7. Thomas Burke	"	"	"
8. Henry Buchannan	"	"	"
9. George E. R. Goodall	"	"	"
10. Nichael Harlen	"	"	"
11. Martin Kelley	"	"	"
12. Patrick Shannon	"	"	"
13. Charles N. Taylor	"	"	"
14. Joseph D. Thomas	"	"	"
15. David Thorey	"	"	"
16. John Timson	"	"	"
17. Albert H. Walter	"	"	"
18. John M. Weaver	"	"	"
19. Maximillian Dehring	"	"	"
20. Francis S. Gordon	"	"	"
21. John Woodruff	"	"	"
22. Francis Raymond	Sgt.	C	"
23. Patrick Rooney	"	"	"
24. Gustave A. Bauer	Crpl.	"	"
25. Patrick Gallagher	"	"	"
26. Henry E. Aarons	Pvt.	"	"
27. Michael O'Gara	"	"	"
28. Jacob Rosenberg	"	"	"
29. Frank P. Sullivan	"	"	"
30. Patrick Smith	"	"	"
31. William Morgan	Sgt.	E	"
32. John Quinn	Crpl.	"	"

No. Name	Rank	Company	Battalion and Regiment
33. George W. Burrell	Pvt.	"	"
34. Timothy Cullinans	"	"	"
35. John Maher	"	"	"
36. George N. Waterbury	"	"	"
37. Alexander Smith	1st Sgt.	H	"
38. Ephraim C. Bissell	Sgt.	"	"
39. George Philip	Crpl.	"	"
40. Michael Sharkey	"	"	"
41. Frank Karston	"	"	"
42. George Davis	Pvt.	"	"
43. Pierre F. Doland	"	"	"
44. Asa H. Griffin	"	"	"
45. Herman Keil	"	"	"
46. James Kean	"	"	"
47. Michael Kinney	"	"	"
48. Delos Reed	"	"	"
49. Thomas M. Madden	Recruit	unassigned	"
50. James Baker	Sgt.	C	2d Cavalry
51. James Kelley	Crpl.	"	"
52. Thomas F. Honigan	"	"	"
53. Adolph Metzger	Bugler	"	"
54. John McCarty	Artificer	"	"
55. Thos. Amberson	Pvt.	"	"
56. Thos. Broglan	"	"	"
57. William Bugbee	"	"	"
58. William Cornog	"	"	"
59. Charles Cuddy	"	"	"
60. Patrick Clancey	"	"	"
61. Harry S. Deming	"	"	"
62. Hugh B. Doran	"	"	"
63. Robert Daniel	"	"	"
64. Nathan Foreman	"	"	"
65. Andrew M. Fitzgerald	"	"	"
66. Daniel Greene	"	"	"
67. Charles Gamford	"	"	"
68. John Giller	"	"	"
69. Ferdinand Houser	"	"	"

No. Name	Rank	Company	Battalion and Regiment
70. Frank Jones	"	"	"
71. James B. McGuire	"	"	"
72. John McColley	"	"	"
73. George W. Nugent	"	"	"
74. Franklin Payne	"	"	"
75. James Ryan	"	"	"
76. Oliver Williams	"	"	"
77. James Wheatley	Citizen		
78. Isaac Fisher	"		

Enlisted Men 18th U.S. Infantry	49
Enlisted Men 2nd U.S. Cavalry	27
Citizens	2
Total	78

Officers of the 18th U.S. Infantry Killed in the Same Action

Capt. William J. Fetterman

Capt. Frederick H. Brown

Lt. George W. Grummond

Recapitulation

	Officers	Sgts.	Crpls.	Pvts.	Citizens	Aggregate
2/18th Inf.	3	7	8	34		52
2nd Cavalry		1	2	24		27
Citizens					2	2
Total	3	8	10	58	2	81

APPENDIX B

Claimed Indian Warriors Killed or Mortally Wounded on December 21, 1866, near Fort Philip Kearny

Name	Tribal Designation	Source
Lone Bear	Oglala Lakota	American Horse; White Bull
Yellow White Man	"	American Horse; White Bull
Horse Looking	"	American Horse
Little Bear	"	American Horse
Eats Meat	Miniconjou Lakota	White Bull
Charging-Crow	"	White Bull
Flying Hawk	"	White Bull
Bear Ears	Probable Miniconjou	White Bull
Little Crow	"	White Bull
Clown Horse	"	White Bull
Male	"	White Bull
He Dog*	"	White Bull
Fine Weather	"	White Bull
Eagle-Stays-In-the-Air	"	White Bull
Broken Hand	"	White Bull
Eats Pemmican	"	White Bull
Bird Head	Arapaho	American Horse
Good Shield	"	American Horse
Bear Robe	Cheyenne	American Horse
Big Nose	"	White Elk; W. Leg; Two Moon†
Strong Wind Blowing	"	Wooden Leg

---

* Miniconjou, not the Oglala He Dog.

† Two Moon gives the name "Swift Hawk" to Little Wolf's younger brother rather than Big Nose.

NOTES

Notes to Prologue

1. James M. McPherson, *This Mighty Scourge: Perspectives on the Civil War* (New York: Oxford University Press, 2007), 63.

2. Ned Blackhawk, *Violence Over the Land: Indians and Empires in the Early American West* (Cambridge, MA: Harvard University Press, 2006), 11.

3. Lee H. Whittlesey, *Storytelling in Yellowstone: Horse and Buggy Tour Guides* (Albuquerque: University of New Mexico Press, 2007), 15, 20.

4. Whirlwind Soldier, review of Joseph M. Marshall III, *The Journey of Crazy Horse*, 2004, Ebsco Host Research Databases, Bibliography of Native North Americans, Summer 2005, #10525505, EBSCOhost.com.

5. Bernard L. Fontana, "American Indian Oral History: An Anthropologist's Note," *History & Theory* 8, no. 3 (1969): 367.

6. Gordon M. Day, "Oral History as Complement," *Ethnohistory* 19, no. 2 (Spring 1972): 99.

7. Joyce A. Kievit, ed., "A Discussion of Scholarly Responsibilities to Indigenous Communities," *American Indian Quarterly* 27, nos. 1 and 2 (Winter–Spring 2003): 3–45.

8. Colin Calloway, ed., *New Directions in American Indian History* (Norman: University of Oklahoma Press, 1988).

9. Kievit, "Discussion of Scholarly Responsibilities," 4.

10. Ibid., 5.

11. Glenda Littlebird to John Monnett, e-mail, December 3, 2003.

12. An Emory scholar, Michael A. Elliot, states, "Multicultural revisionism has not led Americans—non-Indians and Indians away from . . . the Indian Wars but back to them." This era can illuminate many facets of our modern culture. Elliot, *Custerology: The Enduring Legacy of the Indian Wars and George Armstrong Custer* (Chicago: University of Chicago Press, 2007), 6.

13. Shannon D. Smith, *Give Me Eighty Men: Women and the Myth of the Fetterman Fight* (Lincoln: University of Nebraska Press, 2008). Although not yet published at the time of this writing, this study promises to shed more light than any other on the roles of the Carrington wives in shaping the Fetterman story.

14. McPherson, *This Mighty Scourge*, ix.

Notes to Introduction

1. John G. Neihardt, "*Song of the Indian Wars*," *The Twilight of the Sioux: The Song of the Indian Wars—The Song of the Messiah*, vol. 2 of *A Cycle of the West* (Lincoln:

University of Nebraska Press, 1971), 57. All introductory quotes in subsequent chapters are from this epic poem.

2. Adjutant General's Office, *Chronological List of Actions, &c With Indians from January 15, 1837 to January, 1891,* facsimile copy (Fort Collins, CO: Old Army Press, 1979), 25. See also Robert A. Murray, *The Bozeman Trail, Highway of History* (Boulder, CO: Pruett Publishing, 1988), 45–46.

3. Unless an event took place in close proximity to railroads, the politics of Reconstruction occupied the interests of major eastern and midwestern newspapers. See Oliver Knight, *Following the Indian Wars: The Story of the Newspaper Correspondents Among the Indian Campaigners* (Norman: University of Oklahoma Press, 1960), 31–32.

4. For example, *Rocky Mountain News* (Denver) for December 28, 1866, January 2 and 26, and February 1, 1867.

5. Robert M. Utley, *Cavalier in Buckskin: George Armstrong Custer and the Western Military Frontier* (Norman: University of Oklahoma Press, 1988), 194.

6. For the Civil War record of the 18th Infantry in comparison to other regiments of regulars during that conflict, see Mark W. Johnson, *That Body of Brave Men: The U.S. Regular Infantry and the Civil War in the West* (Cambridge, MA: Da Capo Press, 2003).

7. Carrington to Assistant Adjutant General's Office, Department of the Platte, Omaha, NE, "Indian Operations on the Plains," *Senate Exec. Doc.* 33, 40. See also Department of the Army, *The Papers of Ulysses S. Grant*, 26 vols., ed. John Y. Simon (Carbondale: Southern Illinois University Press, 1967–2003), 16:422–23, 17:13–14; and Robert Athern, *William Tecumseh Sherman and the Settlement of the West* (Norman: University of Oklahoma Press, 1956), 90–91. Two investigations were launched.

8. For an overview peruse the "Records Relating to the Investigation of the Fort Phil Kearny Massacre, 1866–67," and Records of the Bureau of Indian Affairs, RG 75, National Archives and Records Administration, hereafter referred to as NARA.

9. Robert A. Murray, "Commentaries on the Col. Henry B. Carrington Image," *Denver Westerners Monthly Roundup* 24, no. 2 (March 1968): 3.

10. "'Unraveling the Mysteries': When Was the Fetterman Monument Built and Who Built It?" *Lookout, Newsletter of the Fort Phil Kearny/Bozeman Trail Association* 9 (Fall 1988): 3.

11. Alternatively, the literature occasionally refers to the "Battle of 100-In-The Hands." See Wolf Feathers (the late Bill Tall Bull), Fort Phil Kearny/Bozeman Trail Association website, http://philkearny.vcn.com/fpk-tallbull.htm.

12. Wooden Leg, in Thomas B. Marquis, *Cheyenne and Sioux: The Reminiscences of Four Indians and a White Soldier*, ed. Ronald H. Limbaugh (Stockton, CA: Pacific Center for Western Historical Studies, University of the Pacific, 1973), 34.

13. Peter John Powell, *People of the Sacred Mountain: A History of the Northern Cheyenne Chiefs and Warrior Societies, 1830–1974, with an Epilog, 1969–1974,* 2 vols. (San Francisco: Harper and Row, 1981), 1:461. For the story of the Northern Cheyenne exodus of 1878–79, see John H. Monnett, *Tell Them We Are Going Home: The Odyssey of the Northern Cheyennes* (Norman: University of Oklahoma Press, 2001); and Stan Hoig, *Perilous Pursuit: The U.S. Cavalry and the Northern Cheyennes* (Boulder: University Press of Colorado, 2002).

14. Susan Badger Doyle, "Indian Perspectives of the Bozeman Trail, 1864–1868," *Montana: The Magazine of Western History* 40, no. 1 (Winter 1990): 60.

Notes to Chapter 1

1. Neihardt's epic poem of the plains begins "The Sowing of the Dragon." John G. Neihardt, *The Twilight of the Sioux: The Song of the Indian Wars—The Song of the Messiah*. Vol. 2 of *A Cycle of the West* (Lincoln: University of Nebraska Press, 1971), 1.

2. Susan Bordeux Bettelyoun, Papers, Nebraska State Historical Society; Susan Bordeux Bettelyoun and Josephine Waggoner, *With My Own Eyes: A Lakota Woman Tells Her People's History* (Lincoln: University of Nebraska Press, 1988), 4; *National Tribune*, March 3, 1910, 7, and January 26, 1911, 8.

3. Connor to Balmer, April 22, 1865, Records of the District of the Plains, NARA, RG 393. For Big Crow see George Bent in George B. Grinnell, *The Fighting Cheyennes* (Norman: University of Oklahoma Press, 1982), 183; and Powell, *People of the Sacred Mountain*, 1:313. Bettelyoun and Waggoner's editor, Emily Levine, identifies Big Crow as Four Antelope but this is contrary to Bent and the military records.

4. Moonlight to Acting Assistant Adjutant General, Letters Sent, Department of the Plains, 1865, U.S. War Department, Records of the Adjutant General's Office, RG 94, Department of the Plains, Letters Sent and Received, 1864–65.

5. U.S. War Department, *The War of the Rebellion: A Compilation of the Official Records of the Union and Confederate Armies*, series 1, vol. 38, part 1 (Washington, D.C., 1880–1901), 276–77.

6. Bettelyoun and Waggoner, *With My Own Eyes*, 84–85, 86, 92. For an account of some of the variations to this event, see Dorothy M. Johnson, "The Hanging of the Chiefs," *Montana: The Magazine of Western History* 20, no. 3 (Summer 1970): 60–69; *Rocky Mountain News*, June 27, 1865, 2; and Will H. Young, "The Journals of Will H. Young, 1865," *Annals of Wyoming* 7 (1930): 421. Desmet was in Europe much of 1865.

7. Young, "Journals," 381.

8. Notable exceptions were 5th and 9th U.S. Infantry and the 3rd Artillery that spent the war years on the frontier.

9. Robert M. Utley, *Frontiersmen in Blue: The United States Army and the Indian, 1848–1865* (Lincoln: University of Nebraska Press, 1981), 211–14.

10. For the U.S. Volunteers see Michele Tucker Butts, *Galvanized Yankees on the Upper Missouri* (Boulder: University Press of Colorado, 2003).

11. Arguably the most famous of these deserters was the indomitable Samuel Clemens, a.k.a. Mark Twain, who left the Confederate Army for the Comstock strikes in Nevada and to launch his literary career.

12. Butts, *Galvanized Yankees*, 216.

13. It is not the purpose of this study to survey in detail the events on the northern plains between 1862 and 1865. The task would require multiple volumes. The best recent account of the military campaigns during these years is John D. McDermott, *Circle of Fire: The Indian War of 1865* (Mechanicsburg, PA: Stackpole Books, 2003).

14. By 1860 the Federal Immigration Commission estimated the percentage of foreign-born white settlers approached 37 percent in the lands west and adjacent to Minnesota alone. *Reports of the U.S. Immigration Commission*, Sen. doc. 756, 61st Cong., 3d sess., 3:444–47. See also Frederick C. Luebke, *Ethnicity on the Great Plains* (Lincoln: University of Nebraska Press, 1980) for an extensive analysis of immigrant population statistics throughout the nineteenth-century West.

15. William Watts Folwell, *A History of Minnesota* (St. Paul: Minnesota Historical Society, 1956), 1:266–304, 350–54.

16. For the life of Jane Gray Swisshelm, see Sylvia D. Hoffert, *Jane Gray Swisshelm: An Unconventional Life, 1815–1884* (Chapel Hill: University of North Carolina Press, 2004).

17. Much has been written on the U.S. Dakota Conflict. A few interesting secondary syntheses are: Micheal Clodfelter, *The Dakota War: The United States Army Versus the Sioux, 1862–1865* (Jefferson, NC: McFarland and Co., 1998); Kenneth Carley, *The Dakota War of 1862* (St. Paul: Minnesota Historical Society, 2001); Gary Clayton Anderson, *Little Crow: Spokesman for the Sioux* (St. Paul: Minnesota Historical Society, 1986); and Gary Clayton Anderson and Alan R. Woolworth, *Through Dakota Eyes: Narrative Accounts of the Minnesota Indian War of 1862* (St. Paul: Minnesota Historical Society, 1988). See also the website of the Minnesota Historical Society, www.mnhs.org/. This site lists the society's collection pertaining to the conflict. Original eyewitness accounts by settlers are linked as are the Henry Hasting Sibley Papers, the most complete original source from the perspective of the Minnesota Volunteers and their commanding officer. One may also view on this site Lincoln's original order, in his handwriting, for the executions of the Dakotas. See also David A. Nichols, *Lincoln and the Indians* (Urbana: University of Illinois Press, 2000), 65–118.

18. An excellent analysis is Louis Pfaller, "The Sully Expedition of 1864 Featuring the Killdeer Mountain and Badlands Battles," *North Dakota History* 31 (1964): 1–54. See also the Sully Papers, 1864, Beinecke Library, Yale University. For the fighting in 1864, see Eugene Ware, *The Indian War of 1864* (New York: St. Martins, 1960).

19. For Sand Creek, see Gary Roberts, "Sand Creek: Tragedy and Symbol" (PhD diss., University of Oklahoma, 1984); Stan Hoig, *The Sand Creek Massacre* (Norman: University of Oklahoma Press, 1961); and Elliot West, *The Contested Plains: Indians, Gold Seekers, and the Rush to Colorado* (Lawrence: University Press of Kansas, 1998).

20. For a secondary source overview of these 1865 campaigns, see McDermott, *Circle of Fire*.

21. For the Bear River Massacre, see Blackhawk, *Violence Over the Land*, 262–65.

22. The campaigns of 1865 are massive and complex. Among the numerous sources are U.S. War Department, *War of the Rebellion*, vol. 48; Grinnell, *Fighting Cheyennes*, 209–11; and J. W. Vaughn, *The Battle of Platte Bridge* (Norman: University of Oklahoma Press, 1963). The most recent and complete synthesis is McDermott, *Circle of Fire*.

23. Kingsley M. Bray, "Teton Sioux Population History, 1655–1881," *Nebraska History* 75, no. 2 (Summer 1994): 165–88.

24. Utley, *Frontiersmen in Blue*, 272–80.

25. Such was evidenced by the overall failures of the Doolittle and Edmunds commissions and the ill-fated Treaty of the Little Arkansas beginning in 1865. In the wake of

the Reconstruction Act and objections by Kansans over the proposed reservation being established in Kansas, the treaty, which would have established a true agency for the Southern Cheyennes, was never ratified by Congress.

26. Utley, *Frontiersmen in Blue*, 332–49.

27. For the sacred covenants, creation stories, and culture heroes of the Cheyennes, see Peter John Powell, *Sweet Medicine: The Continuing Role of the Sacred Arrows, the Sun Dance, and the Sacred Buffalo Hat in Northern Cheyenne History*, 2 vols. (Norman: University of Oklahoma Press, 1969).

28. Winter counts of Lone Dog, National Anthropological Archives (hereafter referred to as NAA), negative no. 3524C (glass negative) (Washington, D.C.: Smithsonian); Flame, NAA ms. 2372, box 12, 08633800; and Swan, NAA ms. 2372, box 12, 08633900. Photographs of these winter counts may be found in Bureau of American Ethnology, *4th Annual Report, 1882–1883* (Washington, D.C., 1886), 120–21.

29. For an excellent overview of this tentative lull in Crow-Lakota relations, see Kingsley M. Bray, "Lone Horn's Peace: A New View of Sioux-Crow Relations," *Nebraska History* 66, no. 1 (Spring 1985): 28–47.

30. Eugene Buechel and Paul Manhart, eds., *Lakota Dictionary: Lakota-English/English-Lakota* (Lincoln: University of Nebraska Press, 2002), 13, 504.

31. Ibid., 41–43.

32. Amos Bad Heart Bull, *A Pictographic History of the Oglala Sioux*, text by Helen H. Bliss (Lincoln: University of Nebraska Press, 1967), 117–87.

33. Bray, "Lone Horn's Peace," 44; Harry H. Anderson, "A Challenge to Brown's Sioux Indian Wars Thesis," *Montana: The Magazine of Western History* 12, no. 1 (Winter 1962): 41; George F. Hyde, *Red Cloud's Folk: A History of the Oglala Sioux Indians* (Norman: University of Oklahoma Press, 1930), 88–95; John C. Ewers, "Economic Warfare as a Precursor of Indian-White Warfare on the Northern Great Plains," *Western Historical Quarterly* 6 (October 1975): 40.

34. For the methodology behind these calculations, see Dan Flores, "The Great Contraction," in *Legacy: New Perspectives on the Battle of the Little Bighorn*, ed. Charles E. Rankin (Helena: Montana Historical Society Press, 1996), 13–15.

35. Russell Thornton, *American Indian Holocaust and Survival: A Population History Since 1492* (Norman: University of Oklahoma Press, 1987), 52.

36. Bray, "Teton Sioux Population History," 172.

37. Ibid., 13.

38. Elliot West, "Contested Plains," *Montana: The Magazine of Western History* 48 (Summer 1998): 2–15.

39. Flores, "The Great Contraction," 16. Accordingly, annual precipitation dropped by 30 percent for nine of the years in the decade following 1846; Dan Flores, *The Natural West: Environmental History in the Great Plains and Rocky Mountains* (Norman: University of Oklahoma Press, 2001), 66; G. J. Wiche, R. M. Lent, and W. F. Rannie, "Little Ice Age: Aridity in the North American Great Plains," *The Holocene* 6, no. 4 (2004). An abstract of this article may be easily accessed at http://nd.water.usgs.gov. Archaeologist Brian Fagan argues that while assessing aboriginal changes centuries ago

during the early stages of the Little Ice Age may be intellectually bankrupt, the evidence shows that climate change is not gradual. It comes in sudden and dramatic shifts that bring about corresponding adaptations by human societies. Thus the changes to a drier climate as occurred on the northern plains beginning in 1846 would be sufficient to cause concern among converging populations of peoples suddenly stressing diminishing natural resources. See Brian Fagan, *The Little Ice Age: How Climate Made History, 1300–1850* (New York: Basic Books/Persons, 2000), xviii.

40. Bettelyoun and Waggoner, *With My Own Eyes*, 77–78; Kingsley M. Bray, *Crazy Horse: A Lakota Life* (Norman: University of Oklahoma Press, 2006), 50. While near the Solomon River in east-central Kansas during the summer of 1857, these Oglalas and Cheyennes suffered defeat at the hands of Edwin V. Sumner's troops during his punitive expedition against the Cheyennes in response to the war that broke out two years previously following the Harney Expedition. Sumner's campaign drove these Oglalas and Cheyennes back toward the Platte and the Powder River country. The best secondary analysis of this campaign and the Battle of Solomon Fork is William Y. Chalfant, *Cheyennes and Horse Soldiers: The 1857 Expedition and the Battle of Solomon's Fork* (Norman: University of Oklahoma Press, 1997).

41. Richard White, *Roots of Dependency* (Lincoln: University of Nebraska Press, 1983), 10–11.

42. Flores, *The Natural West*, 190. See also Dan Flores, "Bison Ecology and Bison Diplomacy Redux," in *American Environmental History*, ed. Louis S. Warren (Malden, MA: Blackwell Publishing, 2003), 160–75. Bray's population study of the Lakotas supports Flores's conclusions that population increased during many of the war years. See Bray, "Teton Sioux Population History," 165–88.

43. John H. Moore, *The Cheyenne Nation: A Social and Demographic History* (Lincoln: University of Nebraska Press, 1987), 127–28.

44. Henry R. Schoolcraft, *Historical and Statistical Information Respecting the History, Condition and Prospects of the Indian Tribes of the United States* (Philadelphia: Lippincott, 1847), 518–24.

45. Moore, *Cheyenne Nation*, 138–40. Although his work is controversial, see also Shepard Krech III, *The Ecological Indian* (New York: W. W. Norton, 1999), 138.

46. Ware, *Indian War of 1864*, 356. For the Camp Weld council, see Hoig, *Sand Creek Massacre*, 113–21.

47. W. Henry McNab and Peter E. Avers, "Ecological Subregions of the United States," www.fs.fed.us/lands/pubs/ecoregions, 8–9. Changes have come to the Powder River Basin during the twentieth century. Ecosystems are threatened by the effects of methane drilling and the absence of buffalo grazing distinguished from that of cattle grazing. For overviews see Abstract of ESA 2003 Annual Meeting, http://abstracts.co.allenpress.com/pweb/esa2003/document/?ID=25625 and http://news.nationalgeographic.com/news/2001/08/0817_NGTmethanemadness.html.

48. David E. Griffin, "Timber Procurement and Village Location in the Middle Missouri Subarea," *Plains Anthropologist* 22, no. 78, memoir no. 13 (1977): 177–85. For additional references see Moore, *Cheyenne Nation*, 143.

49. Ibid., 144.

50. Ibid., 143.

51. Ware, *Indian War of 1864*, 60, 70, 127, 191, 230, 237, 255.

52. James C. Olson, *Red Cloud and the Sioux Problem* (Lincoln: University of Nebraska Press, 1965), 32–33.

53. Robert W. Larson, *Red Cloud: Warrior-Statesman of the Lakota Sioux* (Norman: University of Oklahoma Press, 1997), 30–31. George Hyde and others argued that Red Cloud was born near the Black Hills and only claimed the Blue Water birthplace to give the Lakotas claim to the Platte country. But Larson in his biography makes the best argument for the great Oglala's birthplace on Blue Water Creek.

54. Ibid., 90–93; Frances C. Carrington, *My Army Life: A Soldier's Wife at Fort Phil Kearny* (Philadelphia: Lippincott and Co., 1910), 291–92.

55. A Lakota name for white man but not a description of skin color.

56. Nicholas Black Elk and John G. Neihardt, *Black Elk Speaks* (Lincoln: University of Nebraska Press, 2000), 7.

Notes to Chapter 2

1. Neihardt, *Song of the Indian Wars*, 18.

2. Maynadier to Cooley, March 9, 1866, U.S. Senate, *Annual Report of the Commissioner of Indian Affairs for 1866*, 207.

3. For Red Cloud's early life, and the differences of opinion regarding his birth and name, see Olson, *Red Cloud and the Sioux Problem*, 15–26; and Sheldon, "Red Cloud," 4. The Sheldon mss. are composed of a series of interviews with an elderly Red Cloud in 1893 conducted by Charles W. Allen, typed by Mari Sandoz in 1932, and given to Addison Sheldon of the Nebraska State Historical Society. The 134-page manuscript was published in 1997 as R. Eli Paul, ed., *Autobiography of Red Cloud: War Leader of the Oglalas* (Helena: Montana Historical Society, 1997). It is the best coverage of Red Cloud's life prior to his fighting the whites. In the memoir Red Cloud claims his place of birth as Blue Water Creek, as does Larson in *Red Cloud*, 30–31. George Hyde also thinks differently about much of Red Cloud's early life. He usually did differ with others, often writing in a passive voice and thus avoiding ascription to specific sources. See Hyde, *Red Cloud's Folk*, 85–91. Sioux historian Ohiyesa, Charles Eastman, also writes of Red Cloud's early life, but much of Eastman's work smacks of embellishment and has long been suspect. See Eastman, *Indian Heroes & Great Chieftains* (Boston: Little, Brown, 1918), 1–22. For an assessment of Eastman by George Hyde, see Hyde, *Red Cloud's Folk*, 54.

4. Hyde contends that on both occasions traders had plied the participants liberally with alcohol to encourage the feud. See Hyde, *Red Cloud's Folk*, 53–54. Hyde's contentions are supported by the winter count of Iron Crow for 1841. Iron Crow's drawing was interpreted to mean "While drunk they killed each other." See James Walker, *Lakota Society* (Lincoln: University of Nebraska Press, 1992), 140; and Mallery in *Annual Report of the Bureau of American Ethnology for 1886*, 140–41. See also Olson, *Red Cloud and the Sioux Problem*, 9; and Catherine Price, *The Oglala People* (Lincoln: University of Nebraska Press, 1996), 23.

5. Buechel and Manhart, *Lakota Dictionary*, 305. For an excellent analysis of tiyospayes, bands, etc., see Raymond J. DeMallie, "Teton Dakota Kinship and Social Organization" (PhD diss., University of Chicago, 1971).

6. Price, *The Oglala People*, 26.

7. Eli S. Ricker, interview with Dr. J. R. Walker, Pine Ridge, November 21, 1906, Ricker Papers, Nebraska State Historical Society, tablet 17.

8. Although in the reservation years the Plains Indians traded for scalps and often used locks of hair sold to them by friends, in 1911 an anonymous old Lakota warrior told Richard Nines that during the days of warfare scalps for the shirts were obtained from the enemy. See Nines in Walker, *Lakota Society*, 36.

9. Larson, *Red Cloud*, 73.

10. See Hyde, *Red Cloud's Folk*, 67–68; and Olson, *Red Cloud and the Sioux Problem*, 23–25.

11. Olson, *Red Cloud and the Sioux Problem*, 25–26; Hyde, *Red Cloud's Folk*, 117–18; Vaughn, *The Battle of Platte Bridge*, 37–39; McDermott, *Circle of Fire*, 86; Grinnell, *Fighting Cheyennes*, 216–29.

12. Elsa Spear Edwards, "A Fifteen Day Fight on the Tongue River, 1865," *Annals of Wyoming* 10 (April 1938): 51–58. For Sawyer's extended expedition, see Leroy R. Hafen and Ann W. Hafen, eds., *Powder River Campaigns and Sawyer's Expedition of 1865* (Glendale, CA: Arthur H. Clark, 1961). For a summary see also Olson, *Red Cloud and the Sioux Problem*, 25–26.

13. Maynadier to D. N. Cooley, March 9, 1966, U.S. Senate, *Annual Report of the Commissioner for Indian Affairs for 1866*, 207–8.

14. Ibid.

15. Robert W. Frazier, *Forts of the West: Military Forts and Presidios and Posts Commonly Called Forts West of the Mississippi River to 1898* (Norman: University of Oklahoma Press, 1965), 183–84. Originally Fort Phil Kearny was to be called New Fort Reno, but since the old one remained the name was changed to Fort Phil Kearny before it was constructed after Carrington reached the Piney.

16. Many romantic notions swirl around Mini-Aku. Some contend the girl was in love with an officer at Fort Laramie, perhaps Eugene F. Ware, but pined away from grief when Spotted Tail moved his people from the vicinity of Fort Laramie with the outbreak of the 1865 offensives. See Wilson D. Clough, "Mini-Aku, Daughter of Spotted Tail," *Annals of Wyoming* 39 (1967): 187–216. Lakotas recently recovered the remains of Mini-Aku, long missing from the burial spot, and reburied them on a hill above Fort Laramie in a ceremony conducted by the Brulés on June 25, 2005. See "A Father's Grief . . . A Soldier's Honor," program brochure for the reinterment of Mini-Aku (Fort Laramie National Historic Site, Wyoming, 2005).

17. Larson, *Red Cloud*, 92–93.

18. The quote is from Dee Brown, *Fort Phil Kearny: An American Saga* (Lincoln: University of Nebraska Press, 1962), 38–39. See also, Hyde, *Red Cloud's Folk*, 139.

19. Margaret I. Carrington, *Ab-sa-ra-ka: Home of the Crows*. Philadelphia: Lippincott and Co., 1868), 79.

20. Ibid., 79–80; Brady, *Indian Fights and Fighters* (New York: McClure, Phillips and Co., 1904), 7–8.

21. F. C. Carrington, *My Army Life*, 46–46.

22. Doane Robinson, *A History of the Dakota or Sioux Indians* (Minneapolis, MN: Ross and Hague, 1956), 536–37.

23. F. C. Carrington, *My Army Life*, 291–92.

24. Brady, *Indian Fights and Fighters*, 8.

25. Kingsley M. Bray, "Spotted Tail and the Treaty of 1868," *Nebraska History* 83, no. 1 (Spring 2002): 20.

26. Taylor to Cooley, June 29, 1866, Letters Received, Upper Platte Indian Agency, RG 75, NARA.

27. 40th Cong., 1st sess., *Senate Ex. Doc.* 13, 12.

28. Olson, *Red Cloud and the Sioux Problem*, 37.

29. Chandler to H. B. Denman, January 13, 1867, 40th Cong., 1st sess., Senate Ex. Doc. XIII, 11–12.

30. James D. Richardson, comp., *Messages and Papers of the Presidents, 1789–1897*, 10 vols. (Washington, D.C.: Bureau of National Literature and Art, 1896–99), 6:454.

31. Olson, *Red Cloud and the Sioux Problem*, 40.

32. Carrington Papers, Sterling Memorial Library, Yale University.

33. Ibid. For a concise biography of Carrington's life, see Maguder in Fort Phil Kearny/Bozeman Trail Association, *Portraits of Fort Phil Kearny* (Banner, WY: Fort Phil Kearny/Bozeman Trail Association, 1993), 16–20.

34. For Cooke and his idiosyncrasies, see Otis E. Young, *The West of Philip St. George Cooke, 1809–1895* (Glendale, CA: Arthur H. Clark, 1955).

35. According to historian James McPherson, "The most successful wars in American history have been those with a close congruity between policy and strategies." The "policy" of the federal government in the Powder River country in 1866 was that of a so-called Fabian holding action in an illusory hope that avoiding pitched battles and wearing down the Indians' will to fight over time from permanent fortifications in their country would keep travel safe on the Bozeman Trail and possibly draw Indian attention away from plans to begin construction of the transcontinental railroads through their country. The days of grand offensives such as those in 1865 were temporarily over with the mustering-out of volunteer regiments. The events in the Powder River country in 1866, however, would reverse that policy in 1867 but with few positive results for the whites. Not until 1868 would there start to be sufficient troops on the plains to hold their own with Lakotas and Cheyennes. Never would Fabian strategy succeed. McPherson, *This Mighty Scourge*, 53.

Notes to Chapter 3

1. Neihardt, *Song of the Indian Wars*, 20.

2. Robert M. Utley, "The Bozeman Trail Before John Bozeman: A Busy Land," *Montana* 53, no. 2 (Summer 2003): 23.

3. Ibid., 25–29.

4. Francis Fuller Victor, *The River of the West: Life and Adventure in the Rocky Mountains and Oregon* (Hartford, CT: R. W. Bliss, 1870), 160–61.

5. Clark Spence, "A Celtic Nimrod in the Old West," *Montana* 9 (Spring 1959): 55–56; Utley, "Bozeman Trail Before John Bozeman," 30–31.

6. Among others who vividly remembered the overland journey are James Carrington, Lt. William Bisbee, Sgt. F. M. Fessenden, and Pvt. William Murphy.

7. Fort Phil Kearny/Bozeman Trail Association, *Portraits*, 142.

8. Ibid.

9. Ibid.

10. M. Carrington, *Ab-sa-ra-ka*, 164.

11. Ibid., 182.

12. Ibid., 186.

13. Ibid., 174.

14. James B. Carrington, "Across the Plains with Bridger as Guide," *Scribner's Magazine* 85 (January 1929): 71 (hereafter referred to as J. Carrington's account).

15. Ibid., 70.

16. William Haymond Bisbee, *Through Four American Wars* (Boston: Meador Publishers, 1931), 163 (hereafter referred to as Bisbee's account).

17. Ibid., 41, 44.

18. J. Carrington's account, 70.

19. Bisbee's account, 162.

20. Sgt. F. M. Fessenden in Grace R. Hebard and E. A. Brininstool, *The Bozeman Trail*, 2 vols. (Cleveland: Arthur H. Clark, 1922), 2:95 (hereafter referred to as Fessenden's account). Private Fessenden was promoted to Sergeant by Carrington.

21. The trek from Fort Kearney to Fort Laramie and thence to the forks of the Piney where Fort Phil Kearny was constructed is vividly and minutely recorded in Margaret Carrington's book. It would be redundant to repeat here as a major thrust of this study all of her accounts in their full glory.

22. William Murphy, "The Forgotten Battalion," *Annals of Wyoming* 7, no. 2 (October 1930): 383 (hereafter referred to as Murphy's account).

23. Fort Laramie Post Returns for June 1866, U.S. War Department, NARA, RG 98.

24. Ridgeway Glover, "Letters to Editor," *Philadelphia Photographer* 3 (1866).

25. J. P. Dunn, *Massacres of the Mountains: A History of the Indian Wars of the Far West* (New York: Harper and Brothers, 1886), 485.

26. M. Carrington, *Ab-sa-ra-ka*, 84–85.

27. Ibid. 87.

28. Murphy's account, 384.

29. M. Carrington, *Ab-sa-ra-ka*, 93.

30. Bisbee's account, 167.

31. Murphy's account, 385.

32. Ibid.

33. M. Carrington, *Ab-sa-ra-ka*, 96–97.

34. Brown, *Fort Phil Kearny*, 63.

35. 50th Cong., 1st sess., *Senate Exec. Doc. 33*. This study hereafter refers to Reno Station by its older name of Fort Reno.

36. M. Carrington, *Ab-sa-ra-ka*, 92.

37. Murray, *The Bozeman Trail*, 3.

38. Ibid.

39. William L. Lang and Rex C. Myers, *Montana, Our Land and People* (Boulder, CO: Pruett Publishing, 1979), 40–44.

40. Ibid., 99–101.

41. Murphy's account, 385–86.

42. M. Carrington, *Ab-sa-ra-ka*, 102.

43. Ibid., 106.

44. Murphy's account, 386.

45. Brown, *Fort Phil Kearny*, 71.

46. M. Carrington, *Ab-sa-ra-ka*, 107–8.

47. Ibid., 147–48.

48. Fessenden's account, 94.

49. Ibid., 95.

50. Ibid., 93.

51. Frazier, *Forts of the West*, 84.

52. M. Carrington, *Ab-sa-ra-ka*, 149–50.

53. Bisbee's account, 166.

Notes to Chapter 4

1. Neihardt, *Song of the Indian Wars*, 40.

2. M. Carrington, *Ab-sa-ra-ka*, 94. See also Bray, *Crazy Horse*, 91–92.

3. Interview with George Sword, Pine Ridge, April 29, 1907, Ricker Papers, Nebraska State Historical Society, tablet 39. Students of the Indian Wars are now quite fortunate

to have all the Riker interviews published by the University of Nebraska Press in Richard E. Jensen, ed., *Voices of the American West: Interviews of Eli S. Ricker, 1903–1919*, 2 vols. (Lincoln: University of Nebraska Press, 2005).

4. Virtually all memoirs and reports of the officers at Fort Phil Kearny in 1866 as well as Margaret Carrington's comment on the frustrations faced in combating the guerilla tactics of Indian warfare reflect the naivety of conventionally trained troops once they arrived on the western plains of the 1860s.

5. Bray, *Crazy Horse*, 102.

6. Although some errors as to dates and locations exist, an overview from the Indian perspective of the warriors' tactical maneuvers along the Bozeman Trail during the summer and fall of 1866 is Powell, *People of the Sacred Mountain*, 1:426–61.

7. Black Elk and Neihardt, *Black Elk Speaks*, 8.

8. For a discussion of the extrapolation of the forts from protecting travel routes to seeds of permanent conquest, see Susan B. Doyle, ed., *Journeys to the Land of Gold: Emigrant Diaries from the Bozeman Trail, 1863–1866*, 2 vols. (Helena: Montana Historical Society, 2000), 423–39; 714–15. For a concise overview of travel on the Bozeman Trail, see also Susan B. Doyle, ed., *Bound for Montana: Diaries from the Bozeman Trail* (Helena: Montana Historical Society, 2004). Even though Red Cloud was not yet an itancan, his influence as a war leader was at its zenith.

9. For the sacred covenants of the Cheyennes as well as their beliefs and lifeways, see Powell, *Sweet Medicine*.

10. Statements of Henry Little Coyote, John Stands in Timber, and other tribal elders to Peter John Powell, 1958–61, in Powell, *People of the Sacred Mountain*, 1:426–27. Comments to author by students in Cheyenne Studies classes of Dr. Alonzo T. Spang Jr. at Chief Dull Knife College, Lame Deer Montana, September 24, 2004.

11. "Report of Henry Carrington," 50th Cong., 1st sess., *Senate Exec. Doc.* 33, 9–10 (hereafter referred to as H. Carrington's report); M. Carrington, *Ab-sa-ra-ka*, 103–4; Powell, *People of the Sacred Mountain*, 1:427.

12. H. Carrington's report, 9.

13. Ibid.

14. Ibid.

15. Ibid., 10–13.

16. Ibid., 11. Although H. Carrington's report does not specifically mention Red Cloud as having been in Gazeau's camp the night the Cheyenne peace chiefs were beaten, his wife assumes that he was present. See M. Carrington, *Ab-sa-ra-ka*, 184–85. Powell too assumes that Red Cloud would not have missed such an intelligence-gathering conference. Powell, *People of the Sacred Mountain*, 1:662, n. 15.

17. Murphy's account, 386; John M. Carroll, ed., *"Bisbee, Wm., 'Items of Indian Service,' Papers of the Order of Indian Wars"* (Fort Collins, CO: Old Army Press, 1975), 27; H. Carrington's report, 10–11; M. Carrington, *Ab-sa-ra-ka*, 122.

18. T. J. Gatchell, "Life of John Ryan," *Annals of Wyoming* 31 (1959): 49.

19. Ibid.

20. *Leavenworth Times*, October 20, 1866, 1.

21. U.S. Court of Claims, Indian Depredation Claims, RG 123, nos. 8265 and 10107, NARA.

22. *Leavenworth Times*, October 20, 1866, 1. For Gazeau, see Report of Capt. H. Haymond, Letters Received, Department of the Platte, July 20, 1866, RG 393, NARA; M. Carrington, *Ab-sa-ra-ka*, 87; Hagan in Fort Phil Kearny/Bozeman Trail Association, *Portraits*, 21–24. Barry Hagan gives the several derivations of Gazeau's name as Gazeau, Gazzoux, Gassous, and Gassoux by various writers including the Carringtons.

23. H. Carrington's report, 18.

24. Ibid., 12, 18. M. Carrington asserts the attack on the wagon train took place the following day, July 23. See *Ab-sa-ra-ka*, 124.

25. H. Carrington's report, 11. There were eventually as many as four howitzers at Fort Phil Kearny.

26. "Records Relating to Investigations of Fort Phil Kearny (or Fetterman) Massacre," testimony of Gen. Philip St. George Cooke (hereafter referred to as Cooke's testimony), NARA Microfilm 740, 1 roll. All records "Relating to Investigations" are located on M740 and those records are hereafter referred to as M740, unnumbered. Some individual testimonies before the Sanborn Commission cited in this work are located in the "Records of the Special Commission to Investigate the Fetterman Massacre and the State of Indian Affairs, 1867," catalogued in "Records of the Bureau of Indian Affairs," RG 75, NARA. These records may also be found on Microfilm M740, 1 roll, and are referenced as such in this study. William Markland of Overland Park, Kansas, has done researchers a wonderful service by placing many of the documents of M740 on his extensively researched and documented family history website where they may be easily accessed. The URL address to access the documents is http://freepages.history.rootsweb.com/~familyinformation/#fpk.

27. H. Carrington's report, 11–12. A field howitzer was also procured.

28. Burrowes's Report, July 27, 1966, Post Returns, Fort Phil Kearny, DT, RG 75, M617, roll 910, NARA (hereafter referred to as Burrowes's report).

29. F. C. Carrington, *My Army Life*, 74–75.

30. Ibid., 75.

31. Templeton Diary, entry of July 20, 1866. Peters told Frances Carrington a different story years later regarding this fight. Peters placed Lieutenant Wands as leader of this command and claimed that Templeton rode back with an arrow in his back and soldiers placed him in an ambulance. Peters's account is suspect since Templeton kept a diary of the affair and never recorded that he was wounded; neither does Lieutenant Wands in his report nor Sergeant Fessenden, who later left an account of the fight. Official reports list Lieutenant Daniels and one enlisted man killed and none wounded. Indeed, Peters's 1908 account of this fight is highly suspect in full. F. C. Carrington, *My Army Life*, 69–81; "Records Relating to Investigations, Testimony of Lieut. A. H. Wands" (hereafter referred to as Wands's testimony), like all other Sanborn testimonies, M740; Adjutant General's Office, *Actions & etc., With Indians*, 24; Fessenden's account, 91–92; Dee Brown, however, in *Phil Kearny/The Fetterman Massacre*, 85–87, erroneously accepts Peters's account in Frances Carrington's reminiscences.

32. H. Carrington's report, 12–15. See also F. C. Carrington, *My Army Life*, 74–80.

33. Wands's testimony, M740.

34. Fessenden's account, 91.

35. Ibid., 91–92.

36. Wands's testimony, M740.

37. Fessenden's account, 92.

38. Templeton Diary, July 14, 1866.

39. See F. Carrington, *My Army Life*, 69–81.

40. Wands's testimony, M740.

41. Ibid.

42. Burrowes's report, M617, R.910.

43. Ibid., 4. Burrowes states that he was moving out to Fort Reno on the twenty-third and that he arrived on Crazy Woman Creek that evening. He of course meant Fort Phil Kearny. He uses here the original intent that the new post on the Piney would be dubbed New Fort Reno.

44. For an example of such popular notions perpetuated in trade literature, see Dorothy M. Johnson, *The Bloody Bozeman: The Perilous Trail to Montana's Gold* (New York: McGraw-Hill, 1971).

45. Kingsley M. Bray, "Spotted Tail and the Treaty of 1868," *Nebraska History* 83, no. 1 (Spring 2002): 20.

46. Doyle, *Journeys*, 2:435.

47. Indian Depredation Claims, RG 123, nos. 81 and 474, NARA. No other civilian depredation claims were located in RG 123 for the Bozeman Trail in 1866. For editorial on civilian deaths, see Doyle, *Journeys*, 2:431.

48. Burrowes's report, M617, R.910.

49. Ibid. Again Burrowes refers to Fort Reno when he means "New Fort Reno," i.e., Fort Phil Kearny. He arrived at Fort Phil Kearny at 2:00 PM on July 25.

50. Burgess Diary, July 22, 1866.

51. Doyle, *Journeys*, 433, 563.

52. Burgess Diary, July 22, 1866.

53. Blythe Diary, July 22, 1866; Daily *Rocky Mountain News*, August 21, 1866.

54. *Montana Post* (Virginia City), September 29, 1866; Doyle, *Journeys*, 433.

55. *Montana Post*, September 15, 1866.

56. Doyle, *Journeys*, 434.

57. *Omaha Weekly Republican*, August 17, 1866.

58. F. C. Carrington, *My Army Life*, 74–75.

59. Sawyer Diary, July 20, 1866. All emigrant diaries cited here are from the Montana Historical Society unless otherwise cited.

60. Thomas Diary, July 25, 1866.

61. Ibid., August 7, 1866. The grave was that of George Pease from Pennsylvania. See Doyle, *Journeys*, 2:543, n. 27.

62. *Bozeman Daily Chronicle*, September 19, 1948.

63. Doyle, *Journeys*, 2:537–38.

64. Thomas Diary, endpiece, 1866.

65. Fox Diary, August 2, 1866.

66. Daily *Rocky Mountain News*, August 21, 1866.

67. Willson Diary, July 29, 1866.

68. Ibid., July 26, 1866.

69. Doyle, *Journeys*, 438–39.

Notes to Chapter 5

1. Neihardt, *Song of the Indian Wars*, 40.

2. Carrington's "Statement," 50th Cong., 1st sess., *Senate Exec. Doc.* 33, 9–10, and M740 (hereafter referred to as Carrington's testimony, M740); Hyde, *Red Cloud's Folk*, 144–45; Powell, *People of the Sacred Mountain*, 2:443.

3. Hyde, *Red Cloud's Folk*, 145.

4. Carrington to Litchfield, Letters Received, Dept of the Platte, September 17, 1866, RG 98, NARA; *Omaha Herald*, October 5, 1866.

5. Carrington's testimony; Carrington to Litchfield, August 29, November 5, 1866, RG 98; M. Carrington, *Ab-sa-ra-ka*, 125–26.

6. Carrington to Litchfield, September 17, RG 98.

7. Ibid.

8. Ibid.; Gatchell, "Life of John Ryan," 50.

9. Fessenden's account, 86–97.

10. Glover obituary in *Frank Leslie's Illustrated Magazine*, October 27, 1866, 94.

11. Ibid.

12. Bisbee, *Through Four American Wars*, 70.

13. Carrington to Litchfield, September 17, 1866, RG 98; M. Carrington, *Ab-sa-ra-ka*, 127.

14. Carrington to Litchfield, September 17, 1866, RG 98.

15. Ibid.; F. C. Carrington, *My Army Life*, 90.

16. U.S. War Department, 18th Infantry Regiment, Muster Rolls, September 1866.

17. Hebard and Brininstool, *The Bozeman Trail*, 1:286.

18. 50th. Cong. 1st sess., *Senate Exec. Doc.* 33, 23–30.

19. For Grummond see U.S. War Department, "The War of the Rebellion," *Official Records*, series 1, vol. 38, pt. 2, 495–500; vol. 98, pt. 1, 495–507. See also Robert B.

Partridge, "Fetterman Debacle, Who Was to Blame?" *Journal of the Council on America's Military Past* 16, no. 2 (1989): 36–43; and Shannon Smith Calitri, "Give Me Eighty Men: Shattering the Myth of the Fetterman Massacre," *Montana: The Magazine of Western History* 54, no. 3 (Autumn 2004): 49.

20. U.S. War Department, "The War of the Rebellion," *Official Record,* series 1, vol. 38, pt. 2, 495–500.

21. A short sketch of Grummond's life was written by John D. McDermott in Fort Phil Kearny/Bozeman Trail Association, *Portraits,* 88–92.

22. Francis B. Heitman, *Historical Register and Dictionary of the United States Army from Its Organization, September 29, 1789, to March 2, 1903,* 2 vols. (Washington, D.C.: Government Printing Office, 1903), 1:482.

23. Deanna Umbach Kordik in Fort Phil Kearny/Bozeman Trail Association, *Portraits,* 93–94.

24. See Calitri's introduction to F. C. Carrington, *My Army Life,* Bison Book edition, 2004.

25. F. C. Carrington, *My Army Life,* 85–86.

26. Dee Brown, *Fort Phil Kearny: An American Saga* (Lincoln: University of Nebraska Press, 1962), 117–18.

27. F. C. Carrington, *My Army Life,* 90.

28. Ibid., 96.

29. Heitman, *Register,* 1:251.

30. M. Carrington, *Ab-sa-ra-ka,* 246.

31. Bisbee, *Through Four American Wars,* 161.

32. See McDermott in Fort Phil Kearny/Bozeman Trail Association, *Portraits,* 98–100.

33. M. Carrington, *Ab-sa-ra-ka,* 246–47.

34. Carrington's testimony, M740; F. C. Carrington, *My Army Life,* 120.

35. Carrington's testimony, M740.

36. Carrington to Litchfield, September 25, 1866, and November 5, 1866, RG 98.

37. This is Brown's *assumption* in *Fort Phil Kearny,* 123. But the assumption may have some validity as the Indians made no more demonstrations around the fort for the next three days.

38. M. Carrington, *Ab-sa-ra-ka,* 248.

39. Fessenden's account, 99.

40. Carrington's testimony, M740.

41. Carrington to Litchfield, September 25, 1866, RG 98; Carrington's testimony, M740.

42. Carrington's testimony, M740; M. Carrington, *Ab-sa-ra-ka,* 159.

43. Carrington's testimony, M740.

44. Ibid.

45. Ibid.; Carrington to Litchfield, October 4, 1844, RG 98.

46. Brown states the spokesman was Two Moon but this is unlikely since Two Moon had joined the war faction. Powell states the spokesman was the peace advocate Little Moon. See Brown, *Fort Phil Kearny*, 126; and Powell, *People of the Sacred Mountain*, 1:448–49.

47. Carrington to Litchfield, October 4, 1866, RG 98; Carrington's testimony, M740.

48. U.S. Senate, *Report of the Acting Commissioner of Indian Affairs for the Year 1867* (Washington, D.C.: Government Printing Office, 1869), 289.

49. Powell, *People of the Sacred Mountain*, 1:450.

50. Carrington's testimony, M740.

51. Bray, *Crazy Horse*, 96.

52. Black Elk and Neihardt, *Black Elk Speaks*, 8.

53. Ibid.

54. 50th Cong., 1st sess., *Senate Exec Doc*. 33, 31–33, RG 98.

55. See McWilliams in Fort Phil Kearny/Bozeman Trail Association, *Portraits*, 54–59.

56. 50th Cong., 1st sess., *Senate Exec. Doc*. 33, 31–33.

57. Van Voast to Litchfield, November 2, 3, 21, 1866, Letters Received, Department of the Platte, RG 98, NARA.

58. Cooke to Carrington, telegram, September 27, 1866.

59. Ibid.

60. Hazen to Litchfield, August 29, 1866, RG 98.

61. Litchfield to Carrington, November 12, 1866, RG 98.

62. Carrington to Litchfield, August 29, 1866, RG 98.

63. Carrington to Litchfield, November 5, 1866, RG 98.

64. Van Voast to Litchfield, October 18, 1866, with an appended letter to dispatch; Bridger to W. G. Bullock, November 5, 1866, RG 98.

65. 50th Cong., 1st sess., *Senate Exec. Doc*. 33, 32.

66. M. Carrington, *Ab-sa-ra-ka*, 156.

67. *Omaha Weekly Herald*, January 18, 1867. For a discussion of these events involving the high command during the fall of 1866, see Olson, *Red Cloud and the Sioux Problem*, 44–50.

Notes to Chapter 6

1. The chapter title, *Wau-nee-chee*, means "no good," Margaret Carrington's assessment of the events around Fort Phil Kearny during the autumn of 1866 (*Ab-sa-ra-ka*, 129). The epigraph is from Neihardt's *Song of the Indian Wars*, 40–41.

2. Testimony of J. B. Weston, July 29, 1867, M740.

3. Fessenden's account, 98.

4. Ibid.

5. Bisbee, *Through Four American Wars*, 171.

6. Post Returns, Fort C. F. Smith, November–December 1866.

7. Fessenden's account, 99.

8. Post Returns, Fort Laramie (Scout Reports), November 1866, RG 98, NARA.

9. Bratt, *Trails*, 100.

10. Testimony of Capt. Tenador Ten Eyck, July 5, 1867, M740 (hereafter referred to as Ten Eyck's testimony); Bratt, *Trails*, 96–98.

11. Testimony of George B. Mackey, July 26, 1866, M740 (hereafter referred to as Mackey's testimony).

12. Testimony of Capt. James Powell, July 24, 1867, M740 (hereafter referred to as Powell's testimony).

13. Mackey's testimony, M740.

14. Powell's testimony, M740.

15. Murphy's account, 388.

16. Wands's testimony, M740.

17. See O'Dell in Fort Phil Kearny/Bozeman Trail Association, *Portraits*, 71–73.

18. F. C. Carrington, *My Army Life*, 123.

19. See Fenn in Fort Phil Kearny/Bozeman Trail Association, *Portraits*, 203–9.

20. M. Carrington, *Ab-sa-ra-ka*, 244–46.

21. Bisbee, *Through Four American Wars*, 175.

22. Fetterman makes no mention in any of his correspondence that he previously knew Grummond. Neither do any other original reminiscences of individuals at Fort Phil Kearny in 1866.

23. M. Carrington, *Ab-sa-ra-ka*, 171; F. C. Carrington, *My Army Life*, 119.

24. Terry to Sheridan, May 16, 1876, Records of the Military Division of the Missouri, Letters Sent, RG 393, NARA. For an excellent analysis of the ethnocentric views of Indians and their martial abilities held by officers of the nineteenth-century frontier army, see Smith, *The View from Officers' Row: Army Perceptions of Western Indians* (Tucson: University of Arizona Press, 1990).

25. M. Carrington, *Ab-sa-ra-ka*, 245.

26. Two recent examples of such descriptions of Fetterman's personality are found in Larry McMurtry, *Crazy Horse: A Life* (New York: Viking, 1999); and Bray, *Crazy Horse: A Lakota Life*. "Fetterman was an arrogant young man," writes McMurtry, p. 58. Bray describes Fetterman as a "brash fire-eater," p. 98.

27. For example see Nikolai Wenzel, "The Fetterman Massacre of December 21, 1866," *Journal of America's Military Past* 28, no. 1 (Spring–Summer 2001): 53; and www.army.mil/cmh-pg/books/R&H/R&H-18IN.htm, sect. 645.

28. John D. McDermott, "Price of Arrogance: The Short and Controversial Life of William Judd Fetterman," *Annals of Wyoming* 63, no. 2 (Spring 1991): 43.

29. Ibid., 44.

30. Johnson, *That Body of Brave Men*, 600–607. See also U.S. War Department, *War of the Rebellion*, pt. 1, 527, 558–60, 577–78, 586–88. One need only to peruse any pages in Heitman, *Historical Register and Dictionary of the U.S. Army*, to ascertain the plethora of brevets given out to junior officers during the Civil War, an age when only the Medal of Honor was available as an award for distinguished valor. Fetterman was in no way unique or unusual in his brevets.

31. Brown, *Fort Phil Kearny*, 147–48.

32. M. Carrington, *Ab-sa-ra-ka*, 246.

33. *National Tribune*, June 22, 1899.

34. Ibid., 170–71; F. C. Carrington, *My Army Life*, 120.

35. Ten Eyck's testimony, events of November 7, 1866, M740.

36. Events of November 21–25, 1866; Bisbee, *Through Four American Wars*, 172–73; F. C. Carrington, *My Army Life*, 122.

37. Brown, *Fort Phil Kearny*, 156.

38. Fetterman to Terry, November 26, 1866, RG 393, NARA. See also John D. McDermott, ed., "Wyoming Scrapbook: Documents Relating to the Fetterman Fight," *Annals of Wyoming* 63, no. 2 (Spring 1991): 68. For these confusing events see also McDermott, "Price of Arrogance," 43–46.

39. Fetterman to Terry, November 26, 1866, RG 98.

40. Carrington's testimony, M740.

41. 50th Cong., 1st sess., *Senate Exec. Doc.* 33, 36.

42. Ibid., 33; F. C. Carrington, *My Army Life*, 111.

43. Brown, *Fort Phil Kearny*, 153.

44. George Webber, *National Tribune*, October 21, 1897.

45. For example, Dee Brown states that the "'cocky' Fetterman seemed to be sobered by the events . . . he professed to have learned a lesson." Then Brown states rhetorically, "Unfortunately, Fetterman forgot this lesson, the last he would learn from the Indians." Brown, *Fort Phil Kearny*, 166. See also McDermott, "Price of Arrogance," 19; and Barry Hagan, "Prelude to a Massacre: Fort Phil Kearny, December 6, 1866," *Journal of the Order of the Indian Wars* 1 (Fall 1980): 1–17. In an undocumented statement Michael Straight writes that "[i]n the skirmish of December 6, Fetterman demonstrated both recklessness and insubordination, exhausting his forces in a head-long pursuit of the Indians; firing his revolvers at Indians five miles distant; disregarding the colonel's orders, and swearing in front of his men that their commanding officer was 'either a maniac or a fool.'" Straight, "Carrington: The Valor of Defeat," *Corral Dust: Potomac Corral of the Westerners* 4, no. 1 (December 1959): 27. Nothing could be further from the truth. No original sources support these outlandish claims and the officers who were "reckless and insubordinate" on December 6 were Grummond and Bingham. Fetterman by contrast was praised by Carrington in his report after the fight for his discipline and obedience.

46. J. W. Vaughn, *Indian Fights: New Facts on Seven Encounters* (Norman: University of Oklahoma Press, 1966), 28–43.

47. Ibid., 29–31.

48. Ibid., 31.

49. Hyde, *Red Cloud's Folk*, 146.

50. Vaughn, *Indian Fights*, 32.

51. Both Ten Eyck and Surgeon Hines reported three hundred warriors attacking the train. See Ten Eyck's testimony, M740; and Hines to John Hines, December 15, 1866, 39th Cong., 2nd sess., *House Exec. Doc.* 71, 16.

52. Mackey's testimony, M740.

53. 40th Cong., 1st sess., *Senate Exec. Doc.* 13, 63–64 (hereafter referred to as Fetterman's report). In his report Fetterman wrote that he had about thirty men total, twenty-five cavalry and seventeen mounted infantrymen from Company A (37–38).

54. Vaughn, *Indian Fights*, 34.

55. Wands's testimony, M740. Wands gives the best eyewitness account of Fetterman's sector and the captain's actions in the December 6 fight.

56. Ibid.

57. Vaughn, *Indian Fights*, 35–36.

58. Wands's testimony, M740.

59. Fetterman's report in 40th Cong., 1st sess., *Senate Exec. Doc.* 13, 37–38. If Fetterman had started out with seventeen mounted infantrymen as originally assigned and wound up with fourteen men total, apparently a few of these soldiers either bolted with Bingham's cavalry or were strung out behind Fetterman's pursuit wing.

60. Vaughn, *Indian Fights*, 37.

61. Wands's testimony, M740.

62. Ibid.

63. Vaughn, *Indian Fights*, 37–39.

64. Hines to John Hines, December 15, 1866; Mackey's testimony, M740, roll 1.

65. Mackey's testimony, M740.

66. Fessenden's account, 99.

67. Hines to John Hines, December 15, 1866.

68. Ibid.; Murphy's account, 7.

69. Bisbee, *Through Four American Wars*, 171–72.

70. John M. Carroll, ed., "Bisbee, Wm., Items of Indian Service," in *Papers of the Order of the Indian Wars of the United States* (Fort Collins, CO: Old Army Press, 1975), 79.

71. John Guthrie, "The Fetterman Massacre," *Winners of the West*, September 1939, 8.

72. Compiled by Vaughn, *Indian Fights*, 41.

73. Statement of "Whitewash" in Doane Robinson, *History of the Dakota or Sioux Indians* (1904; reprint, Minneapolis: Ross and Hague, 1956), 359. See also Bray, *Crazy Horse*, 96.

74. Fetterman's report, 37–38.

75. One of the worst detractors is Michael Straight. See Straight, "The Valor of Defeat," 27. According to Carrington and Powell, Fetterman was the only officer to maintain cohesion that day. Powell claimed that it was the actions of Bingham's cavalry that were disgraceful on December 6. See Carrington to Litchfield, December 6, 1866, RG 98; and Powell's testimony, M740.

76. Murphy's account, 389. Also quoted in Brown, *Fort Phil Kearny*, 165.

77. Fetterman's report, 37–38.

78. Wands's testimony.

79. Ibid.; statement by "Whitewash" in Robinson, *History of the Dakota or Sioux Indians*, 359.

80. Reprinted in *Old Travois Trail* 3, no. 3 (1942): 65.

81. M. Carrington, *Ab-sa-ra-ka*, 195.

82. Carrington to Litchfield, December 6, 1866, RG 98.

83. Charles D. Collins Jr., *Atlas of the Sioux Wars*, 2nd ed. (Fort Leavenworth, KS: Combat Studies Institute Press, 2006), map 7.

84. See Vaughn, *Indian Fights*, 43.

85. Carrington's testimony, M740. See also McDermott, "Price of Arrogance," 49.

86. Partridge, "Fetterman Debacle—Who Was to Blame?" 36–43. See also Calitri, "Give Me Eighty Men," 48–50.

87. F. C. Carrington, *My Army Life*, 134.

88. Ibid.

89. M. Carrington, *Ab-sa-ra-ka*, 198.

90. 50th Cong., 1st sess., *Senate Exec. Doc.* 33, 36–38.

91. Quoted in Stanley Vestal, *Jim Bridger, Mountain Man* (New York: Morrow, 1946), 270.

92. M. Carrington, *Ab-sa-ra-ka*, 208.

93. Carrington to Litchfield, December 6, 1866, RG 98.

Notes to Chapter 7

1. Neihardt, *Song of the Indian Wars*, 56–57.

2. White Elk (Cheyenne) to Grinnell, July 16, 1914. White Elk's account of the Fetterman fight is also found in Grinnell, *Fighting Cheyennes* (hereafter referred to as White Elk's account), 234–37.

3. Statement of Whitewash in Robinson, *History of the Dakota or Sioux Indians*, 361; White Bull in Stanley Vestal, *Warpath: The True Story of the Fighting Sioux Told*

in a Biography of Chief White Bull, introduction by Raymond J. DeMallie (Lincoln: University of Nebraska Press, 1984), 54.

4. White Bull (Miniconjou) in Vestal, *Warpath* (hereafter referred to as White Bull's account), 50–54. See also Bent to Hyde, December 5, 1904, William Robertson Coe Collection, Beinecke Manuscript Library, Yale University, New Haven, CT.

5. Bent to Hyde, December 5, 1904, Coe Collection; George F. Hyde, *Life of George Bent Written from His Letters*, ed. Savoy Otisville (Norman: University of Oklahoma Press, 1968), 344.

6. White Elk to Grinnell, July 16, 1914; an unidentified "Cheyenne Old Man" in Marquis, *Cheyenne and Sioux*, 34; and Thomas B. Marquis, *Wooden Leg, A Warrior Who Fought Custer* (Lincoln: University of Nebraska Press, 1986), 14–15 (hereafter referred to as Wooden Leg's account).

7. White Bull's account, 53; Two Moon's account in Hyde, *Life of George Bent* (hereafter referred to as Two Moon's account), 344; and Bent to Hyde, December 5, 1904, Coe Collection; White Elk's account, 244.

8. For the life of Little Wolf see Monnett, *Tell Them We Are Going Home*; and Stan Hoig, *Peace Chiefs of the Cheyennes* (Norman: University of Oklahoma Press, 1980), 123–37.

9. White Elk's account, 244. For more on the roles of transgendered persons in all manners of Indian culture including warfare, see Will Roscoe, *Changing Ones: Third and Fourth Genders in Native North America* (New York: St. Martin's Griffin, 2000); and Sabine Lang, *Men as Women, Women as Men: Changing Gender in Native American Cultures* (Austin: University of Texas Press, 1998). See also George B. Grinnell, *The Cheyenne Indians: Their History and Ways of Life*, 2 vols. (New Haven: Yale University Press, 1923), 2:39–44; Royal B. Hassrick, *The Sioux: The Life and Customs of a Warrior Society* (Norman: University of Oklahoma Press, 1964), 133–35; and E. Adamson Hoebel, *The Cheyennes, Indians of the Great Plains* (New York: Holt, Rinehart and Winston, 1960), 77. Hyde talked about this ceremony with several unnamed Oglalas who claimed that the winkte, whose name is unknown, was a Miniconjou. See Hyde, *Red Cloud's Folk*, 147, n. 6.

10. White Elk's account, 237–38; Wolf Tooth's story as told to John Stands In Timber, in John Stands In Timber and Margot Liberty, *Cheyenne Memories* (New Haven: Yale University Press, 1967), 171 (hereafter referred to as Wolf Tooth's account). See also Hyde, *Red Cloud's Folk*, 147.

11. White Bull's account, 54.

12. Ibid., 55.

13. Wolf Tooth was the great step-grandfather of John Stands In Timber. See Wolf Tooth's account, 172. A number of accounts, mostly secondary ones, along with White Bull's claim that the decision to send decoys was made only after wolves (scouts) had been sent out to check the strength at the fort. This claim seems unlikely since recent raiders were fully aware of the approximate number of soldiers at Fort Phil Kearny. The misconception probably originates with White Bull and the Miniconjous, many of whom had not participated in recent raids or the December 6 fight. Two Moon claimed

to be one of those chosen to spy on the fort for the purpose of assessing troop strength. See Bent to Hyde, December 5, 1904, Coe Collection.

14. White Elk's account, 238; Powell, *People of the Sacred Mountain*, 1:456.

15. White Elk's account, 238.

16. Interview with American Horse, Pine Ridge, June 16, 1905, Ricker Interviews, Nebraska State Historical Society (NSHS), tablets 13, 16, 33. The interview is also found in Jensen, *Voices of the American West*, 280–81 (hereafter referred to as account of American Horse).

17. Interview with George W. Colhoff, ca. 1906, Ricker Papers, NSHS, tablet 17. Sword (Sword Owner) is not to be confused with his brother, George Sword (Hunts the Enemy) (Owns Sword) who was also in the fight but not a decoy. Sword (Sword Owner) died at Red Cloud Agency in 1976. To avoid confusion see also Ella Deloria, "Sword's Acts Related," unpublished typescript, Ella Deloria Papers, Denver Public Library.

18. See the accounts of White Bull, Two Moon, American Horse, Fire Thunder, and George Sword. None mentions Crazy Horse as a decoy.

19. Hyde, *Red Cloud's Folk*, 149.

20. Often chiefs of high influence remained in camp during a large battle, allowing their young warriors to have a chance to attain glory and hence status. See Hyde, *Red Cloud's Folk*; and James H. Cook, *Fifty Years on the Old Frontier* (New Haven: Yale University Press, 1923), 198.

21. Interview of July 30, 1903, referenced in Bray, *Crazy Horse*, 419, n. 45.

22. White Bull's account, 58; White Elk's account, 238–39.

23. White Elk's account, 239.

24. Testimony of Lt. W. F. Arnold and Pvt. George Mackey, M740.

25. Ten Eyck's testimony, M740; Carrington's report, 23; M. Carrington, *Ab-sa-ra-ka*, 18; F. C. Carrington, *My Army Life*, 143.

26. White Bull's account, 60.

27. White Elk's account, 240–41.

28. Ibid., 241.

29. White Bull's account, 60.

30. "Fire Thunder Speaks," in Black Elk and Neihardt, *Black Elk Speaks*, 9 (hereafter referred to as Fire Thunder's account). Fire Thunder was sixteen at the time of the Fetterman fight. In 1931 he told why he went to war: "We are humans too and God created us all alike, and I was going to do the best I could to defend my nation. So I started out on the warpath when I was sixteen years old." Raymond J. DeMallie, ed., *The Sixth Grandfather* (Lincoln: University of Nebraska Press, 1984), 106. White Bull also remembered the Indians' pinching the noses of their horses to keep them quiet. See White Bull's account, 60.

31. Hoebel, *The Cheyennes*, 71–72. See also Hyde, *Red Cloud's Folk*, 148–49.

32. Carrington's report, 22.

33. Vaughn, *Indian Fights*, 45.

34. See the testimonies of Powell and Wands, M740; and Fessenden's account, 100.

35. Carrington's report, 22. Actually Lieutenant Grummond had been drilling the cavalry. This explains why Carrington assigned infantry to Fetterman in response to the captain's request.

36. Ibid.

37. M. Carrington, *Ab-sa-ra-ka*, 201; F. C. Carrington, *My Army Life*, 143–44.

38. 50th Cong., 1st sess., 1888, *Senate Exec. Doc.* 33, 40; Powell's testimony, M740.

39. See statement by Sgt. Alexander Brown, D Company, 2nd U.S. Cavalry in *Winners of the West*, February 28, 1927; Jerome A. Greene, ed., *Indian War Veterans: Memories of Army Life and Campaigns in the West, 1864–1898* (New York: Savas Beatie, 2007), 88–89; Calitri, "Give Me Eighty Men," 47–48; *Chicago Times*, February 2, 1867; Harry Anderson, "Centennial of the Fetterman Fight," *Chicago Westerners Brand Book* 23 (December 1966): 77–80; McDermott, "Price of Arrogance," 52–53.

40. Vaughn, *Indian Fights*, 90.

41. 50th Cong., 1st sess., *Senate Exec. Doc.* 33, 44–45; M. Carrington, *Ab-sa-ra-ka*, 203–4. The orders could have meant not to pursue if the train was still vulnerable.

42. Wands's testimony, M740.

43. Carrington's report, 22.

44. M. Carrington, *Ab-sa-ra-ka*, 201–2.

45. M. Carrington, *Ab-sa-ra-ka*, 201–2; F. C. Carrington, *My Army Life*, 143–44.

46. See Carrington's praise of Fetterman on December 6 in Carrington's report.

47. See Wands's testimony, M740. For Grummond's dubious record for impulsiveness see U.S. War Department, *The War of the Rebellion* 38, pt. 2, 497–500.

48. Vaughn expends six pages reconstructing the Fetterman-Grummond route over Lodge Trail Ridge. See Vaughn, *Indian Fights*, 49–54.

49. Arnold's testimony, M470.

50. Bisbee, *Through Four American Wars*, 173.

51. 50th Cong., 1st sess., *Senate Exec. Doc.* 33, 44.

52. Curtis to Camp, July 15, 1914, item 73, Ellison Papers, CMSS Microfilm no. 35, roll 1, Denver Public Library; Powell's testimony, M740.

53. Bent to Hyde, December 5, 1905, Coe Collection.

54. Testimony of Michael Boyer, M740.

55. White Elk's account, 241.

56. White Bull's account, 60.

57. Smyth to Camp, May 17, 1913, CMSS Microfilm 38, reel 1, item 43, Walter Mason Camp Letters, Ellison Collection, Denver Public Library.

58. Vaughn, *Indian Fights*, 72.

59. Fire Thunder–Neihardt 1931 interview in DeMallie, *The Sixth Grandfather*, 104.

60. White Elk's account, 243; Two Moon's account, 344; Fire Thunder's account, 10; White Bull's account, 60–61, 64. White Bull confirms that Fetterman and the infantry penetrated a little north of the present monument and then retreated back up toward the rocks that are still there today inside the wall that surrounds the present monument. "The infantry quickly fell back up the hill to some large rocks which lay on the slope," he remembered. "They flung themselves down behind these rocks and began to shoot." White Elk too (or was it Grinnell's interpretation?) inferred that the infantry was killed first.

61. Vaughn, *Indian Fights*, 72.

62. Fire Thunder's account, 10.

63. White Bull's account, 63.

64. Statement by Standing Bear, 1931, in DeMallie, *The Sixth Grandfather*, 107.

65. Ibid., 61–62.

66. White Elk's account, 242.

67. Wolf Tooth's account, 172.

68. Strong Wind Blowing was the older brother of Wooden Leg, who was a child at the time of the Fetterman fight. See Wooden Leg's account, 15.

69. White Bull's account, 63. Again, White Bull incorrectly assumed that all of the troops on Monument Hill were cavalry.

70. Ibid., 64–65.

71. White Elk's account, 243, 244.

72. Ibid., 243. Bent relates this story with several factual errors. See Hyde, *Life of George Bent*, 346. See also Crazy Head to Grinnell, September 11, 1908, Grinnell Papers, Southwest Museum, Los Angeles. Big Nose may very well have been wounded earlier in the fight. Despite the source documentation the description of the hill where he was laid to rest is closer to the cavalry fight or perhaps a little north of the infantry's farthest penetration across the ridge.

73. Fire Thunder's account, 10.

74. Fire Thunder in DeMallie, *The Sixth Grandfather*, 104.

75. Account of American Horse, Ricker, tablet 16; Elbert D. Belish, "American Horse (Wasechun-Tasunka): The Man Who Killed Fetterman," *Annals of Wyoming* 63, no. 2 (Spring 1991): 54–57. Surgeon Horton's testimony, M740. Carrington later claimed that Fetterman and Brown shot each other in an act of joint suicide. Carrington is mistaken. Surgeon Horton's autopsy report makes no mention of a gunshot wound on Fetterman's body. Apparently American Horse later gave the war club to his friend, rancher James Cook. The so-called Fetterman massacre club is now on display at Agate Fossil Beds National Monument in Nebraska that used to be part of the Cook ranch.

76. American Horse Winter Count (mnemonic for 1866–67), ms. 2372, box 12, book 08746923, NAA.

77. Wolf Tooth's account, 172–73; White Elk's account, 243–44; Fire Thunder's account, 10. Fire Thunder later claimed the dog was not killed. DeMallie, *Sixth Grandfather*, 104.

78. Hassrick, *The Sioux*, 71–72.

79. White Bull's account, 67. Surgeon Horton later reported, however, that very few men died of gunshot wounds. Most had been killed by war clubs, knives, and arrows. See Surgeon Horton's testimony, M740.

80. Interview with Two Moon by Walter Mason Camp, box 5, envelope 69, Camp Papers, Lily Library, Indiana University–Bloomington.

81. Grinnell, *The Cheyenne Indians*, 2:59. Bunching is a sign of loss of cohesion.

82. This assertion of Crazy Mule's power was told to Marquis by "A [unidentified] Cheyenne Old Man." See Marquis, *Cheyenne and Sioux*, 34; and Wooden Leg's account, 15. Marquis took this claim to mean that some of the soldiers committed suicide so that the Indians did not have to kill them.

83. Statement by Rocky Bear [ca. 1902], Sheldon Papers, box 59, ms. 2039, Nebraska State Historical Society. See also Bray, *Crazy Horse*, 102.

84. Murphy's account, 389–90.

85. Ten Eyck's testimony, M740; Vaughn, *Indian Fights*, 64.

86. Hines's testimony, M740.

87. Testimonies of Ten Eyck and Hines, M740.

88. Hines's testimony, M740.

89. 50th Cong., 1st sess., *Senate Exec Doc.* 33, 45–46.

90. Murphy's account, 390.

91. Ibid., 390–91.

92. Hines's testimony, M740.

93. John Guthrie, "The Fetterman Massacre," *Annals of Wyoming* 9 (1932): 717 (hereafter referred to as Guthrie's account). How Brown was scalped is arguable as he was almost bald. He had some hair but it later was discovered that Brown had been mutilated, perhaps scalped, below the waist.

94. Carrington's testimony, M740.

95. Ten Eyck's testimony, M740.

96. Hines's testimony, M740.

97. Fessenden's account, 2:101–2.

98. F. C. Carrington, *My Army Life*, 146–47.

99. Ibid., 146.

100. Fessenden's account, 2:101–2. Fessenden may have been considering mainly the officers and a few noncommissioned officers. The majority of the men in Fetterman's command were raw recruits.

101. James B. Carrington, "Across the Plains with Bridger as Guide," *Scribner's*

Magazine 85 (January 1929): 71.

102. M. Carrington, *Ab-sa-ra-ka*, 206.

103. F. C. Carrington, *My Army Life*, 152.

104. Brown, *Fort Phil Kearny*, 197.

105. F. C. Carrington, *My Army Life*, 153–54.

106. Fessenden's account, 2:103.

107. Carrington's report, 24.

108. Ibid. Captain Brown had ridden Calico out of the fort on the twenty-first. Apparently the horse had been killed near the cavalry position almost a half-mile from Monument Hill, but somehow Brown had made it back up the ridge to the point of rocks only to finally die beside Fetterman. Perhaps Brown dismounted, turned loose his mount when Grummond bolted, and remained with Fetterman. The circumstances remain a mystery.

109. Guthrie's account, 717.

110. Robert B. David, *Finn Burnett, Frontiersman* (Glendale, CA: Arthur H. Clark, 1937), 127 (hereafter referred to as Burnett's account).

111. *Army and Navy Journal* 4 (April 13, 1867): 546. See also Elmo Scott Watson, "The Bravery of Our Bugler Is Much Spoken Of," *Old Travois Trail* 1 (1941): 21–24. An Indian supposedly gave the bugle to Jim Gatchell for his museum in Buffalo, Wyoming, but it is flattened as if by a heavy piece of farm equipment.

112. Carrington's report, 24; Guthrie's account, 717; Surgeon Horton's testimony, M740.

113. F. C. Carrington, *My Army Life*, 155.

114. Burnett's account, 129.

115. Ten Eyck's testimony, M740.

116. Ibid.

117. Guthrie's account, 717.

118. Carrington's report, 25.

119. Ibid.; Horton's testimony, M740.

120. Fessenden's account, 103.

121. Guthrie's account, 717.

122. Carrington's report, 28.

123. Fessenden's account, 2:103.

124. Testimonies of White Bull, 64; White Elk, 244; Ten Eyck and Hines, M740.

125. Testimonies of White Bull, 64; White Elk, 244; Ten Eyck and Hines, M740; Boyer's testimony, M740.

126. Testimonies of Ten Eyck, Hines, and Boyer, M740.

127. Vaughn, *Indian Fights*, 81.

128. Roberts to Vaughn, June 10 and July 28, 1963, copy in possession of the author courtesy of Douglas Public Library, Douglas, WY.

129. Vaughn, *Indian Fights*, 76–80.

130. Ibid., 79–80.

131. American Horse winter count, MS12, 08746901–08746922, 1866–67, National Anthropological Archives, The Smithsonian, Washington, D.C.

132. Hines's testimony, M740.

133. 40th Cong., 1st sess., *Senate Exec. Doc.* 13, 65.

134. Vaughn to Gerald Keenan, December 24, 1964, and September 27, 1965, copy in possession of the author courtesy of Jerry Keenan.

135. Collins, *Atlas of the Sioux Wars*, map 9.

136. Carrington's reports and the testimonies of all the officers attest to Brown's impulsiveness. Grummond's impulsiveness and insubordination are well documented. They could have impulsively bolted together with the cavalry following en masse.

137. White Bull contended that the infantry were well within the trap as the cavalry advanced but the warriors waited until the cavalry reached the Peno Forks. White Bull's account of the positions of the infantry and the cavalry differs somewhat from the other accounts, probably because of his limited line of sight on the ridge. He contends the infantry were destroyed first but all other Indian sources differ. White Bull is surely mistaken. White Bull's account, 60–61.

138. Conclusions of the Sanborn Commission, M740.

139. Calitri agrees with Vaughn that Carrington may actually have ordered Fetterman to cross Lodge Trail Ridge and pursue the Indians offensively. This possibility is highly unlikely given Carrington's cautions to Grummond not to be lured over the ridge. For this thesis see Calitri, "Give Me Eighty Men," 44–59.

140. Carrington's testimony, M740.

141. Vaughn, *Indian Fights*, 81; Calitri, "Give Me Eighty Men," 44–59.

Notes to Chapter 8

1. Neihardt, *Song of the Indian Wars*, 158.

2. Black Elk and Neihardt, *Black Elk Speaks*, 11.

3. Ibid.

4. Ibid.

5. Post Returns, Fort Phil Kearny for December 1866, RG 98, NARA.

6. Ibid. Indians almost never risked all-out assaults on fortifications in the post–Civil War period. A few feints and halfhearted demonstrations at Fort Wallace, Kansas, in 1867, at Fort Apache in Arizona Territory in 1881, and at a few other places comprise the record. Such fears of a fort actually being attacked were surely a component of the Puritan captivity myths that sprang from tales of besieged forts and communities during the French and Indian War and the American Revolution, and came west in the recesses

of the minds of white pioneers who viewed Indians through stereotypical lenses.

7. F. C. Carrington, *My Army Life*, 158.

8. M. Carrington, *Ab-sa-ra-ka*, 214.

9. F. C. Carrington, *My Army Life*, 159.

10. M. Carrington, *Ab-sa-ra-ka*, 215–16.

11. For biographical sketches of Phillips and his role in delivering the news of the Fetterman fight to the outside world, see Robert A. Murray, *The Army on the Powder River* (Belleview, NE: Old Army Press, 1969), 19–34; and McDermott, "John 'Portugee' Phillips," in Fort Phil Kearny/Bozeman Trail Association, *Portraits*, 126–29.

12. David S. Gordon, "The Relief of Fort Phil Kearny," *Journal of the Military Service Institutions of the U.S.* 49 (1911): 281. Gordon later went on to a distinguished military career, attaining the rank of brigadier general.

13. Palmer to Maj. Gen. C. C. Augur, February 2, 1867, Fort Laramie, Letters Sent, RG 98, NARA.

14. Palmer to Cooke, telegram, December 26, 1866, Department of the Platte, RG 98, NARA.

15. Gordon, "Relief of Fort Phil Kearny," 282–83.

16. For the many myths of "Portugee Phillips," see Murray, *Army on the Powder River*, 24–29.

17. M. Carrington, *Ab-sa-ra-ka*, 213–14.

18. F. C. Carrington, *My Army Life*, 155.

19. M. Carrington, *Ab-sa-ra-ka*, 211. Brown asserts the coffins were there on Christmas Day. See *Fort Phil Kearny*, 201.

20. Curtis to Camp, July 15, 1914, item no. 73, CMSS Microfilm 35, RL1, Ellison Papers, Denver Public Library. Dennis Duffy told Camp in 1915 that "Capt. Brown's private parts were cut off and stuck in his mouth." Interview of Duffy, December 19, 1915, envelope 72, box 5, William Camp Papers, Lily Library, University of Indiana.

21. F. C. Carrington, *My Army Life*, 155.

22. 40th Cong., 1st sess., *Senate Exec. Doc.* 13, 35.

23. *New York Times*, December 27, 1866.

24. M. Carrington, *Ab-sa-ra-ka*, 220–21.

25. *Chicago Republican*, January 3, 1867.

26. *Chicago Tribune*, February 2, 1867.

27. *Chicago Tribune*, January 16, 1867.

28. Anderson, "Centennial of the Fetterman Fight," 73–79.

29. *Frank Leslie's Illustrated Newspaper*, January 19, 1867.

30. Bogy to Browning in "Massacre of Troops Near Fort Phil Kearny," 39th Cong., 2nd sess., *House Exec. Doc.* 71, 1867. Reprinted in Henry B. Carrington, *The Indian Question* (Boston: De Wolfe and Fiske, 1909), 36.

31. Bent in Hyde, *Life of George Bent*, 199–200.

32. 40th Cong., 1st sess., *Senate Exec. Doc.* 13, 16.

33. Testimonies of Cooke and Carrington. For how the politics of Reconstruction affected governmental actions in the West as a whole, see Heather Cox Richardson, *West from Appomattox: The Reconstruction of America after the Civil War* (New Haven: Yale University Press, 2007).

34. 50th Cong., 1st sess., *Senate Exec. Doc.* 33, 41.

35. F. C. Carrington, *My Army Life*, 164.

36. 40th Cong., 1st sess., *Senate Exec. Doc.* 13, 28.

37. Post Returns, Fort Phil Kearny for December 1866.

38. 50th Cong., 1st sess., *Senate Exec. Doc.* 13, 16.

39. Cooke's apology to Carrington (date unknown) is quoted in Otis E. Young, *The West of Philip St. George Cooke, 1809–1895* (Glendale, CA: Arthur H. Clark, 1955), 351–52.

40. For the arduous trek from Fort Phil Kearny to Fort Reno, see F. C. Carrington, *My Army Life*, 173–217; and M. Carrington, *Ab-sa-ra-ka*, 226–43.

41. Carrington's testimony.

42. *Army and Navy Journal* 4 (February 16, 1867): 406; P. M. Shockley, "Fort Phil Kearny, the Fetterman Massacre," *Quartermaster Review* 11 (1932): 28–32.

43. 40th Cong., 1st sess., *Senate Exec. Doc.* 13, 36.

44. Gordon, "Relief of Fort Phil Kearny," 283; David, *Finn Burnett*, 135; Fessenden's account, 2:105; Murphy's account, 392; Shockley, "Fort Phil Kearny," 32.

45. Post Returns, Fort Phil Kearny for May 1867.

46. Murphy's account, 392.

47. Augur to Adj. Gen. W. A. Nichols, Military Division of the Missouri, July 21, 1867, Letters Sent, Department of the Platte, RG 98, NARA.

48. For Hancock's campaign see John H. Monnett, *The Battle of Beecher Island and the Indian War of 1867–1869* (Newt: University Press of Colorado, 1992), 75–92.

49. White Bull's account, 71; Jerome A. Greene, "The Hayfield Fight: A Reappraisal of a Neglected Action," *Montana: The Magazine of Western History* 22, no. 4 (Autumn 1972): 30–43.

50. Greene, *Hayfield Fight*, 31. Palmer was awarded his Medal of Honor in 1896 for action at the Battle of Lexington, Missouri. For Palmer's role in Red Cloud's War see Jerome A. Greene, "Lt. Palmer Writes from the Bozeman Trail, 1867–1868," *Montana: The Magazine of Western History* 28, no. 3 (Summer 1978): 16–35.

51. Greene, *Hayfield Fight*, 7.

52. Ibid.; Henry One Bull to Walter Campbell, June 18, 1936, box 104, item 10, Walter S. Campbell Papers, Western History Collection, University of Oklahoma Library.

53. Greene, *Hayfield Fight*, 8.

54. The best accounts of the action at the Hayfield fight are Greene, *Hayfield Fight*; and Barry J. Hagan, *"Exactly in the Right Place": A History of Fort C. F. Smith, Montana*

Territory, 1866–1868 (El Segundo, CA: Upton and Sons, 1999), 113–36. See also Vaughn, *Indian Fights*, 91–116.

55. White Bull's account, 71–73, 78.

56. Ibid., 72.

57. Powell to post adjutant, Fort Phil Kearny, August 4, 1867, quoted in Jerry Keenan, *The Wagon Box Fight: An Episode of Red Cloud's War* (Conshohocken, PA: Savas Publishing Co., 2000), 40–41. Keenan's book is the most thorough account of the battle. See also Olson, *Red Cloud and the Sioux Problem*, 63–65; and Max Littman's account in Hebard and Brininstool, *The Bozeman Trail*, 2:78–79.

58. Keenan, *Wagon Box Fight*, 52.

59. Ibid.

60. Hebard and Brininstool, *The Bozeman Trail*, 2:53–54.

61. Gibson's account of the Wagon Box fight in ibid.

62. Eugene O'Conner to "Dear Brother," August 2, 1867, "Western Trails" Photo Archives, Wyoming State Archives, Wyoming Historic Preservation Office.

63. Keenan, *Wagon Box Fight*, 33–45.

64. Fire Thunder's account of the Wagon Box fight in Black Elk and Neihardt, *Black Elk Speaks*, 13.

65. White Bull's account of the Wagon Box fight, although filtered through the notes of Campbell, is the most detailed from the Indian perspective. White Bull names many of the participants and lends strong credence that Crazy Horse was one of the principal leaders. See White Bull's account of the Wagon Box fight in Vestal, *Warpath*, 70–83.

66. Braided Locks's statement of July 21, 1927, is discussed in Powell, *People of the Sacred Mountain*, 2:755.

67. For an excellent history of imperial warfare with indigenous peoples comparing America and Africa, see James O. Gump, *The Dust Rose Like Smoke: The Subjugation of the Zulu and the Sioux* (Lincoln: University of Nebraska Press, 1994).

68. George P. Belden, *Belden, the White Chief; or, Twelve Years Among Wild Indians of the Plains, From the Diaries and Manuscripts of George P. Belden*, ed. James S. Brisbin (1870; reprint, Athens: Ohio University Press, 1972), 376. Historians have long discredited Lieutenant Belden as a braggart given to unbelievable self-aggrandizement and claims of superhuman feats. In fact his "authoritative statements" about Indians are riddled with paternalism, lack of understanding, and occasional racist overtones. The large expanse of this fire cannot be verified by any other source and is probably inflated. Belden's book is a good example of why students of history must not take even original sources, especially autobiography and original newspaper accounts, at face value. Original sources often must be scrutinized in light of recent scholarship.

69. Sherman to Assistant Adjutant General, July 1, 1867, Records of the Adjutant General's Office, RG 94, NARA.

70. Monnett, *Battle of Beecher Island*, 75–92.

71. Brian Corkhill, ed., "Skirmish at Goose Creek: Edmund R. P. Shurly's Bozeman Trail Reminiscence," *Montana: The Magazine of Western History* 33, no. 2 (Spring 1983): 60–63.

72. It is not the purpose of this book to detail the fighting south of the Platte during 1867–69 that spilled over from the north. Several secondary works are recommended. See Athern, *William Tecumseh Sherman and the Conquest of the West*; William H. Leckie; *The Military Conquest of the Southern Plains* (Norman: University of Oklahoma Press, 1963); Monnett, *Battle of Beecher Island*; and Jerome A. Greene, *Washita: The U.S. Army and the Southern Cheyennes, 1867–1869* (Norman: University of Oklahoma Press, 2004). For the suffering of Euro-American captives resulting from the Kansas raids, see Broome, *Dog Soldier Justice: The Ordeal of Susanna Alderdice in the Kansas Indian War* (Lincoln, KS: Lincoln County Historical Society, 2003). For the Indian perspective see Hyde, *Life of George Bent*; Powell, *People of the Sacred Mountain*; Grinnell, *The Fighting Cheyennes*; and Donald Berthrong, *The Southern Cheyennes* (Norman: University of Oklahoma Press, 1963).

73. Dee Brown asserts that "[f]or the first time in history the United States Government had negotiated a peace which conceded everything demanded by the enemy and which exacted nothing in return." Brown is mistaken. Brown, *Fort Phil Kearny*, 225.

74. Colin Calloway, *First Peoples: A Documentary Survey of American Indian History*, 2nd ed. (Boston: Bedford St. Martin's, 2004), 294–95.

75. Ibid.

76. Ibid., 295.

77. John Gray, *Centennial Campaign: The Sioux War of 1876* (Norman: University of Oklahoma Press, 1988), 11, 15.

78. Teleconference interview with Charlotte A. Black Elk, September 24, 1992, with author consultants for "How the West Was Lost," VHS, vol. 3, segment 1, "A Good Day to Die." Statement by Black Elk in vol. 3, segment 1.

79. Quoted in Edward Lazarus, *Black Hills/White Justice: The Sioux Nation Versus the United States, 1775 to the Present* (New York: Harper Collins, 1991), 61–62.

80. Powell, *People of the Sacred Mountain*, 2:762–63.

81. Quoted in Calloway, *First Peoples*, 304.

82. Ibid.

83. Quoted in Olson, *Red Cloud and the Sioux Problem*, 74–75.

84. John Stands In Timber Papers, Newberry Library, Chicago.

85. In 1906 Red Cloud told Clarence Three Stars, interpreting for Eli S. Ricker, that the boundaries of the Great Sioux Reservation proscribed in the Treaty of 1868 had not been honored. "It has been a puzzle to me and to the Indian people," Red Cloud stated, "how the line came to be where it has been put." Interview with Red Cloud, November 24, 1906, Pine Ridge, SD, Ricker Papers, tablet 25, Nebraska State Historical Society.

86. Raymond J. DeMallie and Douglas R. Parks, *Sioux Indian Religion: Tradition and Innovation* (Norman: University of Oklahoma Press, 1987), 43.

87. For Red Cloud's later life as a statesman, see Larson, *Red Cloud*; and Charles W. Allen, *From Fort Laramie to Wounded Knee: In the West That Was* (Lincoln: University of Nebraska Press, 1997). An excellent photographic anthology is Frank H. Goodyear III, *Photographs of a Lakota Chief* (Lincoln: University of Nebraska Press, 2003).

88. For culture brokers among former warrior chiefs, see Margaret Connell Szasz, ed., *Between Indian and White Worlds: The Culture Brokers* (Norman: University of Oklahoma Press, 1994).

Notes to Chapter 9

1. Neihardt, *Song of the Indian Wars*, 59.

2. A good example of the exploits of Crazy Horse based almost solely on oral tradition is Joseph Marshall III, *The Journey of Crazy Horse: A Lakota History* (New York: Viking, 2004).

3. Biographer Kingsley Bray gives Crazy Horse's birth year as 1840, making him twenty-six in 1866. Black Elk claims he was nineteen. See Bray, *Crazy Horse: A Lakota Life*, 5–6; and Black Elk and Neihardt, *Black Elk Speaks*, 8. Crazy Horse's close friend Chips told Eli S. Ricker that Crazy Horse was born in 1840. Chips interview, February 14, 1907, tablet 18, Ricker Papers, Nebraska State Historical Society.

4. Vestal, *Warpath*, 68. Some readers may find it surprising that Campbell did not make more of White Bull's brief mention of Crazy Horse in 1866 given that he tried his best to convince his readers that White Bull was the warrior to personally kill Custer a decade later. James H. Howard made the same claim when he translated and edited White Bull's drawings in *The Warrior Who Killed Custer* (Lincoln: University of Nebraska Press, 1968). Ethnohistorian Raymond DeMallie in his introduction to the Bison Book edition of Vestal, *Warpath* (1984), discredited Campbell's assertion that White Bull killed Custer, casting doubt on the credibility of the book. There are no references to such in the Campbell Papers. See Campbell Papers, box 105 (White Bull notes), Western History Collection, University of Oklahoma Library, Norman. See also Stanley Vestal, "The Man Who Killed Custer," *American Heritage* 8, no. 2 (February 1957): 4–9, 90–91; James H. Howard, "The White Bull Manuscript," *Plains Anthropologist* 6, no. 12, part 2 (1961): 115–16; Raymond Bucko in James H. Howard, ed., *Lakota Warrior: Joseph White Bull* (Lincoln, University of Nebraska Press, 1998), v–xix. For a short overview see Charles Vollan, "White Bull, Joseph (1849–1947)" in David J. Wishart, ed. *Encyclopedia of the Great Plains Indians* (Lincoln: University of Nebraska Press, 2007), 218–19. Campbell's lack of concern for the stature of Crazy Horse at the Fetterman fight while placing so much fame on White Bull at Little Bighorn only furthers the question as to Crazy Horse's presence as a decoy on Lodge Trail Ridge.

5. Robinson, *A History of the Dakota or Sioux Indians*, 362, n. 603. This author has been unable to locate any reference to a warrior named White Bear as having participated in the Fetterman fight. Could Robinson have meant White Bull? Roman Nose was a common name among the Cheyennes and other plains Indians. But the famous Cheyenne Crooked Lance warrior Roman Nose was more prominent than any other individual of that name before his death at Beecher Island in 1868. Robinson could not have meant any other.

6. Thomas B. Marquis, *Wooden Leg: A Warrior Who Fought Custer* (Bison Book reprint, Lincoln: University of Nebraska Press, 1986), 14–15.

7. Ibid.

8. Winter Count of Cloud Shield, 1866–67, ms. 2372, box 12, 0874901–08746992, NAA; Rosebud Winter Count, 1867–68, ms. 2001–10, NAA.

9. Joe De Barthe, ed. *Life and Adventures of Frank Grouard* (Norman: University of Oklahoma Press, 1958), 181; Frank Grouard, "An Indian Scout's Recollections of Crazy Horse," *Nebraska History Magazine* 12 (January–March 1929): 72; White Bull's account, 54.

10. Grinnell, *The Fighting Cheyennes*, 234–44.

11. Hyde, *Red Cloud's Folk*, 147, n. 4.

12. Testimony of Two Moon, September 26, 1913, Walter Mason Camp Papers, box 5, folder 15, envelope 69, Lilly Library, Indiana University, Bloomington.

13. Bent to Hyde, December 5, 1904, April 19, 1912, May 20, 1913, Coe Collection; June 7, 1913, Denver Public Library; Bent in Hyde, *Life of George Bent*, 343–46; Hyde, *Red Cloud's Folk*, 146.

14. Hyde, *Red Cloud's Folk*, 146–47. Hyde wrote, "White Bull of the Miniconjous was present, and he states that Crazy Horse led." Two Moon's account in Hyde, *Life of George Bent*, 343–46, makes no mention of Crazy Horse's being in the fight. Two Moon's earlier account, which makes no mention of Crazy Horse, is from Bent to Hyde, December 5, 1904. Two Moon denied personally being in the fight in a statement to Grinnell, September 6, 1908. See Powell, *People of the Sacred Mountain*, 1:666, n. 8. For Hyde's claim in *Life of George Bent* that Crazy Horse made his reputation in the 1870s, see p. 347.

15. Chips interview, 1907, tablet 18, Ricker Papers, Nebraska State Historical Society.

16. George Sword (Hunts the Enemy) (Owns Sword) interview, 1907; American Horse interview, 1906; George W. Colhoff interview, ca. 1906, all tablet 16, Ricker Papers, Nebraska State Historical Society. American Horse told Ricker that Crazy Horse was viewed as dangerous by some Oglalas in 1877. Certainly there was rivalry and jealousy of Crazy Horse at that time. This might account for American Horse's lack of detail about Crazy Horse at the Fetterman fight in his interview with Ricker.

17. For easy access to the Hinman interviews as well as most other early interviews pertaining to Crazy Horse, see Richard G. Hardorff, ed., *The Death of Crazy Horse: A Tragic Episode in Lakota History* (Lincoln: University of Nebraska Press, 2001); or see R. Eli Paul, *The Nebraska Indian Wars Reader, 1865–1877* (Lincoln: University of Nebraska Press, 1998), 180–216.

18. Robinson, *A History of the Dakota or Sioux Indians*, 361, n. 603; Vestal, *Warpath*, 68; Hyde, *Red Cloud's Folk*, 146.

19. Charles A. Eastman (Ohiyesa), *Indian Heroes and Great Chieftains* (Boston: Little, Brown and Co., 1918), 94. In 1922 a journalist named Elmo Scott Watson wrote, "Crazy Horse was chosen to lead the attack on the wood choppers to draw out the soldiers." He mentioned nothing about Crazy Horse as a decoy on Lodge Trail Ridge because that

story had not yet been written by Sandoz. *Record Journal of Douglas County* [Colorado], December 29, 1922, 1–2.

20. Other glaring examples are Marshall, *Journey of Crazy Horse*, 145–52; Fort Phil Kearny/Bozeman Trail Association, *Portraits*, 74–79; and Hardorff, *Death of Crazy Horse*, 34, n. 16.

21. Mari Sandoz, *Crazy Horse: Strange Man of the Oglalas* (Lincoln: University of Nebraska Press, 1942), 199–201.

22. Ibid., 199–200; Mari Sandoz, *Hostiles and Friendlies: Selected Short Writings of Mari Sandoz* (Lincoln: University of Nebraska Press, 1959), 79; Mari Sandoz Papers, Nebraska State Historical Society.

23. Hebard and Brininstool, *The Bozeman Trail*, 297–346.

24. Brown, *Fort Phil Kearny: An American Saga*, 78.

25. Stephen Ambrose, *Crazy Horse and Custer: The Parallel Lives of Two American Warriors* (New York: Doubleday, 1975), 223, 462, n. 14.

26. Powell, *People of the Sacred Mountain*, 1:456.

27. McMurtry, *Crazy Horse: A Life*, 59.

28. Mike Sajna, *Crazy Horse: The Life Behind the Legend* (New York: John Wiley and Sons, 2000), 200.

29. Marshall's convictions of the explicit validity of latter-generation oral tradition passed down through tribal elders are admirable. But trade market published oral histories are perhaps unfortunately ahead of their time in gaining acceptance with wider audiences outside Indian country. Although Marshall lists tribal storytellers in his credits he does not footnote specific events as to the individual oral source. See Marshall, *Journey of Crazy Horse*, 145–71, and 295–98. Another source of modern oral tradition presented to the general public by descendants of Crazy Horse is Tiwahe, Tashunke Witko, *The Authorized Biography of Crazy Horse and His Family*, a DVD in four parts produced by William Matson and Mark Frethem (Reel Contact, 2007). Part Two, "Defending the Homeland Prior to the 1868 Treaty," portrays Crazy Horse's exploits at the Fetterman fight vis-à-vis vintage Sandoz. Ethnohistorian Bernard L. Fontana argues that later oral sources should always be corroborated with original eyewitness accounts whenever possible, in "American Indian Oral History, An Anthropologist's Note," *History and Theory* 8, no. 3 (1969): 3.

30. Bray's closest endnote as sources for Crazy Horse's being chosen as leader of the decoys, and the actions of the decoys in general, are the previously examined Ricker 1906 and 1907 interviews with American Horse and George Sword (Hunts the Enemy) (Owns Sword). Neither of these Oglalas mentions anything about Crazy Horse's being in the Fetterman fight in their interviews with Ricker. The third source Bray cites is a secondary account, an unattributed statement by Powell in *People of the Sacred Mountain*, 1:456, claiming that Lakota chiefs chose Crazy Horse to lead the decoys. Powell, later on the same page, credits Grinnell in *The Fighting Cheyennes*, 238–39, by stating that Crazy Horse rode off with the decoys. But Grinnell makes no such statements in his book or in his papers and correspondence in the Southwest Museum. Again, there are simply no solid original testimonies available to the public or to historians establishing Crazy Horse as a decoy, and certainly there are no original testimonies

ascribing any long, detailed exploits to him in the battle save Gouard's secondhand claim that Lone Bear died in his arms following the fight. The dramatic differential between Crazy Horse's *assumed* actions given a general knowledge of Lakota culture and what details can actually be verified is an example of some of the differences of methodology and viewpoint argued today between ethnohistorians and academic historians. See Bray, *Crazy Horse*, 97–102, 419, n. 44.

31. The elaborate stories of Crazy Horse's exploits as a decoy on Lodge Trail Ridge are still finding their way into fictional accounts of the Fetterman fight as well as into histories. For example see Joseph Marshall III, *Hundred in the Hand: A Novel* (Golden, CO: Fulcrum Fiction, 2007), 302–32.

32. The alleged presence of all but a few important warriors at the Fetterman fight is another example of the differences between historical and ethnohistorical methodologies for evaluating sources. But rather than detract from historical interpretation and dialogue such comparisons serve rather to stimulate debate. Who *was* there? Who was *not* there? Who did what? As with Little Bighorn, such mysteries surround events like the Fetterman fight more pervasively, it seems, than many other topics in American history that are much greater and more significant. And that form of scholarly debate is what keeps the military frontiers of the West and the story of Native American resistance to colonialism one of the most intriguing topics in the American mind.

33. Robert W. Frazer, *Forts of the West: Military Forts and Presidios and Posts Commonly Called Forts West of the Mississippi River to 1898* (Norman: University of Oklahoma Press, 1965), 88.

34. 40th Cong., 1st sess., *Senate Exec. Doc.* 13, 7, 55.

35. For many of the inflated and outrageous newspaper accounts, see Anderson, "Centennial of the Fetterman Fight," 1–3 and 77–79. The Chicago newspapers, especially the *Tribune* and the *Times*, were among the most inaccurate.

36. General Order no. 1, January 1, 1867, Post Records, Fort Phil Kearny, RG 93, NARA; Carrington's testimony.

37. Ibid.

38. Ibid.

39. Ibid.

40. 40th Cong., 1st sess., *Senate Exec. Doc.* 13, 57–74.

41. *Army and Navy Journal* 4 (June 29, 1867): 317.

42. Bisbee's testimony, M740.

43. Powell's testimony, M740.

44. 39th Cong., 2nd sess., *House Exec Doc.* 71, 58.

45. For an analysis of Carrington's and Powell's conflict, much of it speculation but based on mutual dislike and disrespect, see Straight, "The Strange Testimony of Major Powell," *New York Posse of the Westerners Brand Book* 7 (1960).

46. Ibid.; Powell's testimony, M740.

47. Cooke's testimony, M740.

48. Ibid.

49. 40th Cong., 1st sess., *Senate Exec Doc.* 13, 61–66.

50. Heitman, *Historical Register and Dictionary of the U.S. Army*, 1:324.

51. Young, *The West of Philip St. George Cooke*, 352–53.

52. Quoted in ibid., 351–52; Hebard and Brininstool, *The Bozeman Trail*, 1:340; Brown, *Fort Phil Kearny*, 226–27.

53. Carrington's testimony; Cooke's testimony, M740.

54. For an excellent examination of the conflict between Reconstruction needs and those of the U.S. Army and the political implications see Michael L. Tate, *The Frontier Army in the Settlement of the West* (Norman: University of Oklahoma Press, 1999). See also Heather Cox Richardson, *West from Appomattox: The Reconstruction of America after the Civil War* (New Haven: Yale University Press, 2007).

55. For a discussion of the Grant Peace Policy, see Robert M. Utley, *The Indian Frontier, 1846–1890*, rev. ed. (Albuquerque: University of New Mexico Press, 1984), 127–54.

56. Henry B. Carrington, "Explanation of Congressional Delay for Twenty Years," Carrington Scrapbook, Fulmer Public Library, Sheridan WY; Calitri, "Give Me Eighty Men," 52.

57. One edition brought out by Henry Carrington bore his name and was titled *Ab-sa-ra-ka, Land of Massacre: Being the Experiences of an Officer's Wife on the Plains, With an Outline of Indian Operations and Conferences from 1865–1878* (Philadelphia: Lippincott and Co., 1878).

58. Carrington to C. G. Coutant, June 6, 1902, reproduced in Hebard and Brininstool, *The Bozeman Trail*, 1:339–42. The most convenient edition of Margaret's book is *Ab-sa-ra-ka: Home of the Crows* (Lincoln: University of Nebraska Press, 1983).

59. Calitri, "Give Me Eighty Men," 52–53. For Sherman's letter see ms. group 130, microfilm HM136, Carrington Family Papers, Sterling Library, Yale.

60. Calitri, "Give Me Eighty Men," 53.

61. M. Carrington, *Ab-sa-ra-ka*, 171.

62. Ibid., 244–45.

63. Ibid., 248.

64. Ibid., 249.

65. McWilliams in Fort Phil Kearny/Bozeman Trail Association, *Portraits*, 147.

66. Calitri, "Give Me Eighty Men," 54. The government published the reports first in 49th Cong., 2nd sess., *Senate Exec. Doc.* 97, 1887; and U.S. Senate, "Indian Operations on the Plains," 1887, 51–53. The reports are today housed as "Records of the Special Commission to Investigate the Fetterman Massacre and the State of Indian Affairs, 1867," Records of the Bureau of Indian Affairs, RG 75, NARA.

67. George W. Grummond, Pension File no. 23, Widow's Claim 111–143, Records of the Veteran's Administration, RG 15, NARA.

68. Kordik in Fort Phil Kearny/Bozeman Trail Association, *Portraits*, 93–97.

69. Carrington's testimony, M740.

70. M. Carrington, *Ab-sa-ra-ka*, 244–45, 248.

71. Ibid., 249.

72. Shannon Smith Calitri, introduction to F. C. Carrington, *My Army Life*. Bison Book ed. (Lincoln: University of Nebraska Press, 2004), v–xxv.

73. Brown, *Fort Phil Kearny*, 228.

74. Frances Ten Eyck, the captain's daughter, had been urging Carrington to vindicate her father. Others, including writers about the battle, had already been suggesting that Ten Eyck was innocent of any tardiness or cowardice. Carrington agreed, although Ten Eyck was dead by 1908. See F. Ten Eyck to Eli S. Ricker, June 1, 6, 1906, folder 30, box 2, series 1, group 1227, Ricker Papers, Nebraska State Historical Society. Author C. G. Coutant had previously claimed Ten Eyck's innocence in his *The History of Wyoming* (Laramie, WY: Chaplin, Spafford and Mathison, 1899), 574. For a discussion of Frances Ten Eyck's efforts, see Calitri, "Give Me Eighty Men," 55–56.

75. F. C. Carrington, *My Army Life*, 119.

76. M. Carrington, *Ab-sa-ra-ka*, 171. To quote Margaret: "a company of regulars could whip a thousand, and a regiment could whip a whole array of hostile tribes."

77. F. C. Carrington, *My Army Life*, 253.

78. Calitri, "Give Me Eighty Men," 54–55.

79. Bisbee, "Items of Indian Service," 82–83; and Bisbee, *Through Four American Wars*, 175.

80. H. Carrington, "Explanation of Congressional Delay for Twenty Years"; H. Carrington to James B. Carrington, September 9, 1903, Carrington Family Papers, Sterling Library, Yale; Calitri, "Give Me Eighty Men," 55.

81. Brady, *Indian Fights and Fighters*, 23.

82. Ibid., 28.

83. Calitri discusses the many false images that have been perpetuated about Fetterman in modern writing. They include: Brown, *Fort Phil Kearny* (1962); Hebard and Brininstool, *The Bozeman Trail* (1922); fiction by Michael Straight: *Carrington: A Novel of the West* (New York: Alfred A. Knopf, 1960); B. F. McCune, "The Fatal Fetterman Fight," *Wild West* 10 (December 1997); Donald McCaig, "The Bozeman Trail," *Smithsonian Magazine* 7 (October 2000); and Larry McMurtry's best-seller *Boone's Lick* (New York: Simon and Schuster, 2000). Calitri writes of one book reviewer's comments of *Boone's Lick*: "'William Fetterman is an imperious ass who butts head with [the heroine] twice before he rides off into ignominy.'" See Calitri, "Give Me Eighty Men," 58–59. Even the legendary journalist Ambrose Bierce wrote a supernatural tale in 1913 of a fictitious Pvt. Dave Duck, a casualty at Fort Phil Kearny who made a ghostly appearance after he was supposed to be dead. See www.legendsofamerica.com/GH-TwoLives.html.

84. Robinson to Wells, May 10, 1933, Philip Faribault Wells Manuscripts, 1866–1891, H75.134, Fd 1, South Dakota State Historical Resource Center.

85. Ibid.

86. Wells to Robinson, May 19, 1933; manuscript, 1933, handwritten account of Fetterman massacre, Philip Faribault Wells Manuscripts, 1866–1891, H75.134, Fd 1, South Dakota State Historical Resource Center. For Bridger's activities in the early 1870s, see Cecil J. Alter, *Jim Bridger* (Norman: University of Oklahoma Press, 1962), 337; Vestal, *Jim Bridger, Mountain Man*, 296–97; and *The Kansas City Star*, January 18, 1924.

87. Robert W. Witkin, "Irony and the Historical," *Europa* 4, article 3 (1997): 8, available at www.intellectbooks.com/europa/number4/witkin.htm.

88. Alan D. Zimm, "A Causal Model of Warfare," *Military Review*, January/February 2001, 47.

89. Witkin, "Irony and the Historical," 9.

90. Among them are Dee Brown, Michael Straight, and Larry McMurtry.

91. Paramount Pictures, John Ford, producer, *The Man Who Shot Liberty Valance*, 1962.

92. The most damning is Powell's testimony.

93. Young, *The West of Philip St. George Cooke*, 341–53.

94. Sherman to Assistant Adjutant General, July 1, 1867, Records of the Adjutant General's Office, RG 94, NARA.

95. Certainly the plains Indians of that time recognized the military and economic potential of the railroads. For example, see Luther Standing Bear, *My People the Sioux* (Lincoln: University of Nebraska Press, 1975), 6–9.

96. For analyses of these campaigns, see Robert M. Utley, *Frontier Regulars: The United States Army and the Indian, 1866–1891* (Lincoln: University of Nebraska Press, 1984), 110–62.

97. M. Carrington, *Ab-sa-ra-ka*, 171. Margaret Carrington's version was later repeated by Frances Grummond Carrington.

98. Accounts of White Bull, White Elk, Fire Thunder, American Horse, Two Moons.

99. Wolf Feathers/Bill Tall Bull, "We are the Ancestors of Those Yet to Be Born," Fort Phil Kearny/Bozeman Trail Association, 1988, http://philkearny.vcn.com/fpk-tallbull.htm. See also Bill Tall Bull in Fort Phil Kearny/Bozeman Trail Association, *Portraits*, 84–87.

100. See most issues of *Lame Deer Literary and History Journal*, Chief Dull Knife College, Lame Deer, MT.

101. Address given by Robert M. Utley at the Fort Robinson Military History Conference, Crawford, NE, April 2007.

102. http://freepages.history.rootsbeb.com/~familyinformation/#fpk.

103. www.mohicanpress.com/messageboard2/topic.asp?TOPIC_ID=73&whichpage=3.

104. www.firendslittlebighorn.com/Fetterman-Battle-Photos.htm.

105. www.friendslittlebighorn.com/Fetterman-Battle.htm.

BIBLIOGRAPHY

THE PRIMARY SOURCE MATERIALS pertinent to an understanding of the struggle for the Powder River country in 1866 are many. Differing interpretations of this fascinating topic from the military viewpoint may be garnered from federal government original source material alone. Essential to an understanding of the Fetterman fight are the congressional, senatorial, and federal department reports listed below, along with military records from the National Archives and Records Administration (NARA) and the all-important testimonies of the Sanborn Commission (Records of the Special Commission to Investigate the Fetterman Massacre and the State of Indian Affairs, 1867, RG 75, M740, NARA). The books of Margaret Carrington (*Ab-sa-ra-ka*, 1868) and Frances Grummond Carrington (*My Army Life*, 1910) are standard original sources on this event once one considers that both women had personal biases in their descriptions of the actions and ascriptions of responsibility that are reflected in their writings, and thus should be reflected upon by readers of their personal accounts. Most early newspaper accounts of this event are predictably sensational and inaccurate as was typical of the nineteenth-century "yellow" press.

Indian sources garnered from Stanley Vestal's *Warpath* (Miniconjou), Nicholas Black Elk and John Neihardt's *Black Elk Speaks* (Oglala), George Grinnell's *Fighting Cheyennes* (Cheyenne), George Hyde's *Life of George Bent* (Cheyenne), and others examined in this study are easily obtained and remarkably corroborative with official military "forensic" reports, archaeology of the battlefield, and so forth when comparing Indian and white versions in reconstructing the Fetterman fight on December 21, 1866.

But on another level the historiography of the struggle for the Powder River country is equally fascinating as the firsthand story. Beginning with Cyrus Townsend Brady's *Indian Fights and Fighters*, 1904, the Fetterman fight and the character of William J. Fetterman in particular have evolved in imagery much the same as the changing perceptions of George Custer. A perusal of secondary writings in chronological order after 1904 is illuminating in tracing this evolving imagery, especially in historical fiction. Such events as the Fetterman fight present us with mysteries that will never completely be solved and will thus always remain subjects of speculation, educated guesses, and interpretations based on evidential comparisons and logic. This study is but one historian's interpretation of the event based on these criteria as derived from original sources checked against secondary studies. Readers should examine and evaluate the sources below and make up their own minds about the lasting legacy of the struggle for the Powder River country. Their efforts will raise yet further questions to be examined in future studies, thus advancing the scholarship regarding symbolism, significance of myth, and historical irony in evaluating perspectives and cultural viewpoints of Indian peoples and non-Indian peoples within the framework of the American nation and how its diverse peoples remember their history.

Manuscript Collections

Bent, George. Correspondence to George Hyde. William Robertson Coe Collection, Beinecke Manuscript Library, Yale University, New Haven, CT.

Bettelyoun, Susan Bordeux. Papers. Nebraska State Historical Society, Lincoln.

Burgess, Perry A. Diary. S-mss Burgess manuscript. Western History Collections, Nolan Library, University of Colorado, Boulder.

Camp, William. Wm. Camp Papers. Lily Library, University of Indiana, Bloomington.

———. Camp Papers, Ellison Collection, Denver Public Library, Denver.

Campbell, Walter S. Walter S. Campbell Papers. Western History Collection, University of Oklahoma Library, Norman.

Carrington, Henry B. Carrington Papers. Sterling Memorial Library, Yale University, New Haven, CT.

———. Carrington Scrapbook. Explanation of Congressional Delay for Twenty Years. Fulmer Public Library, Sheridan, WY.

Deloria, Ella. Papers: Transcriptions. Colorado Historical Society, Denver.

———. Post Scout Reports, Fort Laramie. Fort Laramie National Historic Site, Fort Laramie, WY.

Ellison, Robert S. Letters to Walter Camp. Ellison Papers. Western History Department, Denver Public Library, Denver.

Fox, George W. Diary, 1866. Mss 27. Wyoming State Archives, Cheyenne.

Grinnell, George B. White Elk to Grinnell, July 16, 1914. Papers and Letters of George B. Grinnell. Southwest Museum, Los Angeles.

Hagan, Barry J. Collection of Fort Phil Kearny/Bozeman Trail Papers. Fulmer Library, Sheridan, WY.

Murray, Robert A. Robert A. Murray Collection. Fulmer Library, Sheridan, WY.

O'Conner, Eugene. Western Trails Photo Archives, Wyoming Historical Preservation Office, Cheyenne.

Riker, Eli S. Ricker Papers. Nebraska State Historical Society, Lincoln.

———. Interview with Chips, 1907, tablet 18; interview with George Sword, April 29, 1907, tablet 39; interview with Dr. J. R. Walker, Pine Ridge, November 21, 1906, tablet 17; Letters. Frances Ten Eyck to Riker, June 1 and 6, 1906, folder 30, box 2, series 1, group 1227, all at Nebraska State Historical Society, Lincoln.

Sandoz, Mari. Sandoz Papers. Nebraska State Historical Society, Lincoln.

Sheldon, Sidney. Sheldon Papers. Nebraska State Historical Society, Lincoln.

Sibley, Henry Hastings. Mss N164. Henry Hasting Sibley Papers. Minnesota Historical Society, St. Paul.

Sully, Alfred E. Correspondence of 1864. Beinecke Manuscript Library, Yale University, New Haven, CT.

Templeton, George. Diary. Graff no. 4099, Newberry Library, Chicago.

Ten Eyck, Tenador. Diary. Special Collections, University of Arizona Libraries, Tucson.

Thomas, William K. Diary. SC 1303, Montana State Historical Society, Helena.

Vaughn, J. W. Letters and Papers. Douglas Public Library, Douglas, WY.

Wells, Philip Faribault. Philip Faribault Wells Manuscripts. Mss H75.134, fd. 1. South Dakota State Resources Center, South Dakota Historical Society, Pierre.

Upholsterer, Frederick. "My Days in Army Life." Manuscript. Carlisle Barracks, U.S. Army Military History Institute, Carlisle, PA.

Willison, Davis. Diary, 1866. Mss 1076. Merrill G. Burlingame Special Collection. University of Montana Libraries, Bozeman.

Correspondence

Littlebird, Glenda. Littlebird to John H. Monnett, e-mail, December 3, 2003.

O'Conner, Eugene. Letter to brother, August 2, 1867. Western Trails Photo Archives, Wyoming Historical Preservation Office, Cheyenne.

Vaughn, J. W. Vaughn to Jerry Keenan, December 24, 1964, and September 27, 1965. Photocopies in possession of the author. Other Vaughn letters in Vaughn Papers, Douglas Public Library, Douglas, WY.

Dissertations

DeMallie, Raymond J. "Teton Dakota Kinship and Social Organization." PhD diss., University of Chicago, 1971.

Roberts, Gary. "Sand Creek: Tragedy and Symbol." PhD diss., University of Oklahoma, 1984.

Records of the National Archives
and Records Administration (NARA)

Records of the Office of Veteran's Affairs. Pension File of Lt. G. W. Grummond. File no. 23, Widow's Claim, 111–43. RG 15.

Records of the Bureau of Indian Affairs. Records of the Special Commission to Investigate the Fetterman Massacre and the State of Indian Affairs, 1867. M740. RG 75.

Letters Received. Upper Platte Indian Agency, 1865 and 1866.

U.S. War Department. Records of the Adjutant General's Office. Department of the Platte, Letters Sent and Received, 1866–67. RG 94.

———. Muster Rolls and Record of Events (Fort Philip Kearny), 1866–67. RG 98.

———. Post Returns, Fort Philip Kearny, 1866–67. M617, roll 910. RG 98.

———. Post Returns, Fort C. F. Smith, 1866–67. RG 98.

———. Post Returns, Fort Laramie, 1865–67. RG 98.

———. Records of the United States Army Continental Commands, 1821–1920. Records of the District of the Plains, 1865. RG 393.

U.S. Court of Claims. Indian Depredation Claims. nos. 81, 474, 8,265, 10,107. RG 123.

Miscellaneous Government Documents

Adjutant General's Office. *Chronological List of Actions, &c With Indians from January 15, 1837 to January, 1891.* Facsimile. Fort Collins, CO: Old Army Press, 1979.

Department of the Army. *The Papers of Ulysses S. Grant.* Facsimile. Vol. 16 of 26. Edited by John Y. Simon, 422–23. Carbondale: Southern Illinois University Press, 1967–2003.

Heitman, Francis B., ed. *Historical Register and Dictionary of the United States Army, From Its Organization, September 29, 1789, to March 2, 1903.* 2 vols. Washington, D.C.: Government Printing Office, 1903.

Richardson, James D., comp. *Messages and Papers of the Presidents, 1789–1897.* 10 vols. Washington, D.C.: Bureau of National Literature and Art, 1896–99.

U.S. Bureau of American Ethnology. *4th Annual Report 1882–1883*. Washington, D.C.: Smithsonian Institution, 1886.

U.S. Senate. *Report of the Commissioner of Indian Affairs for the Year 1866*. Washington, D.C.: Government Printing Office, 1868.

U.S. Senate. *Report of the Acting Commissioner of Indian Affairs for the Year 1867*. Washington, D.C.: Government Printing Office, 1869.

U.S. Senate. *Reports of the U.S. Immigration Commission*. Washington, D.C.: Government Printing Office, 1911.

U.S. War Department. Records of the Adjutant General's Office. RG 94, Department of the Plains, Letters Sent and Received, 1864–65.

U.S. War Department. *The War of the Rebellion: A Compilation of the Official Records of the Union and Confederate Armies*. Series 1, vol. 38, pts.1 and 2, and vol. 98, pt. 1. Washington, D.C.: Government Printing Office, 1880–1901.

U.S. 39th Cong., 2nd sess., *House Exec. Doc.* 71. Washington, D.C., 1867.

U.S. 40th Cong., 1st sess. *Senate Exec. Doc.* 13. Washington, D.C., 1867.

U.S. 50th Cong., 1st sess. "Transmitting in Response to Senate Resolution of February 11, 1887, Papers Relative to Indian Operations on the Plains." *Senate Exec. Doc.* 33. Washington, D.C., 1887.

Winter Counts

American Horse. Ms. 12, book 08746923–0874933. Washington, D.C.: National Anthropological Archives, Smithsonian.

Cloud Shield. Ms. 2372, box 12, 08746901–08746922. Washington D.C.: National Anthropological Archives, Smithsonian.

Flame. Ms. 2372, box 12, 08633800. Washington, D.C.: National Anthropological Archives, Smithsonian.

Iron Crow. *Annual Report of American Ethnology for 1866*. Washington, D.C.: Smithsonian.

Lone Dog. Glass plate, neg. no. 3524C. Washington D.C.: National Anthropological Archives, Smithsonian.

Rosebud. Ms. 2001–10. Washington, D.C.: National Anthropological Archives, Smithsonian.

Swan. Ms. 2372, box 12, 08633900. Washington, D.C.: National Anthropological Archives, Smithsonian.

Lectures and Interviews

Black Elk, Charlotte A. Teleconference interview by author and other consultants for *How the West Was Lost*, September 24, 1992. VHS, three video tapes, six segments, New York: BMG Video in conjunction with The Discovery Channel and KUSA-TV, Denver.

Calitri, Shannon Smith. "Making the Vicissitudes of Peril and Pleasure: How the Cooked Books of Army Wives Massacred the Story of the Fetterman Fight." Presentation at the annual conference of the Western History Association, Fort Worth, TX, October 2003.

Liberty, Margot. Interview by author. Oklahoma City, OK, October 4, 2007.

Students in Cheyenne Studies Seminar of Dr. Alonzo T. Spang Sr. Discussions by author. Chief Dull Knife Memorial College, Lame Deer, MT, September 24, 2003.

Students in the Little Wolf Writing and History Center. Interviews by author. Chief Dull Knife College, Lame Deer, MT, September 24, 2003.

Utley, Robert M. Keynote address given at the Fort Robinson Military History Conference, Crawford, NE, April 2007.

Newspapers and News Periodicals

Army and Navy Journal 4 (June 29, 1867, 317; February 16, 1867; April 13, 1867).

Bozeman Daily Chronicle, September 19, 1948, 16.

Chicago Republican, January 3, 1867, 2.

Chicago Times, February 2, 1867, 2.

Chicago Tribune, January 16, 1867, 1; February 2, 1867, 2.

Frank Leslie's Illustrated Newspaper, January 19, 1867, 19; October 27, 1866, 94.

Kansas City Star, January 18, 1924, 3.

Lame Deer Literary and History Journal. Chief Dull Knife Memorial College. All issues, especially those of 2004.

Montana Post (Virginia City), September 15, 1866, 1; September 29, 1866, 1.

National Tribune, October 21, 1897, 1; June 22, 1899, 6.

New York Times, December 27, 1866, 1.

Omaha Weekly Herald, January 18, 1867, 1.

Omaha [Daily] Herald, October 5, 1866, 1.

Omaha Weekly Republican, August 17, 1866, 1.

Record Journal of Douglas County [Colorado], December 29, 1922, 1–2.

Rocky Mountain News, June 27, 1865, 1; August 21, 1866, 1; December 28, 1866, 1; January 2, 1867, 1; January 26, 1867, 2; February 1, 1867, 2.

Winners of the West, February 28, 1927; March 30, 1933.

Articles

"A Father's Grief, A Soldier's Honor." Program Brochure for Re-Internment of Mini-Aku. June 25, 2005, Fort Laramie National Historic Site, Wyoming.

Anderson, Harry H. "Centennial of the Fetterman Fight." *Chicago Westerners Brand Book* 23 (December 1966): 77–80.

———. "A Challenge to Brown's Sioux Indian Wars Thesis." *Montana: The Magazine of Western History* 12, no. 1 (Winter 1962): 40–49.

Belish, Elbert D. "American Horse (Wasechun-Tashunka): The Man Who Killed Fetterman." *Annals of Wyoming* 63, no. 2 (Spring 1991): 54–67.

Brady, Cyrus Townsend. "The Tragedy of Fort Phil Kearny." *Pearson's Magazine* 11 (1904): 211–24.

Bray, Kingsley M. "Lone Horn's Peace: A New View of Sioux-Crow Relations." *Nebraska History* 66, no. 1 (Spring 1985): 28–47.

———. "Spotted Tail and the Treaty of 1868." *Nebraska History* 83, no. 1 (Spring 2002): 19–35.

———. "Teton Sioux Population History, 1655–1881," *Nebraska History* 75, no. 2 (Summer 1994): 165–80.

Calitri, Shannon Smith. "'Give Me Eighty Men': Shattering the Myth of the Fetterman Massacre." *Montana: The Magazine of Western History* 54, no. 3 (Autumn 2004): 44–59.

Carrington, James B. "Across the Plains with Bridger as Guide." *Scribner's Magazine* 85 (January 1929): 66–81.

Carroll, John M., ed. "Bisbee, Wm., Items of Indian Service." In *Papers of the Order of Indian Wars*, 77–82. Fort Collins, CO: Old Army Press, 1975.

Clough, Wilson D. "Mini Aku, Daughter of Spotted Tail." *Annals of Wyoming* 39 (1967): 187–216.

Cockhill, Brian, ed. "Skirmish on Goose Creek: Edmund R. P. Shurly's Bozeman Trail Reminiscence." *Montana: The Magazine of Western History* 33, no. 2 (Spring 1983): 60–63.

Day, Gordon M. "Oral Tradition as Complement." *Ethnohistory* 19, no. 2 (Spring 1972): 99–108.

Doyle, Susan Badger. "Indian Perspectives of the Bozeman Trail." *Montana: The Magazine of Western History* 40, no. 1 (Winter 1990): 56–67.

Edwards, Elsa Spear. "A Fifteen Day Fight on the Tongue River." *Annals of Wyoming* 10 (April 1938): 51–58.

Ewers, John C. "Economic Warfare as a Precursor of Indian-White Warfare on the Northern Great Plains." *Western Historical Quarterly* 6 (October 1975): 402–10.

Fontana, Bernard L. "American Indian Oral History: An Anthropologist's Note." *History & Theory* 8, no. 3 (1969): 366–70.

Fox, George W. "George W. Fox Diary." *Annals of Wyoming* 8 (January 1931): 580–601.

Gatchell, T. J. "Life of John Ryan." *Annals of Wyoming* 31 (1959): 48–52.

Glover, Ridgeway. "Letters to the Editor." *Philadelphia Photographer* 3 (1866).

Gordon, David S. "The Relief of Fort Phil Kearny." *Journal of the Military Service Institutions of the U.S.* 49 (1911): 281–84.

Griffin, David E. "Timber Procurement and Village Location in the Middle Missouri Subarea." *Plains Anthropologist* 22, no. 78, memoir no. 13 (1977): 177–85.

Greene, Jerome A. "The Hayfield Fight: A Reappraisal of a Neglected Action." *Montana: The Magazine of Western History* 22, no. 4 (Autumn 1972): 30–43.

———. "Lt. Palmer Writes from the Bozeman Trail." *Montana: The Magazine of Western History* 28, no. 3 (Summer 1978): 16–35.

Guthrie, John. "The Fetterman Massacre." *Annals of Wyoming* 9 (October 1932): 714–18.

———. "The Fetterman Massacre." *Winners of the West*, September 1939, 42–46.

Grouard, Frank. "An Indian Scout's Recollections of Crazy Horse." *Nebraska History Magazine* 12 (January–March 1929): 24–29.

Hagan, Barry. "Prelude to a Massacre: Fort Phil Kearny, Dec. 6, 1866." *Journal of the Order of the Indian Wars* 1 (Fall 1980): 1–17.

Howard, James H. "The White Bull Manuscript." *Plains Anthropologist* 6, no. 12, pt. 2 (1961): 115–16.

Hyer, Joel R. "Just Another Battle?: The Significance of the Hayfield Fight," *Annals of Wyoming* 79, (Summer_Autumn 2007): 2–13.

Johnson, Dorothy M. "The Hanging of the Chiefs." *Montana: The Magazine of Western History* 20, no. 3 (Summer 1970): 60–69.

Kievit, Joyce Ann. "A Discussion of Scholarly Responsibilities to Indigenous Communities." *American Indian Quarterly* 27, nos. 1 and 2 (Winter–Spring 2003): 3–45.

McCaig, Donald. "The Bozeman Trail." *Smithsonian Magazine* 7 (October 2000): 88–100.

McCune, B. F. "The Fatal Fetterman Fight." *Wild West* 10 (December 1997): 36–42.

McDermott, John D. "Price of Arrogance: The Short and Controversial Life of William Judd Fetterman." *Annals of Wyoming* 63, no. 2 (Spring 1991): 42–53.

———, ed. "Wyoming Scrapbook: Documents Relating to the Fetterman Fight." *Annals of Wyoming* 63, no. 2 (Spring 1991): 68–72.

Murphy, William. "The Forgotten Battalion." *Winners of the West* 30 (July 1928).

———. "The Forgotten Battalion." *Annals of Wyoming* 7 (1930): 383–401.

Murray, Robert A. "Commentaries on the Col. Henry B. Carrington Image." *Denver Westerners Monthly Roundup* 24, no. 2 (March 1968): 3–12.

Partridge, Robert B. "Fetterman Debacle: Who Was to Blame?" *Journal of the Council of America's Military Past* 16, no. 2 (1989): 36–43.

Pfalfer, Lewis. "The Sully Expedition of 1864 Featuring the Killdeer and Badlands Battles." *North Dakota History* 31 (1964): 1–54.

Shockley, P. M. "Fort Phil Kearny, The Fetterman Massacre." *Quartermaster Review* 11 (May–June 1932): 27–32.

———. "A Forgotten Hero: A Tale of Old Phil Kearny." *Quartermaster Review*, July–August 1932, 17–20.

Straight, Michael. "The Strange Testimony of Major Powell." *The New York Posse of the Westerners Brand Book* 7 (1960).

———. "Carrington: The Valor of Defeat." *Corral Dust: Potomac Corral of the Westerners* 4, no. 1 (December 1959): 25–27.

Spence, Clark. "A Celtic Nimrod in the Old West." *Montana: The Magazine of Western History* 9 (Spring 1959): 55–56.

"'Unraveling the Mysteries': When Was the Fetterman Monument Built and Who Built It?" *Lookout, Newsletter of the Fort Phil Kearny/Bozeman Trail Association*, Fall 1988, 3.

Utley, Robert M. "The Bozeman Trail Before John Bozeman: A Busy Land." *Montana: The Magazine of Western History* 53, no. 2 (Summer 2003): 20–31.

Vestal, Stanley (Walter Campbell). "The Man Who Killed Custer." *American Heritage* 8, no. 2 (February 1957): 4–9, 90–91.

Watson, Elmo Scott. "The Bravery of Our Bugler Is Much Spoken Of." *Old Travois Trail* 1 (1941): 21–29.

West, Elliot. "Contested Plains." *Montana: The Magazine of Western History* 48 (Summer 1998): 2–15.

Wenzel, Nikolai. "The Fetterman Massacre of December 21, 1866." *Journal of America's Military Past* 28, no. 1 (Spring/Summer 2001): 46–59.

White, Richard. "The Winning of the West: The Expansion of the Western Sioux in the Eighteenth and Nineteenth Centuries." *Journal of American History* 65 (September 1978): 330–31.

Wiche, G. J., R. M. Lent, and W. F. Rannie. "The Little Ice Age: Aridity in the North American Great Plains." *The Holocene* 6, no. 4 (2004): 4–36.

Witkin, Robert W. "Irony and the Historical." *Europa* 4 (1997): 1–10.

Young, Will H. "The Journal of Will H. Young, 1865." *Annals of Wyoming* 7 (1930): 402–24.

Zimm, Alan D. "A Causal Model of Warfare." *Military Review*, January–February 2001, 47–53.

Books

Allen, Charles W., with an introduction by Richard E. Jensen, ed. *From Fort Laramie to Wounded Knee: In the West That Was.* Lincoln: University of Nebraska Press, 1997.

Alter, Cecil J. *Jim Bridger.* Norman: University of Oklahoma Press, 1962.

Ambrose, Stephen. *Crazy Horse and Custer: The Parallel Lives of Two American Warriors.* New York: Doubleday, 1975.

Anderson, Gary Clayton. *Little Crow: Spokesman for the Sioux.* St. Paul: Minnesota Historical Society, 1986.

Anderson, Gary Clayton, and Alan R. Woolworth, eds. *Through Dakota Eyes: Narrative Accounts of the Indian War of 1862.* St. Paul: Minnesota Historical Society, 1988.

Athern, Robert. *William Tecumseh Sherman and the Settlement of the West.* Norman: University of Oklahoma Press, 1956.

Bad Heart Bull, Amos. *A Pictographic History of the Oglala Sioux.* Text by Helen H. Bliss. Lincoln: University of Nebraska Press, 1967.

Berthrong, Donald. *The Southern Cheyennes.* Norman: University of Oklahoma Press, 1963.

Bettelyoun, Susan Bordeaux, and Josephine Waggoner. *With My Own Eyes: A Lakota Woman Tells Her People's History.* Lincoln: University of Nebraska Press, 1988.

Bisbee, William Haymond. *Through Four American Wars.* Boston: Meador Publishers, 1931.

———. "Items of Indian Service." *Proceedings: Order of the Indian Wars of the United States.* N.p., 1928.

Black Elk, Nicholas, and John G. Neihardt. *Black Elk Speaks.* Bison Book edition. Lincoln: University of Nebraska Press, 2000.

Blackhawk, Ned. *Violence Over the Land: Indians and Empires in the Early American West.* Cambridge, MA: Harvard University Press, 2006.

Brady, Cyrus Townsend. *Indian Fights and Fighters.* New York: McClure, Phillips and Co., 1904.

Bratt, John. *Trails to Yesterday.* Bison Book edition. Lincoln: University of Nebraska Press, 1980.

George P. Belden. *Belden the White Chief; Or Twelve Years Among the Wild Indians of the Plains*. Edited by James S. Brisbin. 1870. Reprint, Athens: Ohio University Press, 1972.

Bray, Kingsley M. *Crazy Horse: A Lakota Life*. Norman: University of Oklahoma Press, 2006.

Broome, Jeff. *Dog Soldier Justice: The Ordeal of Susanna Alderdice in the Kansas Indian War*. Lincoln, KS: Lincoln County Historical Society, 2003.

Brown, Dee. *Fort Phil Kearny: An American Saga*. Lincoln: University of Nebraska Press, 1962.

Buechel, Eugene, and Paul Manhart, eds. *Lakota Dictionary: Lakota-English/English-Lakota*. Lincoln: University of Nebraska Press, 2002.

Butts, Michele Tucker. *Galvanized Yankees on the Upper Missouri*. Boulder: University Press of Colorado, 2003.

Calloway, Colin. *First Peoples: A Documentary Survey of American Indian History*. 2nd ed. Boston: Bedford St. Martin's, 2004.

———, ed. *New Directions in American Indian History*. Norman: University of Oklahoma Press, 1988.

Carley, Kenneth. *The Dakota War of 1862*. St. Paul: Minnesota Historical Society, 2001.

Carrington, Frances C. *My Army Life: A Soldier's Wife at Fort Phil Kearny*. Philadelphia: Lippincott and Co., 1910.

Carrington, Henry B., *Ab-sa-ra-ka, Land of Massacre: Being the Experiences of an Officer's Wife on the Plains, With an Outline of Indian Operations and Conferences from 1865–1878*. Philadelphia: Lippincott and Co., 1878.

———. *The Indian Question*. Boston: De Wolfe and Fiske, 1909.

Carrington, Margaret I. *Ab-sa-ra-ka: Home of the Crows*. Philadelphia: Lippincott Co., 1868.

Chalfant, William Y. *Cheyennes and Horse Soldiers: The 1857 Expedition and the Battle of Solomon's Fork*. Norman: University of Oklahoma Press, 1997.

Clodfeleter, Michael, *The Dakota War: The United States Army Versus the Sioux*. Jefferson, NC: McFarland and Co., 1998.

Collins, Charles D., Jr. *Atlas of the Sioux Wars*. 2nd ed. Fort Leavenworth, KS: Combat Studies Institute Press, 2006.

Cook, James H. *Fifty Years on the Old Frontier*. New Haven, CT: Yale University Press, 1923.

Coutant, C. G. *The History of Wyoming*. Laramie, WY: Chaplin, Spafford and Mathison, 1899.

David, Robert B. *Finn Burnett, Frontiersman*. Glendale CA: Arthur H. Clark, 1937.

De Barthe, Joe, ed. *Life and Adventures of Frank Grouard*. Norman: University of Oklahoma Press, 1958.

DeMallie, Raymond J., and Douglas R. Parks, eds. *Sioux Indian Religion: Tradition and Innovation*. Norman: University of Oklahoma Press, 1987.

Doyle, Susan B., ed. *Bound for Montana: Diaries from the Bozeman Trail*. Helena: Montana Historical Society, 2004.

———, ed. *Journeys to the Land of Gold: Emigrant Diaries from the Bozeman Trail, 1863–1866*. 2 vols. Helena: Montana Historical Society, 2000.

Dunn, J. P. *Massacres of the Mountains: A History of the Indian Wars of the Far West*. New York: Harper and Brothers, 1886.

Eastman, Charles. *Indian Heroes and Great Chieftains*. Boston: Little, Brown and Co., 1918.

Elliott, Michael A. *Custerology: The Enduring Legacy of the Indian Wars and George Armstrong Custer*. Chicago: University of Chicago Press, 2007.

Fagan, Brian. *The Little Ice Age: How Climate Made History, 1300–1850*. New York: Basic Books/Persons, 2000.

Farwell, William W. *A History of Minnesota*. 2 vols. St. Paul: Minnesota Historical Society, 1956.

Flores, Dan, *The Natural West: Environmental History in the Great Plains and Rocky Mountains.*. Norman: University of Oklahoma Press, 2001.

Fort Phil Kearny/Bozeman Trail Association, *Portraits of Fort Phil Kearny*. Banner, WY: Fort Phil Kearny/Bozeman Trail Association, 1993.

Frazer, Robert W. *Forts of the West: Military Forts and Presidios and Posts Commonly Called Forts West of the Mississippi River to 1898*. Norman: University of Oklahoma Press, 1965.

Goodyear, Frank H., III. *Photographs of a Lakota Chief*. Lincoln: University of Nebraska Press, 2003.

Gray, John. *Centennial Campaign: The Sioux War of 1876*. Norman: University of Oklahoma Press, 1988.

Greene, Candace S., and Russell Thornton. *The Year the Stars Fell: Lakota Winter Counts at the Smithsonian*. Lincoln: University of Nebraska Press, 2007.

Greene, Jerome A., ed. *Indian War Veterans: Memories of Army Life and Campaigns in the West, 1864–1898*. New York: Savas Beatie, 2007.

———. *Washita: The U.S. Army and the Southern Cheyennes, 1867–1869*. Norman: University of Oklahoma Press, 2004.

Grinnell, George B. *The Cheyenne Indians: Their History and Ways of Life*. 2 vols. New Haven, CT: Yale University Press, 1923.

———. *The Fighting Cheyennes*. Norman: University of Oklahoma Press, 1982.

Gump, James O. *The Dust Rose Like Smoke: The Subjugation of the Zulu and the Sioux.* Lincoln: University of Nebraska Press, 1994.

Hagan, Barry J. *"Exactly in the Right Place": A History of Fort C. F. Smith, Montana Territory, 1866–1868.* El Segundo, CA: Upton and Sons, 1999.

Hardorff, Richard G., ed. *The Death of Crazy Horse: A Tragic Episode in Lakota History.* Bison Book edition. Lincoln: University of Nebraska Press, 2001.

Hassrick, Royal B. *The Sioux: The Life and Customs of a Warrior Society.* Norman: University of Oklahoma Press, 1964.

Hebard, Grace R., and E. A. Brininstool. *The Bozeman Trail.* 2 vols. Cleveland: Arthur H. Clark, 1922.

Heitman, Francis B. *Historical Register and Dictionary of the United States Army from Its Organization, September 29, 1789, to March 2, 1903.* 2 vols. Washington, D.C.: Government Printing Office, 1903.

Hoffert, Sylvia D. *Jane Gray Swisshelm: An Unconventional Life, 1815–1884.* Chapel Hill: University of North Carolina Press, 2004.

Hoig, Stan. *Peace Chiefs of the Cheyennes.* Norman: University of Oklahoma Press, 1980.

———. *Perilous Pursuit: The U.S. Cavalry and the Northern Cheyennes.* Boulder: University Press of Colorado, 2002.

———. *The Sand Creek Massacre.* Norman: University of Oklahoma Press, 1961.

Hoebel, E. Adamson. *The Cheyennes, Indians of the Great Plains.* New York: Holt, Rinehart and Winston, 1960.

Howard, James H., ed. *The Warrior Who Killed Custer.* Lincoln: University of Nebraska Press, 1968.

———. *Lakota Warrior: Joseph White Bull.* Introduction by Raymond Bucko. Bison Book edition. Lincoln: University of Nebraska Press, 1998.

Hyde, George F. *The Life of George Bent Written from His Letters.* Edited by Savoy Otisville. Norman: University of Oklahoma Press, 1968.

———. *Red Cloud's Folk: A History of the Oglala Sioux Indians.* Norman: University of Oklahoma Press, 1937.

Jensen, Richard E., ed. *Voices of the American West: Interviews of Eli S. Ricker, 1903–1919.* 2 vols. Lincoln: University of Nebraska Press, 2005.

Johnson, Dorothy M. *The Bloody Bozeman: The Perilous Trail to Montana's Gold.* New York: McGraw-Hill, 1971.

Johnson, Mark W. *That Body of Brave Men: The U.S. Regular Infantry and the Civil War in the West.* Cambridge, MA: Da Capo Press, 2003.

Keenan, Jerry. *The Wagon Box Fight: An Episode of Red Cloud's War.* Conshohocken, PA: Savas Publishing Co., 2000.

Knight, Oliver. *Following the Indian Wars: The Story of the Newspaper Correspondents Among the Indian Campaigners*. Norman: University of Oklahoma Press, 1960.

Krech, Shepard, III. *The Ecological Indian*. New York: W. W. Norton, 1999.

Lang, Sabine. *Men as Women, and Women as Men: Changing Gender in Native American Cultures*. Austin: University of Texas Press, 1998.

Lang, William L., and Rex C. Myers. *Montana, Our Land and People*. Boulder, CO: Pruett Publishing, 1979.

Larson, Robert W. *Red Cloud: Warrior-Statesman of the Lakota Sioux*. Norman: University of Oklahoma Press, 1997.

Lazarus, Edward. *Black Hills/White Justice: The Sioux Nation Versus the United States, 1775 to the Present*. New York: Harper Collins, 1991.

Leckie, William H. *The Military Conquest of the Southern Plains*. Norman: University of Oklahoma Press, 1963.

Luebke, Frederick C., ed. *Ethnicity on the Great Plains*. Lincoln: University of Nebraska Press, 1980.

McDermott, John D. *Circle of Fire: The Indian War of 1865*. Mechanicsburg, PA: Stackpole Books, 2003.

McMurtry, Larry. *Boone's Lick*. New York: Simon and Schuster, 2000.

———. *Crazy Horse: A Life*. New York, Viking, 1999.

McPherson, James M. *This Mighty Scourge: Perspectives of the Civil War*. New York: Oxford University Press, 2007.

Marquis, Thomas B. *Cheyenne and Sioux: The Reminiscences of Four Indians and a White Soldier*. Edited by Ronald H. Limbaugh. Stockton, CA: Pacific Center for Western Historical Studies, University of the Pacific, 1973.

———. *Wooden Leg, A Warrior Who Fought Custer*. Bison Book edition. Lincoln: University of Nebraska Press, 1986.

Marshall, Joseph, III. *Hundred in the Hand: A Novel*. Golden, CO: Fulcrum Fiction, 2007.

———. *The Journey of Crazy Horse: A Lakota History*. New York: Viking, 2004.

Miller, Jay, Colin G. Calloway, and Richard A. Sattler, comps. *Writings in Indian History, 1985–1990*. Norman: University of Oklahoma Press, 1995.

Monnett, John H. *The Battle of Beecher Island and the Indian War of 1867–1869*. Niwot, CO: University Press of Colorado, 1992.

———. *Tell Them We Are Going Home: The Odyssey of the Northern Cheyennes*. Norman: University of Oklahoma Press, 2001.

Moore, John H. *The Cheyenne Nation: A Social and Demographic History*. Lincoln: University of Nebraska Press, 1987.

Murray, Robert A. *The Army on the Powder River.* Belleview, NE: Old Army Press, 1969.

———. *The Bozeman Trail, Highway of History.* Boulder, CO: Pruett Publishing, 1988.

Nadeau, Remi. *Fort Laramie and the Sioux.* Santa Barbara, CA: Crest Publishers, 1997.

Neihardt, John G. *The Twilight of the Sioux: The Song of the Indian Wars—The Song of the Messiah.* Vol. 2 of *A Cycle of the West.* Bison Book edition. Lincoln: University of Nebraska Press, 1971.

Nichols, David A. *Lincoln and the Indians.* Urbana: University of Illinois Press, 2000.

Olson, James C. *Red Cloud and the Sioux Problem.* Lincoln: University of Nebraska Press, 1965.

Ostrander, Alyson B. *An Army Boy of the Sixties.* Yonkers, NY: World Book Co., 1924.

———. *The Bozeman Trail Forts Under General Philip St George Cooke.* Casper, WY: Commercial Print Company, 1937.

Paul, R. Eli, ed. *Autobiography of Red Cloud: War Leader of the Oglalas.* Helena: Montana Historical Society, 1997.

———. *The Nebraska Indian Wars Reader, 1865–1877.* Lincoln: University of Nebraska Press, 1998.

Powell, Peter John. *People of the Sacred Mountain: A History of the Northern Cheyenne Chiefs and Warrior Societies, 1830–1974, with an Epilog, 1969–1974.* 2 vols. San Francisco: Harper and Row, 1981.

———. *Sweet Medicine: The Continuing Role of the Sacred Arrows, the Sun Dance, and the Sacred Buffalo Hat in Northern Cheyenne History.* 2 vols. Norman: University of Oklahoma Press, 1969.

Price, Catherine. *The Oglala People, 1841–1879: A Political History.* Lincoln: University of Nebraska Press, 1998.

Rankin, Charles E., ed. *Legacy: New Perspectives on the Battle of the Little Bighorn.* Helena: Montana Historical Society Press, 1996.

Richardson, Heather Cox. *West from Appomattox: The Reconstruction of America after the Civil War.* New Haven, CT: Yale University Press, 2007.

Robinson, Doane. *A History of the Dakota or Sioux Indians.* 1904. Reprint, Minneapolis: Ross and Hague Publishers, 1956.

Roscoe, Will. *Changing Ones: Third and Fourth Genders in Native North America.* New York: St. Martin's Griffin, 2000.

Sajna, Mike. *Crazy Horse: The Life Behind the Legend.* New York: John Wiley and Sons, 2000.

Sandoz, Mari. *Crazy Horse: Strange Man of the Oglalas.* Lincoln: University of Nebraska Press, 1942.

———. *Hostiles and Friendlies: Selected Short Writings of Mari Sandoz.* Lincoln: University of Nebraska Press, 1959.

Schoolcraft, Henry R. *Historical and Statistical Information Respecting the History, Condition and Prospects of the Indian Tribes of the United States*. Philadelphia: Lippincott, 1847.

Smith, Shannon D. *Give Me Eighty Men: Women and the Myth of the Fetterman Fight*. Lincoln: University of Nebraska Press, 2008.

Smith, Sherry L. *The View from Officers' Row: Army Perceptions of Western Indians*. Tucson: University of Arizona Press, 1990.

Standing Bear, Luther. *My People the Sioux*. Bison Book edition. Lincoln: University of Nebraska Press, 1975.

Stands-In-Timber, John, and Margot Liberty. *Cheyenne Memories*. New Haven, CT: Yale University Press, 1967.

Straight, Michael. *Carrington: A Novel of the West*. New York: Alfred A. Knopf, 1960.

Szasz, Margaret Connell, ed. *Between Indian and White Worlds: The Culture Brokers*. Norman: University of Oklahoma Press, 1994.

Tate, Michael L. *The Frontier Army in the Settlement of the West*. Norman: University of Oklahoma Press, 1999.

Thornton, Russell. *American Indian Holocaust and Survival: A Population History Since 1492*. Norman: University of Oklahoma Press, 1987.

Utley, Robert M. *Cavalier in Buckskin: George Armstrong Custer and the Western Military Frontier*. Norman: University of Oklahoma Press, 1988.

———. *Frontiersmen in Blue: The United States Army and the Indian, 1848–1865*. Lincoln: University of Nebraska Press, 1981.

———. *Frontier Regulars: The United States Army and the Indian, 1866–1891*. Lincoln: University of Nebraska Press, 1984.

———. *The Indian Frontier, 1846–1890*. Rev. ed. Albuquerque: University of New Mexico Press, 1984.

Vaughn, J. W. *Indian Fights: New Facts on Seven Encounters*. Norman: University of Oklahoma Press, 1966.

———. *The Battle of Platte Bridge*. Norman: University of Oklahoma Press, 1963.

Vestal, Stanley (Walter Campbell). *Jim Bridger, Mountain Man*. New York: Morrow, 1946.

———. *Warpath: The True Story of the Fighting Sioux Told in a Biography of Chief White Bull*. Introduction by Raymond J. DeMallie. Bison Book edition. Lincoln: University of Nebraska Press, 1984.

Victor, Francis Fuller. *The River of the West: Life and Adventure in the Rocky Mountains and Oregon*. Hartford, CT: R. W. Bliss, 1870.

Ware, Eugene. *The Indian War of 1864*. New York: St. Martin's, 1960.

Warren, Louis S., ed. *American Environmental History*. Malden, MA: Blackwell Publishing, 2003.

West, Elliot. *The Contested Plains: Indians, Gold Seekers, and the Rush to Colorado*. Lawrence: University Press of Kansas, 1998.

White, Richard. *Roots of Dependency*. Lincoln: University of Nebraska Press, 1983.

Whittlesey, Lee H. *Storytelling in Yellowstone: Horse and Buggy Tour Guides*. Albuquerque: University of New Mexico Press, 2007.

Wishart, David J., ed. *Encyclopedia of the Great Plains Indians*. Lincoln: University of Nebraska Press, 2007.

Young, Otis E. *The West of Philip St. George Cooke, 1809–1895*. Glendale, CA: Arthur H. Clark, 1955.

Electronic and Media Sources

Tiwahe, Tashunke Witko. *The Authorized Biography of Crazy Horse*. Vol. 2, "Defending The Homeland Prior to the 1868 Treaty." DVD produced by Matson, William and Frethem, Reel Contact, 2007.

http://abstracts.co.allenpress.com/pweb/esa2003/document/?ID=25625.

www.army.mil.

www.ebscohost.com.

http://freepages.history.rootsweb.com/~familyinformation/#fpk.

www.friendslittlebighorn.com.

www.fs.fed.us.

www.intellectbooks.com/europa/number4/witkin.htm.

www.legendsofamerica.com.

www.mnhs.org.

www.mohicanpress.com/messageboard2/topic.asp?Topic_ID=73&whichpage=3.

http://news.nationalgeographic.com/news.

http://philkearny.vcn.com/fpk-tallbull.htm.

http://nd.water.usgs.gov/pubs.

About the Author

John H. Monnett is a professor of history at Metropolitan State College of Denver, where he teaches Native American and western history. He has authored, coauthored, or contributed to twelve books on the American West and Native American history.

INDEX

Page numbers in **bold type** indicate photographs.